Evangelism's First
Modern Media Star

Evangelism's First
Modern Media Star

The Life of Reverend Bill Stidger

Jack Hyland

AFTERWORD BY WALTER G. MUELDER

Cooper Square Press

First Cooper Square Press Edition 2002

This Cooper Square Press hardcover edition of *Evangelism's First Modern Media Star* is an original publication. (A portion of this book was previously published in the Fall/Winter 2000 issue of *Boston University School of Theology Focus*.) This book is published by arrangement with the author.

Published by Cooper Square Press
An Imprint of the Rowman & Littlefield Publishing Group
200 Park Avenue South, Suite 1109
New York, New York 10003-1503

Distributed by National Book Network

Library of Congress Cataloging-in-Publication Data

Hyland, Jack, 1938–
    Evangelism's first modern media star : the life of Reverend Bill Stidger / Jack Hyland ; with an afterword by Walter G. Muelder.
        p. cm.
    Includes bibliographical references and index.
    ISBN 0-8154-1187-1 (alk. paper)
    1. Stidger, William L. (William Le Roy), 1886– 2. Methodist Church—United States—Clergy—Biography. I. Title.

    BX8495.S766 H95 2002
    287'.6'092—dc21
    [B]   2001056172

♾™ The paper used in this publication meets the minimum requirements of
American National Standard for Information Sciences—Permanence of
Paper for Printed Library Materials, ANSI/NISO Z39.48–1992.
Manufactured in the United States of America.

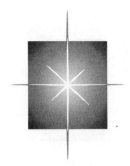

Contents

Acknowledgments

B ill Stidger was extraordinary—volcanic in energy and productivity, and inspiring in his drive to accomplish his goals. He certainly had flaws, but people loved him in spite of them; at the center of it, he showed us all—me, any student, any teacher, or any preacher—that each of us can do incredible things; you just have to believe in yourself and believe in others. I have been immensely impressed and moved by the testimonies of Bill's former students who confirmed the instrumental role he played in their lives. I am especially grateful to the fifty or so of these men and women who helped me with their thoughts and remembrances.

This book has been a labor of love that I began in earnest eight years ago, ready to use whatever energy I had to spare after a normal day's work. I don't regret a moment of the time spent, for it was also a splendid voyage of discovery into myself, the history of my family, the much broader panorama of this country in the first half of the twentieth century, and a detailed look at three extraordinary mortals: my grandfather, Bill Stidger; my grandmother, Iva; and my mother, Betty Stidger Hyland.

Fellow travelers on my voyage who discovered along with me and who helped immensely were my three children, Liza, Jonathan, and Susannah, and their mother, Casey Hyland, who read and kept my writing tethered to earth; Walter G. Muelder, Dean Emeritus of Boston University's School of Theology, who was the wise soul who held my ship to a true course; Pat Frederick, my editor, whose marks of red, green, and blue trimmed the fat from the lean; Eleann Gilhooley, who typed my manuscript cheerfully—innumerable times; Helen Pratt, my agent, whose vision saw more to Bill's story than the telling of it; Larry Wente, my friend, who read every word nearly as often as I and whose judgment helped shape the drama of the book. All were indispensable; but I must also reach out with one hand to grab Bill Stidger's arm and with another to seize Betty's. For, after all, it is their voices, their enthusiasm, and their joy for life itself that makes this little book sing.

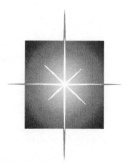

Introduction

It was a time when giants still walked the earth—or, at least I thought so, and I was on my way to visit one—my grandfather Dr. William L. Stidger. It was August 1948, and I was blissfully unaware of anything but my excitement at being on a train as it bore down the tracks bound for Boston. The ride was a long one, overnight, and I had my stack of comic books to entertain me. I was being looked after by a number of friendly strangers, who took an interest in a ten-year-old on his own, stopping to ask where I was going, where I was from, and whether everything was okay.

Too soon, the conductor called out "South Station," as the train slowed and shuddered to a stop. The porter opened the outside car door and lifted the hatch that covered the steps. Then he climbed down carrying a small yellow footstool, which he placed below the lowest step before standing to one side to help descending passengers with their luggage. Once I was on the main platform, I strained to see faces I recognized, while the din of people greeting each other, of train noises, of baggage carts filled my ears.

In the distance I saw two familiar shapes approaching me swiftly. One had the bulk of a football player, head forward, shining bald pate, and glasses with thin silver rims. "Bill"—as everyone called him—Stidger had a presence that brought others up short to watch. My grandmother Iva Stidger walked by his side, tall, flawlessly erect, and as dignified as my grandfather was energetic. Though he plowed ahead while she moved at a stately pace, they crossed the terminal hall as one. My grandfather grinned as he threw his arms around me in a great bear hug, smothering me in his joy. He smelled of peppermint. When he stepped back he reached inside his coat pocket and offered me a

Lifesaver, which I gladly took, from a newly opened roll. Iva stood by patiently, smiling, waiting until his show was over, then held out both arms and gave me a hug.

Standing beside Bill was like being at the foot of a gigantic oak tree that towered over you, that sheltered and protected you. He swept me up in his conversation, and before I realized it we were in front of his brand new Nash Ambassador, a royal-blue machine sitting in the parking lot. It had a curious bulge in the back to accommodate an owner's possible wish to fold the front seat down, turning the inside of the car into a double bed. This feature was short-lived, setting a precedent that no other manufacturer was to follow. But Bill was very proud to possess this innovation. He loved being on the cutting edge. He drove absentmindedly, immersed in conversation with me or in point-ing out the sights as we made our way to Newton, one of the many small towns absorbed by the outward sprawl of Boston.

I was spending a week with my grandparents and pleased to be the only one basking in the attention they showered on me. And I also had the run of the house. My favorite place was my grandfather's office, reached via a back stairway, an almost invisible passage-way off to one side of the refrigerator. It was at the top of the stairs, a modest room, lit mostly by a lamp on his desk. Books were everywhere, rising in vertical stacks from the floor and from the tops of tables until each stack reached a perilous height. Some leaned so precariously that I could barely keep from giving them a nudge as I passed by.

A black Smith Corona typewriter sat on a desk in the center of the room; it always had a piece of paper in it—an article or letter that had been started but not yet finished. When I pulled out the top drawer of the desk, it was heavy with large bronze medals from Bill's victories on the track team at Allegheny College. The room had a musty smell made by the paper and ink of so many books, mixed with a bit of cigarette smoke from the "occasional" lapse. If asked, he would answer, like a good Methodist, that he did not believe in smoking or drinking, yet he smoked frequently, albeit discreetly. As for drinking—well, there were a few exceptions to every rule.

Bill made a furious sound at his typewriter, clacking away, hammering the keys by his two-finger method. I loved the sound of a completed letter being yanked from the black roll on the carriage, as well as the constant chatter he would direct toward me while he was spewing forth a new article.

"Jacky, are you coming to come hear me preach tonight?" And before I could answer he continued, "I would certainly like you to be there."

"Sure, I'll come. But only if I can bring a comic book with me."

"Why a comic book?" Bill asked, always up for a conversation.

"In case I get bored."

"I'd hate to have anyone see my grandson reading while I'm preaching." There was a moment of silence and then he continued: "Do you really think I might be boring?" he asked.

"Maybe," I replied.

"The last person that I would ever want to bore would be you." Then he suddenly made a surprise attack. "Jacky, is there something you'd like to have more than any-thing else?"

I had been pestering my parents for some time for a real wristwatch. So I replied, "I'd like a wristwatch, one that really works."

"Good! I'll make you a deal. You leave your comic book at home, and, if you are bored, I'll get you that wristwatch. But if you find what I have to say interesting, then I don't owe you a watch. How does that sound?"

It was a fair deal, I thought, and agreed to the bet.

We arrived at the church early, at 6:45, for a 7:30 evening service. People were pouring into the church from the parking lot. On the bulletin board near the entrance was notice of the service, the sermon to be given by the "Reverend William L. Stidger." A policeman in the parking lot kept an eye on the crowds, and another stood just inside the front doors.

We took seats about a third of the way back, the last two places on the right aisle. This was my grandmother's place of choice; there she could be close enough to see everything but far enough back from the pulpit so as not to be conspicuous. From her vantage point she had a good view of all the people in the church. She watched every aspect of the service like a hawk and even did a mental count. Though she was Bill's greatest supporter, she never spared him the unpleasant news, if there was any. He did not mind criticism. What galled him was indifference—people who could arrive and leave without his having touched them at all. A minister's greatest sin, he believed, was to be found guilty of boring his congregation.

At 7:00, people were still streaming toward the church from all directions. They headed up the front steps without delaying to chat, hurrying to the remaining seats. Fifteen minutes later, the church was filled. The organ music had begun. The janitor and a number of the ushers were making rustling noises, opening metal folding chairs to put in the aisles to accommodate the overflow.

After the welcome, the readings, the hymns, and the collection, the minister of the church described how pleased he was to have Bill Stidger as his guest speaker. He told the congregation of Bill's prior ministries. Then he covered his accomplishments: the books and articles he had published, his professorship at Boston University, his pioneer work in radio broadcasting. Finally he told the congregation that there was a record number of people present, more than fifteen hundred, many of whom were on folding chairs in the aisles or standing at the rear of the church.

I looked at the expressions on the faces of the congregation; there was rapt attentiveness and eager anticipation. At first, I felt awe as I realized that this vast number of people had come to hear my grandfather speak. Then I panicked. What if they hated his sermon? Could he hold their attention?

The minister completed his introduction and invited Bill to take the pulpit. He rose, and to me it looked like sails being hoisted on an oceangoing schooner. His black robe was in stark contrast to his large round face and bald head. The robe's lavish drapery, his stolid frame, and his exaggerated height in the pulpit, well above the congregation, made him seem like a giant. He stood in the pulpit as if it were the prow of a great ship.

Bill was not bombastic, but he spoke deliberately, one idea piled upon the next. Every word was clear and easy to understand. His first story was about Ethel Barrymore, the famous actress, who had once visited his church despite having a temperature of 104 degrees. She had ignored her doctor's orders to go the hospital, since she had told Bill she would come to his service. She said that when a Barrymore made a commitment to a friend, nothing would get in the way of fulfilling that commitment.

Once or twice I looked at the faces of the congregation. There was silence in the church as we rode the waves of his words. Fifty years later I vividly recall that the theme of his sermon was the strength of families in everyone's lives. The image he used was of a powerful oak, the roots of which fed and nourished all aspects of the tree, just as the family supports its individual members no matter what dangers or hardships prevail.

Then, suddenly, it was over. Bill bent his head in prayer, spread his arms like the wings of an eagle, and invited all present to pause for a moment of silence. There must have been some closing words and music, but I don't remember them. I do recall the congregation standing, turning to their neighbors to talk eagerly about the sermon.

As the recessional music began and the members of the congregation filed out, quite a few thronged around Bill, who walked among them listening to their comments and questions, giving answers, and very much thriving on the attention and congratulations he was receiving. Once the well-wishers had moved on, he retreated to the private rooms behind the altar, where my grandmother and I found him. He was still wearing his black robe and turned to see my grandmother approaching him, an approving smile on her face. As she kissed him, he threw his arms around her. Then he stood back from her, turned toward me, and said, "Well, Jacky, do I owe you that watch or not?"

I looked up at him and declared without hesitation, "I wasn't bored—I guess I don't get my watch."

"I've never had a finer compliment. Thank you." Then he added, making it seem like a casual afterthought: "And, by the way, you'll still get your watch!" He smiled a wide grin, enjoying the startled expression he must have seen on my face.

Looking back, I recall seeing huge perspiration marks on his blue shirt when he removed his robe. I realize only now that this man, who had made no apparent effort, must in fact have worked extremely hard to attract and hold the attention of a church full of people. A mystical transfer of energy had occurred between him and all of us; no wonder the service had drained him.

I was swept along in the wake of this great preacher who was also my grandfather. Years later I began to wonder just how a man can seize the imaginations of so many. How does he learn to give hope and provide humor? How does he know he has this gift? When does he know to what purpose he will put these awesome powers? Questions such as these are not asked or answered by a ten-year-old whose main concern was the ceremonial handing over of the *new, real, wristwatch*. The questions, however, gradually took root in my mind, and over the years I have returned to them, tried to understand why they made such an impression on me, and toyed with answers.

My trip to Boston ended soon after the Sunday service. Little did I know that I would never see him again. He died suddenly of a heart attack the following August. One year and two weeks later, my own father died unexpectedly, and the bottom dropped out of my world. On hearing that he was gone, I remember rushing up to my bedroom and throwing myself face down on my bed, half-smothering myself in the blanket. I screamed into that blanket. It wasn't fair. Why did he have to die? Why did this have to happen to me? There was as much anger as pain. Gradually I cried myself out and then went downstairs into the unreal world that now existed. The next day my aunt took me aside, and we went for a walk. "You know, Jack, your father was a wonderful man, and we all loved him. But, he's gone now, and you'll have to be the man in the family."

It was said so simply, yet so powerfully, that my life changed as we walked. The mantle of responsibility settled firmly on my shoulders, and from then on I wore it. I'm not sure I was even conscious of what had happened. I did know, however, that I had to perform, to be good, to be worthy. And that was the way it was.

School started, and I entered eighth grade with my wound buried. My grandmother came to live with us and to help my mother bring up the three of us. Over the next dozen years I learned much more about my grandfather and my father. Bill, I came to understand, had suffered the loss of his own mother when he had been my age, an incident so sharply etched in his mind that his life and destiny had been changed. He, too, had felt the burden of responsibility as the oldest child. I wanted to know more about this experience that we shared. He had had an extraordinarily close relationship with my mother, as she and I were to have with each other. In some respects, we had much in common.

In that idyllic week in Boston, I experienced firsthand, albeit through the eyes of a ten-year-old, a giant in his world—one who knew his fellow man so well that he could inspire hundreds, even thousands, of people to find better, more confident, and more productive lives for themselves. It is in pursuit of a way to understand him and, through him, to know myself that I peer back through the years to the time when Bill Stidger and his wife, Iva, were alive, vibrantly alive, and when my mother, now also only a memory, was much younger than I am now. And all that follows is what I have learned.

One

The Early Years: Moundsville

High above the town, Bill Stidger sprawled full length, lanky, on the cool earth of Grave Creek Mound. He sank his hands into the dirt. The air was still all around him, and the heat held everything transfixed. Above him the sky shone with a million stars. He was red-headed, freckled and proud of the peach fuzz beginning to cover his face. He heard the rumbling chorus of voices:

> Rescue the perishing. Care for the dying
> Jesus is merciful; Jesus will save!

The thunder of the singing rose from the church below, up the walls of the Mound and reverberated around him, pushing through the hot night, thrusting its joy into his heart. He felt himself drawn into the web of the music. He imagined himself there; he could hear the stamping sound of a thousand feet, pounding the floor in unison; hear the sputter of moths and insects as they darted too near the flames of the kerosene lamps; sense the fluttering of all the fans donated by Jones Funeral Parlor, feel that moment of coolness that almost freezes when a slight breeze stirs, waltzes through an open window and pats your shirt where perspiration has soaked through. The music changed:

> Blest be the tie that binds
> Our heart in Christian love
> The fellowship of kindred minds
> Is like to that above.

Driven by the music, Bill rose to his feet. He ran down the centuries-old stone steps leading from the top of the Mound. The music was louder, and the church was only yards away, glowing with its inner light. The music stopped. The thunder of the voice of the prophets that walked the roads of Galilean times blasted out through the open doors. The preacher, Dr. William Barrett King, sent forth a great outpouring of the Spirit that made the rafters shake. That good old-time religion: "To be washed in the blood of the lamb. Do you hear the call? Anyone. . . . Do you hear the call?"

From the last pew, behind which he was now standing, Bill saw person after person arise, make their way across their neighbors to the aisle and move exultantly toward the altar where they knelt before their preacher. Bill was torn apart inside. Part of him wished to rush forward and join those kneeling at the altar, professing their faith in God. But another part of him, the shy, boyish part, held back. He was afraid, not ready to make the commitment. Before the meeting ended, Bill moved away and headed toward his house. He was deeply moved by what he had heard and seen; there was a compelling force pulling him closer and closer to that altar.

— Betty Stidger, Bill's daughter, describing her father's experience at the 1899 revival in her book, *Those Heavenly Years.*[1]

On that warm summer evening following the revival service at the Simpson Methodist Church, fourteen-year-old Bill Stidger walked the two blocks from the church to his home. Both Simpson Methodist, where his family were regular members, and the Stidgers' modest clapboard house with its wraparound porch were at the base of the ancient Indian mound, which gave Moundsville, West Virginia, its name—a seventy-foot-high mass of earth nine hundred feet around in which two Adena Indian chiefs had been buried two thousand years earlier.

Adjacent to the "Old Indian Mound" was the other dominant feature in Moundsville—a massive stone state penitentiary that held four hundred prisoners. Within its forbidding, crenellated walls there was an occasional execution by hanging. And, every so often, the town would be stirred by the news of prisoners digging a tunnel under the thick stone fortress and escaping in the darkness of the night.

In the early days of the twentieth century, Moundsville had about five thousand inhabitants, having doubled in size from the time Bill was born in 1885. Farming was an important occupation, but there were also jobs in the local shops, as well as employment in the town's few industries—coal mining, glass manufacturing, foundries, and the making of brooms, guns, and buggy whips. Moundsville and other places like it up and down the Ohio River were expectant with opportunity as small businesses sprang up to serve the steel industry, centered in Pittsburgh, eighty miles to the north, which was providing steel for the skyscrapers rising in America's major cities and for the burgeoning automobile industry.

Religion at this time—whether Methodist, the largest denomination, or one of the other mainstream sects—was an integral part of people's lives. This was particularly true during summers, when Moundsville was overrun by as many as six thousand visitors arriving for the annual camp meeting to "partake of the wisdom of the 'exhorters' and evangelists." Camp meetings were first held as early as 1787 in Moundsville itself and after 1824 up the hill at the Methodist Park in the north part of town, beyond the Fostoria glass factory, beyond the cemetery and across the creek. An avalanche of Methodists—and some other denominations as well—poured into Moundsville by train and steamboat on the Sunday before the campground opened.

The boats blew their whistles loudly, and the crowds disembarked laden with baskets of food and provisions. The Baltimore and Ohio Railroad ran special trains filled with families coming to the meetings. On arrival in Moundsville the visitors were greeted by shouts of "Right this way for the campground" from a number of drivers eager for their business. Everyone piled into two-horse wagons that had been outfitted with temporary seats to handle twelve to fourteen people. Usually, however, the wagons were jammed with twenty to twenty-five singing and shouting crusaders, whose rocking movements as they sang made the wagons lean perilously back and forth. Dust kicked up by the heavy traffic rose in vast clouds and hung over the streets and the mile of unimproved road leading to the campground. The old Methodist hymns blasted forth as the revelers made their way across town and up the hill. No one who lived in Moundsville could be oblivious to the contagious enthusiasm of the visitors. Shops closed, and people from town followed the wagons up the hill. The crowds scattered themselves through the beautiful woods to shake off the dust and catch a breath of cool, fresh air.[2]

Most of those who attended the campground's revivals were there to be persuaded to confess their sins—great or small—and be forgiven by the famous evangelists who preached. It was common to see converts walk over the backs of the benches shouting, "I am free!" Many of the preachers who were due to speak would first retreat into the woods and climb the hill. Under the tall beech trees they would wrestle with God, just as Jacob had done in the Old Testament. Then, their battles temporarily won, they would return to camp with shining eyes and glowing faces. The crowd knew that when a preacher had shining eyes and a glowing face, they were in for a meeting in which they were "going to be mightily moved." Such meetings generally ended in climatic showers of "Amens!" and "Hallelujahs!"[3]

Bill was fascinated by the contagious excitement of the crowd, the stamping of feet, the clapping and cheering when one after another of the audience rose to declare a personal conversion. He absorbed a great deal of the technique of fiery oratory and observed its impact on the large number of people who were receptive and willing to be swayed. Each year he circled closer to the religious fire, like a moth drawn to the flame.

In the late spring of 1901, Bill's minister, Dr. King, held his own revival at the Simpson Methodist Church. The *Moundsville Daily Echo* kept daily track of the conversions and gave the revival extensive coverage. On the last day, Bill and twenty-five of his friends experienced personal conversions, which he later described in *Men of the Great Redemption*, published in 1931:

> Came a tall, six-foot giant of a preacher, with gray hair, gray eyes, and a gray mustache, named Dr. William B. King. Came a moving revival service, or "special meeting," as we called it. Came news of a great "outpouring of the Spirit."

Came night after night when boys and girls and men and women knelt at that same altar where my mother's body had lain.

Came a deep feeling of conviction that there was an experience in life that I had not had; that there was something more for me; that I was being called to something; that my mother was calling; that God was calling.

Came a night of loneliness and terror, a sense of isolation from God, which ended only with that sixteen-year-old boy kneeling at his bed promising God that, if the next night ever came, that boy would go to the altars of God.

Came the next night dragging on slow wheels out of the Infinite. The crowd gathered an hour before the time for the service because the whole countryside had heard of the three months' "special meetings"; had heard of the more than six hundred conversions.

The preacher preached. The invitation hymn was sung. It was "I Will Arise and Go to Jesus." A father walked down the aisle of the church toward a red-headed, anxious boy sitting already on the edge of the seat. He, too, had a strange feeling that somebody was after him, that the "giant hour" of his life had come. When that kindly, anxious father arrived he said, simply and tenderly, "Come on, my boy!" And the boy was ready for that simple invitation. The preacher had spoken to the depths of his heart; the invitation hymn had penetrated deep into his subconscious soul. Before he knew it he was out in the aisle of the church, headed toward the altar, utterly unaware of anything, save for his father's leading hand and his mother's voice calling him to arise and take up his journey to the skies, to walk with God amid the stars.

Utterly unaware that others knelt at that altar, battling his own lone way to light and to God; praying, weeping, hoping, waiting, expecting, the boy in his teens knelt.

Then came a voice: "Will you renounce all for me?" It suddenly became clear that only the willingness to renounce stood between that boy and finding God. To that boy came—whether it may be called: regeneration, conversion, cosmic consciousness; words are needless and futile. Came an electrical wave which began at his feet, swept up into his legs, past his knees and thighs, and breast and throat and leaped out of his lips in a great shout of happiness: "Glory! Glory! Glory! Daddy! Mother! Glory!"

Then that boy leaped over the altar at which he had been kneeling into the arms of his father, who whispered: "My boy! My boy! I'm so happy! My boy!"

Later that father said, "I was kneeling inside the altar while you knelt outside. You did not know that I was there. I prayed. I watched you kneeling there—I wanted more than I ever wanted anything in life for you to find God as I had found him—through my own father's help.

"Then God came to you. I saw you rise from that altar and I saw a light in your eyes that I had never seen before. I heard you shout and cry, as I had done before you. The congregation was singing, 'He Fills Me Now,' and He certainly had filled you. That was the happiest moment of my life. I shed a few tears, but they were happy tears. Somewhere, your wonderful mother is looking down on you and is as proud of you as I am."

There is the story. Take it or leave it. It is the first time it has been told in print. It is the great reality of this one life. More real than war, or flood, or famine; more real than any adventure that has come to his life.[4]

For those living in rural areas across the country, such as Moundsville, the experiencing of a personal conversion, which meant a recentering of one's life on the Church, was considered a perfectly normal event and, in fact, was acknowledged as a rite of passage among teenagers. William James, a Harvard University psychologist and brother of the novelist Henry James, wrote *The Varieties of Religious Experience,* which appeared in 1902 and became an immediate best-seller. In this book James devoted two chapters to the subject of conversion, and his discussion of the topic carried over to a good part of the entire work.[5]

Throughout his life Bill believed in the importance of his conversion at Dr. King's revival, in which he had embraced a new Christian life. The customary criticism of revivals was that conversions occurred in the heat of the rhetoric but that in the cold light of day the newly saved "backslid," fell away from the Church. Sensitive to this criticism, Bill wrote fifteen years later to defend his actions and those of his twenty-five comrades: "All of my friends have remained faithful to their vows to remain in the Church and three have even become preachers as I have."

On March 16, 1885, when he was born, William Leroy Stidger was the first of five children of Etta Robinson and Leroy (Roy) Stidger. Roy had left Moundsville in the early 1880s to seek his fortune, stopping in Winfield, Kansas, where he took a job in a grocery store. Etta, a customer, whose family owned the bank in town, was immediately attracted to Roy; they fell in love, married, and returned to Moundsville to raise a family.

Roy fell on extremely tough times when his partner embezzled the funds of their Moundsville grocery store. Rather than declare bankruptcy, however, Roy vowed to repay every penny of his and his former partner's debts by making a success of an ice cream store that he started and at which he worked incredibly long hours. This meant that while Bill was growing up the Stidgers had little or no money. It also meant that Bill barely saw his father. Instead, his life revolved around his mother and his brother and three sisters. With his mother he developed a very close "comradeship."

After her fifth child, May, was born in late 1893, Bill's mother developed an infection in her mastoid, the bone behind her ear. An operation was performed that alleviated the problem but led to a paralyzing stroke from which there was no recovery. Looking back on the incident, Bill wrote: "My mother was dying. She could not speak . . . but she could write. She called us children to her bedside and wrote on a slip of white paper in a sprawling hand, as if it had been written by the broken pinion of a fallen bird: 'Meet me over there!'"[6]

Forty years later, Bill was able to put into words with great vividness the pain which his mother's death caused:

> That was darkness! That was the one great, gloomy, stormy, dark and turbulent March of my boyhood! I did not want to live! I would rather have died and gone with her—my comrade mother! That was my chaos! That was my tomb! But— it was through that experience that my heart was broken; and out of that broken heart a seed of love for my fellowman grew into a flower of service; and it was because of that experience that my heart has always been tender to suffering, needy humanity. That March experience broke my heart but it saved my soul. That experience sent me to the altars of the church a penitent, broken boy. It sent me there because I wanted to make sure that I would see mother "over there" as she asked me to. It sent me from there to my Christ and from Him to school and college and from college into the ministry—a heart full of sympathy and a desire to serve both Christ and my fellowman.[7]

And so, at the age of nine, Bill was without a mother and essentially without a father. It was he who had to care for his brother and three sisters, who depended on him. It was a sobering responsibility, and Bill knew, consciously or unconsciously, that he needed help. Meanwhile, Etta's brothers, with perfectly good intentions, aware that Roy had no money, came to Moundsville and offered to take the Stidger children back with them, to give them homes in Winfield. As Bill would write, however, they found in his father a brokenhearted man yet one determined that he and his children should not be separated. "I want them to have a home together, even if it is a poor one," Roy said. " I want them to grow up knowing each other and loving each other. I could not bear to think of them being scattered. You are good to offer, but it must not be."[8]

Bill always knew where to find Roy, either behind his big desk at the courthouse, where he held a part-time job as clerk of the circuit court, or at the ice cream store. On the mornings when ice cream was being made, the day started at 4 A.M. in the back of the store. If Bill, Read, or their sisters helped churn the four large twenty-gallon containers, which rested on wooden planks above the floor, wet with melted ice impregnated with salt, they got to lick the dashers, which usually yielded a quart of ice cream apiece. It was so rich that "it stuck to the roof of your mouth"; Read got boils from eating too much. None of Bill's friends ever complained, however, about Roy's generosity in dishing out ice cream.

On one late Saturday night, Bill discovered that his father was less than superhuman. He awoke in the early hours of the morning, and seeing a light burning, which he imagined he had neglected to put out, he went to investigate. It was his father fast asleep in a chair in the midst of darning his children's socks for church the next morning, too exhausted to finish. As he looked at his father, Bill felt that he seemed smaller than normal and even somewhat frail. The next morning, though, Roy appeared to be his usual robust self, as he dressed each of his children in clean, well-pressed clothes and walked them to Sunday School. But Bill had seen a vulnerability in his father that he had not known was there.

Providence works in unusual ways, and it was through a new Sunday School teacher that Bill's need for a mother and counselor was filled. Bill met Miss Mary Scott when he joined her Sunday School class in 1895, the year after his mother's death. Mary was seventeen, mature enough to fulfill part of the role his mother would have played, yet young enough to be the friend and confidant that he wanted and needed. To many people, she was "plain of face," but there was a captivating radiance that sprang from her kindliness, selflessness, and generosity that more than compensated for her appearance.[9] "Miss Mary," as Bill always called her, was no Pollyanna; she had clear, hard ideas, and she argued them. She immediately took charge of Bill's life and was a critical influence on him. She drove him to read, read, read, telling him that if he wanted to make his mark on the world he had to travel widely, read extensively, and know great books. There was no doubt in Mary's mind that Bill must go to college—a thought that at ten Bill had certainly not yet had—and, most important, she believed that his life must in some way be conducted in the service of God. Mary also took in hand the destinies of Bill's brother and sisters. Over supper, usually at her parents' house, she would lead the Stidger children in talk on subjects that would shape their lives, and she drew them deeply into the activities of Simpson Methodist Church.

Bill later gave Mary credit for stirring his interest in becoming a preacher. As he later wrote to her, "And best of all, my greatest Friendship, that with my Master, who in these days has come to mean so much more to me, was made there in the old church [Simpson Methodist Church]. I think it was mostly you who introduced me to Him and you who have helped me to keep close to Him."[10] He paid his respects to her publicly by dedicating his book, *Flashlights from the Seven Seas*, published in 1921, as follows:

Dedicated to Mary I. Scott

A Woman Friend who pushed back the horizons of the world and led me to the beginning of the trail that has no end: the Trail of Dreams and Travel.[11]

Bill's father remarried just after Christmas in 1899, providing his children with a stepmother they didn't want and didn't like. After all, in their minds, Mary Scott filled the role of their mother, and they were satisfied with her. Virginia Florence Shaffer was their new stepmother; she was thirty-three years old, five years younger than Roy and two years younger than Etta would have been. She was a stalwart member of Simpson Methodist Church, and the couple had met through church activities. Virginia was very much in love with Roy, and vice versa, but she didn't care much for his children. She won no friends among them by making them sit on the front porch steps on Sundays after church, doing nothing, so as to enforce the Sabbath rules.

Virginia was a God-fearing woman who rigidly upheld all the rules of the Church. Bill was the complete opposite; he cared little for the rules of the Church, and his religious spirit, which was humane and sprang from within, belonged to no specific denomination. Stepmother and oldest son therefore had nothing in common, and Virginia's hold on Roy acted to separate Bill from his own father.

At Moundsville Central High, Bill found that he had a gift for public speaking and debating. He could hold his audience spellbound, and what's more, he thoroughly enjoyed his power to entertain. He also discovered he could write—stories, newspaper reports, and poetry—and the power of the written word was not lost on him. In the last two summers before graduation, he spent time at the editorial office of the *Moundsville Daily Echo*, picking up reporting assignments. His big break came when he was assigned to assist a reporter from the *Wheeling Intelligencer* to cover an execution at the penitentiary. The senior reporter was not at peace with executions; "Bill," he said, "let's get a drink. I can't stand to see a man hanged without having a couple of whiskeys to steady my nerves." Since Bill didn't drink, the reporter had Bill's whiskey as well. Later, in the execution room, "The warden placed the rope around the poor fellow's neck and began to arrange it properly. I heard a slight noise at my side. The experienced reporter had fainted." Bill wrote the story of the hanging, a piece that earned him his credentials as a reporter.[12]

The closer Bill got to the end of his senior year at Central High School in June 1903, the more he was faced with the question of what to do after graduation. His father was beginning to make headway with his ice cream store and hoped Bill would remain to help him. Miss Mary Scott, on the other hand, would have none of this and insisted that Bill go to college—and pointed out that if he did, he would be the first in his family to do. Bill fell quite easily into Mary Scott's line of thinking, since he was ready to be away from home, if only to be rid of his opinionated stepmother.

Mary Scott promoted Allegheny College as the place Bill should go. It was a well regarded liberal arts college of about three hundred students on a beautiful campus in western Pennsylvania, and it was supported by the Methodist Church. Its campus of sixteen acres was on the northern edge of Meadville, a town of eleven thousand, located ninety-three miles due north of Pittsburgh and forty miles south of Lake Erie. By coincidence, a recruiter for Allegheny, named Louie Sherwin, came to Moundsville in late spring of 1903 and was introduced to Bill. Sherwin's stories about the football and track teams at Allegheny and his giving Bill a book on Tennyson clinched Bill's desire to apply.

In September 1904, Bill set out for Meadville, Pennsylvania, with his father's blessing, a check from his mother's brother for $250 to cover tuition, board, and all expenses—and fifty dollars, given to him by Miss Mary, sewn into his undershirt.[13] He was dressed in a cheap blue serge suit and carried with him a Central High School oratorical contest medal. Bill spent two years at Allegheny Preparatory School taking courses that were designed to make the transition to college as easy as possible. Finally, in September 1906, he entered Allegheny College as a freshman, at the age of twenty-one.

At Allegheny, Bill threw himself into football and track as well as most extracurricular activities. The only pursuit he omitted from his kaleidoscopic involvement in campus life was that of scholarly endeavor; this received the shortest of shrifts.

On one cold October day early in his freshman year, Bill was trudging up the hill on his way back to the Allegheny campus from Meadville, deep in thought. A dark-haired, sparkling, brown-eyed girl stood watching him from the brim of the hill. As he reached her, she smiled and said, "Have an apple, fresh, they're from my Dad's farm." Bill's world suddenly took on a new glow—a senior, and a mighty pretty one at that, had laughed with him, a freshman. He already knew she was Iva Berkey and a Kappa Alpha Theta, much too big-time for him. But the glow lingered.

Iva was almost two years older than Bill and came from a respectable family in Ligonier, a small town popular as a summer resort for the Mellons and other wealthy families of Pittsburgh. She had a reputation on campus for being very intelligent, a bit aloof, and willing to speak her mind. Altogether it looked like no reasonable match, there was instant chemistry, which did not dissipate; in fact, it grew as the school year wore on.

Bill and Iva's relationship progressed to the point where they began to plan a life together, even if marriage would have to wait a few years. Finally there came an evening when, judging by the following letter (which does not give the date), everything fell into place, when each spoke from the heart, and lifelong covenants and pledges were exchanged. It was to be a secret between them; no one was to know, not even their respective parents. Bill found he was so excited that he couldn't sleep. He wrote Iva that night and added to the letter the next morning:

11:20 P.M.
Dearest Iva,

I'm going to write you one little note before I seek my bunk. I'm so happy—I feel like slapping all the fellows, on the back. It's too sacred to tell, but I can hardly keep my mouth shut.

Since I left you I have been thinking hard, but I can't think for seeing you all the time in my mind. I'm so glad, glad, glad, you said what you did, on the steps before I left you.

Don't expect this note to be sensible. Just this once—please, allow me to be foolish and say any-thing. I'll be sensible after this, but I must be foolish tonight.

Most fellas, I guess, write poetry at this stage of the game, but I'll use the good, old, honest prose.

You dear girl, if you could only understand how I feel. Maybe this will help you understand at least:

From "A Singular Life":
"The trouble with me, you see," said Helen, "is just what I told you, I am not spiritual."
"You are something better—you are altogether womanly," said the young preacher quickly.
I must go to bed and think. I know you are doing the same thing.

With deepest love,
Will

Saturday morning—7 A.M.
I'm happier this morning.[14]

In early May 1907, the Methodist bishops came to town, and for a week they dom-inated the campus, the chapel, and the attention of the students. They had stern demeanors, accentuated by their being dressed entirely in black, as well as tall black hats, beards, sideburns, and shocks of unruly white hair. Besides their official meetings, the bishops gave a series of addresses to the student body in Ford Chapel covering the state of the Church and its worldwide missions.[15]

The intimate presence of the mightiest movers and shakers in the Methodist Church made a deep impression on the students. It certainly affected Bill, for it was at this time and in this same chapel that he "received his call" to make preaching his career. In some respects, it was the fulfillment of his conversion in Dr. King's church; in other respects, it was what he believed that his mother may have wanted for him; finally, it was certainly what Miss Mary Scott had been preparing him for over the years she had known him. All these factors converged; it was such a powerful moment that when he addressed the Allegheny graduating class in 1923 (he had been invited to commencement to receive an honorary degree), he told the seniors that he could "point out the very chapel seat in which he was sitting when he received his vision."[16] In 1907, Bill could scarcely wait to write the following letter to Miss Mary Scott:

My dear Miss Mary,

I've only time for a few lines. . . . Don't tell Papa, Miss Mary (because I want to surprise him). I am going to be a preacher. It came to me suddenly about two weeks ago (after much study and worry) that God made me for that only. I'm as sure I'm going to preach as I am sure of my name. I'll tell you all about it when I see you. Everything's bright to me and I see my path clearly.

Please don't tell a single person—especially my father. . . .

> *Sincerely,*
> *Will L. Stidger[17]*

Bill may have been exuberant about the certainty of his new calling, but Iva definitely had some questions about his pursuing a career in the ministry and some doubts about her own prospective role as a preacher's wife. While she was dutiful about going to church on Sundays, she was not particularly religious. Bill took a different tack in his effort to persuade her of the rightness of his career choice; he won her over with a flood of romanticism, professions of love for her and evocations of the perfect life they were destined to share. The following letter shows Bill at the height of one of these flights of fancy:

My dear Iva,

I don't know why I'm writing to you just at this time (11:15 P.M.), perhaps it's because I haven't written for so very long and I want to see how it goes. And then again perhaps it's because I can't see you just now and I want to talk, talk, talk, to you. Oh, I could sit all night and talk or just now I could write all night and never tire. I'm as wide-awake as if I had not lost several hours sleep every night for a week.

In some way, I can't tell how or why, I'm way up above the clouds tonight and I'm wild, and free, and happy. It's glorious to be away off like this—up above everybody else so far that all the dirt, and smoke, and smell and filth do not bother. And so far that all the pain and sorrow of earth do not cause one's tears to flow. I'm in my dream world and it makes me bigger and better and purer and cleaner to be here. . . .

And now I must tell you what my dream world is—why, it's all the coming years of my life, and you. It's the joy I feel in anticipation of all the tears I want to dry; of all the broken hearts I want to mend; of all the sad lives I want to make happy—with the help of God and you. That's my dream, just to live because God wants me to make sorrowing men glad of life. *It is good to live and to love and to be loved. Oh, Iva, you'll never know how it thrills my whole being when I stop to think and then realize that you love me. I sometimes wonder if it's true, then it breaks over me like a flood of sunlight: some look I have seen in your eyes or the memory of once or twice when you have bared your soul, unwillingly it may be, to me.*

I'm thinking faster than I can write—about the growth of our Friendship as it gradually developed into Love (and God knows how reverently I say that), about its growth, until now it seems ready to burst into bloom. But it can't open now, it can't burst. It will just keep on growing, larger, and fuller, and sweeter in the bulb until some years have passed. Then if God wills it, and our two lives are spared, it will burst into a full and most beautiful rose of perfect love, when you and I, after all the excitement is over, shall be alone in our own home and shall look into each other's eyes and know that all the world is glad because God is good. Then you'll love me Iva as you never knew you could love, for I'll be good to you and, oh, I can make you happy, I can make you the happiest woman in the world, for I can love you, girl, Iva, my own Iva, more, I believe, than any woman was ever loved.

Why I could write all night but it's one o'clock and I must go to bed, go to church Sunday morning, so I can see you and so we can go out in the evening.

Good night,
Your Will. . . .[18]

When the college year ended in June 1907, Iva graduated and returned home for the summer prior to beginning a job teaching high school in Hollidaysburg, Pennsylvania, about fifty miles to the east of Meadville. It was at this time that Iva introduced Bill to her family. Iva's father, Shepard Berkey, was impressed that his daughter was interested in a man who was going to become a preacher. Berkey was known as a God-fearing man; he sat in the back of his church in the "Amen Corner," so called because of the periodic outbursts of "Amen" resounding throughout the church at pulpit statements that Berkey and his fellow Amen-corner colleagues agreed with. Hannah Berkey, Iva's mother, was far less religious than her husband—who, she said, was "too mighty in prayer." She was won over, however, by Bill's willingness to sit quietly with her in her vegetable and flower garden. While Hannah weeded, giving him tips about seeds and growing vegetables, Bill talked on a number of topics—and polished off the ripest, juiciest tomatoes, salting them with a shaker he brought from the kitchen.

Shepard Berkey owned and ran the general store, located on the north side of the Diamond, the town square. Berkey's store was one of the popular meeting places in Ligonier. In the back was a large pot-bellied stove, surrounded by chairs usually filled with farmers swapping stories and laughing. The Heritage Methodist Church, where the family were regular members, was across the Diamond from Berkey's store. The church was strait-laced Methodist, which meant, among other things, that membership was refused to any family that rented property to anyone who sold liquor.

Iva had been born on August 6, 1883, one and a half years earlier than Bill, and had grown up with rich, brown hair that was often a bit unruly. She had wide-set, large, sleepy brown eyes, the "Berkey" nose (long, straight, prominent), and a firm mouth and chin. Iva stood straight as a die, which, together with her height, five feet eight inches in heels, and her slightly stocky build, gave her a physical presence that commanded attention and could even be a bit off-putting to others. On the other hand, her sense of humor and intelligence attracted people to her.

With Iva off to her new teaching job in Hollidaysburg, Bill returned alone to Allegheny for his sophomore year, but he was joined by his brother Read, who was starting as a freshman.

That fall in the September 1907 issue of *The American Magazine*, there appeared a profile entitled "The Rev. Billy Sunday and His War on the Devil." Sunday was the country's most famous evangelist preacher, and he was still very much a rising star on the American scene.[19]

The American Magazine, a national publication, was particularly well known at Allegheny, since one of its owners, Ida Tarbell, was an Allegheny legend. As a young investigative reporter for *McClure's* magazine, she had exposed John D. Rockefeller's aggressive business tactics so skillfully that a government inquiry ensued, leading ultimately to the breakup of the Standard Oil Trust. Now its in-depth article, nineteen pages long, on Billy Sunday, exploring his preaching and his organizational practices, provided an insight that made obligatory reading for any minister-to-be, and it is entirely likely that Bill Stidger not only read it but studied it carefully.

To most Americans Billy Sunday was first of all the "fastest base runner the National League ever knew." He had had a religious conversion in 1883, given up baseball, and become a preacher who, according to *The American Magazine*, made "more church members than all the ministers in the Middle West working together." While Bill Stidger was never to preach hellfire and damnation like Billy Sunday did, and was no fundamentalist, he came to appreciate Sunday's businesslike approach, especially his understanding of the value of promotion and advertising in building a congregation. Twenty-five years later, Bill was interviewed by a newspaper reporter who asked what the source of Sunday's success (and, indirectly, Bill's own) had been. Bill answered for Sunday and himself: "Publicity."

The opening quotation in *The American Magazine* article laid out a statement by Billy Sunday, one that Bill Stidger himself believed: "The Devil never distilled a wickeder lie into the heart of the world than that the secret of being a Christian is to be solemn and cold and sour."[20]

Bill Stidger found joy in preaching and could never have been "solemn, cold or sour." Sunday's unconventional style exasperated many preachers, and Bill Stidger would later pride himself on his own unconventionality. The Rev. Pearse Pinch, from Fairfield, Iowa, who had been interviewed by *The American Magazine*, said of Sunday: "The man has trampled all over me and my theology. He has kicked my teachings up and down that platform like a football. He has outraged every ideal I have had regarding my sacred profession. But what does that count, as against the results he has accomplished? My congregation will be increased by hundreds. I didn't do it. Sunday did it. It is for me to humble myself and thank God for his help. He is doing God's work. That I do know!"[21]

Even the music in a "Sunday campaign" was no more conventional than the revivalist's preaching methods. Any instrument that made a joyful sound could find use in his services. Brass bands played, and cornet solos were frequently heard. The choir was equipped with tin megaphones, to amplify their voices. The music director was known to have the choir whistle and to encourage the congregation to follow the choir's lead. Throughout his own ministry, Bill Stidger was to know the value of providing a variety of music in his services.

In all matters, Billy Sunday was supremely well organized. He had a pamphlet that was given to the elders of towns that wanted him to accept preaching engagements. It described in great detail his requirements—such as his insistence that a large wooden tabernacle, or shed, be built and outfitted with fixed wooden seats for his meetings. Collections taken during his services went to repay the revival's financial backers and to pay the salaries of the large number of staff needed to run the revivals. However, Sunday specified that whatever was collected on the last night was to be his to keep, as his compensation: "I think that the people who work for Christ ought to be enabled to live as well as those who work for the Devil."[22]

Prior to the beginning of the Fairfield, Iowa, revival, *The American Magazine* reporter followed Sunday as he canvassed the town, calling on shoemakers, druggists, hardware men, butchers, grocers, and news dealers. He was "unaffectedly familiar with quality of goods, with the characteristic traits of the jobbers and wholesale dealers, with current prices and the change in trade conditions." In short, Sunday knew his customers the way an astute businessman would.[23]

As the revival neared its end, about a thousand "sinners" had already come forward, more than any of the town's ministers thought possible. But on the last day, when he spoke at three services, Billy Sunday "was filled with a fierce, almost savage, zeal to bring in all who were without the fold."[24] When he finished his final prayer (while whispering directions under his breath to Rev. Honeywell, his "associate evangelist," to clear the front benches for the reception of the converts), Sunday cried:

> "Now who will be the first to stand up for God and lead the way to salvation for the others who are to come?" A storm of applause and cheers greeted the appearance of one of the leading bankers of the town, striding down the aisle with his head erect and eyes shining, followed by farmers, storekeepers, lawyers, physicians, farmer boys and laborers. Sunday leaned forward over the edge of the platform swaying his arms rhythmically as though to sweep the whole congregation to the front. The ministers and the "personal workers" went out between the rows of seats and labored with those who seemed in doubt. There were eighty converts at the end.[25]

Altogether, Billy Sunday won 1,118 souls away from the devil out of the five thousand people in the town of Fairfield, Iowa, and an additional four thousand in its environs. When

Bill Stidger was himself a teacher of young ministers, twenty years later, he urged his students to hear Billy Sunday rather than more conventional ministers, because, he said, Sunday knew how to bring in huge crowds, and equally important, he knew how to keep them coming. There was a minimum of "backsliding" among people converted at Sunday's famous marathon revival meetings. Bill said, "The one thing that makes me take my hat off to Billy Sunday is that he has survived in the respect of the people for twenty-five or thirty years in spite of his strange methods. Back of his work is a great, genuine sincerity of purpose."[26]

Between his second and third years at Allegheny, Bill was offered a summer job as pastor of three rural churches. The churches were in Erie, on the edge of the vast Lake Erie, forty miles north of Meadville; in Saegertown, six miles north of Meadville on the road to Erie; and in Elgin, a small town about thirty miles to the northeast of Meadville. It meant a lot of traveling and not much contact with Iva, but he was thrilled with preaching. He made his base in Meadville, where he could cover his churches as well as work on *The Campus*, the college newspaper, of which he had been elected editor in chief. Iva, meanwhile, had returned to Ligonier for the summer. There she competed for and won, from a field of five other candidates (all men), the position of principal of the Ligonier high school.

Bill's inattention to his courses finally caught up to him and, as he started his third year, he was still classified as a sophomore. Even though he began to study more diligently, he was overcommitted extracurricularly. Being editor of *The Campus* took an enormous amount of his time, as it was published weekly. He was also associate editor of (and prolific writer for) the *Literary Monthly* and the associate editor of the yearbook, the *Kaldron*. Besides these activities Bill continued with his football and track, although he could only compete in a few of the games or meets due to his low grades.

By the spring semester of his third year, in 1909, Bill was faced with a number of credits to make up and no new extracurricular mountains to climb; he had already scaled every one of them and had been prominently seen on all the summits. Perhaps it was time for a change in scene. If so, as a swan song to his years at Allegheny, Bill published, just before graduation ceremonies in June, an extraordinary issue of the *Literary Monthly* devoted exclusively to his own poetry.

This exceptional offering that Bill let fly upon the student body consisted of twelve of his poems. It was a string of paeans to himself and of barely veiled references to his love for Iva, all of which would have been utterly insufferable except that the pamphlet also included acerbic commentary, which he also wrote (or edited), lambasting his poems and lacerating his skill as a poet.

The need for attention—public attention—at any cost drove him, as did his sense of humor. Miraculously, it worked. It took unusual brashness to put his poetry on view together with the skewering of it. Readers were amused, and Bill was admired for his efforts. The writer of Allegheny College's history, *Allegheny—A Century of Education, 1815–1915*, commented, "The 'Lit' has encouraged in the student body very commendable short story writing. One of the most novel of its issues was that of June, 1909, containing a collection of the early poems of W. L. Stidger, the rival editor of *The Campus*."[27]

The special publication began with this proclamation:

Selections From the Poetical Works of
William Leroy Stidger
(For Many Years a Student at Allegheny College)
Edited with Critical, Explanatory, Exegetical,
Expository and Appreciative Notes and Comments.
For Home Study and for Use in
Kindergartens and Universities

There was a concluding section called: "Notes for Those Students Who Wish to Obtain a True Estimate of the Poet and His Works." In addition there was a further explanation: "These notes are written by a number of our best critics who have made long and laborious research into the various phases of thought, passion and feeling expressed in the several poems here published. We trust they will commend themselves to the reader."

A sample poem and the critical comment about it follows:

I Like the Smell of Burning Leaves

I like the smell of burning leaves,
And I know why I do:
It makes me think of yellow sheaves
When harvest times are through.
It takes me back to boyhood days—
And Oh, those days were good!
We played among the stacked up maize
And in the barren wood.
We hauled the yellow pumpkins in
From field to bursting barn;
We saw our mothers sit and spin
The crimson-colored yarn;
We heard the ghostly stories told—
And Oh, the nights were still.
We knew of Winter's coming cold—
E'en then the nights were chill.
I like the smell of burning leaves,
And I know why I do;
Because it brings back memories
Of times, so good and true.

The critical comment:

According to the best of authorities, this lyric, to be compared only with Coleridge's "Ode on Dejection," is accounted to be our author's masterpiece. The limped movement makes one actually feel as if he were riding on the jolting wagon on top of the pumpkins.

As it is certain that the poet never lived on a farm and as we know that he had a country charge [assignment as pastor], we think that this poem was a result of his long walks through the country to his church. All in all we consider this effort very creditable, yet we find that it has many weaknesses. He says, "And I know why I do." This is accounted for in the fact that it is only a creeping out of his self-confidence. "Yellow pumpkins" is a hackneyed expression, worthy only of a Sophomore. "Ghostly" in the fourth stanza is incorrectly used:—A person is ghostly and stories are ghost stories. This fourth stanza mars the general effect. The first line is the only good one. The word "night" is repeated too much.

In the last stanza he again tells us that he knows why he likes that particular smell. He has kept his secret well. The word "true" in this stanza was put in merely to rhyme with "do." How are those times true? To whom are they true?[28]

Fast on the heels of the appearance of Bill's volume of poetry followed one of the big mysteries in his life. He left Allegheny. Did he flunk out? Was he expelled? Did he simply decide to move on? Allegheny's records are silent on this matter, except that his grades and attendance were just good enough to make the "flunked out" theory unlikely. There was a story that circulated down through the years that Bill and some of his friends—in the tradition of President William McKinley, who was said to have done it first—led a cow up into the bell tower of Allegheny's prized Bentley Hall.

Whether by cow or other prank, or for still other reasons, Bill's experiences at Allegheny came to an end early in the summer of 1909. The college bore no hard feelings toward him, however, and in the summer of 1915 it invited him to return for its hundredth anniversary celebration. At that time he was elected to membership in the national oratorical fraternity. In 1923, Bill was awarded an honorary doctor of divinity degree by Allegheny, as well as asked to speak at the annual commencement vesper service. This recognition meant a great deal to him, and for the occasion he wrote about Allegheny, about friends like Miss Mary Scott, about Iva and ministers who believed in him: "My college has had faith enough in me to give me a degree. That faith in me has made me taller. The faith of my friends has made me taller than I was. Like a mere pygmy I have stood on the shoulders of these giant faiths that my friends have had in me and I have been able to see far. . . . God believes in me. That faith in me has lifted me up until I have been tall enough to touch the stars."[29]

Notes

1. Betty Stidger Hyland, *Those Heavenly Years*, unpublished manuscript, 1955, 1–2.

2. "Camp Ground Sketches of Days of '47," *The Moundsville Journal*, July 29, 1900; newspaper articles compiled by Evan M. Rogerson in connection with the sesquicentennial of Simpson United Methodist Church in 1970.

3. Becky Clutter, *The History of Marshall County, West Virginia* (Moundsville, W. Va.: Marshall County Historical Society, 1984).

4. William L. Stidger, *Men of the Great Redemption* (Nashville: Cokesbury, 1931), 121–31.

5. William James, *The Varieties of Religious Experience* (New York: Random House, 1994), 210–84.

6. William L. Stidger, *Symphonic Sermons* (New York: George H. Doran, 1924), 196.

7. Stidger, *Symphonic Sermons*, 196–97.

8. Iva Berkey Stidger, "The Night of the Little Stockings," *Western Christian Advocate*, May 3, 1916, 8–9.

9. M. Nesbitt, "People We Meet," *The Journal*, Moundsville, West Virginia, July 20, 1896.

10. Letter dated May 29, 1918, from William L. Stidger to Miss Mary I. Scott, author's collection.

11. William L. Stidger, *Flashlights from the Seven Seas* (New York: George H. Doran, 1921), title page.

12. "Dr. Stidger, In Interview, Reviews His Career as Newspaper Reporter," *The Wheeling Intelligencer*, September 30, 1922, 8.

13. Letter dated October 1, 1907, from W. C. Robinson to Ivan Read Stidger, author's collection.

14. Letter, undated, from William L. Stidger to Iva Berkey, author's collection.

15. Ernest Ashton Smith, *Allegheny—A Century of Education, 1815–1915* (Meadville, Penn.: Allegheny College History, 1916), 240–41.

16. "Rev. Wm. L. Stidger Preaches Message of Love at Vespers," *The Campus*, June 20, 1923.

17. Letter dated June 1907, from William L. Stidger to Miss Mary I. Scott, author's collection.

18. Letter, undated, from William L. Stidger to Iva Berkey, author's collection.

19. Lindsay Denison, "The Rev. Billy Sunday and His War on the Devil," *The American Magazine*, September 1907, 451–68.

20. Denison, "Rev. Billy Sunday," 453.

21. Denison, "Rev. Billy Sunday," 454–55.

22. Denison, "Rev. Billy Sunday," 457.

23. Denison, "Rev. Billy Sunday," 459.

24. Denison, "Rev. Billy Sunday," 465.

25. Denison, "Rev. Billy Sunday," 465.

26. "'Gantry' Product of Inflamed Mind, Stidger Charges," unidentified publication, dated November 28, 1927, Stidger Papers at Brown University Library.

27. *Allegheny—A Century of Education*, 435.

28. "Selections from the Poetical Works of William Leroy Stidger (for many years a student at Allegheny College)," *The Allegheny Literary Monthly* 13, no. 9, June 1909, 271–92.

29. Stidger, *Symphonic Sermons*, 142.

Two

Finding Mecca: Boston

I t was a tribute to Miss Mary Scott's strong conviction about a Christian life and education for Bill that after Allegheny his next step was the School of Theology at Boston University. As he was the first in his family to attend college, much less graduate school, Boston University was an ambitious goal. Bill arrived at the imposing entrance of the School of Theology at 72 Mount Vernon Street in the fall of 1909. The "72" was written in ornate gold letters on the lunette above towering heavy doors, with highly polished brass appointments. The brownstone building housing the School of Theology was massive, with five floors on Mount Vernon Street and seven floors on the Chestnut Street side.

The school was located in the quiet, affluent neighborhood of Beacon Hill, a short distance west of the State House with its gilded dome, which shone like a ball of fire hung high in the air. Also, it was within a stone's throw of Boston Common, described by the school's bulletin as "a noble expanse of forty-eight acres of green turf and tall forest trees, in the very heart of the Puritan City." Boston was a metropolis, with a million inhabitants. The city boasted a great library with seven hundred thousand volumes, the largest collection for free circulation in the world; an internationally recognized symphony orchestra; and an outstanding Museum of Fine Arts, with a notable collection of Egyptian and Cyprian antiquities as well as paintings by European masters. With Harvard University, Boston University, and the Massachusetts Institute of Technology, among others, Boston was alive with students and intellectual activity. In addition, there were more than 250 churches within a short radius of the school. Boston was more than a city of the present; it also reverberated with echoes from the past. Near Beacon Hill were buildings almost two hundred years old, such as Old South Church, Old North Church, Faneuil Hall, Paul Revere's house, and the homes or the birthplaces of Franklin, Webster, Emerson, Hawthorne, Longfellow, Whittier, Lowell, and Alcott.[1]

The School of Theology, to which Bill was applying, had been the first Methodist seminary in America. It had been founded in 1839 and had become the core around which Boston University was itself established in 1871. A few other protestant seminaries predated the School of Theology, since the Methodists had been slow to move into education; they believed that it was better for a minister to be made "by the call of God, not by book learning."[2] Many Methodists suspected that seminaries were no more than nurseries for heresy. On the other hand, the gradual shift of America's population from small country towns into the cities put an increasing burden on ministers to be well educated and able to deal with the more sophisticated issues associated with urban life and the times.

Bill therefore lived in an era when the importance of seminaries was coming to the fore. Only thirteen years earlier, in 1896, the faculty at Boston University's School of Theology had persuaded the General Conference of the Methodist Episcopal Church to recognize work done at the School of Theology and at other mainstream theological schools as equivalent to conference examinations—the normal path for most young men wishing to make preaching their careers. While this had been a major advance, skepticism about seminaries remained, especially toward Boston University, whose School of Theology was seen as a hotbed of liberal thought.

Bill presented himself at 9 A.M. on Wednesday, September 15, 1909, to take the school's entrance examinations, required of him because he had not yet graduated from college. He was accepted and placed in the Second Division on a four-year—rather than three-year—track, which meant it was expected that he would in due course satisfy his unfilled requirements, including a working knowledge of Greek, and move into the First Division. Tuition and room were free for candidates for the Methodist ministry.

It is difficult to overestimate the importance of schools of theology to the development of religious thinking in America at this time. The publication of Charles Darwin's *On the Origin of Species* fifty years earlier, in 1859, had introduced the concept of human evolution, which thrust science onto a collision course with the beliefs held by the mainstream religions. Evolution's fundamental assumption was that the history of the earth went back millions of years. This was seen as irreconcilable with the fundamental doctrines of Christianity, including one commonly accepted interpretation of Old Testament chronology that calculated that the creation of the world occurred in the year 4004 B.C.[3] Many people also felt that the theory of evolution belittled and degraded man.

In the rural parts of America, people clung to their established views tenaciously, giving rise to the fundamentalist movement (which became known by that name only in the early years of the twentieth century). Its very reason for existence was reaction to the growing acceptance of science, its products and its ideas, as an integral part of everyday life, especially in the cities.

At the turn of the century, Methodism was the largest protestant denomination in the United States in numbers of members. It had been the most aggressive and well-organized recruiter of people's souls and had sent its ministers on horseback—"circuit riders," they were called—to the constantly westward-moving frontier. As is true of governing bodies of many large organizations, its bishops, whom Bill had seen on the Allegheny campus, tended to be older, more conservative, and more wary of change than many of the younger ministers and intellectuals in the Church.

In order to make a bridge between religious beliefs and scientific theory, there had to be a reinterpretation of the Bible, a softening of the strict reading of its words, an ability to see it as literary or interpretative rather than authoritative. This could best be accomplished in an open-minded environment, such as could be found across the country in a handful of schools of theology, most of which were linked to universities.

Methodism's *primus inter pares* institution was Boston University's School of Theology, which played an important role in constructing a bridge between religion and science and in driving the Church to accept new roles in social responsibility and personal psychology. At this time, Borden Parker Bowne was acknowledged as the school's intellectual giant, and his thinking and writing ranged from dealing with Darwinian evolution to developing a philosophy that emphasized the practical and experiential rather than a deterministic aspect of human life. He called his philosophy "Personalism," and through it and his effective teaching Bowne exerted considerable influence on the thinking at the school, and in wider circles, for years.

There was also an enthusiasm to apply the school's courses "to the work of the minister and the daily lives of his people." As Richard Cameron, the school's historian, has said, "The de-emphasis on the sacred languages had just been consummated; the subsequent emphasis on theology had not yet arrived. . . . Scholarship was mentioned little during this period and 'theological' was almost a dirty word."[4] Even Professor Bowne's philosophical inquiry was used in the service of improving the art of preaching.

For Bill, used to hearing the absolute views expressed by his Moundsville mentor, William B. King, or so persuasively delivered by Billy Sunday, the fresh thought and healthy skepticism of the Boston University faculty opened up a new world. Bill had no aspirations to be a great church intellectual, but his mind churned the new ideas, figuring out how to present them in a meaningful way to ordinary people. Somewhere along the line he defined his objective as "putting the cookie jar on the lowest shelf," which meant he always wanted his message to be accessible to everyone.

Students were each given an opportunity to preach a sermon in the chapel. For that occasion, Bill arranged for Iva to take the train from Ligonier to hear him. He preached a sermon filled with fiery faith that was spectacular—and spectacularly inappropriate, its theme being "The Evil of Women's Beautiful Bodies in Corsets." When he was through and the startled assembly of students and faculty had departed, Professor Knudson, who was new at the school and whom Bill had known at Allegheny, quietly came up to him and said, "Will, you certainly have the fire, the wind and the eloquence, but not the class. Temper the wind to suit the lamb, temper the wind."[5]

Boston and the School of Theology changed Bill for life. He made friends whose paths would crisscross with his for the next forty years, and he had found in Boston a city to love. Furthermore, the school gave Bill many new philosophical paths to travel.

Abruptly, on April 1, 1910, Professor Bowne had a massive stroke in the middle of his class on ethics, collapsed, and died, bringing an era to a close. The school went into a state of shock. For many students the words "Boston" and "Bowne" were synonymous. Bill expressed his own feelings melodramatically in his *Place of Books in the Life We Live*: "When Borden Parker Bowne died, I left Boston Theological Seminary."[6] In fact, he did leave, but on good terms with the school, and he left for two important reasons: he had made a date to get married to Iva in early June, and he had accepted a job as vice president at East Greenwich Academy, a Methodist preparatory school of two hundred students located ten miles south of Providence, Rhode Island. It was a school with a fine reputation but one that had fallen on hard times.

Bill was certain that he had gotten all he needed out of college and theological school. He wanted to move on with his life, especially once he and Iva were married, and he thought that teaching and coaching in a Methodist school made a perfect next step. Iva accepted this plan of action, because they would both have jobs at East Greenwich, she teaching German and Latin and Bill teaching English and theology studies and coaching football. Iva, however, had her own agenda. She understood Bill's impatience but realized that he ought to complete his undergraduate degree. The lack of one had slowed down his pace at the School of Theology, and furthermore, it was an increasingly important credential in any field of professional life. Bill was not at all receptive to this idea and said so. For the time being Iva relented.

The *Ligonier Echo* described the Stidger wedding as Bill and Iva's being "very quietly united in marriage,"[7] at the Berkey home on East Church Street on Wednesday morning, June 7, 1910. Bill had arrived by train from Boston on the prior Saturday. The ceremony was performed by Reverend E. G. Morris, the pastor of the Heritage Methodist Church, with only "a very few immediate friends" present for the occasion and for a wedding breakfast that followed. Iva and Bill then left on the early train to visit his parents; after a short visit they headed to East Greenwich, a married couple joined together for the rest of their lives.

From the Methodist Church's standpoint, when Bill left the School of Theology, he was received on trial by the New England Southern Conference, as recommended by the East Greenwich Quarterly Conference. He was assigned to First Year Studies and appointed vice president and member of the faculty at East Greenwich Academy. Bill's goal now was to be ordained, via studies and examinations, by his conference. (It was not until twenty years later, in 1936, that a seminary education became the officially designated path to ordination.)

In the fall, once classes had begun, Bill learned that the pastor of Warwick Central Baptist Church in nearby Apponaug had died, thereby leaving a position open. He applied for the job when it looked like the Baptists might have trouble filling the vacancy quickly. His own bishop encouraged Bill to take the job. For the Methodists, it was an opportunity for an energetic young Methodist shepherd to place himself in the midst of a Baptist flock. Rhode Island had been a Baptist stronghold ever since the first Baptist church in America was established in Providence by Roger Williams in 1639.

Bill made Warwick Central the testing ground of his ideas. On Memorial Day he invited the few remaining veterans of the Civil War in the Warwick area, members of Thomas Post Eleven of the Grand Army of the Republic. To them and his congregation Bill preached a rousing sermon that he called "The Remnant." The story was about the battered, torn, and bloody flag carried into battle by Bill's grandfather, Capt. John Stidger of Company B of the Second West Virginia Regiment. At the end of the sermon, Bill dramatically unfurled the stained and worn flag and held it high. Most of his congregation, especially the veterans, were patriotically moved to tears. Overall it was a carefully staged and orchestrated event, and it brought many of the veterans back as members of the Warwick congregation.[8]

Bill and Iva were extremely happy in East Greenwich. They loved being together, they both derived great satisfaction from their teaching, and Bill enjoyed coaching the boys in football. Despite his teaching, preaching, and coaching he had leftover energy to burn, and he turned to writing, producing a profusion of articles and poems that found audiences well beyond his immediate circle at East Greenwich.

His *The Lincoln Book of Poems* was published in 1911 by the Gorham Press. It contained twenty-two poems that he had written, suggested by incidents in Lincoln's life, by literary passages referring to Lincoln, and by "thoughts from the author's own meditative broodings over the 'Modern Man of Sorrows.'"[9] One reviewer, distinctly critical, called the book "a collection of amateurish eulogies in rhyme. Harmless outpourings full of obvious, but nevertheless genuine, sentiment."[10] The loyal Moundsville newspaper was more generous to Bill: "The *Echo* has received from the publisher a copy of the book, which is quite an attractive collection of poems . . . portraying . . . in most beautiful word-pictures the beauty, tenderness, sympathy, strength and sorrows of that great man's life."[11] Despite the negative tenor of some of the reviews, Bill was immensely pleased to be in print.

Poem after poem flowed from his typewriter. He wrote individual poems, generally on religious topics, which were published in the various editions of the *Christian Advocate*, the Methodist monthly publication. Then there were nostalgic poems, published in a small volume entitled *The Old Wolf Spring and Other Home Poems*. The book was a home-grown product printed in the Schoolcraft Print Shop of East Greenwich Academy, whose students paid for their education by printing books and postcards and making furniture.[12] To no one's surprise, *Wolf Spring* received a very positive review from the Moundsville *Echo;* somewhat to Bill's surprise, the *Allegheny Literary Review* liked it too.

It took only one year at East Greenwich for Bill to decide that Iva had been right and that he ought to return to college to get his degree. Teaching at a high school was not fulfilling enough for him, and being a pastor in a small Baptist church could only be seen as temporary. Bill was, after all, a Methodist and eager to be given an official assignment so he could move ahead with his career. He did not expect to be ordained for another two years, so completing his final year in college, beginning in the fall of 1911, made sense to him.

In fact, though it was Bill's decision to return to college, Iva's persistence had much to do with it. Bill later readily admitted his indebtedness to Iva and to Miss Mary Scott:

[Miss Mary Scott] told me what I could do, and what I would do and never for a minute did she ever assume that I would do anything other than go to college. It was because of that one woman's faith and hers alone, her great expectations for me, that I went to college.

Then it was because of another woman's faith that I finished, and that was my wife. I was a rebel soul, and I decided that I didn't need to finish college, and that I would show the world that a man could succeed even in the ministry without a degree. But I am glad that I went on and got a degree, and I am here saying that I went on because of my wife's faith that I could and would.[13]

Brown University, in nearby Providence, seemed the ideal place for Bill to apply. It was an institution founded by Baptists and might therefore be receptive to Bill as a minister, especially after his recent work at Warwick Central Baptist Church. Bill was permitted to enter Brown in September 1911, to complete his undergraduate studies. The official record at Brown University stated:

William L. Stidger—Admitted provisionally as member of the Senior class, a candidate for the Ph.B. [Bachelor of Philosophy] degree, having yet to present a letter of honorable dismissal, and a satisfactory certificate of standing, or substitute therefore satisfactory to President Faunce, from Allegheny College.

At some later date the record reported that Bill had been accepted, apparently having satisfied President Faunce, although there was no elaboration on how Bill achieved this.

That fall of 1911 was Bill and Iva's second year at East Greenwich. Iva was teaching Latin, drilling the boys on *"Hic, haec, hoc, huius, huius, huic,"* while Bill plowed through a reading with his students of Shakespeare's *A Midsummer Night's Dream.* Actually, as he admitted to Iva, he was secretly dreaming up new topics for his sermons while he appeared to listen to his boys' recitations. During one of his daydreams, he struck upon a thought that he regarded as an inspiration, and it stemmed from listening to symphonies he had heard in Boston. Why not introduce one idea at the beginning of a sermon, then embellish on it, restate the idea, embellish it further and restate the idea at the end? Bill immediately coined the phrase "symphonic sermon" and tried out the idea on his congregation at Warwick Central Baptist. He chose as his recurring theme:

The soul can split the sky in two
And let the face of God shine through.[14]

The symphonic sermon was an immediate success, and he incorporated it into his repertoire. It was an innovation that Bill credited for further increasing the size of his congregation each Sunday. The symphonic sermon was to earn Bill a wider reputation for innovation in his ministry.

As the fall of 1911 wore on, Iva began to knit "little things" and blushed when she wrote *"puer est agricola"* on the blackboard, causing the boys to giggle. Somehow the news got out that "Mrs. Stidger is going to have a baby." One day, early in 1912, a letter arrived from Ligonier:

Iva, you'd better come home now. I don't think it is proper for you to be around young boys in your condition. Father sends you his love and this ticket. Be sure to pack a nice hamper of food for the trip. Leave all Will's socks darned and his shirts clean. I also am enclosing a ten dollar bill for emergencies, but don't leave it in your pocketbook, pin it to your corset cover. We'll meet the train,

Love,
Mother[15]

As Iva packed, she gave Bill explicit instructions, "When your socks get too holey, throw them away. Wash the lower sheet on the bed and the pillowcase each week. Put the upper sheet on the bottom and the clean one on top. Write often and as soon as school is over, hurry to Ligonier, where Willie, Jr., and I will be waiting for you."

The windup to Bill's year at Brown was noteworthy for the hard work he put into it. In commenting to his daughter Betty years later, he said:

I never did work until I got to Brown that last year and then I had you coming, and I HAD to work or you would have been ashamed of me when you arrived. It isn't the way you begin that counts in the long run but the way you end up.

With Iva home in Ligonier to await their baby, Bill continued to pursue his church responsibilities, his teaching at East Greenwich, and his courses at Brown. All the time, though, he kept his mind open for things in what he saw or read that would provide subjects for sermons or articles.

Bill witnessed a dramatic incident one day on his way to school—and he also saw a larger story in it. Most of his articles and sermons came from such incidents as this one, which he later recalled in a piece entitled "Leaning Against the Wind."

Back in 1912, when I was a student in Brown University at Providence, as I went up the hill to classes I used to stop and watch the workmen walking along the steel girders of a skyscraper. I always expected to see one of them fall, for they were seemingly careless and nonchalant. . . . Then one terrible morning I saw what I had feared would happen. A workman fell from one of those steel girders to his death in the street below.

A crowd quickly gathered around that battered and broken body. I stood on the outskirts and listened to talk about the accident. Finally a man who seemed to be in authority came down from the top of the building on a crude lift, hurried over to the body and said, "The fool was leaning against the wind! I told him to quit leaning against the wind. He was new at this game or he wouldn't have done it."

Later I got that foreman to one side and asked him what he meant by leaning against the wind. Then, seeing that I was an earnest young seeker after truth, he patiently went into some details about one of the occupational dangers of steel workers and said: "Well, you see, along the coast here in the morning hours there is often a strong wind blowing from the ocean, at fifty or sixty miles an hour, and a steel worker high on a building of this type gets to leaning against the wind. It is easier to work that way. You don't have to resist so much. But an experienced worker soon learns that he dare not depend upon that wind, for it may drop at any minute and then he topples to the ground. You can never depend upon the stability of the wind."

There was a parable for you. How many of us get to leaning against the wind in life—or against something which is just as fickle, unstable, and uncertain as the winds that blow. . . . We must learn in life to get something substantial to lean against if we want to do any leaning—the mental and spiritual things; things of character, integrity and honor. These are the rocks of life.[16]

Elizabeth Robinson Stidger was born on a fresh May morning, the twenty-third and a Thursday, at eight A.M. in the morning. An anxious father and mother Berkey assisted the doctor until Betty was safely and soundly ensconced in this world and Iva was declared a healthy mother. Then Shepard Berkey walked into town to Weller's Hardware Store and sent Bill a telegram.

The wire arrived at East Greenwich Academy during Thursday night prayer meeting. The janitor carried it ceremoniously down the side aisle to Bill, who had just begun delivering his sermon. When Bill was handed the wire, he paused in his talk to open and read the contents. He looked up from the paper he was holding in a shaking hand and said half to the congregation and half to himself: "Gosh, I'm a father. Eight pounds." He glanced at his watch and rushed down off the pulpit, saying, "Brother Thompson. Please say the benediction for me. I'm sorry, everyone, but if I hurry I can make the night train!"[17]

When Betty was at Smith College, Bill wrote to her about seeing her for the first time:

Dear Betty,

It is nearing Thanksgiving time—and I'm writing a lot of letters to bishops, and editors and friends who have been a blessing to me. I find that I have to include my own family in the lot. "Ain't that something!" as Amos [of Amos and Andy] says.

First, I have to go back a long way and remember how you were born of Mother's love and mine. I like to think of what you meant to me even before you were born—of how we looked forward to your coming; of how hard I worked that year in East Greenwich in teaching and coaching and preaching—and how my heart was full of song as we waited for your coming.

I remember putting Mother on the train at Providence, and how we wept when she went home to Ligonier. Then the months passed. I had to stay and end up school at East Greenwich and graduate at Brown. Then I went home to you and Mother. When I walked in the front door the first thing I said was: "I want to see my baby!"

Mother took me upstairs and lifted you out of the crib and I took you in my arms—so tiny and frail—and helpless-looking and kissed your cheeks—and wept a little—then kissed Mother—and said: "So that's my baby is it?" with the emphasis on "It." Just like you would say: "So this is Paris" when you first got there.

Then I like to think of the happiness you have brought to me as the years have come and gone. It is good to go back over them and to estimate what a blessing you have been to me—and how thankful I am to have you for my very own daughter—and what a deep satisfaction you have been. I am more thankful for you than anything else on earth—save Mother alone—and you and she belong in the same class.

We accept things from people all along the way and never think to stop to thank them. It's just too bad, isn't it? But not your Dad. He is, at least, letting you know just how much he appreciates you and loves you and how thankful he is just for YOU—and that you are his.

Love,
Dad[18]

The last entry in Bill's Brown University transcript is that he was awarded a bachelor of philosophy degree (Ph.B.) in June 1912, thus ending his near decade-long quest for a college degree. Roy Stidger sent Bill a gold watch with a gold chain and monogrammed fob. Roy didn't feel he could go to the Brown graduation, because his ice cream store was starting to be the success he had hoped it would be and he was reluctant to leave the job to anyone else. He sent the following letter, accompanied by the gold watch:

Dear Willie:

I am sorry I can't come to your graduation. I hope this watch will always be a reminder to you of your Papa who loves you. I am very proud you have decided to be a preacher. I promise I will come to hear you preach someday.

Yours respectfully,
Leroy Stidger[19]

On April 6, 1913, Bill, aged twenty-eight, was elected and ordained a deacon in New Bedford, Massachusetts, by Bishop John W. Hamilton, and was admitted into full membership of the Methodist Episcopal Church as an ordained minister. It would now be only a matter of days, weeks, or months that some pulpit, somewhere in the dominion of the Church, would need a preacher, and Bill would be called. The call came: Bill was given a new church in the Sunset District in San Francisco, and he was to take over in late summer of 1913.

Notes

1. *Boston University School of Theology Catalogue for the Year 1909–10,* 172–76.

2. Richard Morgan Cameron, *Boston University School of Theology 1839–1968* (Boston: Boston University School of Theology, 1968), 2.

3. Since 1658, many Christians have accepted the calculations of James Ussher, an Irish archbishop, who estimated that the first day of creation occurred on October 23, 4004 B.C.E. [Before the Common Era]. *Library of Date Setters:* www.bible.ca/pre-date-setters.htm.

4. Cameron, *Boston University School of Theology 1839–1968,* 45.

5. John Bartlett (1820–1905). *Familiar Quotations,* 10th ed. (Boston: Little, Brown, 1919). Laurence Stone (1713–1768): "God tempers the wind to the shorn lamb."

6. William L. Stidger, *The Place of Books in the Life We Live* (New York: George H. Doran, 1922), 86.

7. "Quiet Home Wedding," *Ligonier Echo,* June 1, 1910, 1.

8. "War Flag Unfurled," unidentified newspaper, Stidger Papers at Brown University Library, Providence, Rhode Island.

9. "Book Talks," *Allegheny Literary Monthly,* 1911, 157–61.

10. "The Literary Sliver," *Town Topics,* New York, March 7, 1912.

11. "Lincoln Book of Poems by Will L. Stidger Just Published," *Moundsville Daily Echo,* undated article, Stidger Papers at Brown University Library, Providence, Rhode Island.

12. *Literary Digest,* New York, April 1, 1911.

13. William L. Stidger, *Symphonic Sermons* (New York: George H. Doran, 1924), 142–43.

14. Edna St. Vincent Millay, *Renascence and Other Poems* (New York: Mitchell Kennerley, 1917), 14.

15. Betty Stidger Hyland, *Those Heavenly Years,* unpublished manuscript, 1955, 10.

16. William L. Stidger, *There Are Sermons in Stories* (New York: Abington-Cokesbury, 1942), 101–2.

17. Hyland, *Those Heavenly Years,* 11.

18. Letter, undated, from William L. Stidger to Betty Stidger, author's collection.

19. Hyland, *Those Heavenly Years,* 7.

Three

The Incredible Electrified Revolving Cross: San Francisco

C alvary Church, in September 1913, was a small, new church located in the sparsely settled Sunset District, just south of Golden Gate Park. The Sunset District was still being reclaimed from miles of sand dunes, and only a few years earlier, it had been called the Great Sand Waste or the Outlands. In Bill's time, the area—like most of San Francisco—had recently been electrified, but streetcar passengers often had to help clear the tracks of drifted sand or, if the drifts were too high, walk for blocks to another car farther ahead.

Calvary Church was a brown wood-shingled structure with a flat-topped steeple, commanding the highest point in a four-mile area. From Calvary's rooftop one could see the Golden Gate and the ships outward bound for the Orient or homeward bound for San Francisco Harbor. Inside the church, there was room for 250 souls with some crowding, although only a handful people made up the new pastor's congregation at the beginning. Bill knew that he had a lot of work ahead of him.

In later years Bill liked to recall that he had only the janitor and a sandstorm on hand for his first Sunday morning sermon. In reality, there was a small but loyal band of "pioneers"—as he called his first congregation—who showed up to support their new pastor. He ambitiously scheduled not one but two services on that Sunday and found himself preaching an evening sermon to six people. He proceeded as if he were speaking to a standing-room-only congregation, whom he asked to adopt the phrase "Calvary—the Little Church on the Hill," to help everyone in the Sunset District who did not have a church home know where Calvary was and that they were welcome. Bill was determined to make his first year a success, which meant dramatically increased attendance and collections, and he had until the next annual General Conference, the following September, to prove himself.

The first item on his agenda was finding a place to live as quickly as possible so he could send for Iva and Betty. He checked out several apartments or houses near the church, but they either cost too much or had no backyards, which Bill felt he needed for Betty to play in. On his third week of hunting, he came across a unique and inexpensive place that, emotionally, he knew was just right; he committed himself on the spot. Bill wired Iva, who was staying with her parents in Ligonier, "House found—right on ocean beach for Betty, inspiration for sermons. Wire what train you can make. Love, Will."[1] Iva immediately reserved two seats on the transcontinental train. On the ride to California, Iva and one-year-old Betty sat next to a woman from a small town in Pennsylvania who said that she was on her way to San Francisco to seek her fortune in one of the finer houses, with their red-velvet interiors, of the infamous Barbary Coast. Directly behind them rode a police officer from California who had handcuffed himself to his traveling companion, a recaptured convict and a three-time offender. This odd group of five passengers spent many hours together as the train made its way west. The food in Iva's hamper gradually spoiled and the crock of milk soured. Betty got fussy, then sick. Iva got sick. Her new pongee blouse became badly wrinkled and soiled. Fortunately the convict loved children and told Betty stories, sang to her, and taught her games to play. Iva's traveling companion took her under her wing and nursed her back to health. As Betty wrote in *Those Heavenly Years*, much later:

> "Now, dearie, a shot of brandy is just what you need, and even if you are against the stuff, you must take some," the prostitute said.
>
> "But my husband's a preacher and we support the Women's Christian Temperance Union," Iva protested weakly.
>
> "Well all I can say, dearie, is that the good Lord turned water into wine and if it was good enough for Him, it's good enough for you. Now you take a slug of this."

When the train arrived in Berkeley, there was no sign of Bill, although he had written to say he would be there. What he actually said was "Nothing in the world could keep me away, so excited am I to see my girls." An hour passed. Another train arrived, emptied its passengers, and once again the station fell silent. The two Stidgers sat on their pile of luggage, waiting for Bill.

Then, off in the distance, abruptly, a tall, redheaded stranger with a most peculiar mustache, a mixture of reds, browns, and yellows, appeared at a dead run.

"Bill, how could you?"

"Iva," he blurted out, "I started out in plenty of time—oh my mustache—you don't like it? Okay, it'll be shaved off first thing tomorrow morning. I guess it scared Betty a bit, didn't it? Yes, I am late, but let me explain. I started early and when I got to the ferry to Berkeley, I realized I had five minutes before I had to get on the boat. So I decided to go in and see the beautiful new plate glass window in the Call Building. It's one huge pane and the view out over the bay is stupendous. We must go there soon."

"Oh, yes," he continued, pulling himself back to the main thrust of his story. "While I was standing there admiring the beautiful picture window and watching boats in the harbor, suddenly I saw my own, the ferry, steaming across the bay toward Berkeley without me on it. I panicked since I realized I had missed it and would be really late for your train. But all I could do at that point was to wait for the next one. I'm sorry, but I hope you'll understand."

Bill loaded the luggage on the ferry, which crossed the bay where the Stidgers boarded a streetcar. At the end of the line, there were no more houses, just an odd turn-around for the streetcar, plenty of sand and clumps of tall grass here and there, a few cracked pieces of sidewalk where the sand had not covered it, and a sign that read "Sunset Estates." Iva bewilderedly picked up a bag and a hat box and fell in behind her husband. Bill plunged on ahead with Betty on his shoulders, shouting back at Iva, "Follow me, save your energy, I'll come back for the bags."

The small procession struggled forward, Bill pushing ahead and Iva panting behind, her high heeled shoes and long, tight wool skirts not helping her much in keeping up. Her feet sank into the holes that Bill's shoes had made in the sand. She didn't have enough energy to look up; but she plugged on. She didn't raise her head until she became aware of Bill's shout: "Well, here we are, Iva. Isn't it great?" Betty wrote:

And there we were. There was the Pacific Ocean dancing and sparkling in the last rays of sun, and there was our home, an abandoned streetcar nestled on the side of a large sand dune. The front door was permanently ajar because the step pedal had become unhinged with the shifting sand. Mother was so horrified that she was literally speechless. The streetcar was partitioned into three rooms: a front kitchen with kerosene burners and a tub on a table. To eat a meal required taking the tub off the table. Mother noticed that each leg of the table was set in a tin can filled with water, which puzzled her until she noticed that every leg of every piece of furniture was in a tin can filled with water. Then suddenly she knew why: sand fleas.

The sitting room came after the kitchen and after that the bedroom. The bedroom held a double bed, a Simmons, made of iron enameled white. There was a white china commode with hand painted forget-me-nots and pink geraniums resting in a shallow pan of water, tucked under the Simmons bed. Mother looked at the commode, which also had to be protected from the fleas, and that sight was the last straw. Dad had stopped giving the tour and now could see the mix of anger, frustration and exhaustion flickering across Mother's face. He realized his mistake: "You're entirely right. This is no place to bring up Betty. I guess I got carried away by the romance of the ocean. Let's go back and we'll spend the night in a hotel. I'll go looking for an apartment tomorrow."

Dad retraced his steps. Mother straddled me over her hip and followed. She stared straight ahead and Dad led the way, loaded with luggage, anxious to give Mother as much room as possible. In silence, they trudged back to the streetcar stop, where they stood and waited. And when the streetcar arrived, in silence they got aboard. Much later in a very small hotel room, I was tucked snugly in a bureau drawer and Mother and Dad were lying tensely in another Simmons bed. Dad finally broke the silence. "Well, Iva, it would have been a fine spot to get inspiration for my sermons. I truly am sorry."[2]

In order to attract people to Calvary, Bill took to the streets with his deaconess, Miss Raynar, knocking on doors, spreading the news about Calvary. He had a flyer printed that said, in capital letters: "We Like Folks, New Pastor at Calvary, 'The Little Church on the Hill,' Come and Hear Him! Nineteenth Avenue, Sunset."[3] Quickly he came to the conclusion that he needed help and better information. On the next Sunday morning, Bill asked everyone to write their names and addresses on a slip of paper and hand them to Miss Raynor, so he could call on each family. He announced he would soon have a visitor's book placed in the church for the names and addresses of all visitors. Also, he said, it was his intention to take a religious survey of the district. Would any of the young people in the congregation volunteer to help with the census?

What followed was an organized effort, based on information gathered from the survey and from the congregation. Bill's efforts yielded the desired results; he was able to count fifty-two people present for the next Sunday morning service. So dominated was he by the desire to increase his congregation that his sermons directly and indirectly carried his proselytizing message: "Finding a Soul" was his morning sermon, "The Supreme Secret" was his evening thought, and "Comradeship" was the watchword for his Wednesday prayer hour.

Bill thought up other ways as well of involving his Calvary congregation in solicitations. He asked each member to send out postcards to friends urging them to come to Sunday service, he harangued his members to make telephone calls to potential members, and he described the heavenly virtues that were available to each person who paid a visit on a neighbor to recruit a larger membership. In short, Bill left no stone unturned.

Iva bore most of the brunt of Bill's disappointment with the torturously slow building of attendance at Calvary. Some nights after a weak turnout, despite his best efforts, Bill would despair. He put up a brave front to his public, who always thought of him as cheerfully upbeat and self-assured. To Iva he showed another side, a sense of vulnerability. Like any great artist, he thought he was only as good as his last performance. She wrote her parents in Ligonier, "We started young people's meeting tonight. It went so poorly—only a few there. But maybe another will be better attended. These are the discouraging things. He is home now and had a nice evening service," the implication being that Bill had rebounded and was taking his work in stride.[4]

After nearly two months of hard work, Bill realized that his efforts had produced a congregation of fifty—sometimes a few more and sometimes, as on Sunday, November 16, 1913, a few less. He observed that people's habits were hard to break, that he had to shock them into seeing that Calvary was there and that it was a place they should attend. Then, on the afternoon of November 17, he had an inspiration. The idea came to him of a lighted cross on top of Calvary's tower—not a stationary object but a *moving,* revolving cross that cast its beams in all directions. He visualized Calvary's tower with its commanding view of the whole Sunset District, from the ocean beach to the hills four miles inland—a permanent light shining on the city of San Francisco for all to see, a beacon. Could it be engineered? Could he pay for such a cross? If he could answer these questions, he thought that he might just be onto a big idea.

Bill called H. W. Hutchinson, a member of his congregation and a mechanical engineer, told him of the plan, and asked him for technical advice on how a revolving cross might work. Then he called George Cuthbertson, another member of Calvary, who was an electrical engineer. Cuthbertson was enthusiastic; he saw how useful the revolving cross might be. Cuthbertson invited Bill to come over to his house that evening after supper to discuss it further, giving him a few hours to think through the electrical aspects of the problem prior to their meeting.

Plans for the revolving cross proceeded rapidly. Bill chose a cross five feet high with a crossbeam three feet wide, all made of heavy sheet iron. A white enamel surface would make the cross effective in daylight and a good reflector at night. There were twelve lights on the cross, and it was turned by a one-eighth-horsepower motor.[5] Engineer Cuthbertson introduced Bill to the Brumfield Electric Company of Seventh Street, San Francisco, which built the cross. The cost of construction was $68; with installation, the total cost would be $300.[6] The expense of operating the cross, with its motor and lighting, averaged one dollar a month. Three hundred dollars was a big sum for Calvary— Bill's annual salary at Calvary, for instance, was only $1,000. He took a calculated risk that the attention the revolving cross would draw would more than pay for its construction and operating cost. He saw the expense as part of what Calvary should spend for advertising and promotion. On the other hand, acquiring a piano for Calvary—also a major event, since it cost $400—was paid for painstakingly over the next year by asking the congregation to increase their giving to include the Piano Fund.

By late December 1913, the cross had been delivered and installed but not yet turned on. Bill advertised heavily in the *Sunset Journal,* in flyers given to his congregation, and in his *Pulpit and Pew Notes.* He turned the dedication of the cross into a spectacle that attracted widespread interest throughout the district. He scheduled a special service immediately prior to the event, so that all people drawn to the lighting ceremony could first sample what Calvary had to offer by way of church service and hospitality.

The newspaper ad stated that after the special service the audience would assemble on the "Boulevard," and the cross would be lighted for the first time. Once lit, the newspaper continued, "It will be seen all over this district from the oceanfront and far out to sea by the sailors, clear down to Second Avenue and by the hill residents." It was unusual for churches to advertise, and some ministers believed that promotion of any kind was not "appropriate." Bill completely disagreed. He needed to attract people, and this was the most effective way he knew.

Well before 7:45 P.M. on Sunday evening, January 4, 1914, Calvary Church was comfortably filled with more than two hundred people, eagerly anticipating the much-heralded lighting ceremony. Bill knew it was essential to deliver on his promise to provide a great service if he was going to convert the new people who had gathered into regular members of Calvary. In addition to his address, he presented a program of music, with Joseph Wesley Gebhardt, a recognized young baritone, and Warren A. Herman, a celebrated violinist. It was Calvary at its best, and he was proud of his work and exhilarated to be preaching to his first full house.

After the service, the crowd surged out of the church and assembled on the east side of Nineteenth Avenue. There were not only the people from the church service but quite a few others from the neighborhood, and they filled most of the street in front of Calvary. Bill called the crowd to silence, said an introductory word, and gave a short prayer dedicating the cross to the people in the district, to the people of San Francisco, and to all the sailors on the sea. "At a given signal, the great cross started smoothly to revolve, its sparkling beams showing first east, then north, west and south," making two complete turns every minute. The effect was "most mysterious with reverence as hundreds of people all over the district watched the cross until it was turned off about eleven o'clock" that evening.[7]

Bill had orchestrated an event that resonated throughout his district. He had shaken the people awake to the presence of Calvary, and he intended to hold on to as many of them as possible. To do this, as he said a number of times, he would make his church services better than good theater. While some people were offended by this statement, most felt that modern and entertaining services were desirable; as one publication said, "Mr. Stidger is animated by a genuinely modern spirit, which makes religion a joy instead of a dire agony."[8]

Within a year, eight churches had installed revolving crosses—with Bill's permission, since he had patented the design. Bishop Edwin H. Hughes, bishop of San Francisco, said, "I wish we had a revolving lighted cross on every church in Methodism. It would give us a unique distinction that would be worthwhile."[9]

News of Calvary's revolving cross found its way into the pages of more than a hundred religious publications, newspapers, and finally, in the summer of 1914, into the pages of *Harper's Magazine,* when a writer in a travel article "told of sailing out of San Francisco Bay through the Golden Gate bound for South America, when the last two things that she saw were the Old Dutch Windmill of the Golden Gate Park and the little Revolving Electric Cross on Calvary Methodist Episcopal Church."[10] When in 1940 *The New Yorker* profiled Bill, it reported that churches in over 380 locations had installed revolving, illuminated crosses, and that the patent royalties had brought "Dr. Stidger something between four and five hundred dollars a year, which he devoted to foreign missions."[11]

As any tide sweeps in, it carries along bits of flotsam and jetsam. So it was that as the Calvary congregation began to build, new members drifted in, bringing their varied backgrounds and diverse talents. Bill watched like a hawk ready to pounce—and then he spotted a new member who could help him fill the church.

Professor Carlos Troyer, a composer who lived on Nineteenth Avenue, quite near Calvary, appeared on a Sunday morning in December 1913, presenting Bill with an opportunity. Troyer was barely recognized in his own Sunset District, but Bill knew about him from the eastern newspapers. Troyer had studied the lives and origins of the Zuni Indians, a cliff-dwelling people in New Mexico, and he had transcribed and orchestrated the tribe's traditional songs. Professor Troyer and his Indian songs had been feted in Europe as well as in New York and other eastern cities, but his music had yet to be performed in the Sunset District. Bill immediately called on Troyer, gathering from him useful information that he duly exaggerated for his *Pulpit and Pew Notes*. He proposed putting on Calvary's first concert, using the professor as his main drawing card. Troyer liked the idea and offered to persuade Miss Sarah Ethel Preble (who appeared in Bill's advertisements with the stage name of "Zahrah"), a "sinuous" dancer who garbed herself in the costume of a Zuni maiden, to repeat her Waldorf-Astoria performance. Bill knew he'd have no trouble getting the men of the district to church to see an "Indian Princess."

Bill wrote the following copy for an advertisement of the concert, demonstrating his skill at promotion:

> The Indian Concert of Songs and Dances by Prof. Carlos Troyer, the composer, will be given in this church to the largest crowd that ever tested its seating capacity. To even get to see and meet a man who is a close personal friend of Theodore Roosevelt; Ralph Waldo Trine, the writer; who knew Jenny Lind and traveled with her through Germany and Holland; who was sent to America by Liszt, the composer; a man who was entertained for three months by Don Pedro, Emperor of Brazil at one time; a man who has a mountain six thousand feet high named for him, located on the peninsula of Southern California, Mount Troyer, would be enough; but to hear him play his own Indian songs while a beautiful Indian Princess sings and dances them, is surely a rare opportunity![12]

The concert was set for Friday, March 13, at eight o'clock in the evening. Bill promised his Calvary congregation a grand show, but he also wanted to let everyone know that Indians and their customs would be treated with dignity:

> We have been asked if these songs and dances will be given in costume. They will: Miss Zahrah Preble has the complete Indian outfit. In some [songs] she will take the part of an Indian warrior and in others of an Indian maid being wooed; in others, of an Indian mother singing her baby to sleep. The church will be decorated with blankets and a tent, and, under Miss Preble's skilled fingers, will look as much like an Indian scene as is possible.
>
> Indian boys will be ushers at this recital or at least our own boys dressed in Indian costumes. . . . Have your children all see this dignified presentation of Indian songs, and let them see that the real American Indian was not a shoddy, cheap, drunken Americanized imitation such as they see at vaudeville and in the moving pictures, but that the real American Indian was a dignified, worshipping man of the open mountains and plains.[13]

Bill announced that Professor Troyer would make an effort "to get a real Indian from the Affiliated Colleges to be at the concert to make fire by rubbing two pieces of wood together, while the Fire Song is sung by Miss Preble. If it is possible to get this real Indian, it will add much interest to the unique performance."[14]

The plan to bring a real Indian to Calvary raised the hackles of several of his congregation. Dissent rumbled around about whether it was appropriate to have Indian songs and a princess in church. Bill defended his concert in *Pulpit and Pew Notes:*

THE INDIAN SONGS AND DANCES

Of course we're Methodists! But these Indian dances are ceremonial dances, and they are to be danced in costume by Miss Zahrah Preble, who for two years has been delighting New York and Boston audiences. Here is what a New York newspaper said about Miss Preble:

The New York Times: Ceremonial songs and dances of the Zuni Indians were the unique features of the entertainment given yesterday at the Waldorf-Astoria Hotel. Miss Zahrah Preble of Berkeley, California, rendered the Indian ceremonies and did it in a most graceful and serious manner, captivating her audience.[15]

And finally on the day of the concert, Bill could not resist issuing another call to those who were still on the fence about attending:

THE INDIAN SONGS TONIGHT

The world has heard the famous Indian songs of Professor Carlos Troyer. They have been sung before kings and queens. . . . They have been heard many times all over California. Every serious musical club in the City of San Francisco has listened to them. But, for the first time in his long residence in this city, Professor Troyer will present his songs to the residents of Sunset District. . . .

The concert is tonight, at 8 o'clock, March 13. If you miss it you will hear people raving about it tomorrow, and you will always be sorry that you were not here.[16]

So, like a great locomotive under a full head of steam bearing down the tracks at top speed, the Indian concert came, and all opposition scattered before the winds. The church was packed for the first time—no matter that the reason the crowd was there had nothing to do with religion. Two hundred fifty paying customers squeezed into the pews; fifty more sat in folding chairs borrowed for the occasion and set up in the aisles. Indian costumes abounded. Ushers and pastor dressed for the occasion in makeshift Indian garb, and there was a festive spirit throughout the church.

After the Indian concert, Bill began a series of sermons on authors: Victor Hugo, George Eliot, Nathaniel Hawthorne, and Alfred Lord Tennyson. He chose the books that attracted maximum curiosity from his congregation. Hugo's *Les Misérables* was

characterized as a story of criminals; *Romolo,* by Eliot, was a story of moral degenera-
tion; *The Scarlet Letter* was Hawthorne's tale of "conscience"; and Tennyson's *Guinevere*
concerned the repentance of a faithless wife. Bill showed the members of his congregation that writers of the world's major literary works dealt with the same moral
Christian themes droned at them by boring preachers, but that the great novelists were
compellingly good storytellers. His congregations kept coming back with enthusiasm
for more of these stories.

Bill proclaimed one Sunday to be Masonic Day, inviting the Parnassus Lodge of
Masons, knowing that if they turned out en masse he could expect two to three hundred
people. Bill was a Mason and wrote a "Masonic Hymn," to be sung to the tune of
"America" (*"Oh, our Fraternity, This night we give to Thee . . ."*). He ordered an extra hundred
chairs put in the aisles of the church to accommodate the crowds, and he was pleased
to be able to fill Calvary with Masons and their families. The event was such a success
that he made it a regular part of his church schedule in subsequent years.[17]

In May 1914 there were five Sundays, and Bill developed a theme for every one. The
first four were "Women," "Mothers," "Go-to-Church," and "Socialism" Sunday. The
fifth and final Sunday in May was Soldier's Sunday. It was Memorial Day, and Bill was
eager to attract as many veterans as possible and have them become regulars. His sermon for the Sunday evening service was his tried and true "The Remnant," the story of
Capt. John Stidger's blood-stained flag.

If May was the month for national causes and constituencies, June saw a drastic
shift in emphasis. Bill set aside the entire month for a series of sermons, at both morning and evening services, on the Abbey Panel Series of Holy Grail pictures in the
Boston Public Library. Bill's fear was the dissipation of his audience to summer vacations. He decided to try a new idea—popular, appealing sermons, *linked,* like a serial
novel. "They are said to be the greatest paintings in America. I will give not only the
Life Lessons taught by these great panels but will also attempt such a description of the
panels as will make them familiar to those who have already seen the paintings and who
may see them in the future." He concluded, with emphasis, "Missing one sermon
breaks the continuity."[18]

Furthermore, he laid down a gauntlet to all: "We have been told that in San
Francisco people do not go to church during the summer months. So far, with the
exception of one or two families who are on vacations, this has not been true with
Calvary, for our crowds seem to be increasing rather than decreasing, and last Sunday
was our most successful day for attendance outside of special Sundays." Bill preached,
and wrote for his *Pulpit and Pew Notes,* the following message:

> We hope that this [attendance] may keep up all summer. The pastor has
> decided not to take any vacation; to stay on the job right through the summer.
> He does this because he wants nothing to interfere with the upward growth of
> Calvary. Things are at the place now where a little carelessness, a little disloy-
> alty, or a letting down on the part of pastor or people will have a marked
> impression on our phenomenal growth.[19]

Bill was relentless. If he sacrificed his vacation, he wanted everyone to know. He was not above laying guilt squarely on the shoulders of his churchgoers. Yet people did take their vacations seriously, no matter that they smacked of disloyalty. In early June, Bill admonished his somewhat diminished flock: "About fifteen of our regular attendants are away on their vacations. This means we must get others to attend church or there will be a slump. So far this has not come. We must not let it."[20] He kept up his drumbeat on the need to come to church. He made a particularly blunt statement: "We are glad that Calvary's folks are discontented. We are glad that they are not willing to sit down and see the church loaf during the summer months, with decreased attendance, small collections and a general lassitude. Instead of that our attendance is growing and our collections are increasing. Which is a very fine discontent in our Calvary folks!"[21] July and August flew by. There were great-painter sermons, on Millet, Raphael, Michelangelo, and Leonardo da Vinci, interspersed with others on socialism and drinking.

Bill kept after his congregation:

If you enjoy a sermon, tell your neighbors about it and invite them to church.
It is safe to say that there will likely be another one like it once in a while.
Your church is beautiful inside. Tell folks about it. The revolving cross is
distinctive enough for *Collier's Weekly* to pay for a picture of it. Therefore,
it must be worth your talking about and your inviting your friends to see it.
Blessed is the man who loves his church enough to advertise it!
    Hand out the sermon topic cards that will be given to you this morning.
Put them in letters and send them. Your pastor writes some days as high as
thirty letters for Calvary. You ought to be able to write one. Let's all boost
Calvary! Let's all advertise Calvary! Let's make the people of this community
know even more than they already do that we are alive![22]

Bill was willing to try almost anything new. At the Young People's Vesper Hour he attracted crowds by promising that he would speak for a minute on any verse of Scripture that was quoted by someone attending the service. At the midweek Bible Study Hour, he gave short lectures on the books of the Bible. He bragged about the prayer meetings: "Visit our Wednesday evening hour and see how different it is. We have a few minutes of silent prayer at first. Then five minutes of church gossip. Then we have a Quaker meeting and speak when the spirit moves us. Sometimes the pastor brings us a poem that has been published or that is just written. There is much singing and the whole [meeting] is permeated with the spirit of Christian friendship and fellowship."[23]

This flurry of diverse programs paid off. On the last Sunday of August 1914, just one month before the end of the church year, which terminated at the Church's Annual Conference, he proudly announced that Calvary had had "Three Century Sundays, which means," he said, "that for three Sunday evening services in a row Calvary Church had more than a hundred people attend its church service, on one occasion mounting up to 120."[24]

Bill made a final stewardship appeal so that Calvary could have a "clean financial year," and he was pleased with the results. He told his congregation, "Last Sabbath and the Sabbath before, the response was so generous that it was almost unbelievable. I felt like the little boy who prayed for a drum and then turned and wondered where the drum had come from when he saw it."

Most people would have stopped there with their statement of thanks, but Bill could not. He continued, "We have the deepest faith in the people of this church. . . . Two more Sundays. Let's pay even more than our obligations! That's the spirit we want in Calvary. Make these two last Sundays the best of the year in payments, and in attendance. It will make your pastor come back to Calvary with a glad heart, eager for the hard field, if he feels that he has the deepest, heartfelt support of the folks."[25]

On Sunday afternoon, a week before the Methodist conference, Bill took the precaution of summarizing his achievements, so that no one—not his board, not his congregation, not the Church itself—would fail to know what he had done in his first year. Bill presented his summary in the *Pulpit and Pew Notes:*

Resume for Calvary

120 members from 6 members.
But one loss by transfer.
Financial obligations paid.
$2,000 raised during the year.
Epworth League organized.
Growth of morning attendance, 6 to 120.
Growth of evening attendance, 15 to 100.
New Four Hundred Dollar Piano.
Church Survey of District made.
Fifteen children baptized.
Cradle roll of 20.
First revolving cross.
New art announcement boards.
$150 furniture for parsonage.
Everybody happy![26]

The official Board of Calvary met and reviewed the work of the year, as well as the budget. It discussed the new budget, in which Bill asked it to set aside $1,000, a portion of which was to provide the Methodist newspaper, the *California Christian Advocate,* to every home in Calvary's membership, and another $100 for church advertising. The board unanimously approved the budget and Bill's plan, but it saved one piece of news for last. Bill was told that the board wished to have him remain as pastor and would recommend that his salary be $1,200 for the year, an increase of 20 percent.[27] He knew that the Methodist Church Conference would certainly accept the board's recommendation. The raise was substantially more than he had thought possible. His mind was already racing ahead to the plans he was making for his second year.

A world's fair was scheduled to open early in 1915 in San Francisco, and no one awaited it more eagerly than Bill. World's fairs showed off the latest technologies and gathered people and new ideas from many countries, and this one was only twenty minutes away from his church by streetcar. The city had fought hard to be chosen as the site and now was dedicating six hundred acres for the Exposition, stretching along the bay from the heart of San Francisco's downtown area to the foot of Presidio Heights. The Exposition's official name was the Panama Pacific International Exposition, honoring the discovery of the Pacific Ocean and the opening of the Panama Canal on August 16, 1914. But from the city fathers' standpoint, having the Exposition take place in San Francisco was proof positive to the world that their city had risen like "the Phoenix from her ashes" from the 1906 earthquake and ravaging fire that had ensued. They were anxious that San Francisco be seen in the first rank of America's cities.

What this exposition might mean to him personally came through to Bill in a moment of enlightenment on a streetcar while he was headed toward the Exposition's construction site, where he liked to watch the buildings rise. He had been reading *The Editor,* a magazine for writers, and had come across this sentence, "Many writers find religious journals and Sunday School papers a valuable field for *marketing* the right kind of copy."[28] The Exposition would be an inexhaustible source for interesting stories. The many Methodist publications he routinely read were stale and needed (desperately needed, he felt) good copy but would surely miss out on the Exposition stories, because there was no way for their editors to be in San Francisco to collect them. Bill's brainstorm was to be the "official go-between" and furnish the stories.

Bishop Edwin J. Hughes was receptive, as was the Exposition's publicity department, which offered to give Bill photographs and "cuts" (engraved printing plates) free, as well as pay the expense of expressing the cuts anywhere in the country. Bill committed himself to write the stories and incorporate the photographs, for which he would charge each publication anywhere from two to ten dollars an article. So it was that, on his initiative, he became the "Official Representative of the Methodist Publications to the Exposition."

His "newspaper syndicate" grew so popular that the Methodist Church publications in Canada and England became members. In addition, the Methodist Book Concern asked Bill to take on all special advertising, consisting of hundreds of full pages of display advertising, for its exhibit at the Exposition. He understood that his getting to know the senior personnel at the Book Concern could certainly help when he first had a book to publish. Bill paid his respects to *The Editor* a year later for inspiring him to launch a major new activity of service to both the Church and the Exposition (and make considerable money from it): "I have earned, in addition to my salary as a minister, which is indeed small, an average of one hundred dollars a month since I read that short sentence," he reported in a letter to the magazine.[29]

The Panama Pacific International Exposition opened on February 20, 1915, and Bill threw himself into it. The Exposition glittered, showed off outdoor search beams and lighting that had not been tried before, and boasted extravagant architecture, including the Tower of Jewels, a 435-foot building covered by 102,000 "novagems," faceted glass jewels backed by mirrors and hung by wires to "gyrate and flash" with every breeze. From the moment the Exposition opened until it closed on December 4, 1915, it was an enormous success. Two hundred fifty thousand people visited on the first day, equivalent to half of San Francisco's entire population, and over the full run of the Exposition, nearly nineteen million people attended.

Bill took Betty innumerable times to the Exposition, even though she was only three, because he hoped that seeing the exhibits over and over would help her remember them. Only two things made a deep impression on her, though: the stately arches of the Palace of Fine Arts, whose tall columns were reflected in the still water of the lagoon; and a man named Lincoln Beachey, who sat on a tricycle seat on top of a broad wing, with "loads of wire ropes holding the thing together." "Betty," Bill said, "That is called an airplane. Someday airplanes will be as common as horses and phones and automobiles. You may even ride in one. Remember this, dear. Our adventure today of seeing the plane is historical." Beachey took off in his monoplane from inside Machinery Hall, flew toward Betty and Bill, and then, with a zooming noise, swooped up, becoming a dot, then descending performed a loop-the-loop, making a complete somersault.[30]

Bill arranged to have an enlarged sepia print made from a *Collier's Weekly* photograph of Calvary Church at night—highlighting the revolving cross—installed in the Methodist exhibit in the Palace of Education. This photograph attracted attention, but it was only a placeholder until an exact replica of Calvary Church, commissioned by Bill, was ready to replace it. The model stood four feet high and had stained-glass windows, "showing forth their colors all day long, reflecting the lights that will be lighted within the little church."[31] The high point, however, was the tiny revolving lighted cross, manufactured by Brumfield Electric Company, which crowned the miniature replica of Calvary. Bill showed off the model to his congregation at Calvary before it moved to the Exposition. He also had hundreds of postcards made of his lighted church for visitors at the Exposition to keep as mementos (and as advertisements for Calvary).

As he lived and breathed the Exposition, he also preached it, urging his congregation to go. When they began to take him at his word, however, attendance on Sunday morning dropped off, and he quickly admonished the offenders in Calvary's *Pulpit and Pew Notes:*

Now Let's Be Loyal!

The pastor hasn't said much about Sunday-going at the Exposition for the simple reason that it isn't done much by Calvary folks—and for the reason that he had not cared to be too narrow in his judgments. But at least this might be a fair stand to take, to say the least, for the few who do go, that they will not let that going interfere with the church services. Could a pastor ask any less? Be loyal to your church! Be loyal to your preacher! Be loyal to what you feel down deep in your heart is right![32]

It may have been the surge of visitors to San Francisco to see the Exposition, providing an irresistible vision of tourist dollars to be spent at the cafes and saloons, but whatever the cause, in April 1915, just two months after the Exposition opened, the saloons and dance halls in the Barbary Coast were permitted to reopen, after having been closed two years before. The reformers had thought that they had put a "lid" on illicit sex and vice in 1913, when James Rolph Jr., the new mayor, in collaboration with a campaign against vice initiated by the *San Francisco Examiner* and aided by clamorous calls for reform from the church pulpits, succeeded in having a resolution adopted by the Board of Police Commissioners that banned dancing in any cafe, restaurant, or saloon where liquor was sold within the waterfront district known as the Barbary Coast. The *Examiner* had run a banner headline on September 23, 1913, "Police Board Signs Death Warrant of Barbary Coast."[33]

The new evidence that organized crime still held the upper hand infuriated the reformers, who referred to the 1915 reopening of the saloons as "the lifting of the lid." Feeling betrayed, the ministers of San Francisco sprang into action, and the *Examiner* enthusiastically printed their outbursts under the headline "Preachers Denounce the Lifting of Lid; City Officials are Scored from Pulpits." Bill's sermon was vivid and direct:

> I am discussing tonight . . . "Vivian the Temptress," one of Tennyson's few vile women. . . . I am reminded how this story parallels the officials of the city of San Francisco in the present lifting of the lid of Barbary Coast. These men have yielded to a Vivian some place. They have been tempted and they have fallen. . . .
>
> There is somewhere hidden in the closet of the present administration a skeleton. . . . It is not the patrolman who has been tempted; it is not the detective; it is somebody "higher up"! . . . A few men have decided that the voice of the people shall be as naught; that the law shall be laughed at; that the Vivian of San Francisco shall flaunt her dirty rags and her painted face fearlessly.
>
> And I contend that men in authority are not doing this merely for the fun of defying public sentiment; they are not doing it because they are helpless; but they are doing it because of the Vivian of graft, or the Vivian of power, or the Vivian of the street has tempted them and they have fallen!
>
> What a delightful thing it would be if we could trust our officials.[34]

A call to action had been sounded, but it was to no avail: the "Vivian" of corruption was too durable and entrenched to be eliminated by the crusaders of the Church and the press. The saloons and dance halls openly allowed the ladies of the night to flaunt their wares.

As the Exposition wound down and prepared to close in early December, Bill preached a sermon entitled "Taps! A Hail and Farewell to the Exposition." On the final day of the Exposition, December 4, 1915, he visited the Methodist Book Concern Exhibit to hear an address that Edwin Markham was scheduled to make. Markham had burst onto the world scene with the publication of "The Man with the Hoe" in the *San Francisco Examiner* on January 15, 1899. The *New York Times* wrote, "The time was ripe for a new poet and a new expression, the yearnings of the country were humanitarian. . . . It was a poem certain to light American enthusiasms, which it instantly did; and, as it turned out, enthusiasms which spread across the world . . ." Markham became "the dean of American poets."[35]

Bill had given sermons on a number of Markham's latest poems, including "Conrad the Cobbler," "The Juggler of Touraine," and "In the Hollow of God's Palm." He knew by heart the two poems that had immortalized Markham: "The Man with the Hoe" and "Lincoln, the Man of the People." But, aside from the poetry, which he loved, Markham's persona completely captured Bill's imagination. He was the very essence of Bill's image of a poet. Markham had a white flowing beard, unruly hair, and piercing dark eyes. He also had a reputation for being a spellbinder of a speaker.

Bill made certain he was at the Exposition grounds early on that last morning and positioned himself in the back of the room while the poet gave an inspiring talk on what he called the three necessities of life: "Bread, Beauty and Brotherhood." The moment he finished, Bill barged forward through the crowd and stood in front of the poet. Although Markham was thirty years Bill's senior, there was an immediate chemical reaction between them, something like the bonding of a father with a young man who might have been his son.[36] Bill told Markham that he planned to make a sermon out of the poet's talk. Markham replied that he was flattered by Bill's intention; then he grabbed Bill's arm and asked for a tour of the Exposition. Bill recalled that they spent the rest of the day together and that somehow each exhibit they saw gave rise to a new topic of conversation that was stimulating to both of them.

When the day was done, Bill couldn't get over the fact that he had met the great Markham. He had wanted to learn all he could from this craggy intellectual Californian who could write so precisely, so beautifully, and with such a spiritual touch. He wanted Markham to see his own poetry, but of course, he had not had the opportunity. In one short day they had met, walked, and talked, acting as if they had known each other for a lifetime.

It took a while, however, for Bill to compose the letter to Markham that he hoped would cement their relationship. Christmas and New Year's came and went before the letter was finished and posted on February 9, 1916. It began:

My dear Father Poet:

I have been calling you that for so long in my heart and in my sermons and in my conversation with folks that it seems impossible to address you in any other way.

The letter noted the "coincidence" of their meeting at the Exposition and recounted the Markham-influenced sermons Bill had prepared and given. He also said he had been "browsing along the foothills, and the fields, and big trees of your *California, the Beautiful*," a book of Markham poetry recently published. Bill said Markham had revealed California as he, Bill, had never dreamed it before.

There are many, many things my heart wants to say to you but I refrain for this time because I do not want to appear either bombastic, or sentimental in my appreciation. At least from pulpit and through our widely circulated Methodist publications all over the country I am speaking of you as "The Greatest Christian Poet of the English language, and the greatest Poet that America has produced." And I mean it! I have a right to speak too, I think, for I have specialized in Literature, graduated at

Brown University, took special work in both Harvard and Boston University, and taught English Literature for three years.

Perhaps I have said too much, but not one word that I do not mean from the bottom of my heart.

Sincerely,

William L. Stidger [37]

While it took Edwin Markham until December 1916, a span of ten months, to answer Bill's heartfelt letter, when it came the message was warm, friendly, and cheering. The poet wrote:

My dear William L. Stidger:

I am just home again [in Staten Island], and my thoughts go at once to you and your gracious letter of some months ago. It warmed my heart to the core, and the glow of it will never fade away; for it was heart speaking to heart.

A friend is one who understands our silence; so I throw myself upon your mercy for not replying long ago to your precious letter. But as you know, it came soon after I reached home from my long absence in California. On my return I found awaiting me hundreds of unanswered letters, scores of books and pamphlets, besides a heavy pressure of neglected business.

In the river rush of it all, your letter was accidentally swept aside and buried in the trench of manuscript, and only a few days ago did I succeed in finding it in an obscure corner.

Markham complimented Bill for giving him such a high place in the "choir of American poets." He went on to say,

I recall with pleasure my meeting with you in San Francisco and I was then struck by the quick earnestness of your spirit. I wish that we could have sat down for an hour's conversation on the great problems of our hope and the greater problems of our immediate duty. If you ever come East . . .

He offered to send any volumes of his work that were not yet in Bill's possession. Then he signed his letter and added a postscript on the first page of the letter:

P.S. I trust that I have made you feel how inspiring and sustaining your words have been to me. I thank you for the noble kindness that prompted them. E.M. [38]

Bill Stidger's impetuousness had paid off, and he could claim an idol as a friend.

An accident of fate now occurred that affected Bill's life as much as had the Exposition. A young Methodist clergyman, the Rev. Paul Smith, arrived in San Francisco to take over the Central Methodist Church. Smith had a passion for reform. No sooner had he assumed the duties of his pastorate than he launched into a crusade against vice; whenever sin appeared, he deluged it with a flood of drama and denunciation.[39] Paul Smith was thirty-one, a year older than Bill, and had been an upperclassman at the School of Theology in 1910, when Bill was a first-year student. They had become friends. Smith's arrival in San Francisco was more than a renewal of a friendship, however; through a peculiar alchemy, Bill seemed able to absorb every ounce of reforming zeal that Smith exuded. In this respect they became almost like blood brothers. They were remarkably similar in other respects, as well. Both came from small towns—Smith from Indianola, Iowa, and Bill from Moundsville, West Virginia. At college both had been officers of their respective classes, had won contests for their oratory, had been athletes and fraternity men, and had served on the staffs of their newspapers and yearbooks.

Smith's church was at the corner of O'Farrell and Leavenworth Streets, on the edge of one of the most vice-ridden areas in San Francisco, the "Uptown Tenderloin." Smith found that prostitutes were brazen enough to solicit business on the steps of his church after his services, attempting to attract the men of his congregation as they left. He denounced this activity from his pulpit but quickly came to realize that corruption penetrated to the highest ranks of the police force and well above that in the city government. Toward certain parlors that were thinly disguised houses of prostitution, and saloons where drinking and soliciting were rampant, the patrolling police turned a blind eye. Prostitutes who paraded on the streets after dark so flagrantly that the police simply had to arrest them were generally released immediately and fined no more than five dollars. Smith had more than reasonable cause to become indignant at the rawness of the area he lived and preached in. Bill, however, had no similar set of circumstances. His Sunset District was sparsely populated, remote from the waterfront; it had no steady traffic of sailors, women, and visitors. Instead, Bill learned by osmosis, through conversations with Paul.

Bill quickly adopted Smith's fervent, almost militaristic, stance against sin and vice. When they both were invited to spend a week giving a series of lectures and talks to the students at the College of the Pacific, a Methodist seminary in San Jose, Bill lectured on the topic, "Is There Sin in the World?" He said:

> You can bet your very life there is sin in the world. Sin is the most real, the most miserable thing in the world. It covers itself with tinsel, and surrounds itself with music and bright lights, and the false-happiness of intoxication, but in the dull glare of daylight, it is indescribably black and loathsome and revolting. It is like the parched sand of the desert, sapping and searing the goodness of life with its burning, hateful, hurtful breath. Sin is like a fever which turns men bleary-eyed and sodden until they can no longer recognize those that love them, and think that all are turned in hate.[40]

Separately or together, Bill and Paul Smith were driven by reforming zealotry. Smith gathered information so he could tackle the big problem at his doorstep—the Uptown Tenderloin—while Bill attacked the corrupt lotteries that were swindling residents of the Sunset District. Together they became involved in a labor–management battle.

In August 1916, restaurant workers in San Francisco were fighting their employers for an eight-hour workday. Bill, Paul Smith, and other ministers threw themselves into the controversy by meeting with the Chamber of Commerce (siding with the restaurant owners) as well as with the Labor Council. The chamber particularly wanted the Church's endorsement of its position that the union should be broken because it kept restaurant owners from hiring nonunion workers. The council went so far as to claim to the newspapers that the ministers had agreed to censure the union. The union officials were angry with the reported position of the ministers and said so to the press, which in turn, questioned Bill and his colleagues as to which side they were on. All but Bill waffled, claiming that they needed time to study the issues. His statement was: "My Church has declared that it stands for the principles for which this fight is being waged, and, win or lose, I have taken my stand with you [the strikers]."[41]

A number of invitations were extended for Bill to address union meetings, one of them an assembly of more than three thousand men. At that meeting, there was prolonged applause when he was introduced and *thunderous* applause when he said: "There is a Church representing five million people in America that is with you, heart, mind and soul in your fight for better conditions. Our Methodist Conference has gone on record that every man has the right to work under decent hours and conditions; the Church favors an eight-hour day throughout this country." The *San Francisco Examiner* wrote: "Never in the history of the Labor Council has any speaker received such spontaneous and prolonged applause. Men stood on their feet and yelled and cheered Rev. Mr. Stidger as he came down from the platform."[42]

By late summer of 1916, toward the end of the Church year (just preceding the Annual Conference), Bill began to hear rumors that he would be asked to become pastor at First Methodist Church in San Jose. He had met its former minister, Dr. George A. Miller, who had been one of the first to add an illuminated revolving cross to his church after Bill introduced the idea. Bill had been impressed by Miller, who had built a beautiful new church building after the old one had been destroyed in the earthquake of 1906. Miller left his pulpit in 1914 at the request of the Church to do missionary work in the Orient.

San Jose was in the Santa Clara Valley and was a town of fifty thousand, compared to San Francisco's five hundred thousand inhabitants. It was prosperous, surrounded by lush orchards whose plums, grapefruit, pears, and other crops had made some of its inhabitants very wealthy. Also, unlike Calvary, First Methodist had a history. It had been founded in 1849 and claimed the distinction of being the first Methodist church established in California—and it had a regular congregation in excess of a thousand people. A man named Crothers telephoned, inviting Bill and Iva to join him for dinner at the Palace Hotel in San Francisco.

When they met, Crothers did not beat around the bush. He said that First Methodist had an opening for a new pastor and that its board had, after some intensive investigation, decided that it would like to have Bill and Iva come to San Jose. Of course, it hoped the Stidgers would welcome the change, and he was authorized to offer a salary of $1,500 a year. Bill said he was very grateful to the First Methodist board for its faith in him, and he accepted. At the Annual Conference, held in late September, Bill's move became official, and the transition to San Jose from San Francisco was swift. On Friday, September

22, 1916, two hundred people gathered at Calvary Church for a farewell reception for Bill and Iva, sponsored by the board. By the next day, the Stidgers were fifty miles south in San Jose. In Bill's opening service at First Methodist Church on Sunday morning, he addressed more than a thousand people, in a relatively new, beautiful, white-stucco building in a Spanish style called "mission revival."

A reporter from the *San Jose Evening News* interviewed Bill on Monday morning, September 25: "A live wire began his ministerial duties in San Jose yesterday." The reporter had found Bill in his office, his coat off and sleeves rolled up elbow high, his head and shoulders deep in his trunk removing his papers and books. The latest-model typewriter sat on his desk, "which he thumped with all the dexterity of a trained newspaper man." To the reporter, Bill appeared to be built from the ground up. "He has a short neck, thick heavy jaws and rather short body set on two sturdy legs. It is not difficult imagining the new minister bucking the line on the varsity for a twenty-yard gain."[43]

Bill decided almost at once that he wanted some changes made in the way things were done at First Methodist. At his first scheduled meeting of the board, which consisted of twenty-five "bright-eyed keen businessmen"—the senior being John Crummey, the chief executive of Food Machinery Company, a major farm equipment producer—Bill proposed an advertising campaign, beginning in the newspapers. The more conservative members on the board hesitated. They wanted to be cooperative with their new minister—but advertise? Bill was persistent: "All right," he declared to the board, "I'll promise from the first Sunday of the advertising campaign not only to pay for the cost of the advertising out of the extra loose collections but I'll double our loose collections in addition to that."

Bill's chairman accepted his proposal, and Bill proved true to his word: on the first Sunday after the start of the newspaper campaign (which cost $5), $68 came in beyond the amount of a normal collection. More important, the church attendance grew with each step-up in the amount spent for publicity. After the third month, through publicity and popular services, First Methodist was never again—during Bill's tenure, according to the church's historian—"big enough to hold all the people."

The advertisements that Bill placed in the newspapers were dramatic and eye-catching. He confirmed his ideas a few years later when he met Bruce Barton, son of a preacher and a pioneer in the advertising industry. Bill asked, "What are the two fundamental advertising rules you think apply for church publicity?" Barton replied, "First, that you advertise your Christ and your Church and your Gospel and not yourself. Second, that you deliver the goods when you get the people. These are also the fundamental rules for good publicity in the business world."

When Bill wrote Edwin Markham on December 11, 1916, ostensibly to say that he had read the poet's poem "The Thinker" the previous night to 1,600 people in "my big church in San Jose," he had more in mind than being informative:

For you will see by this letterhead that like a good Methodist preacher I have itinerated. But in this case, since it was itinerating from the smallest church in the Conference to the largest one I have no objection to adjusting my saddlebag and journeying. And doubly am I thankful because it brings me to your old town, where they are just beginning to awaken to the bigness of their own Poet; which awakening I am trying to encourage, as you will see by the enclosed clipping. That same week I wrote a long article for the San Jose Mercury *on "Edwin Markham, Poet of Democracy."*

As he ended his letter, Bill came to the main purpose for his writing, which was to enlist Markham's cooperation:

Write me a personal letter which I can read to my great San Jose audience [in] the next Edwin Markham Story Sermon I give. Write it to San Jose, like [the Apostle] Paul used to write to the Athenians and Corinthians and etc. It will add a beautiful touch to what I am trying to do in spreading your Gospel and increasing interest in your truly great book, The Shoes of Happiness.

Your profound Admirer,
William L. Stidger [44]

In San Jose Bill was notable for more than his spirited sermons. At the end of 1916, he traded his car in for a new green Nash, a vivid green with a California top. Betty remembered it as being the splashiest automobile in San Jose, if one didn't count the fire chief's or the robin's- egg-blue runabout sported by Bill's doctor and close friend Mark Hopkins. Bill's rapid success in San Jose was evident, particularly in his packed church services, so much so that a complaint was brought against him, as the following newspaper article relates:

POLICE ARE AFTER BILL STIDGER
FOR PACKING HIS CHURCH

"I'm guilty," was Stidger's comment, "and any place I ever go I hope they will always have a chance to arrest me for packing my church. 'I'm guilty!"
The whole fuss started when a number of complaints were turned in to the police charging Stidger with violation of the city ordinance in regard to blocking aisles and exits in public places. The charges made claim that "night after night" the Methodist church is "jammed until it is dangerous." While the pastor pleaded guilty to packing his church, he made it plain that he did not want to break any ordinance, and that he instructed his ushers to keep all aisles clear.[45]

Successful as he was, Bill had "religious" competition, and the press enjoyed focusing attention on the "two lead-horses" in town. On January 7, 1917, the *San Jose Mercury Herald* compared Baptist minister James W. Kramer with Bill: "Sensational Preachers Speed Up Publicity Race." The reporter visited Kramer at his church, at San Antonio and Second, and Bill at Fifth and Santa Clara. Of the similarities he found, "They have the same warm, sincere manner of shaking hands and the same big way of 'looking people in the eye' and making friends. They believe in themselves and in God and in their fellow men, and they believe in work and in advertising." The difference, which the reporter noted, was that while Bill advertised First Methodist and its programs frequently and boldly, if he included his own name in the ad, it was in the smallest possible type and only at the end.

Kramer had a different strategy and bragged about it: "If I am to succeed in the ministry my personality has got to come to the front! It's all right for Stidger to advertise his revolving cross and illuminated window, but you need something new. I'm going to have a searchlight so that everybody in the Santa Clara Valley will say, 'What's that? Why it's Kramer in the First Baptist Church of San Jose!!! I crave to be different, that's why my ads and my sermons have kick, sting and punch. I spend as much time on my ads as I spend on my sermons." He was proud to say that he was the first preacher in America to advertise his church services on billboards, and he followed this by flashing the subjects of his sermons on the screens of the "local moving-picture houses."[46]

By comparison with Kramer's approach, Bill's methods were restrained and conservative. He was, however, just as strong an advocate of advertising as Kramer. The reporter said of Bill, "Advertising has BROUGHT the crowds there. The strong, magnetic personality of the 'reporter preacher' and his eloquent spiritual message have kept them and brought them back again. . . . He is a true democrat, and he makes prizefighters and barkeepers whom his ads entice into the church feel that they have 'found a friend.' There is not the slightest suggestion of the 'holier than thou' attitude about Mr. Stidger, and the men, women and children who crowd around him at the close of his 'spellbinding' sermons know it and 'go on their way rejoicing.'"[47]

The reporter concluded that the long lines of automobiles in front of both men's churches each Sunday proved the efficacy of their strategies. "In the words of Dr. Kramer himself, they have 'cut the mustard.'"[48]

Notes

1. Betty Stidger Hyland, *Those Heavenly Years*, unpublished manuscript, 1955, 23.

2. Hyland, *Those Heavenly Years*, 26–28.

3. Advertisement, 1913. Scrapbook given on September 20, 1914, by William L. Stidger to T. S. Garrett, Trustee, Calvary Methodist Church. Scrapbook is in possession of Calvary Church (Stidger scrapbook).

4. Letter dated May 11, 1914, from Iva Berkey Stidger to her mother, Mrs. J. S. Berkey, author's collection.

5. "First Revolving Cross in City," undated newspaper article in Stidger scrapbook, 22.

6. "The First Revolving Cross Ever Erected on Any Church," article dated December 27, 1913, in Stidger scrapbook.

7. "Lighting of Cross Draws Large Crowd," undated newspaper article in Stidger scrapbook, 22.

8. "Cheerful Churches," newspaper article in Stidger Papers at Brown University Library.

9. Bishop Hughes comments in promotional material on revolving cross, author's collection.

10. William L. Stidger, *Standing Room Only* (New York: George H. Doran, 1921), 137–38.

11. "Talk of the Town," *The New Yorker*, March 2, 1940.

12. "The Indian Concert Near," *Pulpit and Pew Notes*, March 8, 1914, Stidger scrapbook, 60.

13. "Talk! Talk! Talk!" *Pulpit and Pew Notes,* March 1, 1914, Stidger scrapbook, 60.

14. "The Indian Concert Near," *Pulpit and Pew Notes,* March 8, 1914, Stidger scrapbook, 60.

15. "The Indian Songs and Dances," *Pulpit and Pew Notes,* February 22, 1914, Stidger scrapbook, 59.

16. "The Indian Songs Tonight," *Pulpit and Pew Notes,* March 13, 1914, Stidger scrapbook, 7.

17. "A Masonic Hymn," *Pulpit and Pew Notes,* April 19, 1914, Stidger scrapbook, 29.

18. "Art Sermons for June," *Pulpit and Pew Notes,* May 31, 1914, Stidger scrapbook, 66.

19. "Art Sermons for June," 66.

20. "Art Sermons for Today," *Pulpit and Pew Notes,* June 7, 1914, Stidger scrapbook, 66.

21. "Calvary's Discontent," *Pulpit and Pew Notes,* June 14, 1914, Stidger scrapbook, 67.

22. "The Promissory Note Cards," *Pulpit and Pew Notes,* August 9, 1914, Stidger scrapbook, 73.

23. "Wednesday Evening Prayers," *Pulpit and Pew Notes,* July 19, 1914, Stidger scrapbook, 70.

24. "Three Century Sundays," *Pulpit and Pew Notes,* August 30, 1914, Stidger scrapbook, 73.

25. "Responding Nobly!" *Pulpit and Pew Notes,* September 13, 1914, Stidger scrapbook, 74.

26. "Resume for Calvary," *Pulpit and Pew Notes,* September 20, 1914, Stidger scrapbook, 75.

27. "Resume for Calvary," 75.

28. William L. Stidger, "The First Syndicate of Religious Journals," *The Editor,* February 12, 1916, 178.

29. Stidger, "The First Syndicate of Religious Journals," 178.

30. Hyland, *Those Heavenly Years,* 37.

31. *Pulpit and Pew Notes,* Stidger scrapbook, 85.

32. "Now Let's Be Loyal!" *Pulpit and Pew Notes,* August 1, 1915. Stidger scrapbook, 89.

33. "Police Board Signs Death Warrant of 'Barbary Coast,'" *San Francisco Examiner,* September 23, 1913, 1.

34. William L. Stidger, "The Lifted Lid," *San Francisco Examiner,* April 19, 1915, 12.

35. "Edwin Markham, Child of Nature," *New York Times Book Review,* June 11, 1933, Section 5, page 2.

36. Letter dated February 9, 1916, from William L. Stidger to Edwin Markham, Markham Collection, Horrmann Library, Wagner College, Staten Island.

37. Stidger to Markham.

38. Letter dated December 3, 1916, from Edward Markham to William L. Stidger, author's collection.

39. Herbert Asbury, *The Barbary Coast* (New York: Capricorn, 1933), 307.

40. "Judge's Decision Was Body Blow to Crusade," *College of the Pacific Weekly,* January 30, 1916.

41. "Clergy Gains New Light on Labor in S.F.," *San Francisco Examiner,* August 26, 1916, 5.

42. "Unusual Equipment of New Minister of First M.E. Church," *San Jose Mercury Herald,* September 23, 1916.

43. "Labor Unions and Revivals are Both Liked by Preacher," *Evening News,* September 25, 1916.

44. Letter dated December 11, 1916, from William L. Stidger to Edwin Markham, Markham Collection, Horrmann Library, Wagner College, Staten Island.

45. "Police Are After Bill Stidger for Packing His Church," newspaper article, Stidger Papers at Brown University Library.

46. Emily Chynoweth, "Sensational Preachers Speed Up Publicity Race," *San Jose Mercury Herald,* January 17, 1917, 1.

47. Chynoweth, "Sensational Preachers Speed Up Publicity Race," 1.

48. Chynoweth, "Sensational Preachers Speed Up Publicity Race," 1.

Four

Waxing Fiery over Sin: San Jose

I n the midst of Bill's acclimating himself to his new church in San Jose, he received a call from Paul Smith, who was gearing up his antivice crusade to close down the Barbary Coast and Uptown Tenderloin in San Francisco. Though it meant splitting his time between the two cities, Bill had no intention of remaining a passive bystander and missing the excitement of being Smith's coconspirator. He was therefore at Smith's side as much as he could be during the month of January 1917, and he was never sorry that he was.

The Barbary Coast, with all of its racy color, sex, and physical danger, traced its origins to the discovery of gold in 1848 at Sutter's Mill, in central California, and the ensuing gold rush of 1849. The flood of miners flush with cash into San Francisco supported a large number of saloons, dance halls, and gambling establishments, concentrated in a several-block area called the Barbary Coast. Commercialized prostitution had a semilawful status in San Francisco for more than sixty years; in fact, whether laboring as a streetwalker, inmate of the brothels, decoy in the saloons, or performer in the dance halls or peep shows, the prostitute was the key to what attracted men to the Barbary Coast. The red-light district settled along the Embarcadero dock area and pushed westward to Powell Street and southward to Commercial Street. There were many blocks containing nothing but saloons and "parlor houses."[1]

From time to time, "red light" beachheads in other areas were established, only to be beaten back by indignant property owners and angry families who resented the intrusion. The only small colony of prostitutes that did succeed in gaining such a foothold was in the Uptown Tenderloin. There gambling houses, shady saloons, and cabarets established themselves on Mason, Larkin, Eddy, Ellis, O'Farrell, Powell, Turk, and other streets leading northward or westward from Market Street, the principal business and traffic thoroughfare in San Francisco. The Uptown Tenderloin was also the center of the city's more reputable night life, as many of the important hotels, restaurants, and theaters were in this area. The brothels of the Uptown Tenderloin were regarded as being of a higher class than those of the Barbary Coast, which meant that their prices were higher, they were more elegantly furnished, and the girls tended to be more attractive and accomplished.

Girls came to the Barbary Coast and the Uptown Tenderloin from all over the country. Most were from small towns, brought to San Francisco by procurers. Women who started in parlor houses, the aristocracy of the red-light district, were usually able to retain their youth and beauty for only a half dozen years, after which they became streetwalkers or went into the cribs (small, individual cubicles) or cowyards (groups of cribs under one roof, sometimes accommodating as many as three hundred women).

Every crib, cowyard, or parlor house was marked at night by a red light that burned near the front door from dusk to dawn, and during the day by a red shade behind one of the front windows. Often there were gaudily painted signs that gave the name of the house or information about the girls. For instance, Madame Gabrielle's establishment on Commercial Street had an ornate sign of a huge insect lying happily in a bed of fragrant flowers surrounded by simpering cupids. Her place was called the Lively Flea. Another, owned by Jerome Bassity, had a cast-iron rooster painted a brilliant scarlet with a red light burning in its beak. Still another house had a copper plate engraved "Madame Lucy, Ye Olde Whore Shoppe."

Inside the parlor houses were erotic paintings or photographs, garish couches, and gilded chairs and tables. An automatic or electrical musical instrument, fed by coins, was in a corner of the parlor to provide lively music, and in some cases there was dancing. When a "gentleman caller" crossed the threshold of a parlor house, he was greeted by the madame, who encouraged him to purchase liquor, supply coins for the player piano, and state his preferences. The madame would then stride to the foot of the stairs and call out, in as sweet a voice as she could muster, "Company, girls!" One by one the "professionals," decked out in nightgowns or costumes, or even flimsy underwear, would troop downstairs.[2]

Though Bill and Paul did not have access to the full facts, they guessed that many of the city authorities were "on the take" in a big way. Reform, therefore, had never had much of a chance. In a memoir, Nell Kimball, a brothel owner, discussed the extent of the corruption and graft she had encountered:

I didn't do as well as I should have in S.F. Not that I'm crying. I was in the business to do well and I got by with a hefty bank balance and a few good city lots put by. But the police and politicians were pressing the houses hard all the time for the boodle and the graft. The payoffs got very heavy. I paid a fixed grift for each girl I had working. I gave City Hall a cut in the likker sales. And at one time (till I cured a political boss's son of the clap caught from a college girl by sending him to the right doc) I had to let the police take all the coins from the player piano. I didn't blame them—everybody has his hand in the till in big cities.

However I knew how to get top protection from judges and city and state capital members; so while I paid out heavy, I didn't pay as much as some to inspectors, cops, ward heelers, night court judges, reporters (a few go for a free ride) and firemen. I'm used to human greed, to the dirty use people in power make of their office, their official position. I never knew anyone in politics—and I've seen them all from Vice President on down in my places—who didn't want power, money and the right to push people around. I never knew one that was Simon pure and just working for the good of the city or state or country. Don't say that I only got the wrong 'uns. I could give you a list of lily white reformers, law makers with the habits of zoo apes. Lots of those who made the eagle scream with their love of country at picnics and Fourth of July rallies—yet they wanted their nookie free of charge.[3]

By January 1917, Smith, in collaboration with Bill, believed that they had amassed evidence enough to stir the public to action. The two of them had toured the underworld, visiting the saloons, dance halls, parlor houses, and restaurants. They had also observed the "hands-off" attitude of the police. Smith knew, and Bill agreed, that they had to go public with their information. Only by securing the support of powerful groups of citizens, and through them the support of a broad base of the population, did they stand a chance of achieving meaningful reform. Otherwise, the entrenched interests—the police and some city officials—would stonewall and frustrate any progress.

Paul and Bill crafted an open letter to the mayor, the police commission, the district attorney, and the police judges; Smith provided it to the *Examiner* on Saturday evening, January 13, 1917, in time to make the Sunday papers. The letter appealed to all church people, labor unions, lodges, and civic organizations to join in a campaign of reform to shut down the Uptown Tenderloin and the Barbary Coast. Smith persuaded three leading ministers—a Presbyterian, a Baptist, and a Congregationalist—to cosign his letter. His own position as president of the San Francisco Federation of Protestant Churches gave substantial weight to his words. The open letter set forth ten demands that its writers considered crucial to clean up San Francisco and to remove the city from the grip of "authorized vice control."

Smith's Demands

1. The immediate repression of the "uptown tenderloin" centered on Mason Street.
2. The vigorous and immediate repression of all street solicitation, with arrest and full penalties for repeated offenses.
3. The immediate repression of vice in all residential districts.
4. Uniform enforcement, without special favors, of California's two o'clock [A.M.] drink law.
5. Elimination of pernicious special permits and privileges.

6. Immediate repression of the common practice of unescorted women, both employees and guests in cafes, of "picking up" men and drinking with them.

7. The separation of the vicious combination of public drinking and public dancing, in accord with a policy indicated by frequent action of the Police Commission.

8. Suppression of the common custom of serving drinks in cafes without bona fide meals, a practice which makes some cafes practically saloons for women.

9. Abolition of the vicious curtained booth in all restaurants and cafes and elimination of private dining rooms with adjoining bedrooms.

10. Closer supervision of the rooming houses and hotels, making it more difficult for men to take young girls to them.[4]

"The time certainly is ripe," Paul exhorted from his pulpit, "to move against the parasitic underworld minority and their financial beneficiaries who are menacing our youth." He added that church and various law enforcing officials had "for months" known that vice conditions were extremely bad and were rapidly becoming worse. "We decided that it was time to take some concerted action. The people of San Francisco must know the truth concerning the city."[5]

Smith stated that "accompanied by a committee," he had toured the "carefree and tragic life of the underworld" and that he would be reporting on his findings. Simultaneously, Bill, the other half of this "committee," told of his observations and impressions. The *Examiner* printed his story on Sunday, January 14:

> It was three o'clock in the morning . . . when we got to "The Mason" on Mason Street. They call it "the Bucket of Blood" because, so one of the girls told us, there had been a murder there. It was the dirtiest hole physically I ever saw. I pitied the human beings who were there. The detective who was with us bought two beers. This was about 2:30 A.M. and we two preachers had our tenth "lemon sour." I never will be able to look a "lemon sour" in the face again.
>
> "Spider Kelley's" was no worse; no better. We were in there about one o'clock. It was dull. The girls with whom we talked apologized for that. "Come around Saturday nights. We tear loose then!"
>
> At 40 Mason Street we entered what is called "A Parlor House." The obsequious "Heathen Chinee" who met us, shot us upstairs in an elevator. About six extra girls were ushered in. They tried hard to entertain us; but I'm afraid we were a pretty dull crowd. Once or twice I thought I detected a look of suspicion on the face of one of the older girls, especially when one of them, I think it was "Evelyn," was telling me about being picked up by a "Bull," as she called him, on the street because she was only seventeen, and I carelessly admitted knowing Detective Redmond and Sergeant Goff of the traffic squad. It looked for a minute as if I had "spilled the beans" but our own detective switched the conversation just in time to save the situation.
>
> "Daisy," in answer to some questions that I asked her before my break, admitted that there were twelve girls in the house and room for thirty; that about

twice that many were "on call." I asked her what she meant by that and she said, "Oh, married women and young girls at home, who leave their telephone numbers and when we're all busy the landlady telephones to them to come in. They're not reg'lar y'a know; just fill in to make a little spending money."

"Do you actually mean that married women have their names on call in here?"

"I certainly do; lots of them. There's one right over there now, talking with that tall guy with you."

Then I asked her what happened when they were picked up on the street. "Oh, they soak us five dollars and let us go. That's the regular price. Everybody knows it."

The girls discussed with us freely that "D——d preacher" who was raising all the trouble over the red light district, and had their curious and psychologically interesting explanations for why he was doing it. But the unanimous, and final, comment always was, "Oh this will blow over; we're in right in this town. It's the only wide-open town, except New Orleans, in America. We're all right. The police wink at us."

I said to "Mazie," a girl down in "The Bernard" on Leavenworth Street, "What do you think of what Police Commissioner Roche said about having lived in this city for twenty years going up and down this section without being approached by a girl; and insisting that there is no 'Uptown Tenderloin'?"

She laughed aloud at that. Then she kept on laughing. And she didn't seem to be able to stop laughing. It was a huge joke to her that the Police Commission did not know that there was an "Uptown Tenderloin" in San Francisco. And it was to me also after I had, with these men, visited no less than fifteen wide open places, ranging from Spider Kelley's to that Parlor House at 160 Eddy Street. Yes, it is a huge joke; but something more than a joke it will become, I suspect, before this fight is through.

Commissioner Roche wants the evidence; and we have it; stacks of it.[6]

The war waged by the ministers was wholeheartedly joined by the *Examiner*, and it escalated rapidly. The *Examiner* sent its own teams, incognito, out to investigate. Since the prostitutes thought they were protected by the police, they were amused at the efforts of the reporters and inquiring clergy. The war on vice struck a responsive chord with reforming groups across the city but was opposed immediately by the authorities. Police Commissioner Roche reiterated his denials about which Bill had quizzed Mazie at the Bernard:

I have been travelling at night through the district of this church for 15 or 20 years, and I do not believe the condition of affairs alleged by the Reverend Paul Smith exists. The reverend gentleman will have to convince me that San Francisco is not the cleanest city of its size in the country. I say that after studying conditions in New York, Chicago and other cities.[7]

Smith stepped up his charges and moved on to a new line of attack—he threatened to expose the anonymous owners of the buildings in the Uptown Tenderloin, some being well-known, upstanding citizens making handsome profits from the rent and leases. Smith said he would name these absentee landlords in his public "Roll of Dishonor" unless there was evidence of a cleanup "either by official or voluntary action." He identified the fifteen hotels and apartment houses that he and Bill had prowled through, gathering more than enough evidence to close them under the Red-Light Abatement Act. He said he also had affidavits, one of them from his church janitor, B. F. Felton, of instances of women soliciting in the neighborhood of Central Methodist Church. Smith said, "You can order up a young girl very much as you might order up a beefsteak."[8]

Mayor James Rolph Jr. summoned Police Commissioner Theodore J. Roche for a late-night conference to discuss what to say publicly in view of the rising storm of protest. Church after church, one woman's club after another, the YMCA, and many prominent citizens stepped forward demanding action. Chief of Police D. A. White complained that Reverend Smith's charges "were greatly exaggerated in some respects and wholly unfounded in others."[9] Roche stridently said that there were no "intolerant" vice conditions in the Uptown Tenderloin. White concluded, "Nothing will be gained by indiscriminate abuse of the police by clergymen or other over-zealous crusaders."[10]

The *Examiner* reported Smith's condemnation of the police chief:

> If he [Chief White] be sincere when he says he does not know of law violations during past months, then he has certainly outlived his usefulness to San Francisco as a police official. If Chief White and the Police Commission do not know of conditions as they exist and have existed for some time, I am sure that most everyone in San Francisco knows. Those who do not know, including the police heads, will know, however, before the Committee of Eighteen is through.[11]

Smith was referring to his "Citizen's Committee of Eighteen," which he was forming as a permanent watchdog commission, to be composed of representatives of the churches, women's clubs, and labor, civic, and business groups. Its first mission was to call for a "mammoth mass meeting" to be held the following week, on Thursday night, January 25, 1917, in Dreamland Rink on Stainer and Post Streets. The mass meeting would demand that the police wipe out the "dives and hotel resorts of the Uptown Tenderloin and enforce uniform regulations for all establishments where liquor is sold."

Over the weekend before the mass meeting, the labor unions and women's clubs held their own mass meetings in support of the vice campaign; four bills "aimed at the saloon traffic"[12] were introduced in the lower house of the California state government at Sacramento. Smith read the full list of names on his "Roll of Dishonor" at his Sunday night service. He said that these citizens were "fattening [themselves] on the vice of the city."[13] The *Examiner* began running a series of vice reports made by its own investigators, reports that corroborated Smith's charges.

"Satisfactory to everybody" was the phrase used by Roche the next day when he promised that the Police Commission would announce a "policy" within the next few days "in respect to the flagrant and vicious evils of the liquor-selling business in this city."[14] Separately, in an all-day conference on Wednesday (which issued an announcement in the evening, so that it would appear in the newspaper on the morning of the mass meeting), the mayor and the police commissioners decided to accept, almost in entirety, the ten demands Paul Smith had made in his open letter to the mayor on January 13.

Finally, late on the Wednesday afternoon, the telephone rang for Paul Smith. It was an unidentified female caller:

"Would you receive a visit from us and listen to our story?" the caller began.

"Yes, of course I will. How many of you will come?" he asked.

"Only a few," the caller replied hesitantly.

"Does that mean only five or six?" he persisted.

"Only a few," the caller replied again, this time firmly. "We'll come to your church at eleven tomorrow morning."

On Thursday morning, the day of the mass meeting, Paul awaited with great curiosity the arrival of the prostitutes. Bill was not present, as he was in San Jose; an afternoon train would put him in San Francisco in time for the meeting at the Dreamland Rink.

Promptly at 11 A.M., an orderly, silent delegation of over two hundred women, all habituées of the Barbary Coast and Uptown Tenderloin "alley" houses, filed through the doors of Central Methodist Church and took their places in the pews. A reporter from the *Examiner* described them: "Their eyes blinking at the unaccustomed morning light, their clothes of the best in their wardrobe, their manner defiant." The reporter wrote:

It was an amazing audience that faced the Methodist pastor when he ascended his pulpit.

Hats of the latest mode set off faces defiant, faces simple to the point of childishness, faces indicating much more than average intelligence, faces showing all the signs of the night life's ravages, and faces yet untouched by its harrowing experiences.[15]

Paul Smith looked out over his audience and asked for the woman who had telephoned him to rise. Mrs. M. R. Gamble, better known as "Reggie," arose. She was a co-owner in one of the richest "parlor houses," located at 40 Mason Street, and she walked forward and ascended the pulpit. She was smartly attired in a checked, tailor-made suit. "Her face was pale with nervousness, her dark eyes brilliant with intensity. When she spoke she showed all the signs of an extraordinarily keen intelligence and a neat command of language."

Reggie Gamble did not discuss the cleanup of the Uptown Tenderloin nor the eradication of openly condoned immorality. Instead, she spoke eloquently about the reasons women became prostitutes, the social and economic forces that drove innocent women into their "sad" calling. Smith was caught entirely off guard by her speech. He stated afterward that facing that church full of fallen women was "the most dramatic moment of my life." She said:

These women are better off in these houses than they would be out in the world of ordinary work, for here, at least, they have the protection of their houses and have sufficient money on which to live themselves and to support their dependents. Yes, nearly all these women before you are mothers, support-ing children. Do you know that? What's going to happen if you stop their opportunities? They were driven into this life by economic conditions.

One of these women, now in this church, before she came into this life, wrote her brother, a Methodist minister, told him of her troubles and asked him what to do. He wrote back, "to trust in God." Well, you can't "Trust in God" when shoes are ten dollars a pair and wages six dollars a week.

You are asking to have this bit of town around your church cleaned up. Well where are you going to send these women? Have you chartered a ship for them, and where are you going to ship them?

There are men in your sphere of life who smile knowingly at the notion of "sowing wild oats." These women here are the products of such sowing. Leave these women alone and teach the people who are raising the coming generation that they must inculcate in their children a different attitude. . . . Do these things and you will do good. But leave these women alone.[16]

Paul Smith was "palpably affected" by Reggie Gamble's moving address and strove to regain control of the meeting, bringing the discussion back to the primary subject. "How many of you have children?" he asked, to which three-quarters of those present raised their hands.

"How many of you earned less than eight dollars a week before entering . . . your night life?" To this question, all women present raised their hands. In answer to another question, they said that they considered that twenty dollars a week should be a minimum wage. "But statistics show," Smith said, "that family heads all over the country receive an average wage below that."

"That's why there's prostitution," stated Reggie Gamble, definitively.

Smith said, "Have you considered housework?" With this, the entire congregation of women convulsed with laughter. He tried again, "I think you should be able to live and remain virtuous on ten dollars a week." This time the church was filled with raucous laughter.

"Come on, girls, there's nothing for us here," Reggie said. The women all arose and filed out of the church as they had come in, quietly. Outside, a crowd had gathered, many of whom were reporters, intensely curious at what had happened inside. The women dispersed, walking or taking taxis, but protecting their identities by pulling down their hats or raising their coat collars to hide their faces.

Paul confided later to Bill that it had been the saddest gathering he had ever seen in his life, yet it had taught him many things, including the importance of throwing his efforts into achieving a minimum wage for women. He was incensed when he learned that the delegation had been ordered to march on his church by the bosses of the "underworld." This had been no voluntary meeting by the prostitutes. Reggie had got-ten the word around that every woman was to attend the church meeting or forfeit her room privileges. When Paul and Bill realized this, they fully appreciated the cynical intent of the "higher-ups" who were engaged in fighting against the vice crusade. This publicized, obligatory march of the prostitutes on Central Methodist Church had been intended to create sympathy among the people of San Francisco for the "fallen women" and thereby soften the resolve of the crusaders.[17]

Paul and Bill had little to worry about, however. By eight o'clock that evening Dreamland Rink was filled to overflowing with seven thousand people, and an equal number was milling around outside unable to get in. Paul was the featured speaker, and the vast crowd applauded him for a full minute when he rose to speak. He launched, with fervent but not overly flamboyant oratory, into a "hammer and tongs" presentation of the facts that "he and his fellow clergymen" had valiantly brought to light as justification of the battle against open vice. A resolution was adopted, firmly and unanimously, demanding action by Mayor Rolph to appoint a vice commission "to investigate and report upon the whole problem of liquor selling, vice and the social evil."[18]

Smith was overjoyed with the results of the mass meeting. Bill cautioned him that continuous vigilance would be necessary to make certain that the mayor picked a blue-ribbon committee that would see the reform through and keep the movement on track. Smith agreed, and he told the *Examiner* that he would not let up.

Two weeks later, in early February 1917, the police raided and closed every brothel in the Uptown Tenderloin and instituted a blockade on the perimeter of the Barbary Coast. No man was permitted to enter unless he could show he had a legitimate reason; the prostitutes were ordered to vacate "the cribs, cowyards, and parlor houses." Eighty-three brothels were closed, and 1,073 women were driven from their quarters. Forty Barbary Coast saloons and dives were shut down for lack of business, and within a week the remainder closed as well. The Barbary Coast and Uptown Tenderloin were declared as dead as "the proverbial doornail."[19]

In subsequent years efforts to resuscitate these areas were made from time to time, but on each occasion the police stamped out whatever modest fire had been lit. As one writer observed in 1933: "Of its ancient glories nothing remains excepting a few battered facades, the tattered remains of signs, and the plaster nymphs and satyrs in the entrance lobby of the old Hippodrome, now befouled by dirt and penciled obscenities."[20]

Bill and Paul felt that they should share with the world what they had learned about rooting out illicit sex and vice from its sordid lair—and what better medium by which to tell their story to vast audiences than the motion pictures? In the months following the Dreamland Rink meeting, the enterprising preachers made a deal with the San Rafael Movie Studio, raised forty thousand dollars to meet the budget for a first film, and hired a writer and some actors. Paul had a grand vision—a series of films depicting vice crusades in major cities across the country, the proceeds from the sale of tickets going for the building of a brand new Methodist church in San Francisco on Market Street near Ninth, seating two thousand people and costing $225,000. The first film, *The Finger of Justice,* was in full production by October 1917; the screenplay was by Miss Grace Sanderson of San Francisco, and the leading actor was Crane Wilbur, who played the hero in *The Perils of Pauline.* Bill made his film debut as a policeman on the morals squad, and Bill and Paul promoted themselves as the first two ministers *ever* to finance and produce a movie. *The Finger of Justice* dupli-cated the conditions, cafes, and "bosses" of the underworld that they had encountered in the vice campaign in San Francisco. The scene of a "sensational" raid involving several hundred women was staged with professional movie actors plus a large group of extras from the congregation of the California Street Methodist Church, which featured a revolv-ing illuminated cross, throwing its light across the night.[21]

The Finger of Justice, though completed and distributed, did not turn out to be the success its two aspiring producers had hoped for. Paul Smith never recaptured the moment of glory he had achieved in his triumphant Dreamland Rink rally. He left the Methodist Church altogether in 1921 and moved to New York to become president of the International Church Film Corporation, a company producing films with religious themes. According to one source, he ultimately wound up as a car salesman—that was far off in the future, though. Bill, for his part, by the end of January 1917 had already plunged deeply back into the responsibilities of his new church in San Jose and was cooking up an agenda for himself.

One early item on this agenda was to shame Edwin Markham into replying to his letter of the prior December. Bill shot off a plea for attention on February 23, 1917:

Dear Brother Markham:

Busy Man! Too bad a Poet has to be so busy, but I understand. But you mustn't be so busy that you forget your Disciples. . . . You mustn't forget that you promised to write a letter . . . addressed through me and my church to your former Neighbors of San Jose. Soon I am going to have a Markham Sunday. I want a big picture of you—as large as you can send me to have on my pulpit that day. Then I want the letter you promised me to read from my pulpit that evening.

I have already given a series of four Markham sermons, copies of which I sent you and am planning four others because they were so popular. Now you must cooperate with me. When you find a young fellow in this materialistic age who truly understands and appreciates your great verse and wants to spread its beauties and teachings, lay not one stone, aye, even the stone of indifference in his way, busy as you are.

"How long, Oh Lord, how long" must I wait?

> *Faithfully,*
> *William L. Stidger*[22]

Markham replied this time in a letter to Bill dated March 9 in which he confessed to being "as busy as a whirlpool," giving lectures and readings up and down the East Coast. "Be assured that I stand ready to cooperate with you in any way I can. I need ten brains and twenty hands to do the work that is pressing upon me like a mighty pyramid. . . . Use my letter [which he sent to Bill ten days later] to the San Joseans in whole or part. As for a photograph of Markham, we will send you one."[23]

The "Open Letter to San Jose," as Markham called it, was dated March 19, 1917, and it did all for Bill, with respect to publicity, that he hoped it would. The *Mercury Herald* printed Markham's letter to Bill, as well as his "Open Letter," and advised its readers that

Bill would read Markham's "Open Letter to San Jose" in his service as well as preach another of his Markham-story sermons. In his open letter, Markham wrote of his long span of years spent in San Jose, his pilgrimages back to it, his "good friend" Bill Stidger, and provided a long statement of his ideas about Christianity and its obligation to achieve a better and more equitable social order.

There was a major war being fought in Europe. Its roots were in a conflict between Austria-Hungary and Serbia, commencing with an assassination on June 22, 1914, of an Austrian archduke, Frances Ferdinand, by a Serbian student (who was part of a militant group called the "Black Hand"). The United States had held itself aloof. This neutrality began to unravel with the sinking by the Germans on May 7, 1915, of the *Lusitania*, a British ship, which took the lives of more than one hundred Americans. For some time after the *Lusitania* incident, Germany refrained from similar attacks, during which time President Woodrow Wilson attempted to seek a diplomatic end to the war, in which he was unsuccessful.

Then, on February 1, 1917, Germany announced that it would sink on sight all merchant ships, enemy or neutral, found near the British coast. President Wilson dismissed the German ambassador and recalled the American ambassador to Germany. In addition, the United States government intercepted a secret proposal by Germany to Mexico offering Texas and other American territory as spoils to Mexico if it joined with Japan in attacking the United States. Neutrality had now become impossible, and Congress formally declared war on Germany on April 6, 1917.

Provision was immediately made to enlarge the U.S. armed forces by one million soldiers, to be drawn by lot from the pool of young men between the ages of eighteen and thirty-one. Shipbuilding began in earnest to provide troopships for our forces; armaments in far greater number were needed; food supplies were collected to feed the soldiers. Whether by having a member of the family—or a friend—conscripted, or by seeing one's business increase as a result of the military buildup, everyone was affected by the war, long before American men began to die on the front lines.

As the long fingers of war and of patriotism were reaching the Santa Clara Valley, Bill was in the midst of launching drives to clean up "vice conditions" in San Jose. He burst onto the front pages of the San Jose newspapers on June 4, 1917, hotly waging not one but two vice crusades. Bill said that he had evidence of saloons illegally serving or selling liquor to servicemen, a violation of the army "dry" bill. The police commission had issued an order declaring the serving or selling liquor to uniformed men would be subject to prosecution. He was also indignant about the upcoming Round-Up, San Jose's annual Fourth of July celebration, complete with rodeo, cowboys, street carnivals, and prostitutes imported from San Francisco. He was unsuccessful in stopping the Round-Up, though he did provoke the police to raid a number of parlor houses, arresting quite a few young men from the Round-Up as well as many prostitutes.[24]

When the Round-Up was over, it was evident, as Bill had predicted, that there had been a large influx of prostitutes. Reverend Kramer, Bill's rival, saw a way to get at Bill by throwing his support behind the Round-Up, much to Bill's irritation. Kramer said, "I desire to thank the Round-Up people for their assistance in helping to make my Sunday evening service such a phenomenal success. They played fair and square with me."[25] Bill's tack, however, was to increase the pressure on the police. He claimed that they were bogging down in their pursuit of closing the parlor houses and hotels. Bill called for help from his fellow muckraker, Paul Smith, and the former state senator Edwin E. Grant, a moving force behind California's enactment of the Red-Light Abatement Act of 1913 and head of the California Law Enforcement league. The three men toured the saloons and parlor houses making up San Jose's "sin belt," which paled in comparison to San Francisco's former Barbary Coast.

With the evidence collected and without a moment's hesitation, Bill announced to the newspapers that he would be holding a "great general mass meeting" on the next day, Sunday, at First Methodist. It would be called "The Smash That Kills the Round-Up and Kindred Vices in San Jose." Bill promised that Senator Grant, District Attorney Arthur M. Free, Reverend Paul Smith, and possibly City Manager Thomas H. Reed would make addresses.[26]

Bill proceeded with a recklessness that came from strident self-confidence. He did not pause to consider the differences between the Barbary Coast and Uptown Tenderloin crusades from the situation in San Jose, or to think about the readiness of the people for reform. There had also been a ten-day period of buildup to the mass meeting in San Francisco, with headlines in the newspapers every day, creating a fever pitch of which the mass meeting was the culminating event. The process in San Jose was so foreshortened that it was difficult to whip the people into a highly charged state that could push reform through. Finally, there was a preoccupation that diminished the level of attention people could give to vice crusades—the United States was now in a world war in Europe, and American fighting men's lives would soon be at risk.

Still, the "great indignation meeting" held Sunday evening, July 8, at First Methodist attracted plenty of attention, and the church was jammed to the very doors of the building. "Startling" charges against prominent inns like Hotel Vendome and Lamolle House, the "baring-to-view of vicious and unthought-of crimes," all based "on purely irrefutable" facts, and a demand that the people of San Jose "turn bloodhounds of relentless publicity upon the vice masters and the white slavers until they are driven from the state or placed behind prison bars" made up Paul Smith's incendiary speech from First Methodist's pulpit. He recited the stories of young girls made drunk in the barroom and other rooms of the Hotel Vendome and then taken out into the gardens of the hotel grounds until early morning hours and brought back debauched; another girl had been fed liquor in Lamolle House then taken to rooms above, where she had been "virtually raped." He charged the police department with full responsibility for the existence of these "seething conditions of vice." Smith called "for using the red-hot rays of publicity to scorch out the vice dens."[27]

The big audience seemed in tune with the presentations of Paul Smith and Senator Grant. The newspapers reported, however, that when "the Rev. Dr. Stidger during his flaying of the police department stated that 'the police and the sheriff's office must answer to the city for its sin,' the applause was almost unbelievable."[28]

After the big meeting, Bill left San Jose for Yosemite for a vacation with Iva and Betty, and while he was away, the steam seeped out of the vice crusade machine. Raids stopped, and there was no more news on the subject to print. On his return, Bill grabbed the reins of the vice crusade as soon as he alighted from the train on July 16, announcing that a San Jose public official having "direct influence and control of the police department" was the "higher up" to whom bribe money from the "houses of ill repute" was funneled. The police, prompted by Senator Grant's investigation, filed charges before the City Council against the Lamolle House, and numerous married women of "ostensible respectability" were arraigned. By Wednesday, July 18, 1917, Bill had turned over to City Manager Reed a dossier containing fifty names of men and women, all implicated in one way or another with sin and vice, listing their ages, their places of residence, the color of their hair and eyes, and "everything that will give your police department accurate clues so they may investigate. . . . It's up to your department now."[29]

While it should have come as no surprise to him, Bill's aggressiveness created an undercurrent of opposition, which surfaced in *Town Talk* on July 21, 1917, in an article entitled "The Stidgering of San Jose":

> Our professional purifiers are exploiting the model hometown of San Jose. This is punishment fitting the crime of tolerating a Stidger in the Garden City . . . .
>
> Then he [Stidger] turned himself loose in San Jose where he has been very busy. He attacked Louis O'Neal and inveighed against the annual "Round-Up" as an enterprise detrimental to public morals. San Jose has been in a ferment ever since, a sort of storm-centre of reform, with Stidger's pals—Paul Smith and former State Senator Grant—lending him their aid. It was bad enough to have Stidger bellowing his nauseating buncombe from the Methodist platform, but to have him buttressed by two such reformers as Smith and Grant, each vociferating his favorite style of appeal to the I.W.W.'s [Industrial Workers of the World] of puritanism, has set the town by its ears.
>
> Resolutions [by the Merchants' Association affirming the innocent character of the Round-Up] are not satisfactory instruments wherewith to brand or scatter cattle of the Stidger-Smith-Grant variety. These troublesome busybodies require something more effective than plain English to acquaint them with the folly of their methods of keeping themselves in the public eye, and it wouldn't surprise me if in the mild-mannered town of San Jose they received a lesson that might improve their manners. For in San Jose there are some red-blooded men and women who think pretty well of the town and who regard libels on the town as libels on themselves. San Jose has been pictured in Washington as a city too depraved to be within twenty miles of a military camp. The Lamolle House must be closed, says Purifier Edwin Grant, who confesses he has been . . . listening to private conversations over a telephone, all in the interest of public morals. . . .
>
> I'd not take his word for a conversation which he listened to over a phone, but if I were interested in a woman calumniated by him I'd be inclined to take him to one side and admonish him with a club. Perhaps there are men in San Jose who might feel similarly inclined.[30]

A second article lambasted "Grant and Stidger," suggesting that the former's spying tactics should "have treated ex-Senator Grant to a coat of tar and feathers and they might not have spared the Reverend Doctor Stidger either." The writer admitted not knowing Bill, but "I do know the breed. They are the moral scavengers that infect every community. The warmth of the sun, the good fresh air, the buds, the flowers, the beauties, they neither see nor enjoy; but in the blackness of night, they wander and grope in the back alleys and ash cans for the foul, sickening refuse of city life. And not content with befouling themselves, they must bring forth the reeking rot and filth to lay on your breakfast table or to tell on Sunday [in their churches]."[31]

The summer intervened, and August and September were relatively quiescent, but a story broke on Friday, October 5, 1917, that brought Bill vividly back into everyone's minds in San Jose. At a meeting of women of the YWCA the night before, Bill had accused City Manager Reed and Chief of Police J. N. Black of "official negligence" for failing to warn the citizens of San Jose of "worse than a great plague" existing among the soldiers at Camp Fremont. This was no innocuous topic. Thirty thousand soldiers were arriving at the newly opened Camp Fremont, one of the army's big new bases, less than twenty miles away from San Jose at Palo Alto. On the one hand, the San Jose merchants were understandably enthusiastic about a huge number of weekending servicemen visiting the town and spending their money, while on the other hand, families in town were beginning to appreciate the significance to their daughters of a flood of single males in uniform.[32]

It is hardly surprising that Bill's startling accusation produced an effect equivalent to detonating a bomb in the middle of the town square. According to his information, the police and city officials had been told by the officer in command at Camp Fremont that over two hundred men recently arrived from the Philippines had been segregated because they were infected with "the worst vicious disease that man can have." The officer asked the San Jose police chief to warn "the women of the underworld" that these men, with pay in their pockets for the last three months' work, were expected in San Jose this weekend. Bill was flabbergasted that Camp Fremont had not seen fit to warn everyone. Obviously, the danger was not only to prostitutes but to all young women in the town. "The afflicted men [will be] coming into contact with young girls in dances and other functions given both here and in Palo Alto for these men. They are being invited into our homes and the problem is immense and terrifying. If the city manager and police chief have not the backbone to tell the people, feeling that they must choose their words in order not to offend, then someone else must tell them," he declared at the meeting.[33]

Angry knots of soldiers on leave in San Jose gathered on street corners and voiced their anger at Bill. Several times over the weekend and on Monday, October 8, 1917, the San Jose police were notified that soldiers had been asking where Bill's church was located, and there had been threats openly made to drag him bodily from his pulpit and raid the church. The anger smoldering among the businessmen for Bill's attack on the Round-Up fed their reaction to his current attack on the military. At a meeting of the City Council that Monday, resolutions were passed expressing regret for the attack Bill had made upon the "moral character of enlisted men of the Eighth Infantry now stationed at Camp Fremont." Bill departed on the 9:20 P.M. train for Los Angeles, where he had a "brief and important matter of business"; the *Examiner* reported that "the minister left suddenly for Los Angeles," fueling rumors that he had taken flight. Those in San Jose who were fed up with his crusading ways found in the aspersions he had cast upon the army ammunition to attack Bill.[34]

The Chamber of Commerce held a meeting on Tuesday evening during which one of its directors stood up, shook his fist toward the heavens, and said—referring to Bill—in a loud clear voice, "The defamer must be asked to leave the city willingly," then he added, "and if he does not leave willingly, then he will leave by force."[35]

When Bill returned from Los Angeles on the Wednesday morning train, he found matters were careening out of control. He was met at the train by reporters, who told him about the Chamber of Commerce meeting; that it had been filled with bitter denunciations against him from beginning to end, with motions made to "tar and feather" him or to "ride him out of town." The reporters asked for a statement, and Bill replied: "I don't propose to back down one inch even in the face of this unfair and ill-informed criticism. When all the facts are known I will be vindicated."[36]

Bill called the members of his church board together and was quickly assured that he had their support, which was formally stated as follows:

> We do hereby endorse the stand taken by our pastor, the Rev. W. L. Stidger,
> in the matter of the recent controversy, believing that he acted from principle
> and for the good of the entire community. We have full confidence in him and
> in his leadership. We further know that this entire controversy was stirred up
> by the enemies made by Mr. Stidger during the recent vice campaign.[37]

Then, in his organized way, he sat at his desk before his Corona typewriter and punched out a message for the newspapers:

> The actual facts of what I said and the conditions under which I said them have
> been greatly distorted. Instead of speaking to a great crowd of young women at
> the YWCA as has been reported I spoke to ten or fifteen mature woman in a
> social service class. Anything further I have to say will be said in a church ser-
> vice Sunday night when I speak on: "The Curse of the American Army Which
> Is Worse Than War." I promise to deal frankly with this problem.[38]

Bill delivered his message to the *Evening News* on Wednesday evening, October 10, together with two other important items for the paper: a copy of his Board of Trustees' resolution expressing confidence in him, and his request to present his case before the Merchants' Association at its meeting on Thursday morning. The request was granted by the association.

Bill knew that the Merchants' Association meeting the following day was important to his survival in San Jose, since the City Council, the Labor Council, and the Chamber of Commerce had already weighed in against him, and the great majority of the merchants appeared ready to condemn him as well. During the night, the large electric sign outside Bill's church was destroyed. Because of that and rumors that someone might kidnap Betty or cause the Stidgers bodily harm, the police detailed three detectives as bodyguards; they "attended the Merchants' meeting to protect Dr. Stidger."[39]

When he took his seat at the Merchants' Association meeting the next morning, the room came to an embarrassed silence. Chairman Howel D. Melvin was noticeably ill at ease. Though a petition had gone around to summon the merchants to vote on whether Bill was an "undesirable resident in the city," Melvin hit his gavel on the podium, cleared his throat, and asked nervously, "What are we here for?" Bill recognized at once that no one wanted to be the first to speak or to cast the first stone. It was his chance to take the initiative. He jumped to his feet and, pretending that the alarming circumstances he found himself in were of no consequence, said: "Mr. Chairman, I volunteer to set the ball rolling, if I may have the privilege of the floor."

Melvin polled the membership, and there was no objection. Bill smiled at the assembly of hostile faces and began, "I am here to stay, men. You know that, and let this be final. I am here to do a work to which I have been called and until that work is done no man shall take me from it. How soon that work will be completed I do not know, but I am here to stay."

> All that I ask of you is a fair deal and I have come to you to meet you face to face that we may understand each other. You do not understand me nor do I understand many of you. I want you to be good sports in the same sense that we were all good sports in college days and though we may disagree in many things, let there be no animosity personally. For my part there has never been any [animosity], not even do I feel it for the person, whoever he may be, who destroyed the beautiful and costly [electrically lighted] bulletin board in front of my church during the night. I know the passion that rises in a fight like this and it is regrettable, but I do not feel hatred for the one who committed the act.[40]

Bill continued, "I am glad to make this statement of facts in regard to the discussion that has been stirred up over my statement at the YWCA for there has been so much exaggeration, and misstatement of what I said and where I said it, and the spirit in which I said it, that I feel that when the people know all the facts, at least the thinking people will approve, rather than condemn me."

> In the first place I made the talk before a very small group of mature women in the YWCA. I am sure that there were not more than fifteen at the most, and not "100 girls" as one of the statements set forth. I would never have made any statement in regard to the question I discussed to a crowd of girls. I would have trusted their mothers, and their fathers, to do that.
>
> In the second place, the group was supposed to be a social service class organized for the purpose of discussing such problems. I had been asked to discuss the question: "How the YWCA and the Church can Best Serve the

City" and one of my headings was, "We can serve the city by warning the young girls of the city of certain conditions that always exist in armies and that exist according to a statement recently made by a Camp Fremont captain to Chief Black of this city." This statement I followed up with the facts as they were given to me by the chief.

Two things are in the minds of the people, neither of which was in my heart: that I insulted the girls of San Jose, and that I insulted the soldiers of Camp Fremont. In the first place I neither had it in my heart, nor did I say anything that would even remotely impart that I did not trust the women of this city. Only distorted and malicious reports of my talk make it seem like that. I was simply warning of a condition that a captain at Camp Fremont had said existed. If I knew that two hundred or ten or fifteen cases of small pox existed I would feel the same duty to warn people.

In regard to the soldiers, I want to call attention of the thinking people to the fact that the real things that I stated about the soldiers no reporter took to his paper. I said: "There never has been a cleaner, finer army since Cromwell's great Christian army which saved England to the common people. Not only is our present army the largest that was ever raised in the history of the world, but it has the highest standards of decency. Colonel Slade said . . . that the first man caught drinking would be dropped from the camp, that no officer was fit to hold in his hands the lives of our boys who was a drinker. . . . Eleven hundred of these officers signed the YMCA Covenant of Personal Cleanliness. . . . These officers know they are engaged in a serious life and death business and that the high and holy task of the leadership of this great, clean new army is worth any man's taking to the task a clean mind and a clean body with a clean soul back of it."

I hereby say to the San Jose public and to the soldiers at Camp Fremont and to anybody that feels hurt, that if they had heard my address they would have gone away saying "That man is the best friend the army has; and that fellow is the best friend this city has!"

I have nothing to say against the men who have taken this up and have criticized me. I know them, at least many of them, to be honest men. They are indignant simply because they did not have all the facts. When you have all of the facts I know your judgments will be reversed.

Bill was almost finished, but he needed to touch on two sensitive subjects. "I suspect that there is an underlying, unspoken element in this controversy. What happened in the Round-Up fight should be forgotten when we think of this current problem. Let us agree to differ but also let us agree not to hold grudges."

Finally, I would like to refer to the resolutions passed against me by the Labor Council. I am still the friend of those men no matter what they may say about me, and as long as I am here I shall fight for the laboring people just as much as I will fight for the capitalist for I am mediator for both if I do my duty. They may criticize me and you may criticize me, but I shall still stand on the great principles for which I fight. I thank you men from the bottom of my heart for the privilege of meeting you face to face and although I know we will many times disagree, yet I feel you will be fair. I must carry this through, not because I want to fight, but because it is my path of duty. That is all. Thank you.[41]

He sat down. Almost immediately Karl Stull, Joseph De Simone, and Colonel Bryant rose in their turns to voice their denunciations of Bill. But the mood of hostility in the room had perceptibly shifted, Bill thought, to a neutral or even positive bias. These three men had barely regained their seats when John Crummey, a senior member of Bill's church and respected because of his wealth, power, and seriousness of purpose, asked to address the group. Chairman Melvin acknowledged him immediately. Crummey had a stern demeanor, when he wished to, and this was such a moment: "I have been asked by Mister Stidger to read you a telegram from Bishop [Adna W.] Leonard of the Methodist Church." Whereupon Crummey read the following:

San Francisco, Cal.
October, 1917
Rev. William Stidger
201 North Twelfth Street
Pastor, 1st M.E. Church, San Jose

Press reports indicate that efforts are being made to displace you. Know nothing definite regarding merits of local controversy. It appears, however, that because of your campaign against vice the plan is to intimidate you and to do so under the guise of patriotism. Stand your ground. I believe in you and so does the Methodist Church.

A. W. Leonard[42]

Crummey concluded, "I have shortened an important trip across the States on business hearing of this controversy and wanting to give you my thoughts. I do not know precisely what Reverend Stidger said but I have two daughters and I would want them to know the truth. I stand with him."

The shift in sentiment in the hall now seemed evident. People were no longer in a lynching mood, but they were unclear how the meeting should be resolved. The chairman recognized J. S. Williams, a merchant, who stood in his place and looked around the room, "Mr. Chairman, I was one who signed the petition but I confess that I did so without fully understanding the facts. I am abjectly sorry that this meeting has been held at all. We have mistreated a minister who was trying to do what he believed—as I now believe—to be right. I apologize to Reverend Stidger and I move that this meeting be adjourned."

One by one the merchants in the room rose to give their agreement, and Chairman Melvin declared the meeting concluded. Many came up to Bill to shake his hand. He returned their greetings heartily and with a generous spirit. He was exultant; the meeting to condemn him had been transformed.

Public opinion swings like a pendulum, and as far as it had swung against Bill, it now moved in his favor, even to the point of turning him into a local hero. On the first Sunday after the Merchants' Association meeting, Bill arrived at his pulpit to find a huge bouquet of white chrysanthemums with a card attached from the women in his congregation stating that they had complete faith in his work and the fullest confidence in him. An editorial in the *San Jose Mercury Herald* complimented Bill for taking the high moral ground: "Mr. Stidger has performed a real public service, for which he is entitled to the commendation of all good people."[43]

As the summer of 1917 progressed, the effects of the war became more evident and more real in the United States. The headlines of American newspapers spoke in bold black letters about the "war in Europe": ships being torpedoed by German submarines; local San Francisco and San Jose boys in army training camps preparing to head to the front lines in France; London suffering an air attack; talk of an allied offensive across Flanders that could bring the war to an early end. The *Evening News* had asked Bill whether ministers who preach to their congregations to aid the war should be exempt themselves from war duty; he replied, "We would be unfair to our teachings if we claimed exemption from the duties of war. Ministers must do their share."[44]

The idea of service to the country to spread democracy and "smash the Hun" looked appealing to Bill. Besides, there was little more for him to do where he was; he presided over a successful, large church in a small city. San Jose's citizens were well-to-do, and there were no large problems to solve. He began to read every book on the war he could get his hands on, steeping himself in the action and the thinking, and for the *Evening News* he wrote reviews of these works, such as *Our Soldiers in France, The Cross at the Front,* and *The Soul of the Bishop.* He urged readers to obtain still other books, such as *Over the Top,* by Donald Hanky, and Robert Service's *Rhymes of a Red Cross Man.* Also, he introduced the theme of war and service into his sermons in a series he called "Help for the War."[45]

It came as no surprise to anyone who was close to him, especially his family, when Bill asked his Board of Trustees at a meeting on December 9, 1917, to grant him a six months' leave of absence so that he could depart "at once for Paris and the western battle front to serve in YMCA war work."[46] The YMCA had offered its services to President Wilson to provide specialized manpower to the armed forces in the fields of religion, engineering, and entertainment. Men and women volunteered to serve in the war with the YMCA; the senior of these were called "secretaries." They were paid for their work, signed on for specific time periods, and endured conditions similar to those in which our fighting men lived, including risk of their lives. They did not, however, carry guns. The board granted his request, with reluctance, and agreed to continue to pay him, provided he returned to First Methodist at the end of his tour of duty. Bill readily agreed.

On his last Sunday, December 30, 1917, before leaving for France two days later, Bill fired off the following letter:

Dear Edwin Markham:

My, my, when will I ever get through asking favors of you? But it is again that I come asking that you will be kind enough to give me written permission to quote from your poetry in my new book, proofs of which you have seen. . . .

I am expecting to be called to France any day now and my hope is that I may be able to get this book in condition to leave behind for the printer.[47]

Bill had written during 1917 a series of articles entitled "Poet Studies for Preachers"; they had appeared in the *Advocate,* and he was fashioning them into a book to be called *Giant Hours With Poet Preachers.* The book contained his essays on American poets (Markham, Vachel Lindsay, Joaquin Miller, Alan Seeger) and English poets (John Oxenham, Alfred Noyes, John Masefield, Robert Service, Rupert Brooke). It was Bill's first serious, published work, and he dedicated it to Markham. The poet wrote a gracious introduction.[48]

Bill's services at First Methodist in December, especially that last Sunday, were unusually packed, "literally bulging out of the great auditorium and Sunday school room of the church." On December 30, 1917, he preached a sermon entitled "Keep Home Fires Burning," which had most of his congregation in tears at one time or another, including himself. He was melodramatic about his own fate:

I tell you this night with the serious thought that it may be the last thing that I shall ever have the privilege of saying to you that there never was a war in the world that was such a worthy war as this, the great war; there never was a cause so high and just; there never was a war fought so magnificently for humanity. . . . I tell you that it is a glorious thing to be chosen for this war. . . . Give our boys a slap on the back and a word of cheer and a song of inspiration and throb of courage as they go. Don't whine over them. Give them courage. They need your letters and they need your sweaters[,] . . . but Ah God of Love, they need your word of confidence. . . .

And it is for that reason that I feel the call imperative to go to France. The one thing that those who love me and know me best fear most is that which they put in their own words, "I'm afraid that when you are there you'll see the need and will enlist and get into the trenches." I do not know. All that I know is that I am going to do that thing the YMCA and the Army officials . . . . feel is the most important thing: . . . to keep up "the morale" of the troops. . . .

If the fire of courage burns feebly at home it will burn feebly across the waters. Rather let your courage like a beacon light be on the waters day and night for the boys "over there." I know how hard that will be. A man went out of my church service a week ago. Somebody had noticed that when we read the names of the soldiers and they prayed for them, he put his hand to his face and sobbed aloud. As he passed me this morning at the church door he told me why. He said, "Oh, Doctor Stidger, I just lost my boy, and it is so hard."[49]

Betty's recollections follow:

The parting was very hard on Mother. The story has been told to me so often I feel I know what happened.

We three went down to San Francisco the night before Daddy left. We went to the "Pig and Whistle" for supper. We were very gay. Then we went back to a room in the hotel. I remember Mother lying across the bed and weeping. Dad was holding her in his arms and weeping a little, too, I think.

I was sitting on the floor cutting paper dolls. It was very quiet. They weren't speaking, just lying there talking with their eyes and hearts.

I climbed up suddenly and threw my little body between them, one arm around Dad's neck and the other around Mother: "Now, Daddy and Mother, don't cry—look at me, I'm brave and we'll get along."

Callous infant, never realizing the immensity, never anticipating the loneliness, the fear of eternal separation![50]

The tantalizing question is why Bill would choose to leave his family and church for a war in Europe when he did not have to go and would be a noncombatant in any case. Perhaps unknowingly, he provided the answer himself by frequently quoting Thomas Carlyle, speaking of mankind: "Stands he not thereby in the center of immensities, in the conflux of eternities?" By 1918, twenty-four nations across the world were aligned against the Central Powers, consisting of Germany, Austria-Hungary, Turkey, and Bulgaria. At this point in time the "center of immensities" was sharply defined as the front lines of the world war, and Bill simply had to be there. Throughout his life he had always wanted to be not only in the game but in the middle of it.

Bill vastly underestimated the perils of his decision to go to the front, and he overestimated the contribution that he might make to the war effort. He was driven by a romantic vision of man's bravery, of war, of foreign places where he had never been. Therefore, early to volunteer and to secure a leave of absence from his pastorate, Bill was one of the vanguard to leave for France to serve his country. The arrival of American forces was seen as the critical factor in shifting the balance from the Central Powers to an allied victory. However, while victory was a brave and triumphant expectation, the Americans, including Bill, soon learned that their expectations were naïve and that victory was not a sure thing.

Notes

1. Herbert Asbury, *The Barbary Coast* (New York: Capricorn, 1933), 232–33, specific quotations and general descriptions.

2. Asbury, *The Barbary Coast*, 232–47.

3. Nell Kimball, *Nell Kimball: Her Life as an American Madam, by Herself* (New York: Macmillan, 1970).

4. "Pastors Join in Demand to Clean Up City," *San Francisco Examiner*, January 14, 1917, 1.

5. "Pastors Join in Demand to Clean Up City," 4.

6. "Pastor Visits Homes of Vice," *San Francisco Examiner*, January 14, 1917, 4.

7. "Expose Owners, Vice War Threat," *San Francisco Examiner*, January 15, 1917, 1.

8. "Ministers Put Responsibility for Vice on Officials," *San Francisco Examiner*, January 15, 1917.

9. "Citizens Anti-Vice Crusade On Today," *San Francisco Examiner*, January 17, 1917, 1.

10. "'Baseless,' Says White of Charges," *San Francisco Examiner*, January 17, 1917, 5.

11. "Pastor Ready to Give Chief White Lesson," *San Francisco Examiner*, January 18, 1917, 4.

12. "4 Bills Up in Legislature to Curb Saloon," *San Francisco Examiner*, January 20, 1917, 1.

13. "Owners of Vice Dens to be Exposed," *San Francisco Examiner*, January 20, 1917, 1.

14. "Police to Act on Law Violations, Says Roche," *San Francisco Examiner*, January 23, 1917, 1.

15. "Women Coerced into Call upon Pastor," *San Francisco Examiner*, January 26, 1917, 3.

16. "Women Coerced into Call upon Pastor," 3.

17. "Women Coerced into Call upon Pastor."

18. "Thousands in Mass Meeting Demand Reform," *San Francisco Examiner*, January 26, 1917, 1.

19. Asbury, *The Barbary Coast*, 313.

20. Asbury, *The Barbary Coast*, 314.

21. "Pastors Plan for Vice Film," *San Francisco Examiner*, October 16, 1917, 5.

22. Letter dated February 23, 1917, from William L. Stidger to Edwin Markham, Markham Collection, Horrmann Library, Wagner College, Staten Island.

23. "Rev. Mr. Stidger, Pastor of First M. E. Church, Has Letter for San Jose From Poet Markham," *San Jose Mercury Herald*, March 19, 1917.

24. "Pastors Try to Pry Rodeo from July 4," and "Hotel Liquor Case Probed by Pastors," *Evening News*, June 4, 1917, 1.

25. "Wind-up of Round-up Brings Out Many Pros and Cons in San Jose," *Evening News*, July 5, 1917, 2.

26. "Stidger Back; Attacks Rodeo; Hits Redlights," *Evening News*, July 7, 1917, 1.

27. "Redlight Mass Meeting Held," *Evening News*, May 9, 1917, 3.

28. "Redlight Mass Meeting Held," 3.

29. "Redlight Evidence Is Given Reed by Stidger; Slaver Given 3 Years," *Evening News*, July 18, 1917, 1.

30. "The Stidgering of San Jose," *Town Talk*, July 21, 1917, 8.

31. "The Poll-prys of San Jose," unidentified newspaper, July, 1917, in Stidger Papers at Brown University Library.

32. "Stidger Denounces Policy of Silence about Fremont Men," *Evening News*, October 5, 1917.

33. "Stidger Denounces Policy of Silence about Fremont Men."

34. "Attack on U.S. Men Resented," *San Francisco Examiner*, October 8, 1917.

35. "Pastor Attacks Soldiers; His Removal Asked," *Evening News*, October 9, 1917.

36. "Rev. W. L. Stidger To Fall His Accusers," *Evening News*, October 10, 1917.

37. "Stidger Upheld by His Church in Resolutions," *Evening News*, October 11, 1917, 3.

38. "Rev. W. L. Stidger to Fall His Accusers."

39. "Stidger Defies San Joseans to Oust Him," *Evening News*, October 11, 1917.

40. "'Silent Influence' in San Jose Affairs Hit at by Pastor's Friends," *Evening News*, October 11, 1917, 1.

41. "Stidger Replies to Accusers," *Evening News,* October 10, 1917, 1.

42. "The Rev. W. L. Stidger Converts His Foes into Friends," *San Jose Mercury Herald,* October 11, 1917.

43. "An Unwarranted Attack on a Pastor," *San Jose Mercury Herald,* October 11, 1917.

44. Undated article, author's collection.

45. "Stidger Writes Review of War Books for News," *Evening News,* December 18, 1917, 7.

46. "Pastor Stidger Will Go to Battle Front," *Evening News,* December 9, 1917.

47. Letter dated December 30, 1917, from William L. Stidger to Edwin Markham, Markham Collection, Horrmann Library, Wagner College.

48. William L. Stidger, *Giant Hours with Poet Preachers* (New York: Abingdon, 1918), 7–10.

49. "Keep Home Fires Burning, Urges Mr. Stidger in Farewell Sermon," *San Jose Mercury Herald,* December 31, 1917.

50. Betty Stidger Hyland, *Those Heavenly Years,* unpublished manuscript, 1955, 50–51.

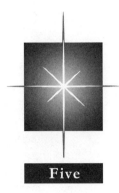

Five

The Center of Immensities: France

"Have been under the shadow of leaving Betty and 'Mother' all day but have been eager for the Great Adventure of 'over there' in France."[1] These were the first words that Bill wrote in his war diary which he began on January 1, 1918, the day he left his home and church in San Jose, California, for a six-month commitment on the front lines of the world war.

As the transcontinental train pulled out of the station bound for New York, Bill waved to Iva and Betty as long as he could see them, "and then some."[2] He was bitterly lonely. By the third day, however, after Salt Lake City and before the immense mountainlike piles of yellow and white corn in Kansas, he had begun to pound out on his new Corona typewriter, a present from his congregation, stories of his "Adventures on the Way," as well as a poem called "East Bound":

EAST BOUND

William L. Stidger

Written on a Transcontinental Train on the way "Over There" on the crusade of service. Dedicated by this clergyman to the YMCA in appreciation of the privilege of service he found through it.

East Bound! East Bound! East Bound!
And we thank Thee, God, for the urge of it;
For the swing and the swirl and the surge of it;
For the game of it;
For the flame of it,
For the call and the thrall and the care
Of this giant job "Over There."
East Bound! East Bound! East Bound!
And we thank Thee, God, for the thrill to it;
For the wish and the want and the will to it;
For the sweep of it,
For the deep of it;
For the hope where men grope 'mid the flare
Of the light in the world "Over There."
East Bound! East Bound! East Bound!
And we thank Thee, God, for the chance of it
For the reach, for the risk, and romance of it;
For the worth of it,
For the girth of it,
For the hand in a land that will dare
With a sword for the right "Over There."
East Bound! East Bound! East Bound!
And we thank Thee, God, for the right of it;
For the love and the lift and the light of it;
For the guns that play,
And the men who pray;
In the mud and the thud and the air,
For the hope of the world "Over There."[3]

In New York, which he found to be bitterly cold, short of coal, and jammed with people, Bill spent time shopping for his war gear, getting inoculations for typhoid and a vaccination for smallpox, as well as obtaining his visas (French and English) and his passport. With Peter Clark MacFarlane, the writer for *The Saturday Evening Post* who had befriended him through Calvary Church, he explored the teeming immigrant areas in the lower part of the city, as well as the long stretch of large apartment buildings on

Riverside Drive. The knowledge that he would soon be headed to France and to the war front occasionally swept over him, bringing with it waves of loneliness. On such a day, a Sunday, Bill went to church at Dr. Charles Jefferson's Broadway Tabernacle. Inside, he saw hundreds of soldiers, like him, lonely and apprehensive. In its tranquil sanctuary, the choir and congregation joined together to sing:

> Peace, perfect peace;
> With loved ones far away,
> In Jesus' keeping, we are safe, and they.

Bill wrote that a great sense of peace settled over his heart and that he was comforted, as he knew the other soldiers were, too.

The wait for his orders and the longer wait for his ship, the *Niagara,* to sail were trying, but eventually he learned that his departure date had been set for the third week in January. Loaded down with his war equipment—which consisted of three blankets, a gas mask, a mess kit, a poncho, trench boots, and a raincoat, all of which he had purchased himself—Bill boarded the *Niagara* at about six o'clock in the evening on Thursday, January 24. He was pleased that Bishop Francis J. McConnell, one of the most highly regarded of the Methodist bishops—and a brother of Bill's good friend from Boston University, Pat McConnell—would be a fellow passenger.

The ship was awash in rumors, the most optimistic one being that French liners were not targeted by German submarines because they carried German spies. Another widespread rumor was that the *Niagara* would not be attacked because it would travel in convoy all the way across the Atlantic. But some passengers were not so optimistic. They pointed out that the *Niagara* was an ideal target for a well-placed German torpedo. If so, it might suffer the same fate as the *Lusitania,* whose sinking had helped to provoke America's entry into the war. When the *Niagara* finally sailed the next morning, Friday, January 25, at 7 A.M., in a dense fog, it appeared to Bill that they might not even make it to the Atlantic, for suddenly out of nowhere, camouflaged with paint, heading straight for the *Niagara,* "shot a big freighter." Both ships frantically maneuvered; the *Niagara* "only missed the freighter's midships by about four feet." Bishop McConnell, who was standing on the deck near Bill, said, "I held my breath, that's the closest I ever saw a boat come without a smash." Bill noted in his diary that he guessed that his adventures on the high seas had started off "with a jump."[4]

On his first day at sea, it was surprisingly warm for January, warm enough to walk on deck without an overcoat, because the ship's southern route took them through the Gulf Stream. Bill wrote, "It has been a wonderfully beautiful day with warm sunlight sparkling in the deep blue water. I shall never forget the look of the sun shining on the ocean way off from the ship after striking some clouds. It gave a glory to the water that was celestial. Hereafter when I hear the expression 'A Great Light' I shall know what it means. The waves are rolling so high that they splash over the first deck—great deep blue mountains of wonderful water with green tops when the sunlight burns through them. I watched the white gulls playing with the ocean, taunting the waves, sweeping down their crests as with a dare and just as the waves were about to pounce they would glide away with a wild triumphal cry. How helpless Man is in the grip of the ocean compared with a gull."[5] The beauty of a calm sea was shattered by the fury of a terrific storm, with an accompanying dose of seasickness, demonstrating just how wide the range of weather in an ocean voyage can be.

Readers of the *San Jose Mercury Herald* learned about Bill's trip on board the *Niagara*:

It has been an exciting voyage. We have already been out of New York ten days. It takes so much longer to cross because we have zigzagged across the Atlantic and made detour after detour to avoid German submarines which have constantly menaced us. This ship, which is French with French officers, has constantly traveled under wireless secret orders from shore and patrols.

We have five inch guns with an expert gun crew—all from the French navy, and they have already had several encounters with the U-boats in all of which they came off victors. The captain has several medals for sinking German subs. He is a daring rascal, much to our discomfort, for he will not accept a convoy like most of the other trans-Atlantic ships. We did not know this until we were outside New York harbor.

We have not had a light on board at night since we left New York, and the last three nights even the red and green lights on the front of the ship have been extinguished, and we have sailed in total darkness. I presume we change course every three minutes to make ourselves a difficult target. No one is permitted to smoke because we are told, "The Germans can sight the light of a cigar a long distance through their periscopes."

Submarines have harassed us for days. Two nights ago such a lurch came to the ship as threw everybody about in their staterooms. We thought it was a storm until the morning came, and we were informed that it was a sudden lurch to avoid a submarine. The voyage has been full of uneasiness, and now we are coming to the most dangerous part of it, the submarine zone.

It's no joke to be sailing the Atlantic these days, especially when you have to sail within 200 miles of the Azores, which the Germans on the day before we left New York declared to be a new forbidden zone. The supposition is that they have established a submarine base there. Any man who comes home and tells you that he wasn't afraid of subs on the Atlantic . . . is a liar or a fool, for the officers of this boat themselves are constantly alert. We have been sleeping in our clothes for two nights, with no lights and constantly on edge with apprehension.

Yesterday everybody was on deck. It was Sunday afternoon. Suddenly off to the east several spots appeared on the horizon. What were they, friendly craft or enemy ships?

Nobody knew, not even the captain. There was a wave of uneasiness over the boat. Speculation was rife.

Then we saw the signal boy go aft, and in a moment the tricolor of France was fluttering in the winds, and we knew that the approaching craft were friendly. Then through powerful glasses we could make them out to be long, low-lying, lithe, swift destroyers coming out to meet us. They were a welcome sight. Like "hounds of the sea" they came, long and lean. Headed straight for us, they came like the wind. Then suddenly a slight mist began to fall, but not enough to obscure either the destroyers or the sun. Through this mist the sun burned its way, and almost as if a miracle had been performed by some master artist, a beautiful rainbow arched the sky to the east, and under the arch of this rainbow fleetly sailed those approaching destroyers.

It was a beautiful sight, a Silhouette of the Sea, never to be forgotten while memory lasts. The French flag fluttered, the band started to play the "Marseillaise," and a ship-load of happy people sang it. A sense of peace settled down over us all. The rainbow, covenant of old, promise of the eternal God to His people, seemed to have new significance that memorable day.[6]

Bill was told that the patrol boats which had joined them could do thirty knots and that "the subs slink away when they heave into sight."

During the trip, Bishop McConnell gave a series of lectures, "The Background of the War," and on one occasion congratulated Bill saying, "Your poem ['East Bound'] is the best I have read of yours, Stidger," of which Bill wrote in his diary, "That pleased me, of course."[7] Then, on the last Sunday at sea, there was an Episcopal communion service, at 6:30 in the morning, followed by a talk given by French chaplain G. F. Lauga, who described his three years in the trenches. Bill wrote about this man, who much impressed him:

We all liked the young chaplain. He was more than six feet tall. His hair was light, his eyes blue, and there was a pert, clean-cut stubby little mustachio to set off his straight-as-a-tree military appearance.... Lauga said, "I have known the worst places of our western front. Everywhere it is hell! In Verdun one battle was raging for days and nights. Huddled in a shell hole with me were a Roman Catholic priest chaplain, a French officer and a private, with thirty shells a minute bursting all around us. I asked the priest if we all had a common God at a moment like this. He grabbed my hand and said that we did. I looked over at the French officer who had his back to the enemy and was trying to stop the flow of blood that was fast ebbing out the life of the soldier. The difference between officer and private was swept away there in the shell hole in Verdun. We were just comrades; brothers in the face of death.[8]

Bill was thoughtful after he had heard Lauga, whose expression "Everywhere it is hell!" seemed so remote and out of place from the conditions on the *Niagara,* which was then sailing smoothly on a calm and peaceful sea. Bill did a double-take. "Like a flash," he said, "my mind was brought back to the lurking submarines that might at any moment turn this great peaceful scene into a holocaust of terror and hate and hurt. Yes, the chaplain was right—'Everywhere it is hell!'"[9]

That evening, February 3, the ship reached the Bay of Biscay, near France, but it was still not in sight of the shore. Bill spent a sleepless night on deck in his clothes, as did most of the ship's passengers, because the perils were great this close to land. Then, at last, France! Bill saw land heave into sight as the "lights along the shore appeared against the blackness of the night. I shall never forget the great ship without a single light threading its cautious way through the mines and lurking danger zone and through the submarine net at the mouth of the river. I will never forget the ride up the river to Bordeaux: the two masts of the torpedoed *Quebec*, the torpedo boat destroyed speeding out into the sea on patrol duty, the thousands of American boys cheering us from the banks of the river: 'Where are you Yanks from?' 'New York'; then: 'Where are you going?' From the shore; the answer: 'To Paris, then to Berlin!' Or I could never forget the little children standing at attention and saluting; or the German prisoners; or the black Liberians in French uniform; or the great tower of the Cathedral St. Michael with the wireless outfit and observation platforms on top; or the great cathedral itself; or the marvelous amount of work done by the Americans in wharf construction in only six months."[10]

Bill rode from Bordeaux to Paris in a railroad car compartment from midnight to dawn with Bishop McConnell, Gen. William E. Sweet, and a drunken Canadian soldier on leave to Ireland; no one was permitted to take a sleeper unless he was sick or wounded. Bill, McConnell, and Sweet were put up at the Wagram Hotel, where Bill enjoyed his first washup and warm bath in several days. His impression of Paris as a newcomer to the City of Light was one of rain; gray skies; wet, muddy pavements; wounded soldiers with arms, legs, and faces half shot away; mourning women; Red Cross nurses; English, Australian, French, American, Belgian, and Russian soldiers walking everywhere on the streets of a city that feared being overrun by the Germans.

Bill reported to the Religious Work Department of the American YMCA, located at 10 Rue de l'Elysée. The executive secretary of this department was Dr. Robert Freeman, who had been minister of the First Presbyterian Church in Pasadena. With much in common, Bill and Freeman became immediate friends. The department had only begun its work with the American Expeditionary Forces, or AEF, as the U.S. military presence in France was called, as of January 1, 1918. About 1,700 people, three hundred of whom were ministers, had already reported to the YMCA for duty, and many more were expected. Consequently, conditions in the Religious Work Department were chaotic, and Bill was told it would take several days—or longer—to be given his assignment.

In fact, it took only two days. On Friday, February 8, Bill was told to report to Soissons, northeast of Paris and near the front. He understood that Soissons was the focus of important military action and that he would be in the heat of it at once. He wrote Iva that he had accepted the assignment "with a hope in my heart and a prayer in my soul that I may be worthy of this trust."

Almost immediately he got a change in assignment, to the town of Gondrecourt, where the staff of Gen. John J. Pershing, commander of the AEF, was located. He was told to be prepared to wear his helmet and his gas mask.

When Bill left Paris by train for the front lines, the American army he was joining comprised about 300,000 soldiers, with more arriving every day. Many of these men had not yet been in battle or even exposed to trench warfare. To date, the American divisions had been assigned to work with French formations, under French commanders. An anticipated major German offensive, thought likely to happen in early March, would be the Germans' "big push" to destroy the Allies and end the war. This led the Allies to unify the French, British, Italian, and American troops within a high command, under Marshall Ferdinand Foch. Ready or not, the Americans soldiers were suddenly thrust into battle alongside their allies.

Bill arrived in Gondrecourt about 2 P.M., only to find that the American army was pulling out and moving on to Toul. He was told to take the train to Toul and meet the army there. With several hours to kill in Gondrecourt before the train to Toul would arrive, Bill explored the town. He later described his experiences on his way to the front lines in an article, which he called "A YMCA Preacher-Secretary's First Night," for the readers of the *San Jose Mercury Herald*. This story appeared on May 5, 1918, and was among the earlier firsthand reports by Americans of life in the Great War.

As I stepped off the train from Paris [in Gondrecourt] there it was, my first battle plane; a whoppin' big fellow with a spread of wings that made it look like the wings of the Palace of Fine Arts in San Francisco if those wings were straight rather than crescent. It was a tri-plane. It had run out of gas, for it had been up all day, and it was now evening. I saw it swoop down on a high hill, and finding that I had time, I climbed that high hill to see it. There were three Frenchmen in it. One was the pilot, one an observer and one the fellow who handles the machine-gun. After climbing the hill I was also privileged to climb into the machine, for the French aviator was a fine, courteous fellow and was friendly enough to explain everything about the big bird to me. He himself was dressed as if he had just stepped out of a band box and seemed more like an opera star aviator than a real, honest-to-goodness war-time aviator. But he was all of that and then some, for he had a record, as his medals plainly showed.

As he stood talking with me on top of that hill, with the fair fields of France below us dotted with American camps, threaded with thousands of American soldiers, suddenly he pointed into the sky over the front lines and there, on my first day down the line, I saw a battle between two German machines and one French machine. For once in my life I had thrill enough and to spare for a few minutes. The French fellow climbed above one of the German planes. It was enough to take your breath away to see him climb, up, up, up. Then it actually did take your breath away to see him suddenly swerve and drop, drop, drop straight down like a bullet toward one German machine. As he dropped suddenly he began to pop, pop, pop at the Boche [German]. The air was full of white puffs of smoke where the air [antiaircraft] guns from below were doing their share to shoo away the intruders. Then a great black cloud came between us and this air battle. We could hear the shots, but we could not see the ships. To make a truly complete story I ought to describe how one of the German machines was dropped, but I have promised myself that not one whit or jot of thrill shall get into a single one of these adventures that is not true, so I shall have to leave the thrill of actually seeing a German machine fall for another story. . . .

By the time I got back to the depot it had gotten dark. My train pulled in and on I climbed. We rode in complete darkness for 40 miles. . . . As I, under the weight of my big sleeping bag and a ten-ton suitcase, stumbled into a compartment, in the darkness I noticed two soldiers with helmets and rifles. I waited a while until my eyes came to be familiar with the darkness and determined that they were French. But much to my joy one spoke to the other and they were American boys who had already seen three periods in the front trenches. They soon saw that I was new and took great delight in showing me the points where our train went nearest the front lines. Once we were within ten miles of the lines and at that point for several miles we could distinctly hear the rumbling of the guns and the flashes of the air rockets [fired to burst in the air, illuminating the sky to reveal enemies]. The nearest thing that I can use for simile to get these air rockets over to my readers is that at that distance, ten miles away, from a train window, traveling through war country in total darkness, is that they looked like heat lightning back at home of a summer evening. For miles and miles, every minute or so these rockets went up, forming a great sheet of light along the horizon. The boys in the compartment told me that down on the actual front these make the trenches and "No Man's Land" as light as day. I saw several great fingers of fierce, white light flashing across the skies. Then suddenly these fingers turned themselves into ladders of light and seemed to climb up into the very source of all light to burn against as beautiful a star-lit night as I ever saw.

"They're searching the skies for German planes," my friends, the American soldiers, said to me.

"Are they expecting an air raid tonight?" I asked in my freshman ignorance.

"Sure, Mike! We have them every clear night like this in these parts. We've had them now for five straight nights!"

It all seemed too good to be true; an air battle, the sight of the guns firing and the rockets, a three-hour ride on a long train without a single light on it; the great searchlights scanning the sky and the possibilities of an air raid. Once again I am tempted to use that new American, and most expressive, phrase, "Can you beat it?"

. . . From the time I clambered aboard my train until we began to pull into the yards of the city of my destination I had not seen a human soul save those American boys. . . . Nobody appeared to tell me where to get off or to help me with my ten-ton suitcase. One has to find out everything for one's self in war time. Fortunately for me, the American boys knew where I was to get off and knew the place for it was the last town before the front lines, and they had been through it several times. . . .

I found the city [Toul] in total darkness save for pocket flashlights. There was no cab and no taxi and no English-speaking human in sight, and it was midnight. The YMCA headquarters was a mile away. It was up to me to find my way through those little crooked, Boston-like streets (this is a slander on Boston streets as bad as they are) to headquarters.

I wandered around like a lost duck lugging that suitcase. I tried to talk to every Frenchman that I met in order to find my way to my destination but once again I found that they don't understand their own language, and they didn't know their own city. Midnight and poor me wandering around. . . .

Then to make matters really interesting suddenly the sirens began to wail. There were about 50 of them. Groups of excited people rushed out of their homes just like California folks do when they have an earthquake. They were all looking up into the sky. And there was I; with a typewriter in one hand and a 10-ton suitcase in the other; nobody to talk English to; lost, strayed or stolen and an air raid on. I stepped up to one group and asked what was the matter. They whispered excitedly: "Germans, Germans, Germans!" and pointed into the sky. But they didn't need to do this for suddenly my heart stood still and I dropped both the typewriter and that suitcase kerplunk in the street and ran for an arched driveway that I saw. I used to take my clothes off and dive in "The Old Sheep Hole" like that only in those days I couldn't get up so much real speed. I used to make 50 yards in a little better than five seconds but I made that 50 yards in just two and a fraction seconds. I heard the machines overhead. There's no sound just like an airship. A motorcycle tries to make one but it can't do it quick enough nor powerfully enough. It sounded to me as if there were 10 of them. Then flash, flash, flash, we saw the lights in the sky over us; and bang, bang, bang, after each flash, and I was right under my first night air battle between the French and the Germans. It was glorious! It was thrilling! It froze your blood cold one minute and then it burned you up with joy and excitement. It was a spectacle such as the gods of old might have envied. There above me, nobody knew how far away or how high, I was seeing an air battle at night. At each flash we could catch dim outlines of the planes. Then flash, flash, flash, flash, and bang, bang, bang, bang in another part of the city, and there were two battles in the air at once. Evidently the Germans had entered from two sides. It was keen strategy, and it was a great show. The sky was the stage and the entrances were east and west. As each German machine came on, it was the cue for a French machine to speak its part and speak they did with fire and shrapnel and thunder.

As the battle progressed I found that in the excitement of the thing I had forgotten my first desire for safety and I was out in the street wandering about with the other fools looking up at the fights with my mouth open, my eyes staring and my heart thumping. The first that I knew that I had wandered from the archway was when I stumbled over my suitcase and typewriter. Then I suddenly realized that I was in danger. But I had hardly realized this before there was a new sound. It was something like a whistle or the shriek of a murdered woman and the cry of a sick child and the wail of a siren and the hisses of escaping steam, and the rush of an express and the hiss of a snake were all put into one sound. I jumped, for the sound that followed this strange hiss was like that of ten thousand earthquakes combined. I jumped. Then I heard another. Then another. Then another. I asked what it was in English and an American voice answered out of the crowd in the dark street.

"Those are the bombs they're dropping now. I've counted ten already."

I stepped over to that fellow. I needed some American to talk to in a time like that. I never remember having heard music that sounded sweeter than that voice. . . .

It was a YMCA secretary. I didn't exactly kiss him, but I am sure he was afraid I was going to.

Then to add a bit to my initiation on my first night "down the line" the Germans came back for an encore about three o'clock in the morning. After that anything seemed tame. But I'm glad I'm here, anyhow.[11]

The secretary showed Bill to YMCA headquarters, where he was given a room to sleep in. He threw his sleeping bag on his cot, climbed in, and had a "great old sleep," proud of being the nearest to the front lines any "Y" secretary had ever been. The entire American force was there, with as many as five soldiers a day being killed. The soldiers were in huts and dugouts right "on the line." Bill wrote, "It's a great old game, and I'm glad I'm in it."

Bill's exuberance at being in the Great War was not yet grounded in any reality. No one who had been to the front lines found it romantic. The truth was that the war had become static, an unromantic war of attrition where men lost their lives to gain inches of terrain. Since the major German drive culminating in the Battle of the Marne in September 1914 had been thwarted and Germany's strategies to destroy the Franco-British forces or capture Paris had been foiled, a battle line had been drawn across the northeastern part of France, with the Germans on one side and the Allies on the other, with only a no-man's land between them, in some places no wider than forty yards. Three years had passed in this stalemated head-to-head confrontation. Fortified trenches on either side had been constructed with elaborate tunneled passageways. Soldiers were relatively safe in these uncomfortable, muddy, and unsanitary trenches, and unsafe anywhere else.

A call by a superior officer to leave the trenches to attack was seen, virtually, as a death sentence. It was no surprise that an increasing number of mutinies began to occur as the soldiers' frustration increased. In fact, desertions and mutinies among the French troops became a serious matter in the latter part of 1917. The arrival of the Americans, beginning in the early months of 1918, about the time Bill arrived, was a material factor in the pickup in British and French morale. It was the prospect of vastly increased resources that the Americans brought to the Allies that led the Germans to plan a major military push toward Paris in early March; they realized time would no longer be working in their favor.

Bill was up at 6:30 A.M. on his first day "on the front lines." His job that morning was not shooting Germans but helping to unload a railroad car of its boxes of chocolate. It was stevedore work, and he labored alongside several other ministers and a big six-foot athletic director named Gossen, whom Bill had last seen at his church in San Jose. The weather had turned. It rained all day, and it was cold, wet, and miserable. He admitted that night that he was exhausted.

Bill's YMCA barracks were on the ground floor of an abandoned brewery, so the workers referred to themselves as the "Brewery Gang." At Bill's first mess, his leader, "the count," arose and let his dislike for preachers show. Knowing Bill was a preacher, the count introduced him saying, "Gentlemen, 'Angel Face' is with us." Bill hated the name he had been given, but he did not complain; he just went to work.[12]

On his second day Bill helped in the building of a stone road; he later said that he felt like a convict and looked like a bum but never was so satisfied with himself as when he returned with cut hands, a sore ankle, and a dirty face. The impetus for working on one's hands and knees was summed up by the count: "Old man, you may not be used to hard labor; especially you preachers; and you may think that unloading boxcars isn't very heroic, but you must remember that every stove you lift down out of that truck is going 'down the line' to make some of those poor lads warm; that every time you lift a back-breaking box of chocolate you are boosting it nearer that lad's reach; that every unbearable burdensome case of soap you strain yourself to lift into the warehouse is helping to make the almost intolerable conditions of the lads in the trenches a little more comfortable. And God knows he needs every little thing you can do for him."

While Bill was getting used to the labor, he could not accustom himself to the weather. He would recall feeling that it was as cold as Iceland and that on the prior night "I had on six blankets, two sweaters, a heavy bathrobe, a helmet, sleeping socks, pajamas, my sleeping-bag and my poncho." He settled into a routine of long days, working from 7:30 A.M. until 9 P.M. or later. After two weeks, he was assigned truck duty. One of his favorite truck runs was up and down the trenches throwing oranges to soldiers and officers alike.

> Imagine, if you can, a big Ford Camionet truck, loaded to a pyramid peak with orange boxes, each with two hundred oranges in it. . . . I had the honor to be perched on top of the pyramid. On the way to the trenches, we passed a French ammunition train on their way to the front. Each wagon was drawn by eight or ten horses in pairs and each pair of horses was ridden by a French soldier with two soldiers on the seat of the wagon. As we passed them I pitched two oranges a piece for the men. The French soldiers were not used to catching and many of the oranges wound up in the mud. The whole French train stopped with officers and enlisted men scrambling for the fallen fruit.
>
>   The truest pleasure for us was leaving fifty boxes of the oranges down in the trenches for the lads who were there. This was like a shower of gold to these American boys. If those who gave the YMCA the oranges could have seen the look of gratitude on the faces of these boys they would have been amply repaid for their generous gift.[13]

Bill was promoted to truck driver. There were always two drivers, one behind the wheel and the other riding shotgun, on the lookout for trouble. Bill later described the conditions:

> One of the favorite outdoor sports of this preacher for a month was to lie on his stomach on the front mud-guard of a big Pierce-Arrow through the war-zone road, bumping over shell-holes, with a little pocket flashlight playing on the ground, searching out the shell-holes, and trying to help the driver keep in the road. It is a delightful occupation about two o'clock in the morning, with a blizzard blowing, and knowing that the truck is rumbling along within sight of the German big guns.[14]

Three weeks after joining the Brewery Gang and having won a place with them, Bill—who was now called "Doc"—was assigned a new arrival as a fellow driver on his truck. On the first morning it was pouring down rain, and the newcomer was told by the count that he must ride outside on the top of the truck. He didn't like this and said, with obvious annoyance, "I'm sick of seeing a lot of god-damned preachers sitting around doing nothing! Why don't you make them ride out in the rain?"

Bill took a quick walk around the truck to calm down. Then his anger, which had not been tamped down at all, erupted. He grabbed the brawny bully by the throat, backed him up against a wall, and said between clenched teeth: "You're going to take back what you said! I've been around here for three weeks, and I don't kick when the rest of this gang kids me. I take my medicine just like the rest of them, for they're men and they've won the right to kid. But you have just arrived and your vile remark about the ministers is indication that you think we're a lot of mollycoddles. You won't get by with it. Take it back, every word of it, or I'll knock you into that snow bank and rub your face in the mud. Then when you get up I'll knock you down again, and again, until you do take it back. Speak quick!"

The newcomer sized Bill up, saw the fight in his eye, and backed down. "Ah, that's all right. I didn't mean it. I take it back."

"All right, then," said Bill, "We'll be friends." That was the end of the incident, but Bill wrote that he was ashamed of himself all day, disappointed that he had lost his temper, despite the provocation. He went off in his truck on the assignment to the trenches, and when he returned late, the rest of the gang were at mess. Word of Bill's fight had gotten around, and when he entered the dining room, muddy and dirty from a twenty-mile drive, everyone fell silent. The count arose and said, with reference to Bill, "Gentlemen, Gyp the Blood." (Gyp the Blood was a ruthless gangster operating for a group of criminals known as "Eastman's Gang" in Brooklyn at the turn of the century.) The name stuck.[15]

The Brewery Gang also was in charge of building YMCA huts for the soldiers. These huts were warm, well-lighted canvas-and-wood shelters, built as near the front-line trenches as possible. One of Bill's assignments was to assist in constructing a hut; when Bill's crew arrived at the site, it was greeted by hundreds of soldiers who rushed to help unload the YMCA trucks. The prospect of providing heat, light, church services, and fellowship to fighting men who had been living with rain, snow, mud, and artillery shells filled Bill and his fellow workers with great satisfaction, despite the continuous danger of being near the trenches.

One late evening after mess, the count asked for a truck crew to volunteer to make a delivery to the farthest hut in the trenches. Tom Norton, Bill's codriver, raised his hand offering the two of them to go. Bill's description follows:

"Come on, Doc; it's 'down the line' again for us to-night," said the big husky guy named Norton with whom I worked.

I felt like complaining. Three trips down the line in one day I thought was enough for ordinary human beings to be asked to take, and then to add a night trip with the probabilities of not getting back until two in the morning to the sum total of an already full day's work seemed a bit heavy to me. But here was a man much older than I bucking up to it with a smile, and his smile was contagious.

Before I knew it we were lumbering out of town in our great truck, gliding along the heavily burdened French roads with our truck full of provisions for the lads at our front-line hut.

Overhead the air seemed to be full of observation balloons and scouting planes. All the American and French planes available seemed to be up. The whole horizon was lighted up like daylight with Vereys [flares] and bursting shells and range-finding lights. It looked like Broadway in its heyday off to our right as we drove down.

We had never seen traffic heavier than it was that night on the French road. An ammunition train [truck convoy] was hurrying along the road. Back of this train rambled several truck-loads of boys "going in." Then there was a great supply train that stretched back along the road for miles. When we got to the divisional headquarters town we saw a line of ambulances—some two hundred of them—lined up along the road waiting for orders.

"I tell you, there's something big in the air to-night," Tom muttered.

Officers shot past us on their fleet-footed horses bound "down the line." There seemed to be anxious looks on their faces as they rode by, glancing at us. Motorcycles flashed by like streaks in the night on their important errands.

"I tell you, there's something in the air, Doc!"

And sure enough he was right. He had hardly spoken before a shell from the German batteries on the hills to our right whined like a crying child over our heads on its way to the American batteries which were to our left. The road at this point was down the center of a triangle with the German lines on one side of the triangle and the American lines on the other. The shells from both batteries then began to whine over us—high in the air, to be sure, but over us, just the same. It seemed that thousands of them were being exchanged. It sounded like a north wind blowing around the corner of an old barn for a half-hour. Off in the distance a deep, dull thud followed each whine. It was the weirdest sound I ever heard. Then, to add to the discomfort of the situation, an old Frenchman got ahead of us with an ox-team drawing a big cart. He planted himself right in the middle of the road. We were not permitted to use our horns. Then a dull thud near at hand and we knew that a gas shell had struck dangerously near. We stopped the truck and adjusted our gas masks.

Gas can be seen in the daytime but not at night. The first indication that gas is about is the abominable scent of the treacherous stuff. Then it is too late, and you're dead. The gas mask can save your life and the further burning of your lungs, but one whiff is dangerous. You feel nauseated for a night and a day and then for weeks and weeks suffer with what you think is an interminable cold.

After this Tom speeded up. We didn't like that canopy of shells over our heads. One might drop out of the arc any time like a great stone. Then again we came to the Frenchman leisurely driving along in the middle of the road.

We couldn't toot our horns, and now that we had our gas masks on we couldn't even argue. The Frenchman seemed utterly oblivious to the fact that the shells were whining overhead. Evidently he was used to this evening "strafing." He didn't move one bit faster, and so for half a mile we had to drive along behind his slow ox-team.

That was the longest half-hour I ever put in. The saliva ran out of my mouth, because I couldn't swallow with the teeth-grip of the mask occupying most of my mouth, and the sweat ran down over my face. I never felt so much like downright murder in all my life. I could have seen a German bomb drop on that Frenchman's head without a quiver of pity. The road was already packed with shell-holes, and into these from time to time we bumped. I have no recollection of any place in all my life out of which I was so anxious to get and out of which I was getting so slowly. I thought of those old boyhood dreams where one is climbing a great steep hill with the Indians after him and something seems to be holding his feet back. That was the way we both felt on that road with the Frenchman in front of us.

Two boys jumped on our truck going to the line. One boy told of a half-dozen Americans who had been killed by a shell on "Dead Man's Curve" a half-hour before. That was encouraging for we were just approaching "Dead Man's Curve" with that Frenchman in front of us.

"One guy got killed and the other had his head blowed off," one of the lads said to me.

"What happened to the one who had his 'head blown off?'" I asked, for even in our desperation the boy's way of putting the news amused me— "one got killed and the other had his head blowed off."

Then we all laughed. But it was a laugh tempered by the consciousness that one of those whining shells over our heads might drop out of the procession any time into our pathway. The Frenchman ahead of us plugged leisurely on.

Some who read this story will wonder why we did not drive around the ox-team. There was a very good reason: four-foot ditches on either side of the road over which we were driving, into one of which we had bounded one night out of a shell-hole and worked all night to get the machine out again. No, we didn't have any intention, at all, of going around the Frenchman. We were going to keep right on behind him as long as he held out.

Tom began to swear a blue streak. He cursed France in general for being so leisurely, for taking two hours off in the middle of the day for "soup," for a lot of things that didn't fit in with his American notion of the way of doing things, and he cursed that particular Frenchman in very positive and eloquent language. When he was through and had turned to me, I said:

"Yes, Tom, 'there's something in the air' to-night all right, and it's blue."

Then we both had a good laugh, in spite of our danger.

One of the boys who had climbed up to get a ride said, "No swearin' for me after what I escaped to-night."

I asked him what he had escaped.

He said: "I was with that gang at the 'Curve,' and I saw the guy beside me lose his head. Just like that: slam, bang, whoop! And it was off! I had been talking to him at the time, and it certainly made me feel funny when I came to from the shock."

Then he paused a few minutes as we rumbled along behind the Frenchman, and added: "It wasn't my time to die. I guess the Lord is going to give me a chance to get a German or two. He didn't bring me over here for nothing."

Then a side road came, and we saw, with a sigh of relief, the Frenchman turn out. From that moment on, in spite of shell-holes, we made about thirty miles an hour. It was like "shooting the chutes" at Coney Island to do it, but we felt just in the mood for that—all of us. We had wasted too much time already. As it was, we would not make it back home until morning.

When we drove up to the underground hut, a cautious voice hailed us.

"You guys make it quick to-night, and don't make a sound, for there's something 'in the air.'"

It was the voice of the sentry using Tom's own words.

We unloaded that truck in mighty quick time.

Each load meant climbing down a pair of stone steps, pushing cautiously aside big heavy canvas curtains (for not a ray of light must escape), stumbling over twenty boys lying on the floor because the passageway was too low to stand in, and dumping the boxes of oranges, chocolate, and tobacco on the soft mud floor.

"The boys think there's something 'in the air,'" the secretary in charge said to us in a whisper.

"The big drive?" I asked.

"Maybe."

Then we started back. As we did the sky was white with the light of exploding shells. The great observation balloons loomed majestically against that lurid background. No Man's Land was flaring with star shells and machine-gun explosions.

We were shooting homeward as fast as we could go with the heavy traffic on the road, and we were nearing "Dead Man's Curve" when an explosion came that made the steering gear swerve in my hands, for I was driving back. It just felt as if there had been an earthquake and the earth had wrenched the front wheels. I fully expected to turn turtle, but, much to my relief, we were still on our wheels and in the road.

Around the corner of the dangerous curve we shot. Fifty feet beyond we saw a black pile of debris in the road. We got down from the truck and found a supply wagon smashed to bits lying in a broken mass at the side of the road. Two mules were lying in the field dead, two boys dead, and four boys who had been getting a ride in the back of the wagon were killed. It looked as if the shell had hit squarely in the middle of the wagon seat and the two boys driving had been killed outright.

Tom went for an ambulance and I stayed behind. One of the lads was seriously wounded—in fact, he was dying. He wanted one of us to take his mother's address and write her if he passed on. With my flashlight I wrote it down in my notebook to comfort him. The next day he died in the evacuation hospital, and I wrote to his mother. He said, "Well, it's my time to go 'west,' I guess, and I want you to write my mother that I have read my Testament every day and that I died ready."

That night as we drove into the Brewery, where we kept our trucks, and climbed down out of the seat about three o'clock in the morning, Tom said, "I told you there was something in the air tonight."

And even as he spoke the siren blew in the old Cathedral, warning the sleeping people of Toul that there was another visit from the Germans imminent.

"Yes, Tom, old boy, you're right: there's certainly 'something in the air' tonight and if we don't hurry home they'll drop something on us too."[16]

The days dragged on into the bitter winter. Bill's work was grueling in the cold rain, snow, and mud, and all the while men were dying around him. He also developed a fierce sore throat, which, he would later learn, was the first side effect of the exposure to poison gas that he and Norton had sustained. It was at this time that Bill began to resent the role he was playing—everywhere around him men were fighting, while "we are carrying sweaters and oranges. I have spent little time in my life on the sidelines and I don't like it."

There were occasional moments of beauty, as when the battlefield was covered by a thick white blanket after a heavy snowfall that masked the sad reality:

One group of hills which I had heard were the most heavily fortified in all France, loomed like two huge sentinels before the city. The Germans knew this also, and military experts say that that is the reason why they did not try to reach Paris by this route in the beginning of the war.

We were never permitted on these hills, but we had seen them belch fire many a time as the German airplanes came over the city.

But on this morning, after three days of snow, those great black hills were transformed, covered with a pure white blanket. The trees were robed in white. Not a spot of black appeared. Even the great guns on the top of the hill looked like white fingers pointing toward Berlin. The roads and fields and hills of France had suddenly been transformed as by a magic wand into things beautiful and white.[17]

Despite the snow's deceiving whiteness and apparent peacefulness, bloodshed and death went on:

The ambulances were running in a continuous procession. We had seen things that few days and nights that made our hearts sick. We had seen every available room in the great evacuation hospital crowded. We had been told that a hundred surgical cases were in the hospital, mostly shrapnel wounds, and that every available doctor and nurse was working night and day.

We had seen, under one snow-covered canvas, six boys who had been killed by one shell early that morning—boys that the night before we had talked with down in a front-line hut—boys who had been killed in their billet. We had seen a captain come staggering into our hut wet to the skin, soaked with blood, his hair disheveled, his face haggard. He had been fighting since three o'clock that morning. He had been shell-shocked, and had been sent into the hospital.

"My God!" he cried, "I saw every officer in my company killed. First it was my first lieutenant. They got him in the head. Then about ten o'clock I saw my second lieutenant fall. Then early in the afternoon my top-sergeant got a bayonet. And a hand-grenade got a group of my non-commissioned officers. Half of my boys are gone.

"But, thank God, we licked them! We got them six to one, and drove them back! No Man's Land is thick with their beastly bodies. They are hanging on the wires out there like trapped rabbits!"

Then the thought of his own officers came back.

"My God! Now we know what war means. We've been playing at war up to this time. Now we've got to suffer! Then we'll know what it all means."

War is black. War is muddy. War is bloody. War is gray. War is full of hate and hurt and wounds and blood and death and heartache and heartbreak and homesickness and loneliness.[18]

As Bill and Norton drove their truck one evening in the early days of March, they came across a sight that transformed Bill:

One dark midnight in France on the Toul line, when I was driving a truckload of supplies to the front lines, we got lost. I climbed down from my truck at a French crossroad, and walked over to a little French shrine. I knew that there would be directions carved on a little stone.

When I got to the shrine I turned my flashlight on the markings and got my directions. Then I flashed that light above the stone marker to have a look at the shrine itself. It was a beautifully carved figure of Christ on a cross, and above that figure were carved these significant words: "Traveler, hast thou ever seen so great a grief as mine?"

Those words stunned me. Then I looked away across the fields. I could hear the great shells rumbling in a continuous roar of hate and suffering. I could also see the dim flare of Verey lights over No Man's Land. Within a few hundred yards of that crossroads was the first little American cemetery, in which we had buried from time to time our dead, including the first American soldier killed in the World War.

As I stood there in the darkness I suddenly felt for the first time the terrible meaning of war. I realized all its foolish waste of human life, its useless suffering, sacrifice and sorrow. I stood there and all the faces of all the mothers in the world flashed by me.

I saw again all the wounded boys I had seen in hospitals with their faces shot away, trembling with shell shock, husky with burned out throats.

Then I turned again and flashed my light above that wayside shrine and read again that cryptic sentence: "Traveler, hast thou ever seen so great a grief as mine?"

That night I knew for the first time all that war meant then and means now. Up to then for me it had been a glorious adventure of flag-waving, band-playing, bugle-blowing, high-sounding public addresses. But never again! From that sacred moment I knew what war meant. It meant hate, hurt, mud, rain, midnight darkness, wounded and dying boys in their teens, broken homes and hearts.[19]

Almost a month to the day after Bill had received his first assignment to proceed to the front lines, he was ordered back to Paris, to work at the YMCA headquarters. Truthfully, he was glad to leave the trenches; the weather had not improved, and he still had a sore throat, accompanied by bouts of nausea. He departed Toul on the evening of Friday, March 8, heading by train for Chaumont, General Pershing's headquarters.

Bill interrupted his trip when he met an American military policeman who said he was getting off the train at Domremy-la-Pucelle, a small town in the Vaucouleurs—the "valley of colors," named for its beautiful hues, which shine in the summer sun. There Joan of Arc had been born in 1412, was baptized, and later heard the voice of God calling her to save France. Bill was overwhelmed by the contrast between Domremy and Toul:

> One day on the Toul line, a train by night, and the next morning so far away that all you could hear was the singing of birds. Peasants quietly tended their flocks.
>   Children played in the roads. The valley was beautiful under the sunlight of as warm and beautiful a spring day as ever fell over the fields of France. I stood on the very spot where the peasant girl of Orleans caught her vision. I looked down over the valley with "the green stream streaking through it," with silence brooding over it, a bewildering contrast with the day and the month that had just preceded.[20]

His interlude in the quiet, peaceful valley, where winter already seemed to have lost its power, was a tonic to his soul. Bill moved on to Chaumont, and on Monday, March 11, at 5 P.M., after a day at General Pershing's headquarters, he took the afternoon Paris Express, thus ending his experience of living and working "on the front."

In a twist of irony, Bill found Paris to be almost as dangerous as the front lines. As the Paris Express pulled into Gare de l'Est at about 9 P.M., the sirens blew, announcing a German bombing raid. Lights across the city were doused, and Bill found himself in the huge train station without a light. He searched for a taxi, only to find that they had all melted into thin air. There was the sound of bombs dropping and shrapnel bursting all over the city. Bill had a heavy suitcase that he could only carry a short way, so he ducked down into the Metro, but he found its service halted by the air raid and its platforms teeming with people seeking shelter. The raid lasted until 1 A.M., with more than a hundred Parisians killed. Bill was spotted in the Metro by a fellow YMCA secretary, who guided him to the enlisted man's hotel, the Pavilion, where he was to live while in Paris. He had a single room all to himself, with hot and cold running water.

Bill was assigned to the Publicity Department, which reported to Fred Shipp, the YMCA general secretary in France. The work consisted of writing articles for magazines and newspapers back home and facilitating the efforts of U.S. reporters who were in France to write on the war to visit American troops. The German "big push" had now begun, and fierce fighting was occurring along the front lines that Bill had left. Paris itself was an object of nighttime air raids and occasional daytime bombings. Many believed that the Germans were likely to overrun Paris, and news of allied losses and of German victories sent the city into fits of panic and despair.

The situation of the allies was grave. Bill wrote that "there were more men killed on the Somme lines along the road to Baupaume in one week than at any other similar time in all the history of the earth. Officers and men with whom I talked told of the streets of Amiens running red with blood; told of the German hordes pushing the

English and French back toward the Channel ports, told of blood flowing until the rivers ran red." Men, women, and children, old and young, sick, wounded or healthy were pouring into Paris, evacuating the towns to the north and east.[21]

Friday morning, March 22, 1918, was a day that as it dawned would become forever etched in Bill's mind, and in his view, it would impress the world as well. It was the first time that a large gun had been used that was able to fire a shell more than seventy-five miles, and it raised havoc in Paris. A German air raid had kept residents of Paris up most of the night; and now, to cap it off, at 7 A.M. a second, unexpected bombardment commenced utilizing the new and mysterious weapon. The bombing raids by German planes Paris was used to; this new weapon was particularly ominous, because there was no telltale plane overhead to alert the inhabitants that the city was about to be attacked.

Bill talked with a number of military men that day. The city was roiled with controversy and disbelief. Army officers, artillery men, and gunners from battleships were incredulous that such a long-range weapon—which became known as "Big Bertha"—could exist, especially one that the allies had not invented. Apart from the impressive technology, this new German weapon was extremely dangerous; it was linked to the "big drive," which seemed to have Paris as its goal. All business in the city stopped, shops closed, subway trains and streetcars were at a standstill, and people sought cover in the *abris* (sewers). Bill wondered if he might be better off (and safer) on the front lines. The German shelling of Paris by Big Bertha coincided with the start of Holy Week, which began with Palm Sunday and ended with Good Friday and Easter Sunday.

The shelling by the long-range guns continued the next day, commencing promptly at 7 A.M., with shells coming in regularly every twelve minutes. At the first concussion Bill leapt out of bed, not particularly in a mood, as he wrote, to thank the Germans for the efficiency of their wake-up call. "There was also an air fight later in the day. Thousands of Parisians watched and applauded the French pilots by name because they knew each pilot by the color of his plane's lights. The French spectators became so involved with cheering for their hero pilots that they seemed oblivious to the impact of the falling bombs."

The third morning of the shelling of Paris by the long-range guns was Palm Sunday, March 24. Church went on despite the bombardment. Bishop McConnell preached at the American Church in Paris, on "How the Spirit of Christ Comes Back After It is Apparently Crushed." McConnell told in his sermon of his having spoken to a thousand Scottish Guards the day before the big drive began. His sermon to the soldiers had been "How Men Die"; within a week, he remarked sadly, most of that group to whom he talked had made the supreme sacrifice. Bill wrote, "While the bishop was preaching three shells fell so close to the church that their explosion shook the windows. We were a restless crowd, and it is no small tribute to the eloquence and power of the man that he kept that great audience of English-speaking people there at all, for the shells were too close to be safe. The newspapers humorously called it 'Bomb Sunday.'"[22]

By the next day Bill realized how exhausted and sick he was. He had been up half the night with air raids and had gone to bed early with a sore throat and a nauseous feeling. A loud explosion occurred nearby at 6:30 A.M.; a shell tore the top off a building just a square away. Later he walked to Les Invalides with Bishop McConnell to look at two German planes that had been shot down. The "machines" were no more than smoking, burned-out hulks, but according to Bill, they were "whoppers" in size, with room to seat three men in each; they were biplanes, and each had two engines.[23]

Paris quickly became a city of evacuation. People, old and young, couples and singles, were panicked and fleeing. The Germans were about to enter Noyons, only thirty-five miles away. Bill later wrote, "We have been notified as to where we shall get truck transportation in case the city is officially evacuated. Hand luggage only, allowed. I visited the Gare du Nord today. It is piled to the ceiling with the baggage of men and women fleeing Paris. I saw old men and women in wheel chairs by the hundreds, men and women who had never been out of Paris in their lives." Bill sold his Corona to raise cash to buy goods for the "boys in the hospitals." He also saw what he called a "war sun," a great blood-red ball that burned through the heavy smoke and mist that covered Paris. For some peculiar reason, the air raids had let up, and there had been no more shelling from the long-range guns. Was this a move by the Germans to provoke diplomatic negotiations? Or was it to save Paris for themselves?[24]

News reached Paris that Noyons had fallen to the Germans, as had Baupaume and Peronne. There was betting among the French that the Germans would possess Paris within two weeks. The British admitted that the situation was serious. Yet as the day wore on, the news seemed to shift, giving both French and British room for hope. Bill spent the evening in a makeshift hospital:

All night long a group of Red Cross and YMCA men and women had been feeding the refugees from Amiens. There were two thousand of them in one basement room of the Gare du Nord. They had not eaten for forty-eight hours. Most of them were little children, old men, and women of all ages.

Two hundred or more of them had been in the hands of the Germans for two years, and when a few days before it came time for the Germans to open their second big Somme drive, they had driven these women and little girls out ahead of them, saying: "Go back to the French now, we do not want you any longer."

For two days and nights these refugees had tramped the roads of France without food, many of them carrying little babies in their arms, all of them weary and sick near unto death.

The little children gripped your heart. As you handed them food and saw their little claw-like hands clutch at it, and as you saw them devour it like starved animals, the while clutching at a dirty but much-loved doll, somehow you could not see for the mist in your eyes as you walked up and down the narrow aisles of that crowded basement pouring hot chocolate and handing out food. The things you saw every minute in that room hung a veil over your eyes, and you were afraid all the while that in your blinding of tears you would step on some sleeping, starving child, who was lying on the cold floor in utter exhaustion.[25]

The Germans, who had advanced farther than the allies had expected, seemed suddenly to have slowed or stopped. It was too early, however, to celebrate, especially since the shelling of Paris resumed. Other news was also breaking. Bill wrote that a "new revolution for the freeing of Russia [from the Bolsheviks] is being hatched in Paris and the men engaged in it are here in the YMCA office every day. We are, as Carlyle says, truly at the Center of Immensities—at the Conflux of Eternities."[26]

Bill published the following account, drawn from his diary for Good Friday, March 29, through Easter Sunday, March 31, 1918:

> I have never spent a Good Friday in my life when I felt more in the atmosphere and memory of Christ's sufferings long ago than I have today. In addition to the poor refugees with whom I worked all day and night: the piteousness of their suffering haunting me; I spent half an hour in the Madeleine [the Roman Catholic church of St. Mary Magdalen, near the Paris Opera] this afternoon. The church was crowded with soldiers of every nation, and men and women from everywhere. The service was strangely filled through and through with the "Presence." It was as if He were here; as if He were on earth again in a strangely human fashion of the suffering of the world, in the dying of the thousands up yonder. "Up yonder." It means so much to us and to the world. The cathedrals and churches are crowded today. Half of the French who are pouring into them are wearing black. Thousands of women and little children with weeping eyes who are passing through their Calvary, pass me as I stand at the steps of the Madeleine or of Notre Dame. It is a stirring day. This morning as I came home from an all night's work with the refugees, before daylight, about four o'clock, I stopped at a church where workingmen gather and it was packed to the limit.
>
> About fifteen minutes of three I left the Madeleine to walk down the boulevard toward the hotel. I thought of all the millions of human beings at that hour who were kneeling in memory of the crucifixion of their Lord. I thought of those who were at that moment kneeling in the sacred places of this great city, such groups as I had just seen in the Madeleine. I thought of my own loved ones at home as many a thousand American boys were doing at that minute.
>
> The big gun had been silent most of the day, but suddenly this afternoon I heard an explosion. I knew it was the big gun. Its sound was different from anything else. I looked at my watch and noticed that it was three o'clock almost to the dot, "the ninth hour" of biblical computation.
>
> The windows rattled about me. The earth seemed to shake as with convulsions. This may have been my imagination, but that shell somehow seemed nearer and heavier than any that I had felt before.
>
> Then the news came. It spread like fire over Paris. That shell had thrust itself on this Good Friday afternoon, like the spear thrust into the side of

Jesus; had thrust itself into the side of that ancient and beautiful church St. Gervais, at three o'clock, "the ninth hour"; at the exact moment when millions of people were kneeling in memory of the hour that Jesus cried and gave up the ghost; at the same moment that hundreds of people were kneeling in this particular church, and more than seventy-five lives were snuffed out like the blowing out of a candle. More than a hundred others were terribly wounded. I was on the spot an hour later and what I saw shall haunt me forever.

Women's furs, baby shoes, baby carriages, broken hats, coats; clothes of the poor and clothes of the rich; all buried in the three feet of stone that had fallen from the arch of the church when the big shell, weighing a ton, went through the ancient walls. The explosion followed and blew out the roof. It was a horrible sight. Bloodstains were everywhere.

As I stood there looking down on the awful ruin of this Good Friday afternoon and thought of the terrible Passion Week [properly, the week before Holy Week] through which we were passing; thought of the refugees; thought of the thousands of boys who had given their lives up there for me this week; thought of the cross and the cannon ball up on the Baupaume road; thought of the thing that had just happened at three o'clock, the phrase of the old, old story came flashing into my heart. "And at the ninth hour there was darkness over all the land. And the veil of the temple was rent in twain, and the earth shook and the rocks fell."

"And I heard the voice of Jesus crying amid the blackness of that hour, 'My God, my God, why hast thou forsaken me?'"

And as I stood in that ruined cathedral this afternoon, with the spear thrust through its sacred side, I heard the voice of the Christian nations crying out, "My God, my God, why hast Thou forsaken me?"

Then came Sunday, the Resurrection Day.

I am not trying to force this parallel of Passion Week. I am trying to keep from forcing it. To do that I am quoting from my diary: "Something has happened since Good Friday, when all was so dark for the Allies. The tide has turned. The English and French are holding. The Americans are coming into the line. Hope is in the air. The dawn seems to be about to break."

"Paris rests easier today than it has for two weeks. The news from the battlefront is more than good. The tide seems to have turned. All Paris is out in gala attire along the boulevards. The day is glorious. The sun is shining. The trees have opened over night. It is a glorious hour."[27]

Although the spirit in Paris was rising with the hope that the German offensive had been stopped, Bill's diary contains worried references to his own health—which was not good—and his gradual understanding of what his problem was:

EASTER SUNDAY, MARCH 31.
I have a terrific cold in my lungs which I got in that close, vile smelling basement at the Gare du Nord the last three nights helping the refugees. Went
out, had dinner with Budd. Came home feeling even worse and took a lot of
drugs. Dreamed that I was captured by the Germans and put in the front line
trenches. A few nights ago I dreamed that I was in a boat which was torpedoed
and I was swimming in water and at last went down. This afternoon as I sat in
my room, the long distance guns banged away three times and scared the wits
out of me, the final crash was so unexpected. I don't like that gun at all—at all.

MONDAY, APRIL 1ST.
Came home this afternoon sick and went to bed. It is a cold that I have had
(almost) constantly in France, and which I don't seem to get rid of. I have
wondered what it was and discovered today. I had a slight gas attack when I
was driving at Toul. Norton, my driver, had the same experience as I did and
the other day he had to go to the hospital where they told him that he had had
a slight touch of gas. Barnes, one of our fellows, is ruined for life by gas and
another boy I know died from it last week. I remember now when I got it. I
was sick to my stomach all night and the next day and for two weeks my
throat and nose and lungs were sore. I have never gotten entirely over it and
my cold is an indication of it all. Had a big shelling this afternoon, while I was
sick in bed, and I felt too bum even to get up. I have certainly felt rotten.[28]

Bill was asked by his boss, Fred Shipp, if he would be willing to spend ten days with
a group of men who were driving trucks carrying American soldiers to the front lines.
He said that he would take the job gladly, but he had to decline, because he was afraid
that he was not up to it; he was still waking up in the middle of the night in a cold sweat
and feeling nauseous. Gradually, however, the fevers and nausea subsided, and after a
week of rest, Bill had regained enough of his energy and vigor to conclude that the
worst of his illness was over. In mid-April he was offered a new assignment by Shipp;
he was to become the religious director of St. Nazaire, one of the principal ports of
entry for the arriving American soldiers. He said that he would be thrilled to take it. In
a letter written much later to Miss Mary Scott, Bill described what his new job was like:

YMCA—A.E.F.
Headquarters, Base No. 1
Wednesday, May 29, 1918

My Dear Miss Mary:

*Your fine letter came to me here at St. Nazaire where I am now located; and have been for a month
and a half, as Religious Director of the Division that centers around this great Port of Entry. I had
the honor to succeed Dr. W. H. Crawford, the President of Allegheny College, as the Religious*

Director here and I am to be succeeded by Dr. Merle Smith, the man who took Bishop Matt Hughes' church in Pasadena.

I think that I wrote you last when I was in Paris in the Publicity Department. Shortly after that I was given this responsible position and have been here all this time, enthused and challenged by my job. I am not permitted to tell you how big my assignment is; or, rather, how many men I have in it, for the censor would not allow that, but I am permitted to tell you that it runs from St. Nazaire (this Port of Entry) to Nantes (where the Edict of Nantes was signed) sixty five miles and east and west as far. I cover it in a motorcycle and feel, as I have said many times, like a REAL Methodist now for I am a true "Itinerating Bishop" of this area. When I first started driving it, I put some of Uncle Sam's finest soldiers in their first real danger but at least I didn't put them in the hospital. I can't tell you the number of Religious Directors I have altogether but I have about eight Methodist preachers among them. I speak on an average two times a day and three times on Sundays and ride night and day at about fifty miles per hour in my motorcycle with a side car attached, in which I carry my religious literature. It is SOME life and just to my liking.

I have several hospitals in my area and the other night I was visiting in the Shell Shock ward of one of them. The boys there were shaking as if they had the ague and stuttered as well. I never saw such an awful sight and yet it has a touch of hope for about sixty percent of them actually get well enough to go back to the frontlines again and they are all the most cheerful bunch that I have ever seen in a hospital here in France.

I knew one of the boys from California. The last time I saw him he was standing on a platform addressing a crowd of young church people. And there he was, his six foot three frame shaking from head to foot like an old man with palsy, and stuttering every word he spoke. He had been sent to the hospital in Amiens with a case of acute appendicitis. The first night he was in the hospital the Germans bombed and destroyed it. They took him out and put him on a train for Paris. This train had only gotten a few miles out of Amiens when the Germans shelled it and destroyed two cars.

"After that I began to shake," he said simply. "We call ourselves the 'First American Shock Troops,'" my friend from the West said with a grin.

"I guess you are 'shock troops,' all right. I know one thing, and that is you would give your folks back home a good shock if they saw you."

Then they all laughed. Laughter was in the air. I have never met anywhere in France such a happy, hopeful, cheerful crowd as that bunch of shell-shocked boys. It was contagious. I went there to cheer them up, and I got cheered up. I went there to give them strength and came away stronger than when I went in.

They laugh and tremble and stutter and cry and your heart aches for them. I spent more than two hours with them for I saw that they were hungry for a good visit. Just as I was leaving I said "Boys, I am not much of a mollycoddle but I would like to pray with you." They said, "We'd like it, Sir."

Then I prayed the prayer that had been burning in my heart every minute as we stood there in that dimly lit ward, talking of home and battle and the folks we all loved across the seas. All that time there had been hovering in the background of my mind a picture of a cool body of water named Galilee, and of a Christ who had been sleeping in a boat on that water with some of His friends, when a storm came up. I had been thinking of how frightened those friends had been of the storm; of the tossing, tumbling, turbulent waves. I had thought of how they had trembled with fear, and then of how they had appealed to the Master. I told the boys simply that story, and then I prayed:

"Oh Thou Christ who stilled the waves of Galilee, come Thou into the hearts of these boys just now, and still their trembling limbs and tongues. Bring a great sense of peace and quiet into their souls."

The nurse told me the next day that after I had gone the boys went quietly to bed; that there was little tossing that night and no walking the floors, as there had been before.

I have the great joy here of meeting and giving a word of welcome to the men as the transports land. It is a privilege to speak a Christian word to them. It is the first voice they hear in France. On Mother's Day I heard that several transports were to land so I took an automobile and scurried around our Divisions and gathered up five or six thousand Mother's Day Folders such as the YMCA issued and when the boats landed I tied a rope to the folders, even before the boats were "Cleared" and swung them up to the transport YMCA secretaries who were aboard. Those homesick American boys, on their first day in France, were handed Mother's Day Folders, on MOTHER'S DAY. That was a great privilege.

And so it goes. The days and the nights are full of the chances to serve, serve, serve, somebody else and just as I used to write you eighteen years ago I still "Thank God for the chance to work." But more especially do I thank Him now for the chance to work for somebody else.

You will be glad to hear that I have had a request from the Macmillan Company to submit several of my stories like "The Louvre of the Atlantic" with the idea of putting them out in book form. That of course does not mean that they will be PUT out but it does mean that this big company has seen enough in what I am writing to be interested in my stories at least. I hope that you have read my Giant Hours With Poet Preachers. *I see that it is out now. The Methodist Book Concern is also going to put out a book under the title of* The New Calvary *for which I have gathered the material over here.*

My present plans are to sail about July first for America. I have been urged to stay another six months but feel that just now the thing that I MUST do is return as per my promise to my church and my bishop and then, if the war continues, to come over again for "The Duration of the War." I can be of great use to the YMCA at home now for six months and to my country too I feel certain.

I will be in Moundsville, of course, with Betty and Iva, on our way west and one of the great pleasures of that visit will be to see you and Miss Norma and your dear Daddy. The quiet, seldom voiced, and yet constantly sympathetic influence of your Father's life I have always felt.

Please let my Father read this letter too and, if there is anything that you think is of public interest, cut out the personal parts and let the Moundsville Daily Echo *have it for I haven't the time to write many letters.*

With love,
Will[29]

Everyone, whether having just arrived or combat-hardened, thought longingly of home. On an evening when Bill was particularly struck with thoughts of Iva and Betty, he wrote a poem, which was published and read widely by other servicemen:

WHEN THE WEST WIND BLOWS

The west wind is the homebound wind
As it blows across the sea
And every breeze bears a breath of love
From a lonely heart to Thee.

And the west wind sings as it sweeps along
And it plays with the white cap foam
But it will not stay for it bears a song
And the theme of the song is "home."

And the west wind whispers soft and low
As of old in the lullaby
And a father hears as it starts to blow
The sound of a baby's cry.

Then he sends a kiss to his little child
And the west wind bears it home
And the soldier lad to his sweetheart
Wings a kiss in the lengthening gloom.

For France is the east and the wind is west
And the sea is a long, long way
But the bridge of the sea is a wish of love
At the close of a lonely day.[30]

Though busy with his speaking in YMCA huts and hospitals, Bill found time to write articles for "the folks back home." The warm, even hot, late spring weather gave him the zest to write, and the freedom from constant bombardment gave him the peace of mind to turn his attention to producing a steady flow of articles about life in the Great War. To most of his readers, Bill's articles were as close as they would ever get to the front lines, and his stories were eagerly received. A comment by the *San Jose Mercury Herald* illustrated the interest his writing created:

MR. STIDGER'S LETTERS FROM FRANCE

Quite naturally everyone is reading the letters of the Rev. Dr. Stidger to the *Mercury Herald* and to his own congregation, for not only are they beautifully written but in other respects are so illuminating in the information they contain that the veriest dullard could hardly fail to find them interesting. From a clergyman one expects an overplus of preachment, since that is the duty of the clergyman in the vicinity of the trenches; but while Mr. Stidger regards as vital the spiritual mission he has gone to perform, the bills of flotsam and jetsam that drift into his and every man's life in France have a peculiar significance to him because doubtless of his newspaper training which has educated him to scent the joys and miseries which alternate in one's experiences more or less proportionately in such a place and under such circumstances. For example, could anything more beautifully impressive be written than this little story of the death and burial of a German lad, picked up by the Americans and brought into camp:

"The day before I left the front I helped to bury several American soldiers and a German lad. We secretaries had been given the detail by the major in charge of digging the graves and arranging for the funeral. When we had buried the American private and the squad had blown taps for him, and when we had buried the American captain and had blown taps for him, it was time to bury the German prisoner. The lads on the funeral detail saluted the chaplain and said: 'Sir, shall we blow taps for the German?'

"The chaplain was a big, broadminded fellow, I am thankful to say, and saw his opportunity. He saluted the boys in return and said in a few words, 'Yes boys; we are not fighting this poor dead German boy; we are fighting the German government. The German lad shall receive the same honorable burial as the American captain beside whom he lies. Blow taps for the German.' And there in that open field, near a beautiful woods just bursting into spring life and leaves, in the quiet of a moment undisturbed by gunfire, the clear sweet notes of taps blew over that German lad's grave."

. . . Dr. Stidger's letters are a pleasure to all who read them; and with others of his friends the *Mercury Herald* sincerely hopes for his safe return to his congregation and to this city which is proud of him.[31]

The American military censor looked through all his papers, his diary, and his carbons, stamped them on June 15, 1918, and cleared Bill to leave France. Two plain-clothesmen from the intelligence office in Paris arrived without advance notice, demanding to search his luggage and papers. He passed their inspection and assumed that they had been sent because he had worked for the Publicity Department and had written so extensively on the war.

Bill boarded the *Matsonia* on Thursday afternoon, June 20. He and Bobby Freeman shared a stateroom and bath; a stateroom was a "virtual palace" compared with most of the places he had stayed while in France. As the ship sailed, a soldier whom Bill knew from California shouted to him from his truck on the dock, "Don't forget to tell Mother we're all right."

Bill and Bobby were assigned to a submarine watch in the ship's crow's nest. They had to climb about sixty-five feet straight up a ladder that, Bill said, had been "constructed for monkeys" and not for human beings. He had never been so afraid of anything in his life as climbing that pole:

It was the four-to-eight A.M. lookout. Seamen call it the "Morning Watch." We climbed sixty-five feet in the darkness into the crow's nest, with the great transport swinging in the waves and on its zigzag course, and the wind blowing such a terrific gale that I thought I would fall to the deck every time the ship swung. For a pure landlubber the feat of climbing a mast is no easy before breakfast exercise. When I started up that pole, it looked a good mile and a half to the top. When I got half-way up, the rungs took a dizzy notion to travel clear around the mast. As one of my fellow sufferers who was following me up the mast said "I would have gone back, but that would have been doing the impossible twice." At last, by sheer will power, we reached the top, crowded through the little hole in the floor of the crow's nest, and took the next half of the four hour watch recovering from the climb. The Ledge Trail at Yosemite looks easy compared with that climb into the crow's nest. But, like the Ledge Trail, this climb was well worth the effort when you reached the top.[32]

It was a beautiful moonlit night, a perfect occasion for the "steel fish," as the men called the submarines. Bill spotted a black object that looked like a bale of cotton fifty yards off the port side and telephoned the bridge. Then he sighted forty or fifty more objects floating on the water and several boxes and some liferafts—evidence that a ship had been sunk nearby. He was ordered to keep a close lookout for boats and bodies but sighted none. Just before dawn he saw the *Manchuria,* an Allied battleship, along with five camouflaged destroyers accompanying the *Matsonia,* silhouetted in the moonlight. The ships were escorting the *Matsonia,* which was making about fourteen knots.

On Bill's next morning watch, sunrise was about 5 A.M. One by one from out of the rising sun came ten destroyers, their "lithe low lines" cutting the water. The destroyers that had protected the *Matsonia* had left in the middle of the night. Bill watched the new destroyers through his binoculars as they came out of the east in single file like a caravan of the sea. Then, suddenly, there appeared from the west, where the moon still shone, several black patches of smoke. He knew the smoke to be from the convoy that the destroyers were out to meet. In a few minutes, coming up over the western horizon, toward which the *Matsonia* was bound, one by one, the outlines of transports' masts appeared, then the hulls of the ships, until twenty large vessels were in sight. A cruiser was leading them. The transports were laden with human freight, American soldiers on their way to France to "make the world safe for democracy." Bill said, "It was a tremendously impressive sight, one not to be forgotten in a life time." The destroyers swung around and in the dawn flashed messages back and forth with their searchlights; then they wheeled into a column and steamed off eastward as an escort for the transports. The entire thirty-six-ship convoy steamed on toward France.

The passage across the Atlantic was not all in calm weather. On one particularly stormy night, Bill wrote the following:

> The *Matsonia* was cutting its way through three dangers: the submarine zone, a terrific storm beating from the west, and a night as dark as Erebus, with no lights showing.
>
> I had the midnight to 4:00 A.M. watch on the "Aft Fire Control." Below me, on the aft gun deck, as the rain pounded, the wind howled, the ship lurched, I could see the bulky forms of the boy gunners, two to each gun, two standing by with phone pieces to their ears, and six sleeping on the deck, ready for an emergency. Our ship was carrying back to America a precious cargo of wounded officers from France.
>
> For an hour I heard no sound from the boys below me. I watched their silent forms with a great feeling of respect and affection. The ship lurched

through the storm on its zigzag course. Then suddenly I heard a familiar sound coming from one of the boys below me. It was from big, rawboned "Montana" as they called him. The sound was low at first, and because of the storm and the vibration of the ship I could not make it out, although the melody was strangely familiar. Then the boy on the port gun took the melody up, followed by the gunners on the starboard, and I caught the old familiar words of:

Jesus, Saviour, pilot me
Over life's tempestuous sea;
Unknown waves before me roll,
Hiding rock and treacherous shoal;
Chart and compass came from thee;
Jesus, Saviour, pilot me.

Above the creaking and vibrations of the great ship, above the thunder of the storm, those American boy gunners all unconsciously, in that storm-tossed, tumultuous, turbulent sea, were singing the old hymn which came back to them from their boyhood memories in little churches across our continent. I think I never heard that wonderful hymn when it sounded sweeter or more appropriately sung than it did that night, as the second verse wafted up to me when I stood my watch on the aft gun deck of the old transport *Matsonia*.

We heard a good deal in the days of the war of how our boys sang "Hail! Hail! The Gang's All Here," "Where Do We Go From Here, Boys?" "There's a Long, Long Trail A-Winding," "Keep the Home Fires Burning"—and they did. But when you got those boys in a serious, thought-ful mood you found them singing the great hymns of the Church. Indeed, most of us, under circumstances of storm and stress, doubt and night, find ourselves with the old hymns ringing in our hearts. They give us a sense of peace and security in this too turbulent, storm-tossed world. How much we all need a place of peace and quiet in these tumultuous days! And that, my friends, is God.[33]

Two days before landing, the ship was diverted to Newport News, Virginia, disap-pointing Bill and everyone on board; all had been looking forward to a triumphal entrance into New York Harbor, passing the Statue of Liberty and Ellis Island. After their unceremonious arrival in Newport News, Bill caught a train to New York City, where he reported to the YMCA headquarters to be "decommissioned," after which he planned to go straight to Ligonier to see Iva and Betty.

Bill described his stay in New York in a letter to Edwin Markham. It covered his whirlwind of activity in the latter half of July 1918:

I spent three weeks in New York. I only had expected to be there three days, but I was called on to address the Salmagundi Club. Men who heard me speak there—Editors—sent for me to come and see them. The result was that I stayed in New York at the request of Charles Scribner's Sons to write a book which I call *Soldier Silhouettes on Our Front.* They are at work on it now. I also wrote and sold six stories to *The Outlook,* the first of which appeared in the issue of August 7th called "Ship Silhouettes." I sold three to *The Independent,* the first of which will appear in the issue of August 10th. I wonder if you saw either? I wrote an article at the request of *The American,* two for *Leslie's* and several for *Association Men.* A second book at the request of the Methodist Book Concern kept me a week longer. In all, I was about exhausted when I got through and longed for the cool air, white fogs and sea breezes of California.[34]

Bill hastened to "explain" his incredible volume of writing to a poet known for approaching each sentence with painstaking care:

You who work so carefully and so wonderfully will feel that I have done careless work in turning out so much copy in such a short time, but you will forgive me when you know that it is all war stuff and only has its warm vital message just NOW and cannot wait for more finished workmanship. I do not hope or expect this work to live but I do have hopes that it will go out to the mothers and fathers of the boys "Over There" as a message of comfort and hope.

I am hoping to get to see the new poetry that you are writing for I have been longing to hear your voice in this great moment of the nation's need of real spiritual leadership.

P.S. I hesitate; but am making bold to send you a copy of a sermon of mine that I got down in the trenches on the front lines and which I preached to the boys in France and which the Christian Advocate *of New York published in full.*[35]

Bill was consumed by a furious energy to set down and disseminate his thoughts on the war as rapidly as humanly possible. He checked into the Prince George Hotel, "only a few steps away from the Marble Collegiate Church," locked himself in his room with his typewriter, and did not emerge for twenty-four hours. When he did, he had the complete draft of his new book, *Soldier Silhouettes,* in his hands.

In October 1918, *Soldier Silhouettes on Our Front* was published through Charles Scribner's Sons, to very favorable comment by reviewers. This was followed some months later by a second book, also on his war experience, entitled *Stardust from the Dugouts,* from the Abingdon Press (the Methodist Book Concern). The foreword to the *Stardust* book was by Bill's good friend and writer for *The Saturday Evening Post,* Peter Clark MacFarlane, and Bill cherished it. The foreword concludes:

I used to think the deepest thing I saw in France was mud, but Stidger was always seeing the deeps in hearts. He has touched this war with his human hands; he has measured the current of its emotions through his heart, and some of that touch, of that measure, is here in the book, told with a simple sincerity that is power.

Peter Clark MacFarlane[36]

Afterword

Becoming a civilian again was not easy for Bill. Some years later, Betty Stidger reminisced about her father's return:

Dad was gone 7 months.

Mother cried every time they played the "Star Spangled Banner," and I saw Charlie Chaplin in a movie where he caught a thread of his stocking and his whole stocking unraveled.

Dad sent pictures of himself in uniform, in helmet and mud, in flying clothes. There were rumors about him being called "Gyp the Blood." His reputation was, "He got the oranges through."

Later, much later, we all laughed at the time when he was driving a truck through a tiny French village at three A.M. on a cold morning and the gate was down to block the road. The gatekeeper was an old crone who went to bed at sunset and wouldn't open the gate for love or money. Dad couldn't persuade her for all his haggling. He yelled at her from her yard in his pig French and she let loose torrents of provincial French from her latticed window.

Finally, Dad sighed, and said, "Well, old lady, I was trying to be Christian, but to hell with it!" He got back in his truck, floored the accelerator and the old gatekeeper was without a job and the road was without a barrier in less time than that!

Being back from the "center of immensities" was extremely difficult for Bill. He had his memories of American soldiers suffering and dying, perhaps needlessly, and he relived his own brushes with death. In addition, he had had such a soul-changing experience in France that returning to his pastoral duties in provincial San Jose made him restless. To be fair to the citizens of San Jose, they were not to blame. Bill realized that every serviceman returning home anywhere in the country felt out of sorts with life around him. War changed each participant, creating a gulf between him and those who had remained at home. He focused on this subject in *Stardust from the Dugouts*. He called it his "reconstruction" book, meant to help "the preacher and the church worker, together with the parents" understand the state of mind of the two million soldiers as they returned from the front lines. Finally, until the war was over, while

Americans continued to die, it was especially difficult for Bill to find satisfaction in his safe routine at home.

Bill was entertaining the idea of a second assignment on the front lines when "on the eleventh hour of the eleventh day of the eleventh month in the year 1918," armistice was declared, and the world war was over. Genuine jubilation swept across the country, and Bill described it in one of his radio broadcasts nearly twenty years later:

Armistice Day in 1918 meant a good deal to me. I had been in France working with our American soldiers. I had close friends in every Division of the
American Army and on the high seas. I knew that many of my dearest
friends were at Chateau Thierry in the Belleau Woods during the Argonne
Battle. I myself had returned to my home in California a month before
the Armistice.

One morning we were all sound asleep on our San Jose sleeping porch,
just before daylight when the most unearthly noise broke out—automobile
horns, factory whistles, fence poundings. Even the town fire alarm was going
full blast, which sounded for all the world like the warnings of an air raid to
which I had become so accustomed in France. A tumult of sound literally
bombarded the morning stillness like the guns of the Hindenburg line. I
jumped out of bed, half-asleep and half-awake. We were all bewildered, and
Mrs. Stidger called out: "What has happened? What is it?" in a terrified tone.
Then the answer came to us out of that grey California dawning above the
din of the noise. The answer came from next door when we heard a
woman's voice with a shriek of almost hysterical relief, joy and ecstasy:
"My God—it's the Armistice!"

We knew what that Armistice meant to her, for we knew that her son
was in the thick of the Argonne Battle the last we had heard from him. My
heart sank as I heard the pathetically wild cry of that young mother, for I
knew too well that all of her joy of that morning might well be turned to
ashes in a week or so. Fortunately my fears were never realized for, in due
time, that lad came home to his mother and his friends, unscathed, in spite
of the fact that on the very morning of the Armistice he had heard that terrifying whistle from his Battalion Leader which called him over the top.

He went over, and he came back. But somehow, whenever I hear the
world "Armistice" every year since that morning, I can hear that mother's
shriek through the grey dawn: "My God, it's the Armistice."

To some people the Armistice meant one thing; to others it meant
something else.

There was the young American who came home with a long scar running from his ear to his chin, down across his check. One of his friends
asked him one day how he had received that scar.

He replied: "I got it the night of the Armistice in Paris."

"How in the world did you get it?"

"I jumped through a plate glass window," he replied, with a reminiscent grin.

"What in the world did you do that for?" his friend asked.

"I don't know, it seemed a good idea at the time."

We all chuckled over that story, for a good many foolish, joyous, laughing, wild, hilarious things seemed good ideas to most of us on that high and bold dawning. It was a relief of tension such as the world never experienced before up to that time; and little do we blame any soldier for having done wild-eyed, foolish things.

To me that Armistice morning meant and has always meant the bringing back of one rich memory. It comes from Chaumont; General Pershing's Headquarters where I once drove a truck load of supplies in my big Pierce-Arrow. I was billeted with an English Tommy [soldier] who had been wounded at Gallipoli [in Turkey, in 1915] and had been invalided out of the British Army, his lungs gassed. But he was so anxious to remain in the war that he got a job with the American YMCA and was stationed at Chaumont. That night before he went to sleep we had a long chat about the war and his experiences.

"Yank, I'm only twenty-eight but I'm an old man," said my English Tommy just before we piled into our cots on the coldest night that I had ever experienced in France. And his terrible cough added fatal testimony to his statement.

There was not a minute when he was not coughing; I thought he would tear his lungs out. I went to sleep, aching for that fine lad. About midnight I awoke shivering. From his coughing I knew that he was awake also and I carelessly said to him: "Tommy, I never was so cold in my life. I didn't know I could shiver inside as well outside." He laughed between his coughs and we went to sleep again.

An hour later I was again awakened by his violent coughing. To my surprise, I seemed warm and wondered if the wind had changed, but from its constant whistling I knew that it had not. The snow drifted in on us. I reached out over my body and felt two extra blankets on me which I knew had not been there an hour before. I suspected whence they had come by the more violent coughing of my comrade from England.

I immediately got up from my cot, carried those two extra blankets over to his cot, threw them over his body and said to him: "Tommy did you put these blankets on me? You, a sick man, coughing your lungs out and still you gave me your blankets?" He replied: "Yes, Yank, I did, for you said that you were cold."

"But what about *you,* my friend?"

"Oh, me—I'm used to the cold and you're new at this war game."

"Well, all I've got to say is, thank you old top, but if you do that trick again I'll throw you out of that window into the snow and let you freeze to death."

And that is the memory which always comes back to me on Armistice Day for that little act of kindness always seems to me the spirit of Armistice, Peace and Good Will. If the whole world could have this spirit in its heart, none of us would ever go to war again for anything.[37]

In stark contrast to the joy of the millions of soldiers returning to their homes in about thirty countries was a deadly pestilence that accompanied them. Influenza quickly infected populations across the world, killing in only a few months twenty million people, although the actual number of dead may have been double that number. Those felled by the flu greatly exceeded the eight million men and women who had lost their lives over the four years of the world war. The virus was thought to have mutated from an influenza in China, and it spread rapidly among the soldiers on the battlefields. It was ironic that with armistice came such a cruel and horrible plague, wiping out both soldiers who had been spared on the battlefield and their families.

In the San Francisco area, the first case was noted on September 23, 1918; thereafter the caseload doubled every two days until late October. Within eight weeks, 2,200 people died. Overall, more than 675,000 people died in the United States from the flu. There was no effective medical response to the epidemic except to let it run its course. In San Jose, schools, theaters, and all public gathering places were shut down for six weeks; church services were forbidden, and an ordinance was passed requiring everyone to wear gauze masks. With the threat of rapid death (within hours) affecting young as well as older members of the population, fear gripped the people of San Jose. Bill was sick at his helplessness in the face of this disaster and felt that more than ever before, people needed both their churches and their ministers—yet the churches were closed by law. He called his electrician (as he had two years earlier when he wanted to light the church's window from the outside); they met and walked through the empty church, which echoed with their footfalls. They estimated and measured, and finally the electrician said, "I can illuminate every one of the windows from the inside pouring the light to the outside, for about one hundred dollars."

"Let's do it," Bill told him, and in a week he advertised in the newspapers that, beginning at the customary time for church services, the street would be flooded with light from every one of the eight stained-glass windows from the inside the church. That Sunday night the streets around First Methodist were crowded. It was the only church in the city that was "preaching to folks during the flu shutdown and doing it in a reverent way without endangering lives, for the people were all outside in the fresh air." Bill said that it was a curious sight to see thousands of people standing on the streets with their masks on, looking at the beautiful lighted windows.

As the years passed, and regardless where the paths of his life took him, Bill was to be periodically haunted by recurring images of the suffering and death he had seen in the war. In France, he had summed up his thoughts in a poem evoked by the vivid images of the cross he had seen near the battlefield and of a grief-stricken mother.

He sent this poem, which was one of his favorites, to Betty in May 1931, when she was a freshman at Smith College, with the following note:

I had a poem in Zion's Herald *this week which I want you to see so I am enclosing it in this letter for you to read. I wrote it in France, with the query in my heart as to whether the World War—after all—accomplished much or was even in the least degree worthwhile. I had that feeling one evening when I saw a woman walking through a national cemetery where her boy was buried. Look it over, and, if you have any criticisms, tell me when you get home for I value your viewpoint and your criticism of my verse.*[38]

"TRAVELER, HAST THOU EVER SEEN?"

William L. Stidger

INSCRIBED upon a crucifix,
A wistful wayside shrine:
"Traveler, hast thou ever seen
So great a grief as mine?"
In Flanders Field I saw it,
Beside a stricken way:
A golden sunset lingered
Reluctantly that day.
Mute shadows in the twilight,
Mute crosses on the plain,
Mute symbols of ten thousand dead
Who died perhaps in vain.
Dead trees, a gaunt reminder
Of war and hate and hurt;
Deep scars across the summer fields
With poppy belts begirt.
Deep pits like pockmarks, desolate;
The wounds of shot and shell;
A tale of tragic circumstance;
Footprints of hate and hell.
A woman walks along this way
Of crosses row on row
In Flanders Field, and kneels
Besides a grave where poppies grow.
And will the world remember,
Or will the world forget,
The march of martial music,
The hate and hurt and fret?
The grief and lonely anguish
Of mothers in all lands;
The ugly wounds of battle;

The bloodstains on the sands?
In Flanders Field I saw it,
Beside a stricken way;
A golden sunset lingered
Reluctantly that day.
Inscribed upon a crucifix,
A wistful wayside shrine:
"Traveler, hast thou ever seen
So great a grief as mine?"[39]

Bill knew he needed to move on to a new assignment; he had outgrown San Jose. His writing on the war and his reputation within the Church had grown sufficiently that by the late spring of 1919 he had a fistful of telegrams from boards of churches across the country asking him to become their minister. He expected that one of these might provide him with the challenge he wanted to take on; yet he yearned to get some world travel under his belt.

Notes

1. William L. Stidger, "War Diary," 1918, author's collection, 1.

2. Stidger, "War Diary," 2.

3. William L. Stidger, *Christian Advocate,* January 24, 1918, 104.

4. Stidger, *Christian Advocate,* 25.

5. Stidger, *Christian Advocate,* 26.

6. William L. Stidger, "Stidger's Ship 'Sub' Quarry," *San Jose Mercury Herald,* 1918, author's collection.

7. Stidger, "War Diary," 27.

8. William L. Stidger, "Human Adventures from 'Over There,'" *Christian Advocate,* May 23, 1918, 648.

9. Stidger, "Human Adventures from 'Over There,'" 648.

10. Stidger, "War Diary," 36.

11. William L. Stidger, "Adventures 'Over There'—a YMCA Preacher-Secretary's First Night," *San Jose Mercury Herald,* May 5, 1918, 1.

12. William L. Stidger, "Finding Old Friends in France," *Epworth Herald,* June 15, 1918, 1.

13. William L. Stidger, "Orange Day, Somewhere in France," author's collection.

14. William L. Stidger, *Soldier Silhouettes on Our Front* (New York: Scribner's, 1918), 176.

15. William L. Stidger, "Down Where Shells Are Thickest," *Independent,* August 10, 1918, 191–92.

16. William L. Stidger, "Something in the Air," *Outlook,* December 11, 1918, 596–97.

17. Stidger, *Soldier Silhouettes on Our Front,* 125–26.

18. Stidger, *Soldier Silhouettes on Our Front,* 39–40.

19. Stidger, *Soldier Silhouettes on Our Front,* 28–41.

20. Stidger, *Soldier Silhouettes on Our Front,* 81–82.

21. Stidger, "War Diary," 87.

22. William L. Stidger, "Calvary-France-1918," *Christian Advocate,* April 10, 1919, 457–59.

23. Stidger, "War Diary," 84.

24. Stidger, "War Diary," 85.

25. Stidger, *Soldier Silhouettes on Our Front,* 130–31.

26. Stidger, "War Diary," 87.

27. Stidger, "Calvary-France-1918," 459.

28. Stidger, "War Diary," 90–91.

29. Letter dated May 29, 1918, from William L. Stidger to Miss Mary I. Scott, author's collection.

30. William L. Stidger, "When the West Wind Blows," "War Diary."

31. "Mr. Stidger's Letters from France," *San Jose Mercury Herald,* undated editorial, author's collection.

32. William L. Stidger, *Stardust from the Dugouts* (New York: Abingdon, 1919), 76–77.

33. William L. Stidger, "Ship Silhouettes—The Midnight Watch," *Outlook,* undated article, author's collection.

34. Letter dated August 15, 1918, from William L. Stidger to Edwin Markham, Markham Collection, Horrmann Library, Wagner College, Staten Island.

35. Stidger to Markham.

36. Stidger, *Stardust from the Dugouts,* 12.

37. William L. Stidger, "Getting the Most Out of Life," radio broadcast on the Yankee Network, November 11, 1937.

38. Letter dated Mary 27, 1931, from William L. Stidger to Betty Stidger, author's collection.

39. William L. Stidger, "Traveler, Hast Thou Ever Seen?" *I Saw God Wash the World* (Chicago: Rodeheaver-Hall Mack, 1934), 76.

Six

Flashlights from the Seven Seas:
The Orient

The invitation to travel the world, all expenses paid, came, according to Iva, "out of a clear sky, but it was what we had been hoping for." The telegram was addressed to Bill and arrived on Sunday morning, August 23, 1919:

> The Centenary Program is in great need of your services. We need someone like yourself who can see things in the big and write them up for both church and secular press. I will give you home field or send you abroad. We will give you $4,000 and all expenses of travel. Would like to have you for year, if possible. You might take leave of absence from your church. Trust you may give me favorable reply as church needs your services. If you think favorably of matter, will arrange conference. Write me at Wawasee, Indiana, before Tuesday morning. John G. Benson.[1]

The Methodist Episcopal Church had been actively engaged in raising funds in 1918 and 1919 to commemorate the hundredth anniversary of the founding of the Methodist Missionary Society (now called the Board of Missions) and to use the money to build new churches both in the United States and abroad. The fund-raising was done under the name of the Centenary Fund, and by May 1919, the Church had pledges in excess of $100 million. It was said that no church had ever attempted a campaign of such magnitude.

Throughout the day that the telegram came, Iva said, "We burned with wonder, would we or wouldn't we go?" Bill's bishop said that it was in the interest of the Church that Bill accept the call, and Bill's board agreed. Iva wrote, "Our hearts sang yes!"[2] After a trip to New York to work out the terms of his arrangement, which involved touring most of the countries in the Far East for the better part of a year, visiting Methodist missions and writing home about them, Bill booked passage on the *Empress of Asia,* one of the fastest ships of the Canadian Pacific Line. The *Empress* was due to sail from Vancouver on October 30, 1919, bound for Yokohama.

In preparing for the voyage, Iva read in the *Ladies' Home Journal* just what a "seafarer should wear" and insisted that her family dress accordingly. On the sailing day, it was boiling hot, and the October sun beat down with an August intensity. Nevertheless, Iva—with firm determination to be dressed in proper style—wore a brown wool suit and a mink stole (a gift from one of Bill's wealthy parishioners) and carried a heavy, brown woolen coat with a dark brown velvet collar as well as a steamer robe. Perched on her head was a brown felt sailor hat with a dark brown velvet lining and two stiff brown feathers jutting out on high.

Betty wore a blue serge sailor dress, a heavy coat, and a floppy hat; she carried Iva's hat box in one hand and Nemo—her plush monkey—in the other. Bill followed Iva and Betty with his coat over his arm and his big Graflex camera slung on a leather belt over his shoulder. He had his arms free, he said, so that he could "handle any situation."[3]

No sooner was land was out of sight than the ship encountered heavy seas off Puget Sound. The bad weather was unrelenting, tossing the ship and everyone on board around violently. Just about all the passengers were seasick and confined to their cabins until the fourth day, when the ocean calmed down. Both Iva and Bill felt well enough to go to the dining room. That night, however, the rough weather returned with a vengeance, as Iva's letter home relates:

Bill and I took a long promenade and had a grand time, congratulating ourselves on the joys of a sea voyage and to bed as usual. But again, in the middle of the night, we awoke in the midst of a storm and how sick we were. Then Betty took sick and has been sick ever since. She ran a fever of 103 for three days. The doctor said it was from an abscessed tooth but I didn't think so. The doctor gave her silly little pills and finally I said "castor oil." Neither the doctor nor Bill could get Betty to keep it down and I was too sick. I got desperate. I did it and the castor oil stayed down. As a result Betty is better, fever down and all. Her mouth is covered with fever sores, her nose is a sight, her eyes discolored, but I truly believe it was all stomach poisoning, only with added seasickness. I wished and wished we had never heard of the Orient.[4]

Finally, in calm water and within sight of land, Bill wrote his father:

I want to write to you before we land in Yokohama which we expect to do tomorrow morning. The great mountains of Japan are in sight, and the almost innumerable fishing smacks are already sailing past us. It is a beautiful day and we are quite happy to be landing after ten days of awful weather.

The captain of this big 30,000 ton steamer says that it is the worst trip he has ever taken. Iva and Betty and I have been in our berths seasick about eight days out of ten days. Betty has had her first serious illness and she has been in bed the entire voyage with a temperature running from 101 to 103 for about seven days straight. The ship doctor's diagnosis is septic poisoning, from bad teeth. We will have them tended to at once in Yokohama.

Her temperature is normal again this morning, and we feel greatly relieved. I have been up with her every night on an average of fifteen times a night. In addition to her sickness the ship has been rolling and tumbling about so much that it has been a Hell on the seas for all three of us.

There are four thousand passengers on board with about three hundred Chinese coolies who have just returned from a year's service in France, and who are now on their way to Russia.

We expect to spend a month in Japan and after that will go to China where we will stop for another month and then go to Manila where we will be permanently located for a few months.

I have thought of you many times during the voyage and have wished you might have the pleasure of seeing all that we are seeing. . . . During this long period of Betty's illness I have come to know again and again something of that anxiety that must have been in your heart as you—alone, without any mother for us kiddies—watched us through our sicknesses. As we grow older and have children of our own we more and more appreciate all that you have done for us and all that you mean to us now. . . . You have been a dear good Father to us, and I only hope that in our successes you are getting some pay.

With deepest love,
Will [5]

Bill and Iva checked into the Grand Hotel in Yokohama, choosing a room with a fireplace and a view of the ocean. On their first evening in Japan, Bill typed out his impressions for an article to be published in the *Evening News* in San Jose:

Three rickshaws were plodding through the streets of Yokohama. It was pouring down rain, a cold drizzling November rain. The rickshaw men had on such thin shoes that they might have been called nothing but black stockings. They paddled through the mud and water and rain uncovered.

I do not mind saying that one of the hardest things I ever did was to climb into a rickshaw and let another human being act as a beast of burden for my comfort. It did not and it does not seem right. No social condition can be right that makes it necessary for another human being to be a beast of burden for a more fortunate brother. I felt I would like to get between the shafts myself and let the worn, old, gray-haired rickshaw driver climb in and ride.

Why am I not cold and wet? Why am I not unshod like a horse between two shafts pulling a rickshaw? Because of the economic and social blessings that have come to me through Christianity. That's why. I want to pass that on. God helping me I will. That's what we are doing in the Methodist Church today, thank God.

It is night now.

Off to the east, that is really west the other way, is home. The lights are shining on the docks. A great ship is landing to take its place at the docks vacated a few hours ago by the *Empress of Asia*. It is the *Venezuela*. Its lights sparkle in the night. Smoke belches from its funnels. Off beyond it I can see the white lighthouse with the white light at King's Point flashing through the darkness as I sit in a warm hotel room writing.

I am wondering, as I look at the lights of the newly-docked ship, how many missionaries it carried; just how many men and women the Church of God sent out on this boat to bring the light into this economic and spiritual darkness.

Out of the hotel window this evening there is an old man fishing. It is pouring rain. It is cold. It is so cold that we have donned our wools and we have a coal fire burning in our grate. The evening is nearing darkness, but the old man patiently fishes on. Betty is watching him with much curiosity.

"Why is he fishing so late at night?" is her first question.

It goes unanswered, but the boy who is making the fire and who speaks a little English looks up as if he would like to answer the child's question.

"And why does he have no shoes and stockings on when it is so cold?" flies a second question, as the little, warmly dressed, well-fed, much loved American child presses her face to the window.

The boy who is making the fire turns again from his task. I nodded to him. He answered.

"He catcha fish for he baby. He no catcha fish he baby no eat tonight. He have no shoes because he too poor. Everybody in Japan too poor. Not like America. Everybody too poor. Everybody cold; everybody hungry."

And long after night had fallen that bare-legged old man of Japan stood on the cold stones of the docks below the Grand Hotel fishing for the evening meal of his children. And a little child could not forget him as we ate a bounteous dinner that night. She spoke of the "poor man" all through the meal and the little children at home waiting for their dinner. When we came back to the room at eight he was still fishing.

"What if he does not get any fish?" the child asked.

"He no eat tonight," the boy at the fire answered. "He no eat."

And who cares?

Certainly not that cold, unemotional bronze Buddha, as cold and uncaring as Mount Fuji. Neither has done a single thing for the people who worship them. They are cold, unfeeling. The economic, the social, the spiritual welfare of these peoples, have never improved under the cold stare of these unfeeling monuments of worship.

But somebody cares. A little American child cares. And the Methodist Church cares for this poor fisherman, who typifies an economic condition that Christianity always relieves. Yes, the Methodist Church cares, and it has so expressed itself in the practical pledge of the Centenary.

Yes and Jesus Christ cares—for Jesus so loved a poor fisherman once that he called him to be one of his intimates forever.[6]

Bill's and Iva's plan was to move directly from Yokohama to Tokyo where they would stay at the Methodist Missionary Compound, located "within a stone's throw" of the emperor's palace on the grounds of Aoyama Gakuin, the Methodist College. While still in Yokohama, however, Bill was invited to accompany Bishop Herbert Welch and Pat McConnell, a friend of Bill's from Boston University, on a two-week trip into the remote regions of Japan. Iva said she was willing to go on to Tokyo with Betty so that Bill could join the bishop's party. Therefore, for two weeks, Bill traveled in the extreme northern part of Japan visiting the island of Hokkaido, where lived the last remaining Ainu, a race of white Indians who were the original inhabitants of Japan. The Japanese, who were "crowding over into Hokkaido at the rate of about 400,000 a year," were squeezing the twenty-five thousand Ainu into smaller and smaller space—pretty much, he wrote, "like we Americans treated our native Indians. All Japanese mythology," he added, "is the story of how the 'brave' Japanese drove these helpless people from their rightful possessions."[7]

Bill arrived in Tokyo bearing gifts for Iva and Betty, including a nest of lacquer boxes, five ermine skins, and a Russian wolfskin for a rug, on the day before Thanksgiving, which he celebrated at the Methodist Compound with Iva. Then he left almost immediately for a three-week trip through Korea, which he described to the readers of the *Evening News* in San Jose:

Editor, The News: *December 15, 1919*

I promised you that I would write a letter for The News *once in awhile, so I shall do so this morning. I am in Seoul, the capital city of Korea, as I write, sitting in Bishop Welch's home on a mountainside looking down upon the city. Just back of this house towers a mountain. A ridge of mountains surrounds the city. On one side of the city is a great peak.*

The Fire God used to use this peak, according to Korean legend. And according to real Korean custom it was from this peak that the signal fires used to flare out each night telling the emperor that all was well within his borders. . . . Running along the top of this mountain ridge surrounding the city is the old city wall, a massive piece of masonry which was built in thirteen hundred A.D., two hundred years before Columbus even discovered our young upstart of a country. Even before Columbus was born, Korean slaves were toiling up this old hill building this wall. . . . At the northern wall of the city there is a pass cut in the mountains by human hands, a Herculean task, and it is called the Peking Pass since through this pass the road runs to Peking, China. . . .

Outside of the climate in mid-winter, figuratively speaking, this is about the warmest spot on earth; or rather I should say, politically speaking. Wartime in France has nothing on peacetime in

Korea. No wonder the eyes of the world are focused on this peninsula and the one opposite: Shantung (China). Said eyes had better be. There are many things I'd like to say, but the Japanese censorship is very rigid, and I might get thrown into prison, so I'll keep mum about that part of it.[8]

Bill chose not to write publicly about an incident he witnessed on his first day in Korea, which he later described in his book. He and Pat McConnell had been walking down the main street from the train depot when a squad of Japanese soldiers drew alongside them. In front of Bill and Pat, a poor Korean workman was walking slowly pushing a heavy cart that looked like a wheelbarrow. Apparently under orders from the officer in charge, the squad edged over to the Korean worker. As the Japanese soldiers reached the Korean they pushed him to the ground and kicked his wheelbarrow over as they passed by. It was the first example of a number of acts that Bill saw of deliberate brutality by the Japanese.

Bishop Welch told Bill that Korea at the time he arrived in 1916 was a tinderbox waiting to explode. The Koreans hated their Japanese masters—who had controlled Korea since 1905. The Japanese, for their part, went so far as to propose "assimilation" of Korea by making Japanese citizens of all the Koreans, an extremely unpopular idea to a people as nationalistic as the Koreans were. Ten months before Bill arrived in Korea, the explosion that Welch thought was imminent occurred on March 1, 1919, when thirty-three Korean men (fifteen of them Christians) met in the "Great Bright restaurant, issued a Declaration of Independence for the country, notified the police of their whereabouts, and calmly awaited arrest."[9] Demonstrators for a free Korea took up their cause all over the country, and the rebellion became known as the Independence Movement.

Both Korean and Japanese police cracked down forcefully and at once. There were widespread reports of brutality, of shooting, burning, and torture. Because a number of the Great Bright demonstrators were Christians, Bishop Welch and nine other senior members of foreign churches were summoned by the Japanese government, which asked them to use their influence to stop the demonstrations. The missionaries flatly refused and even suggested that the Japanese relax their tight grip on Korea, permitting the Koreans to meet together publicly and to publish their views without fear of arrest. Shortly before Bill arrived, Welch said, the Japanese prime minister had promised greater freedom to the Koreans and changed the leadership of its administration in Korea, naming Baron Minoru Saito as the governor-general.

Bill, at first, withheld his criticism of the Japanese in deference to Bishop Welch. The bishop, whom Bill sincerely admired, believed in working within the system to obtain reform. Bill, on the other hand, was always on the lookout for boats to rock and, when he found one, he rocked and rocked it until he had created a good-sized wave. He did recognize, however, that he, Bishop Welch, and the entire missionary community owed the existence of their missions to the forbearance of Japan. Moreover, Japan was not only the most powerful economic force in the Far East but the center of the American missionary movement in the Orient. The official Japanese position was that Japan was at peace with its neighbors, and the American church representatives had to be especially careful about casting doubts on the truth of the Japanese assertion. (A few weeks after Bill's visit, Welch's house burned to the ground on a cold January night. As the bishop would write, "Many thought it a case of arson by Japanese or Koreans; I preferred to regard it as an accident." If it was arson, Welch conceded, "It was the only penalty inflicted on me" for his criticism of Japanese actions during the Independence Movement.)[10]

Bishop and Mrs. Welch, Pat McConnell, Bill, and a few others set out across Korea by motorcycles and Ford cars on a tour of the missionary settlements, from Seoul on the west coast to Kangnung on the east coast, a distance of 180 miles. They stopped after seventy miles at the Methodist frontier mission station in Wanju. Bill sent a description of his trip to both the *Evening News* and the *Christian Advocate:*

> We had counted twenty-five stark-naked babies between Seoul and Wanju. It was mid-winter and bitter cold. I had on two pairs of thick woolen socks, two suits of woolen underwear, three shirts, two sweaters, two pairs of trousers, and a woolen helmet that covered every inch of my face, in order not to freeze on the trip by motorcycle. The rice fields, the ponds and even the rivers were frozen solid. We had to break ice half an inch thick to ferry three rivers. And yet in spite of that we saw naked children everywhere on the way. "But they get used to the cold. It doesn't bother them like us," some missionary is always quick to say in defense of the national custom. Pat McConnell scoffed: "You can't tell me that they get used to it. When a baby's stomach aches, it hurts him; when a baby hasn't any clothes on in this kind of weather, that baby is a cold baby. They don't get used to it; they die!"
>
> "You are right," said Dr. A. C. Anderson, who runs the Methodist hospital at Wanju. "They do die! I called on a mother the other day and she pointed to her sick baby, 'I have lost seven altogether. They live to be about five and then get sick and die. This one is going the same way.'" Dr. Anderson also explained other problems he deals with: "Many of my operations are to remove needles that some Korean doctor has inserted into the body of a patient. I took four out of a man the other day; they are copper needles and they sterilize them by running them through the hair. Another Korean medical custom is to cure convulsions of children by burning a hole in their heads. Tiger's-bone and deer-horn drugs are about the only drugs they use. They also depend a lot on witches and sorcerers." I asked him, "How big a practice do you have, doctor?" His answer was sharp and to the point. "I have 500,000 people, and am the only doctor serving them. In fact, I am the only doctor this side of Seoul. I have forty villages in sight of my hospital and I see the smoke of twenty thousand homes from my office window."
>
> The valley below the mission compound at Wanju was rapidly filling with smoke as evening advanced. The smoke was swifter than the shadows of that December evening and much more beautiful. It floated silently up from a thousand thatched roofs in spirals and then, when it was about fifty feet above the houses, it seemed to spread out in a great blanket of gray and floated against the mountain sides as if to cover the village with a blanket of gray wool

for the night. I said, "What makes all the smoke so suddenly?" for the smoke seemed quickly to have risen, as a fog does at the close of day from a swamp. "That is the smoke from the evening fires. The Koreans build fires under their houses each evening about this time to warm the floors for the night."

"The evening fires, the white blanket of smoke, the valley, the purple mountains beyond, the mission house looking down in blessing upon the village, and the white moon shining over all; ah, it is beautiful," I said. "But there is something else down in that village besides the beautiful," said Bishop Welch thoughtfully. "There are hunger, and cold, and ignorance, and heartache, and misery. There are little children, and women, and men who need God."

"Yes, and they need fires, and clothing, and handkerchiefs, and bathtubs, and shoes," added Pat McConnell, the member of our party who introduces the practical to bring some of the rest of us back from the clouds of theory and generalities.[11]

From Wanju, we took our noisy departure early the next morning, with frost in the air and on the ground and on our noses; bound on the second lap from "Seoul to the Sea." All that day we sped over the rocky roads. We crossed innumerable valleys, through scores of villages, over three great mountain passes, the last of which was a mile high, until at last, about four o'clock, we shot around a bend at the top of the range of mountains that forms the very backbone of Korea, and there before us lay the Eastern Sea [the Sea of Japan]. Down we chugged, around mountain turns as sharp as any curves I have ever navigated in our highest Sierra Mountains, overlooking precipices that would make a Californian green with envy, along mountain roads that if a car were to achieve them in mid-winter in America the maker of that car would use the matter for publicity for a month thereafter, down, down, down, until dark came. Then our lights, the lights from our three motorcycles and two Fords, rivaled the full moon that presently came up out of the sea to keep us company.

When we reached Kangnung, the coast town for which we had been bound for two days, even though it was after dark and bitterly cold, we found all the members of the Christian church lined up along the road to greet us. It was a strange sight. Our yellow headlights lighted up the two lines of Koreans one on each side of the road. I do not know what the temperature was, but I know that the water alongside of the road was frozen and that snow had been flying in our faces for an hour. They had been waiting to welcome us for two hours. But these hospitable and faithful Koreans had come out to greet the bishop and his party of Americans and they would stay if it froze them. That is their way. This is the reason why the Independence Movement will never die in their souls. That is their way.

The spirit of these Christian Koreans! It mattered not that, on the way to Kangnung, villages were pointed out to me where "Forty Koreans were brutally shot down last Spring in a peaceful celebration just because they shouted their national cry, Freedom." It mattered not that I had visited the parents of some of these brave fellows who were killed in that terrible and brutal week of massacre by the Japanese. I had forgotten all of that for the time in the glory of what this little church on the far eastern shores of Korea was trying to do for us.

We were given a banquet that meant a supreme sacrifice on their part. Then on Sunday morning, the sun came out and the folks gathered and crowded the front yard of the church; they came with their grandfathers, their sons and daughters, babies and relatives. And they came with their dignified, white robes flowing as they walked with folded arms, across the fields.

It was wonderful to hear Bishop Welch speak to the people gathered, this eloquent man in his own nation, fitting his language to these people, making it so simple that anyone could understand it. There were meetings scheduled all day, morning, afternoon and evening; they were not going to waste any time. Then the Centenary pictures were taken. And I watched the faces of those eager, hungry, soul-hungry and body-hungry Koreans as they heard the story of this great Centenary which plans to bring the gospel to them in a large, fuller way; this Centenary that is to bring them new light, and I said again to myself, "Surely this too is 'declaring the glory' of God to these people." Never was it more truthfully illustrated to me that "The world is our parish" than that wonderful night in Korea, two hundred miles from a railroad, on the shores of the Pacific.[12]

After his motorcycle trip Bill spent two weeks in Seoul, and with every missionary or Korean he met, there were new stories of insult or abuse by the Japanese. He kept notes, which he knew that some day he would use.

Bill returned to Tokyo for Christmas and New Year's, then he, Iva, and Betty departed by train for the ancient city of Kyoto, with its hundreds of Buddhist temples and Shinto shrines. They were making their way to Kobe to catch the *Empress of Asia,* which was due to sail on January 9, 1920, for Manila. As the sailing date of the *Empress* drew near, Iva grew concerned about another sea voyage, loading up Bill, Betty, and herself with Epsom salts, which she had read would steady their constitutions in case of heavy seas.

Once the *Empress of Asia* had sailed, it stopped to refuel in Nagasaki, where a tender came alongside, and Pat McConnell climbed aboard the liner. Bill and Iva knew that Pat was on his way to Peking to attend the Methodist Conference about to begin there. Bishop Welch had tried to persuade both Bill and Pat, when they were traveling together in Korea, to join him in Peking and to travel in China afterward, but Bill had declined so that he could accompany Iva and Betty to Manila.

With Pat so close at hand and going to China, Bill was torn between his wish to be with Iva and Betty and by his need to be in on the action. Iva later wrote that he stewed and fidgeted, then made up his mind. In a letter to her family, she said:

Bill has decided to get off our ship in Shanghai, and Betty and I are going to Manila alone. What do you think of that for nerve? Bishop Welch wanted Bill to do this all along but Bill thought Betty needed a warm climate, and he couldn't send us alone.

But I told him I wasn't afraid to try it. I'll wireless when we get in communications with Manila for a reservation at the best hotel until I can get a good place to stay by the month. I'm not going to go so many places on account of Betty. The climate doesn't seem to agree with her at all, and there are so many diseases everywhere.[13]

The *Empress* made a stop in Tsingtao, the major port city in the province of Shantung, to discharge 2,500 coolies who were returning from France. They had been as part of 150,000 coolies from Shantung who had been China's contribution to the Allies in the World War. Iva and Bill watched as the Chinese were put ashore, lined up, and each given ten silver dollars, then marched to a waiting train that would take them to a demobilization camp and eventually to their homes.

In 1897–98, Germany had acquired a concession of territory in Shantung—the bay of Kiaochow and fishing village of Tsingtao—as compensation for the killing of two German missionaries by the Chinese. Germany had then built Tsingtao into a great port and military and commercial center, with golf courses, hotels, clean streets, and miles of paved roads. Eventually the whole province came under German economic control. In return for the Japanese capture of Kiaochow from the Germans during the World War, Japan demanded of China, and was given by the Peace Treaty of Versailles, the German economic concessions in Shantung. Control of Shantung by the Japanese incensed the Chinese, because this province was the spiritual center of the country as well as an important commercial region, with thirty million inhabitants.

The *Empress* pulled out of Tsingtao's harbor and anchored for the night nearby in the mouth of the Yangtze River—in order, Iva and Bill guessed, to keep the large cache of silver bullion aboard from falling into Japanese hands. The silver belonged to the Chinese government and was being carried by the *Empress* to Shanghai. While at anchor Betty developed a raging fever and a temperature of 104 degrees. Iva tried remedies of oil, enemas, and cold sponging, but to no avail. The ship's doctor said Betty must be made to "sweat," so Bill and Iva surrounded Betty with hot water bottles and wrapped her in blankets. She slept but became delirious; finally, around four in the morning, she threw up and the fever broke. This incident convinced Iva that going on to Manila with Betty instead of into the frigid cold of China was the right decision.

Bill and Pat left the *Empress* in a tender when the ship reached Shanghai the next day; Bill and Iva did not see each other again for six weeks. During this time Bill traveled extensively in China with Bishop Welch and Pat McConnell. On February 3, 1920, he checked into the Astor Hotel in Shanghai for what he described as an "orgy of writing." Six days stretched out in front of him before his ship sailed for Manila, and he intended to do nothing but write from morning to night, catching up on his notebook, his articles, and the book he was sketching out.

Before Bill's trip concluded in Shanghai, he had the opportunity to meet Dr. Sun Yat-sen, perhaps China's most revered statesman, through T'ang Shao-I, a leading Chinese businessman and financial backer of the Chinese patriot. Bill had, in turn, met T'ang Shao-I through George Sokolsky, an American newspaperman who was close to the inner circle of the Chinese Republic. Sun Yat-sen was elected president of the

Chinese Republic shortly after Bill's meeting with him. As Bill wrote, "He [Sun Yat-sen] was in exile, and Japan had a price on his head. They would have executed him on sight. But at that time the French Concession was a haven of refuge for all exiles, and there he lived with Madame Sun Yat-sen, sister of the present Madame Chiang Kai-shek.

"When I was ushered into Sun Yat-sen's private library, Mrs. Sun Yat-sen, looking for all the world like a rare piece of Chinese porcelain, brought in tea.

"In that conversation, Dr. Sun Yat-sen, a slender man, small of stature, with a little black mustache, then streaked with gray, told me of the long fight for Chinese independence and the overthrow of the Manchu dynasty, which was exploiting and throttling China."

Bill told Sun Yat-sen of his trip to Korea and of the friendship he found there for the United States, relating that he had heard over and over from Koreans, "America is our only hope! We have always trusted and loved America!" Dr. Sun Yat-sen replied, "America has always been China's staunch friend as well. America we trust. America we love. America is our hope. America is our model." Bill asked Dr. Sun Yat-sen why he looked to the United States for help, and he gave this answer: "It is because so many of our young men have been trained in your colleges and because so many of us feel that the United States is our second home. It is because you have sent so many missionaries to help our people, to teach us, to live with us, to share our problems and suffering. The very name 'America' is a sacred passport to the Chinese heart."[14]

Bill's descriptions of his experiences in China were vivid and impressionistic. While he had almost a sensory overload, he conveyed to the readers back home that—through it all—he was captivated by the Chinese people, their spirit and their fondness for America. He wrote the following while he was at the Astor Hotel:

> The streets and fields and highways are jammed with people, dogs,
> babies, donkeys; a few horses; cats, birds in cages; pets of all descriptions;
> paper flowers, Peking carts, creaking wheelbarrows; women in every style of
> dress on earth; men in every state of robing from ten layers to one; going,
> coming, walking, running, carrying loads that would tax a horse; camel trains
> in Peking; human trains in Shanghai; everywhere are sights that fascinate one
> and fill one with continuous wonderment and amazement. It is like going to
> a theater to walk along any street any place in China, in any city or village, by
> day or night, for action never ceases.
>
> You may be riding along on a train, and looking out of a window and see
> a canal that was built ten centuries ago; a dozen city walls in a day; fifty beauti-
> ful pagodas that excite the artistic admiration of your soul; pagodas out in a
> field alone; pagodas gracefully rearing their silhouettes above a city wall against
> a crimson sunset. You may see a Yellow or Yangtse River tearing through the
> lowlands. You may see mountain beauty, such as the world knows not of
> elsewhere, and stretches of plains that rival the West in America. You may
> see ten thousand graves in an hour with their little conical mounds rising like
> ant hills man-high for hundreds of acres; graves massed on valley and hill-
> side running up in waves to the very peaks of mountains. You may see

unburied coffins awaiting the "lucky day" for burial, sometimes waiting so long that that "lucky day" never comes and the coffins rot and the bones lie scattered along a city street, as I saw in Shanghai. You may see color in crimson, red-skinned oranges and persimmons. You may see a dozen human beings hitched and harnessed to wagons like beasts, in any city in China at any time of the day, almost on any street! You may see coolies swarming like flies with their rickshaws everywhere; the mouth of the Yangtse by day with its hundreds of little flat boats, jamming even this wide water-way, with whole families living on deck, cooking, sleeping, eating, sewing clothes; children playing horse; men playing cards; or you may see this same river by night with these little boats lighted up with a myriad of everlasting flares in the bow of the boats and human figures silhouetted against those flares. You may see monoliths, temples, arches, pagodas everywhere in one unending panorama of motion, drama, hope, life. And some of the sights that you see you may like and some you may not like, but "you can't help liking the folks."

It is two o'clock in the morning. We have alighted from a train in a little village in Shantung, China. The missionary has kindly met us. Suddenly a strange sound greets our ears. It is a bugle blowing. It comes with a strangely beautiful music through the night air.

The music of bugles you hear all over China these days, by day and night. You hear too the tinkling of temple bells in the winds; you hear the "tum, tum, tum," a monotonous and hollow beating of the Buddha drums; you hear the wrangling and crying of rickshaw men out of your hotel window all night long. It never ceases. In an American city at a certain time in the night, sounds more or less cease, even in New York. But not so in the Orient. Sounds never cease there, for the "struggle for existence" never ceases and men must work night and day. At any time you happen to be walking along what seems a deserted village street in China and hear family looms buzzing and men hammering at their work. Beggar whines are so practiced and so subtle in their plea that you never get out of range of their sounds. Once I heard the priests in the Lama temple chanting their services. There were hundreds of little boys with high tenor voices and one or two big, deep bass voices that seemed to come from some unearthly depth. I would like to hear one bass voice I heard in the Lama temple sing "Rocked in the Cradle of the Deep." One such bass voice could support a hundred sopranos and tenors. It was thrilling to hear their mournful chanting with its chorus of tenors suddenly cease, all save one beautiful tenor that sounded like a far-off echo in some hidden part of the temple. But the sweetest music I ever heard in the Orient was a Chinese boy whistling "Jesus, Lover of My Soul," crossing a bridge in Shanghai one evening. Yes, you may, or you may not, like all of the sounds that you hear in China, but "you can't help liking the people."

The smell of incense is always in the air hovering over China. Old temples and pagodas are saturated with it, for it has burned at their altars for untold centuries and has drifted out over the land until it too is saturated with this beautiful, lotus-like, stupefying odor. The water smell will always be with you and the smell of fish in some stage of freshness or decay; chickens that have been varnished and hanging in shops for months; and eggs as fresh or as ancient as the case may be. The smell of close, stifling city and village streets; the smell of lacquer shops, and burning wood; varnish and toy shops; meat shops and animal stalls, where birds and beasts are for sale; burning charcoal; the beautiful scent of spices, flowers of every odor; mountain winds; tea with jasmine leaves boiled in it—yes, you may or may not like the scents of China, but "you can't help liking the folks."

They win you. You may hate the smells or you may like them. You may be indifferent to the sights and sounds or you may be charmed by them; but you cannot be indifferent to the people of China. They win you. The little rascals of beggars win you. One little girl followed us about all one afternoon in Shanghai. She whined at our feet. We tried half-heartedly to drive her away, but she just smiled and stuck to us. We discovered that she was afraid to have her picture taken. The superstition is that the camera steals your soul. So when we pointed that at her she scurried away, but she always showed up again with her smile and her whine.

And those little children at the Lama temple. They were just a few dozen of regular boys, although they were dressed up in stately robes, and a lot of patriarchal priests chanted the dignified service with them. It was a very solemn occasion at least to the priests, for there were foreigners about. But I decided to try the boys out and see if they were human, so in the midst of their solemn chanting, I winked and smiled at them and every last one of them winked and smiled. The old priests, who looked like gnarled old trees, thundered admonition and threats at them, but they were just boys and kept on winking and smiling. Then when the service was over they piled out to visit with me and were so eager that two of them fell and the rest piled on top of them like a football scrimmage. They pummeled each other on their little bald heads and acted for all the world like a lot of American children loose from school.

And who could pass up that group of a dozen little rascals who followed us through the ruins of the old summer palace? Who could resist their quaint imitations of everything that we did? I sneezed and the little rascals sneezed too. I counted "one, two, three, four" in adjusting my Graflex and they counted "one, two, three, four" also. We fell in love with the dirty-faced rascals. They looked to be a nuisance when we started and I wanted them driven back, but before we were through they had become the most interesting part of the trip. Sure enough we emptied our pockets of pennies and some soft [paper] money, but it was worth it. The little fellow who was in his bare feet in spite of winter winds and looked as if he had been shoeless forever, had a philosophy about his poverty that was full of fun, for when he saw us looking at his dirty feet he said through the interpreter, "These are my leather shoes and they will last all my life!" That was humor with a vengeance. No, you can't help liking the people.

And after all helping the people is what we are in China for, we Methodists; that is why Centenary funds are being spent in this land of four hundred million folks; that is why our missionaries are giving their lives for them.[15]

The Japanese occupation of Shantung had sparked a mass demonstration against the Japanese by more than five thousand Chinese students in Tiananmen Square in Peking on May 4, 1919, eight months before Bill's visit. The students had burned a pro-Japanese cabinet minister's house and seized and beaten the Chinese minister to Japan. The police had attacked the protesters, who had then called a student strike, and sympathetic demonstrations had sprung up in a number of major cities. Some students were killed, many were wounded, and many more were jailed.

The student movement turned out to be a powerful weapon against the Japanese; it focused Chinese sentiment against the Japanese presence in China. Outbreaks of student street demonstrations continued; some occurred while Bill was in Tientsin and in Peking. Bill said that he saw "keen, alert young Chinese men addressing the crowds admonishing them not to buy Japanese goods in Chinese shops." Most Chinese merchants, from the lowest shopkeeper to owners of the chain stores, responded by putting away Japanese-made goods and refusing to sell them. The governor of Tientsin had a number of students arrested, which precipitated terrible riots that Bill described as "war to the death." Several students were killed, and the public uproar became so great that the governor was compelled to release the imprisoned students. Bill was incensed at the Japanese and wrote an editorial for the Peking *Leader,* which he also sent to the *Evening News* in San Jose.

When his article was received in San Jose six weeks later, R. L. Burgess, the editor of the *Evening News,* understood the explosive nature of the material he was dealing with and in a statesmanlike manner prepared a preamble to accompany Bill's article. This disclaimer was meant to defuse Bill's words, but Burgess became carried away with his own rhetoric, and he succeeded only in fanning the flames. His introduction and Bill's editorial follow:

The following heartfelt impression from the rapid pen of Dr. Stidger the noted pastor-journalist, regarding the Boycott and Student Movement in China, in no way represents a deliberate attempt to prejudice the Japanese in the eyes of the world. From long years of friendship we can well say that the writer is too robust a cosmopolitan and too practical an idealist to look at the Sino-Japanese Crisis with any bias. His criticism is rather directed against that gang of Japanese exploiters, financial and concession hunters that harass China by playing on the weakness of the officials. In other words, the writer, like many liberty-loving Europeans or Americans, deeply resents the idea of seeing China sacrificed as a Fat Lamb before the altar of secret diplomacy, aggressive imperialism and conscienceless militarism such as are dominating the militaristic and bureaucratic Japanese statesmen of today.

* * *

All day long I have seen on the street of Peking groups of students discussing the all absorbing questions of the treatment of their fellow students down in Tientsin.

I have not understood the characters printed on their banners, for they have been printed in a language that I cannot read. But I have understood the light in Young China's eyes. I can understand that language and that light, for it is the light of freedom, and justice, and liberty. I am an American. I know that light when I see it, and know, too, that it is a light that can never be snuffed out. It is a light that prison walls cannot hide and that authority cannot dim. . . .

Figuratively speaking, the Chinese students are themselves dumping into the seas everything Japanese that comes to these shores[,] and all success to them. If every ship that sailed the seas were to be brought to Pacific waters and loaded with Japanese goods I should hope and pray that that fleet should not discourage the students of China.

I should hope that there would be enough loyal patriots among these 400 million people to sweep down on the port cities and dump every last case of Japanese goods into the sea. That would be a Chinese "Boston Tea Party" that would go down in history with a splash.

I have just come from Korea. I spent a month in that desolated, exploited, unhappy country. I shall have more to say of that later. I spent six weeks in Japan. Not all of Japan is bad. I found much good in that country and many good people. But the Japanese that I find in the process of exploiting Korea and China I do not like. I do not trust them because I have seen them in action. They are uninvited guests in both China and Korea, uninvited guests who take the rugs and furniture and food in the house.

The weapon that most worries the Japanese I should say is the boycott that the student movement has inaugurated. I was in both Korea and Japan when the boycott in China started. The Japanese Government never had anything that quite worried it so much. It is a weapon that is worth a thousand battleships or fifty divisions of soldiers. It is a weapon that will, if used continuously and consistently and faithfully, bring a money-loving nation, like Japan, to her knees and send her scurrying, finally, like a whipped cur, with her tail between her legs, back home.

I have talked with chair bearers down at the Sacred Mountain at Taishan. I said to these chair bearers, "What do you think of the Japanese taking over your land of Shantung?" They smiled and said: "We like to get their money. We play with them and then when we get ready we drive them out. . . ."

I was in Tientsin the day the students were arrested and their meetings forbidden. I do not wonder that they were indignant. This is not freedom of speech to the American way of thinking. This is what we would call "suppression of free speech."

But judging from the talks that I had with students and with those who know the students better than I, this is only stopping up the flood of waters at one point to have it break out at another point. The Student Movement is like the Yellow River. It is in flood. It will not be denied. You may think that you have it dammed up, but you will find out tomorrow that it has swept away your dams.

I hope that the matters of the Student Movement and the boycott may finally be brought to the attention of the League of Nations. If the students hold on and keep their faith and their courage the League will listen to their just case in the International Court.

I have found no Americans with whom I have talked in China who believe for one moment that Japan ever intends to give up Shantung unless the public opinion of the world forces her to. I have talked with businessmen, missionaries, Englishmen, men of long-standing in China; I have talked with Chinese coolies, with Chinese statesmen, teachers, preachers and businessmen and I have yet to find a single person who will believe Japan when she says that she intends to give up Shantung. Therefore I believe that the greatest contribution that the Student Movement can make to China is to keep up the agitation until the whole world sees Japan in her true light. Publicity, glaring, flaring publicity, is the one thing that Japan is most afraid of. She is afraid of it in her own country, as is evidenced by the fact that she continually suppresses newspapers in Japan. She is afraid of it in regard to her Korean affairs as I have found out and am ready to substantiate. She is afraid of publicity in regard to Siberia, Mongolia, Manchuria, Shantung, Korea and her own internal condition.

And just because Japan is afraid of publicity is the very reason that the Student Movement can use this weapon to its utmost.

On with the boycott! On with the Student Movement! On with both to the Judgment Seat of the League of Nations, and above all, to the Judgment Seat of the Public Opinion of the whole world![16]

Bill boarded his ship for Manila on February 9, 1920, and recorded in his diary: "As the great ship swung about in the muddy waters of the Yangtze and turned southward, the bitter winds of winter were blowing across her deserted decks. But in two days one felt not only a breath of warm tropical winds on his face but he also felt a breath of warmer friendship blowing into his soul as he thought of the Philippines and America."[17]

Iva, who had preceded Bill by six weeks, was finding Manila—well, glorious! If Tokyo had been dark, cold, somber, and rainy, Manila was bright, full of clear skies and sunshine. Bill arrived from China just in time for the thirteenth annual Philippine Conference of the Methodist Episcopal Church. After the conference, he took a short trip to the far northern end of the island of Luzon, to visit a tribe of Negritos in the jungle. Bill was accompanying Dr. E. A. Rader, a leading minister in Manila, and Mr. Oscar Huddleston, a missionary who had been in the Philippines for a number of years.

The Negritos were short, dark people who lived in the trees. They ate roots and nuts and hunted with bows and arrows. The day of the trip was unbearably hot, and Bill felt the tropical heat pouring down on him with each step on the way up the mountainside to the Negrito village. Without a proper cork helmet, the intense heat was penetrating, and Bill felt his head begin to pound like a pile driver until he finally collapsed unconscious on the trail. When he revived, he was able to continue, with support from his colleagues, to the village, where the Negritos swarmed around their party. As Bill described the scene: "They were a horrible looking crowd; stark naked, filthy with dirt; starved to their skin and bones; and animal-like in every look and move."[18] Too sick to eat lunch, he lay on his back trying to regain his strength. As the rest of the expedition ate, the Negritos, with hungry eyes, crowded closer.

One old man was in the forefront of the natives. Bill remembered that he was "so hideous looking that he was sickenly repulsive to me as I looked at him crouched as he was like an animal with a streak of sunlight playing on his face. This streak of sunlight, with ruthless severity, made the ugly scabs of dirt stand out on his old, wrinkled face. His whole body was covered with dirt and sores."[19] The visitors compared notes on wild tribes they had seen across the world and concluded that this old man broke the scale. The old man did not know, of course, that he was the object of the conversation; he just sat looking at the missionaries with his animal-like eyes as they ate, and at Bill as he lay under a tree trying to recover his strength for the trip back. The meal over, the missionaries started to hand out what was left of the food. Huddleston offered a sandwich to the old man. To the group's astonishment he did not eat it but took it over behind a tree, where another old man was timidly watching, and gave it to him. Again and again he returned for more food, and each time he gave it to another tribe member. Then he suddenly disappeared.

In half an hour he returned with an armful of broad palm leaves. He spread these out on the ground in the shade of a tree and motioned to Bill to lie on the bed he had made. Then he disappeared again, bringing when he reappeared a long bamboo tube full of clear, cool water that he had gotten from a mountain spring. With the water, this "most hideous man" cooled Bill's fevered burning head, and he made him drink. For the entire group of missionaries, it was a revelation: even in this naked savage, whom they had decided "was the lowest human being on the earth," there was a "spark of the Divine" that made Bill and the others recall that "God never did and never shall make a man to live on this earth that He did not have some purpose in making him."[20]

Iva had made reservations, beginning April 1, for two months in a mountain retreat in the town of Baguio. Bill planned to remain with them until April 9, when he would leave on his last big trip before they all returned to San Jose. While Iva and Betty remained in Baguio, Bill departed for Singapore, Borneo, Java, Sumatra, and French Indochina. He described part of the trip for the *Evening News*:

> I left from Singapore one Saturday evening on the *Merkeus,* a small Dutch
> boat, bound for Borneo. The sun was setting and we were sailing directly
> away from it. As we left the straits a lighthouse flashed its white light against
> that golden path of glory. Black clouds dripped from the upper heavens
> against this gold background. If the gracious Lord ever forgives me I'll never
> do it again for crossing the South China Sea in a boat of less than 500 tons is
> no joke at any time.
>
> Two days and a night and we sailed into the mouth of the Kapuas River
> bound for a town called Pontianak. The little grey monkeys and the big red
> fellows were playing in the trees and having the time of their lives shooing

the boat along and chattering at us as we stood on the upper decks watching them play. Brilliant plumaged birds flashed through the green avenues of palms and river trees and they, not content, planted their trunks far out into the muddy tropical water.

Red, brown, yellow orchids flashed in the sunlight. At times the ship went so close to river banks that I could reach out and grab a limb of a tree, much to the indignation of the monkeys who chattered at me as if I had stolen something. Now and then a big lazy alligator slid into the water from the muddy banks as the wave wash from our propeller frightened him.

The first town at which I landed on this island was Pontianak and in that Dutch village, for two days, while waiting for the boat to unload her cargo I sat astride "Mr. Equator" with my feet hanging over. Little did I know that down here in Borneo, where I am writing this story, has been started a most interesting piece of real pioneer missionary work by an unusual man.

His name is Worthington. He is the only missionary in West Borneo. He and his wife are living here alone with no other American nearer than Singapore, five hundred miles away, across the China Sea. But here they stay, lonely as it is, without seeing even an American newspaper for months. They go their way among the head-hunting Dyaks, the Malays and Chinese, hunting hearts instead of hunting heads. I have lived with them a week. I have seen them in action, and my heart has been strangely warmed at what I have seen happening and I have a deep sense of pride in my heart.

After a drive in an automobile, we left it in the road and took off through the jungle for several miles under a burning equatorial sun. The sun goes through even a cork hat as water goes through a sieve. We had to reinforce heavy cork hats with wet leaves and rags to save our lives.

Mr. Worthington had sent word to the Dyaks that we were coming and a reception committee awaited us with bolos, spears, swords and other killing devices conspicuously stuck in their belts. But I later learned that they had been used for making a wider and a more comfortable track for us through the jungle, incidentally killing a few snakes and animals that might have grabbed one of us off for lunch that day as we passed through the jungle grasses, fording black jungle-bred streams, climbing dank, bamboo lined hills.

Our escort was a motley crowd of old men. Off through the jungle we could hear firecrackers going off and the wild yelps of the Dyaks. I can't say that I enjoyed the sounds. They smacked too much of utter abandonment and I had a thought that, on a New Year's day celebration like this was, they might in their drinking hark back a generation or so and decide that it was a pleasant day for taking a head or two since here were two perfectly good American ones which none of the head hunters had in their collection.

The only consolation I had was that both Mr. Worthington and I are bald and the Dyaks always like lots of hair on the heads that they take. It happened to be New Year's Day at the first compound of Dyaks we visited.

New Year's does not come at the same time for each tribe. It follows the harvests. When a tribe gets its crop in, then it is New Year's.

It is a blistering hot May morning. It is the end of a jungle trail which opens into a wide, cleared space in the forest of tall palms. In front of us is the Dyak house.

It is a long narrow house, built in one piece, community style, every room joining, and running in front of every room is a long front porch. It is a big wide platform, about thirty feet across and it is the common meeting place of all who live in that compound. People step out of the privacy of their rooms onto the common platform, floored with narrow strips of bamboo and here all the community events take place.

"There are fifteen doors to this compound," said the head man of the crowd to me, with a certain element of pride, for that meant he was the chief of fifteen families. The doors were swung on ropes from above and had no hinges. At the end of the platform, which was raised from the ground about ten feet, a bamboo log ladder, with notches cut in it for the feet, was the method of getting up and down.

As we approached from the end of the jungle trail, little children by the dozens were scurrying down that bamboo ladder like so many monkeys. It was hilarious to see them do it. So they thronged this May morning swarming like a lot of bees about Mr. Worthington. I soon learned the reason, for he began to reach into his pockets and out came a handful of picture cards, such as we gave out in the primary department in our Sunday schools at home.

He was the Pied Piper of Hamlin. Those little bare brown children followed him about clinging to his hands, pulling at this coat, calling him "The Picture Man" over and over. I thought of Jesus entering Jerusalem in triumph. Missionary Worthington was entering this Dyak compound in triumph.[21]

Java, to the southwest of Borneo, was Bill's next port of call. He again recorded his impressions for the *Evening News:*

Southbound on a Dutch boat on a Saturday evening with the great white southern cross directly in our pathway, we crossed the equator without feeling a single jar on our way to Java.

Sunday morning and Java. Yonder on the wharf at Surabaya stands a young man, not yet out of his twenties. It is J. B. Matthews. I found this entire mission manned by men and women mostly under 30. As one bishop said, "It is a team of ponies down there in Java."[22]

Not far from Surabaya was the giant volcano of Java, Mount Bromo. Bill, Matthews, and a colleague named Archer started out at three o'clock in the morning on ponies. Bill later wrote, "White flashes of light leapt up from Bromo at frequent intervals in the darkness as we traveled on little rugged Javanese ponies along the tropical jungle trail, upward. The flashes of light were called 'Nightblooming lilies.'" There was something "beautifully weird in their white wonder against the night[,] . . . sending out a sweet odor which mingled strangely with the odor of sulfur from the volcano."[23] It took the group until daylight to cover the eight miles to the crater's edge. All the while that they were traveling, they could hear the volcano's thundering and rumbling, "as somber as suicide":

> At daybreak we reached the mile high cliff which looks down onto the world-famous sand sea. It was a sea of white fog. I have seen the same thing at the Grand Canyon and in Yosemite looking down from the rims. I thought of these great American canyons as I looked down into the Bromo sand sea. By noon this was a great ten-mile long valley of silver sand which glittered in the sunlight like a great silver carpeted ballroom floor. Tourists from all over the world have thrilled to its strange beauty. Like the gown of some great and ancient queen this silver cloth lies there; or, like some great silver rug of Oriental weaving, it carpeted that valley floor at noon.[24]

From Bromo, they went on to visit one of the great monuments of the world, the temple of Boroboedoer:

> This great temple built in the seventh century A.D., by the Javanese under Hindu culture, has, instead of the plain surfaces of the great pyramids in Egypt, one mile of beautifully carved decorations, with 2,141 separate panels depicting the life of Buddha from the time he descended from the skies until he arrived at Nirvana, or perfect isolation from the world. A history of more than a thousand years is told in its stone tablets by the sculptor's chisel, told beautifully, told enduringly, told magnificently.
>
> There are four ledges to this hill temple and above each ledge or stone path are rows of Buddhas hidden in great 5-foot stone bells, and, at the top, crowning the temple is a great 50-foot bell in which Buddha is completely hidden from the world, symbol of the desired Nirvana that all Buddhists seek. . . .
>
> The fire dies out of the sky. It is late evening and all day long we have been climbing the ancient ruins. The several terraces of the stone temple begin to blur into one great and beautiful pyramid. Only the innumerable stone bells stand out against the starlit night; stone bells with the little peepholes in them, through which the stolid countenances and the stone eyes of many Buddhas, in calm repose, look out upon the four points of the compass.
>
> The shadows seem to wrap its two thousand exquisite carvings, and its bells of Buddha in loving and warm tropical embrace. But no warmer is the embrace of the shadows about the Temple than the naked embrace of a score of Javanese boys who hold to their hearts naked Javanese beauties who sit along the terraces looking into the skies of night utterly oblivious to the passing of time or the presence of curious American strangers.

Love is such a natural thing to these Javanese equatorial brown brawn and beauties that unabashed they lie, on Buddha's silent bells, breast to breast, cheek to cheek, and limb to limb; as if they have swooned away in the warmth of the tropical night.

The southern cross looks down upon lover and tourist as we all fore-gather on the topmost terrace of that gigantic shadow-pyramid of granite.

The sound of the innumerable naked footsteps of all past ages seems to patter along the stone terraces. Now and then the twang of the Javanese *angklong* and the beautiful notes of a flute sweep sweetly into the shadowed air.

Then comes the dancing of a half dozen Javanese girls, naked to the waist, their crimson and yellow sarongs flying in the winds of night, as, in slow, graceful movements, facing one of the bells of Buddha they pay their vows and offer their bodies and their souls to Buddha; and, evidently, also to the Javanese youths who accompany them in their dances. Their very naked-ness seemed to fit in with the spirit of the night; a spirit of complete aban-donment to beauty and worship. In their attitudes there seemed to be a mingling of religion and earthly passion; but it was so touched with rever-ence that we felt no shock to our American sensibilities.

All night long we wandered about the terraces of the old Temple. We wondered how long the Javanese girls would remain. When we watched the sun rise, they were still there as fresh as the dawn itself in their brown beauty, the dew of night glistening in their black hair and wetting their full breasts. And across from Boroboedoer, the sun, in its dawning splendor, was trans-forming belching and rumbling old volcanic Merapi into a cone of gold.[25]

Bill visited missionaries in Medan, Sumatra, where he witnessed priests scalding sick children with red hot irons to burn the devils out of them, usually killing the children in the process, and made a short trip up the Saigon River in French Indochina, where he saw Chinese boatmen steer their small boats directly across the bows of larger boats to throw the river devils off their trail. Finally, he wound up in Hong Kong to await Iva and Betty's arrival.

Iva and Betty left the Philippines suntanned and happy, joining Bill at the Grand Hotel in Hong Kong. They sailed from Hong Kong on June 6, 1920, on the *Equator,* under Captain Yardley, bound for Yokohama. Yardley had told Bill that he doubted he would have enough room on board to take them to Honolulu and that they would have to wait in Yokohama for another ship that was not fully booked. However, when the ship landed in Yokohama, Japanese police boarded the *Equator,* asked to see Bill and ceremoniously informed him that he was not welcome on Japanese soil. This was the government's revenge for Bill's sharp criticism of its actions in Korea and China. Captain Yardley made room for the Stidgers on the *Equator* and arranged transporta-tion for Iva to go to Tokyo and retrieve the trunks and belongings they had stored at the Methodist Compound.

The final leg of their trip home was to Honolulu. A vacation there of three weeks gave Bill time to work on his book, *Flashlights from the Seven Seas.* In the foreword Bill expressed his exuberance about his year in the Orient as well as the sensuousness—as it seemed to him—of its places and the peoples:

> That vast stretch of opal islands; jade continents; sapphire seas of strange sunsets; mysterious masses of brown-skinned humanity; brown-eyed, full-breasted, full-lipped and full-hipped women; which we call the Orient, can only be caught by the photographer's art in flashlight pictures.
>
> It is like a photograph taken in the night. It cannot be clear cut. It cannot have clean outlines. It can only be a blurred mass of humanity with burdens on their shoulders; humanity bent to the ground; creaking carts; weary-eyed children and women; moving, moving, moving; like phantom shadow-shapes; in and out; one great maze through the majestic ages; one confused history of the ancient past; emerging; but not yet out into the sunlight!
>
> . . . The facts, fancies, and fallacies of this book are gleaned from the rovings and ramblings of a solid year of over fifty-five thousand miles of travel; through ten separate countries; across seven seas; after visiting five wild and primitive tribes; face to face by night and day with new races, new faces, new problems, new aspirations, new ways of doing things, new ways of living, new evils, new sins, new cruelties, new fears, new degradations; new hopes, new days, new ways, new nations rising; new gods, and a new God!
>
> And this author, for one, is honest in saying that, in spite of careful investigation, in spite of extensive travel and a sympathetic heart, he sees but dimly. The very glory of it all, the age of it all, the wonder of it all, the mysterious beauty and thrill of it all; the thrill of these masses of humanity, their infinite possibilities for future greatness; like a great blinding flash of glory, dims one's eyes for a time.
>
> But, now, that he has, through quiet meditation and perspective, had a chance to develop the films of thought, he finds that he has brought back home pictures that one ought not to keep to one's self; especially in this day, when, what happens to Asia is so largely to determine what happens to America.
>
> So, out of the dark room, where they have been developing for a year, and out of the dim shadows of that mysterious land whence they came, they are printed and at the bottom of each picture shall be written the humble words: Flashlights from the Seven Seas.[26]

The book covered all aspects of Bill's travels and experiences. One of these aspects, his exposure to the dark and cruel side of the Japanese, received extended treatment under the chapter "Flashlights of Frightfulness." He dealt plainly and directly with the ruthlessness and brutality of the Japanese, as well as with the resistance by the Koreans and the Chinese to the tyranny of their masters:

> I found the Japanese scorned and hated from one end of the Orient to the other. As far south as Java, as far east as Suez; as far north as the uttermost reaches of Manchuria and Siberia; as far this direction as Hawaii. . . . While

I was in Java some high dignitaries in the Japanese Navy arrived in Batavia. The Chinese coolies who lived in Batavia absolutely refused to carry any Japanese officers or sailors in their rickshaws. It was a striking indictment of the Japanese nation. In Singapore the distrust and hatred of the Japanese is unanimous. In the Philippines it is the same. In Hong Kong you see few Japanese. They are not wanted and they are not trusted. In Shanghai and Peking it is the same. The student movement, one of the most powerful weapons that has ever arisen in any nation in the world, has focused the Chinese sentiment against selfish aggression in China. . . .

And after due consideration, and after a year to think it over carefully, I am here to say, that I never saw, or heard of anything worse happening in Belgium under German rule than that which I saw and heard of happening under Japanese rule in Korea, Siberia and Formosa, while I was in the Orient.

Suffice it to say, at this point, that the Japanese is hated by the whole Orient. I do not believe that the German Hun in his worst day was ever hated more unanimously for his inhuman practices than is the Japanese Hun hated by the whole Orient to-day.[27]

Flashlights from the Seven Seas was published around Christmas in 1921, a little more than a year after he returned from the Far East. By this time Bill was minister of a new church, St. Mark's, in Detroit. Shrewdly, he had invited one of the most powerful Methodist bishops, Bishop McConnell, to write the introduction. McConnell's last sentence read, "The contagion of youth and energy are in this book: it will reach and stir all who read."[28]

Japanese-controlled newspapers were stirred all right, but in fury, at the accusations Bill made against Japan. Several American missionaries also wrote denouncing *Flashlights from the Seven Seas*. The following article appeared in the *Seoul Press* on Sunday, July 30, 1922:

THE STIDGER AFFAIR

We call the attention of our readers to letters published elsewhere today written to us by two eminent missionaries here in regard to the Rev. Mr. Stidger's preposterous criticism of the Japanese administration of Chosen [the Japanese name for Korea]. It will be seen therefrom that they are heartily disgusted with the writer and his utterances. It remains to be seen what steps the Methodist Church in Chosen will take. . . . To us it seems that Mr. Stidger ought to be summarily disowned by that Church.

We need scarcely say that great indignation has been expressed by many Japanese here at Mr. Stidger's monstrous charges. Some of them even go the length of saying: "I told you so," insinuating thereby that we were wrong when, during the independence agitation, we defended the missionaries against the oft-repeated charges that they were behind the movement. We would remind these Japanese readers of ours that there are black sheep even in the best of flocks. It is unwise to conclude that, because one or two bad elements appear at times, the missionaries in Chosen are wrong as a body.[29]

The two letters referred to above were from Methodist missionaries J. S. Gale and Edward J. Urquhart. Gale had said, "I take this occasion to disassociate myself from the man Stidger and the missionary who became his mentor here [Bishop Welch]. He makes his brutal charges from beyond the sea where no one can answer, and gives as his authority someone who hides behind the whole missionary body. The dishonor done His Excellency the Governor-General and his associates, who, we know, have been most anxious to right every wrong and give the Korean, as well as the missionary, every opportunity possible, puts us all to shame."[30]

A few days later, the *Seoul Press* printed a letter written to the editor by Bishop Welch, who felt he had to reply as "Stidger's mentor" whether or not he supported Bill's position:

The recent articles and letters concerning Rev. W. L. Stidger's book, Flashlights from the Seven Seas, *have been of especial interest to me not simply as a foreigner residing in this country and as a missionary, but as a representative of the particular church of which Mr. Stidger is a minister.*

Mr. Stidger came to the peninsula in the late fall of 1919 and remained on Korean soil, if I am not mistaken, precisely sixteen and a half days. In that period of tense excitement he heard many tragic stories of the wretched happenings of the first months after the outbreak of the Independence Movement. He is a man of quick sensibilities and powerful impulses; and even at that time he expressed his intention of writing a book on Korea—a purpose from which more than one friend tried to dissuade him. His knowledge was so slight and his immediate reaction to tales of injustice and brutality was so fiery, that it was quite evident that any statement which he might make would be fragmentary, one-sided, unfair.

He had published a book or two on his experiences in France during the War which displayed a gift for picturesque and persuasive writing, and he had therefore been sent out by our Mission Board to gather "human interest" stories of missionary life and Christian work. But instead of confining himself to this legitimate and useful task, he felt called upon, both here and in China, to discuss national questions on which his information was exceedingly limited; and he has thus brought embarrassment and humiliation upon the Methodist Episcopal Church and in particular upon its American representatives in Korea.

The volume from which the quotations are taken refers to all of Eastern Asia. It is florid and inaccurate in minor and in major matters alike, and is certain not to be taken seriously by careful students of Oriental affairs. There is in Mr. Stidger a tender and poetical side, and a directness, virility, optimism, and courageous sympathy which account for his large popularity as a speaker and as a friend. But here admirable qualities afford no excuse whatsoever for rash and exaggerated statements which amount to nothing less than slander upon an entire nation.

His sweeping condemnation of the Japanese Government and the Japanese people is deplorable. Most unfortunate of all are his aspersions upon the administration of the present governor-general, Baron Saito, whose policies mark a new spirit and a positive advance and who enjoys so deservedly the respect and confidence of all elements of the population. Mr. Stidger has already been taken sharply to task by representatives of our church, both publicly and privately, for his unjust and unchristian treatment of situations of which he knows so little.

While it is quite natural for us to know the facts more fully than Mr. Stidger could possibly know them, to disavow and repudiate such an untrue presentation as he has made, I must demur to any suggestion that the missionaries of Korea, or any group of them, have any accountability in this matter. Mr. Stidger's articles in our church press were only on themes of Christian service and not open to criticisms, at least on the score of their tone and contents; his objectionable book was put forth not by our publishing house but by an independent concern. He is a free man whose utterances can not be controlled by any of us in this country, no matter how deeply we may regret them.

The missionaries and church authorities of Korea have no more responsibility for Mr. Stidger than the Japanese Christians have for some men of their number who may slander America. Where injustice has been done, however, or words spoken which might alienate individuals or nations, I believe that we all should use our diligence to right the wrong and to promote friendly understanding. Hence these lines. Thanking you for the use of your columns, I remain,

Sincerely yours,
Herbert Welch [31]

Bill stood his ground; he had reported the facts as he had found them. Was he in fact "taken sharply to task" by representatives of the Methodist Church, as Bishop Welch claimed? There was no evidence of this. Ironically, the two men remained friends for the rest of their lives. It is likely that Bishop Welch found much of what Bill had to say of the Japanese attitude and actions throughout the Far East more true than false, but within Korea, he and his fellow missionaries had to be extremely circumspect if they were to be effective.

On September 9, 1922, an "Official Statement on 'The Stidger Affair'" was published in Tokyo. The statement claimed that Bill's descriptions of the Japanese administration of Korea were "utter fabrication, woven in the desire to defame Japan." The statement then quoted several "monstrous" passages in Bill's book that had been reproduced in the *Seoul Press* and said that Bishop Welch had made "special investigations and declared that the charges in the book against Japan were entirely groundless." The statement concluded:

> It is most criminal for the author thus to try to place the Japanese Government in bad odor by deliberately disseminating falsehoods. . . . Since Formosa [Taiwan] and Chosen came under her dominion, Japan has constantly exerted herself to enhance the welfare of their inhabitants, and to promote their standard of civilization. . . . In the face of all this, it is most regrettable that facts are often twisted and abuses indulged in at the expense of the Empire.
>
> It is to be hoped that anyone wishing to criticize Japan's rule in her new possessions will do so fairly and squarely on the strength of hard facts. Just and honest criticism is always welcome to Japan and the Japanese.[32]

In December 1922, Japan evacuated Shantung and gave up all its interests there as a result of an armament-limitation agreement made at the Washington Conference of that year. Bill might have said, "I rest my case." (Unfortunately, Japan was to release its stranglehold on Korea only in 1945, when it surrendered to the Allies.)

One year later, in September 1923, a devastating earthquake, tidal wave, and fire struck Japan, creating unprecedented destruction and loss of life. On September 4, Bill wrote about Japan's tragedy for the *Detroit Times*. He was given banner headlines and a full page to describe the situation in Japan. Bill recalled with fondness the street scenes familiar to him in Yokohama and Tokyo, which were now in ruins. In Yokohama, after the earthquake a fire had started on the Bund, the street that wound around the waterfront, where the Grand Hotel was located (and where the Stidgers had stayed). The red-light section, Yoshiwari, had been destroyed. "The Hill," with its buildings owned by wealthy Americans and the missionaries, had survived the fire and tidal waves.[33]

The railroad station, Shinagawa, in Yokohama, with its trains to Tokyo, had been swept away by a tidal wave. Tunnels, factories, houses—all were lost. The Ginza of Tokyo, with its myriad of little flaming lights, its shops, was now a highway of charred and burning ruins.

Earthquake, tidal wave, and fire: these were the three horrifying fates of Japan in 1923. When Bill wrote this article for the Hearst papers, he was moved more by the tragedy of the Japanese people than by his anger at Japanese policies. He genuinely liked the people and never hinted in his report that Japan might be harvesting the pain and suffering that it had inflicted on its neighbors.

Notes

1. Iva B. Stidger Scrapbook, "All on a Sunday Morning," 1919–20, author's collection, 1.
2. Stidger Scrapbook, 1.
3. Betty Stidger Hyland, *Those Heavenly Years,* unpublished manuscript, 1955, 57–58.
4. Letter dated November 9, 1919, from Iva B. Stidger to her family, author's collection.
5. Letter dated November 10, 1919, from William L. Stidger to Leroy L. Stidger, author's collection.
6. William L. Stidger, "Flashlights of the Orient," *Evening News*, December 12, 1919, 1–2.
7. William L. Stidger, "Stidger Greets S. J. Friends in Note to News," *Evening News*, January 24, 1920.
8. Stidger, "Stidger Greets S. J. Friends in Note to News."
9. Herbert Welch, *As I Recall My Past Century* (New York: Abingdon, 1962), 84.
10. Welch, *As I Recall My Past Century,* 87–88.
11. William L. Stidger, "From Seoul to the Sea," *Christian Advocate*, February 26, 1920, 280–82.
12 Stidger, "From Seoul to the Sea," 324–46.
13. Letter dated January 9, 1920, from Iva B. Stidger to her family, author's collection.
14. William L. Stidger, "I Visit Dr. Sun Yat-sen in Shanghai," *More Sermons in Stories* (New York: Abingdon-Cokesbury, 1944), 35–36.
15. William L. Stidger, "You Can't Help Liking the Folks," *Christian Advocate*, June 24, 1920, 855–56.
16. William L. Stidger, "Micawber's Column," *Evening News*, March 20, 1920, editorial page, and March 22, 1920, editorial page.
17. William L. Stidger, undated letter, author's collection.
18. William L. Stidger, *Flashlights from the Seven Seas* (New York: George H. Doran, 1921), 56.
19. Stidger, *Flashlights from the Seven Seas,* 57.

20. Stidger, *Flashlights from the Seven Seas,* 60.

21. William L. Stidger, "Heart-Hunting among Borneo Head-Hunters," *Evening News*, July 8, 1920, 6; July 9, 1920, 8; July 12, 1920.

22. William L. Stidger, "Journeying in Java," *Evening News*, July 16, 1920, 8.

23. Stidger, *Flashlights from the Seven Seas,* 22.

24. Stidger, *Flashlights from the Seven Seas,* 36.

25. Stidger, *Flashlights from the Seven Seas,* 44–48.

26. Stidger, *Flashlights from the Seven Seas,* ix–xii.

27. Stidger, *Flashlights from the Seven Seas,* 79–80.

28. Stidger, *Flashlights from the Seven Seas,* viii.

29. "The Stidger Affair," *Seoul Press,* July 30, 1922, author's collection.

30. "A Wolf in Sheep's Clothing," *Seoul Press,* July 30, 1922, author's collection.

31. "The Stidger Affair," *Seoul Press,* August 2, 1922, author's collection.

32. "The Stidger Affair, Official Statement Published in Tokyo," *Seoul Press,* September 9, 1922, author's collection.

33. William L. Stidger, "Dr. Stidger Describes Quake Zone," *Detroit Times,* September 4, 1923, 1.

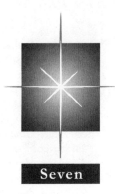

Seven

Standing Room Only: Detroit

The words of Bishop Theodore S. Henderson, presiding bishop for Michigan, came drifting back to Bill as he stood on the Detroit train station platform. The bishop had been persuading Bill to become pastor of a new church in Detroit: "We need you to see Saint Mark's through its first financial period. Your task will be to get a crowd, a membership, a constituency; to put Saint Mark's into the consciousness of the city and the Methodist Church, to meet the bonds as due, and to get the interest paid each week."[1] Bill was scheduled to give his first sermon at St. Mark's the next morning, October 3, 1920. The church had only recently been completed, in May 1920; the building was a very large one, and it had a debt in proportion to its size. It had been described as a white elephant—and this white elephant was now his to deal with.

Bill proceeded through the Michigan Central Terminal, taking in the scuffling sounds of people walking, the muffled noises of many conversations, and the smells of food drifting in the smoky air coming from the restaurant. He stopped briefly at the newsstand and bought Saturday's paper to read.

His destination was the Statler Hilton, where he had booked a room for that Saturday night. No one had met him at the train, and he was a stranger in the city. Iva and Betty were still in Ligonier, with all the luggage for their new life in Detroit, and wouldn't arrive until later in the week. As he sat in the hotel lobby, he glanced through the newspaper. He came across a small item about an accident that had befallen eleven-year-old Marjorie Allen.

It seemed that Marjorie had a job selling newspapers and had also been babysitting her younger sister and her cousin. Late the prior afternoon, she had been at her stand when a man called out to her from across the street, asking her to bring him a paper. Marjorie obliged and crossed the street to deliver a newspaper to him, making certain to be well ahead of a streetcar that was advancing down the block.

Just before she reached her customer, an unexpected movement caught her eye, and she turned around to see what was happening. To her horror she realized that both children in her charge had followed her and now stood directly in the path of the oncoming streetcar. Marjorie rushed to push them out of danger but found herself trapped instead. The streetcar, unable to stop in time, ran over Marjorie, dragging her about ten feet before grinding to a halt. She was taken to the hospital, but doctors had to amputate both her legs. The newspaper reported that the doctors were not certain that "Marjorie would last the night" and that even if she did, her life had been inalterably changed.

Bill was deeply moved by the story and by the terrible predicament that her family must now be in. He tried to think about other subjects, even about his sermon for the next day. But his mind kept returning to this gruesome, sad accident. "This article says the child was selling papers," he thought. "Evidently her people are poor. Maybe I can do something to help." The article gave the Allens' address, and Bill asked a bellhop to tell him where to find their apartment. He took a taxi there at once.

When Marjorie's father appeared at the front door in answer to Bill's knock, Bill explained to him that he was new in Detroit, had read of the tragedy, and come to offer his sympathy. The family had once been Methodist, Mr. Allen said, but since arriving in Detroit they had not attended any church. They were brokenhearted and baffled as to what to do. What could Marjorie make of her life, faced as she was with poverty and a terrible handicap? Her parents told Bill how bright she was. "And no one," Bill said, "needs to tell me that she has courage!"[2]

As Bill talked with the family, an idea occurred to him. "Would you permit me," he said, "to tell my congregation tomorrow morning of Marjorie's accident? I think some decent folks will want to help if it is brought to their attention." The Allens were completely agreeable. After an hour, Bill left them and returned to the Statler.

The next morning, well before it was time for church to begin, Bill took a cab out Jefferson Avenue to the corner of Garland Avenue. There, near Waterworks Park, was St. Mark's. He was shocked at what he saw. St. Mark's was a huge building, and it seemed even larger than it was, since there was no planting around it yet. In fact, it looked like a massive government office. "Architecturally, it's an ugly church," Bill said to himself.[3] He paid the cab driver and walked in the front entrance.

A second shock awaited inside. He was unprepared for the cavernous interior, with its gigantic auditorium able to seat more than three thousand people. He knew there were over a hundred rooms in the building. On top of it all was a $300,000 debt, which was his to pay off. It seemed truly to be a white elephant, perched squarely on his shoulders.

When the service began, Bill found himself addressing about three hundred people. This was a reasonable number for a young, new congregation, but St. Mark's looked emptier with three hundred than Calvary in San Francisco had looked with six. At the end of the service, Bill remembered his promise to the Allens from the night before. He told Marjorie's sad story, giving all the gruesome details, because he wanted the congregation to feel the Allens' pain, just as he had when he read about it. In concluding, Bill said, "Brave, unselfish Marjorie Allen! Do you wonder that I forgot my own small worries in the face of a tragedy like that?" He added that he would like to have everyone in the church come forward. He wanted to shake each person's hand. "And," he said, in what may have seemed like an afterthought, "please help me to educate this child that she might be able to live a useful and happy life in spite of her handicap."[4]

One by one the members of his new congregation filed by; Bill introduced himself and asked their names. The three hundred men, women, and children—none of them rich—left over three hundred dollars on the table for Marjorie.

Her story did not end here, however. After the service, Bill returned to the Statlers and went into the dining room to have lunch. There he was paged by a newspaperman who had heard of his gesture to raise money for Marjorie. He said he wanted to have the other newspapers interview Bill, and by later that afternoon reporters from many papers in Detroit had spoken to him. The next morning his picture was in one of the papers, and there were articles in a number of other papers covering what he had done. The effect of the newspapers' joining in on this mission produced over ten thousand dollars for the Marjorie Allen Educational Fund over the next several weeks. Bill said to a writer for *The American Magazine,* "I suppose if I had deliberately planned to advertise myself in Detroit, I couldn't have chosen a better method. But I had no such idea in mind; I wanted simply to help Marjorie Allen—and to help my own people! And there is no surer way of reaching people and of inspiring them to *action* than by touching their emotions." Detroit had had its first exposure to William L. Stidger.[5]

Almost immediately after arrival, Bill, or "Brother Bill," as he was soon nicknamed, made changes at St. Mark's. The first thing he did was to contact the Brumfield Electric Company in San Francisco to construct a large illuminated revolving cross, his signature piece. Within a relatively short time, he built an enthusiastic and capable team headed by the Rev. O. R. Grattan, who undertook the role of St. Mark's business manager and religious director. Adeline Cambridge was the church secretary and chief of the information bureau. Adeline carried out Bill's wish to develop innovative and interesting weekly church bulletins. William Kemp was director of music. Kemp worked closely with Bill to build a program of soloists, the "Big Sings," which involved the full congregation, and to carry out musical programs suitable for special services.

The athletic facilities were fully utilized and brought men, women, and young people from all over Detroit to St. Mark's. Irene Lampkin was the instructor for women's sports, R. L. Vanderschow directed the gymnasium classes, and R. C. Carlson supervised the St. Mark's interchurch basketball league, which played four or five games each Thursday evening. Nonchurch teams were allowed to schedule games any other evening except Wednesdays, when the entire church was given over to activities related to the weekly prayer night, which Bill called "Food, Faith, and Fun." With the largest gymnasium in the city, two first-class bowling alleys, and rooms for wrestling, Boy Scout activities, and various club meetings, St. Mark's became a center for community activity—so much so that within three months Bill could say that the number of people using St. Mark's was running over ten thousand each week.

Bill instituted a day care center, one of the first ministers to do so, and a newspaper reported on this innovation: "The raucous voice of a disgruntled baby no longer interrupts the minister's sermon. . . . The pastor of St. Mark's has established a 'church nursery' for care of little children while their parents are attending services. A room in the church is set aside for that purpose and two young women, Miss Luella Anderson and Miss Bernice Krieger, are assigned to the care of the children. But this is not all: 'Brother Bill,' always a step ahead, has provided a sandpile, picture books, toys and everything to keep the children contented and quiet. . . . As Brother Bill says, 'It is no more than right. It enables the woman who has no maid to attend church and not fear her baby may interrupt the sermon. All healthy babies cry. It's part of their make-up.' Other churches have taken up Brother Bill's plan to care for the children, but it remained for Rev. Stidger to provide a sandpile—and everything."[6]

To attract different groups to St. Mark's for special occasions, Bill began advertising in the Detroit papers. Two of the target groups were the Odd Fellows and the Masons. He invited neighborhood lodges of both fraternal orders on January 9, 1921, promising them a special Masonic and Odd Fellow sermon, and giving their officers a place on the program. Masons and Odd Fellows served as ushers and collectors.

Both groups dressed in their uniforms and marched behind their bands in a parade down Jefferson Avenue to St. Mark's. People began streaming into the church two hours before the evening service began, Bill's first fully packed service at St. Mark's. The church had more than three thousand people seated, every inch of standing room taken, and a collection of "loose money" of close to four hundred dollars. Special bulletins were printed (Masonic and Odd Fellows souvenirs), and Bill introduced two hymns: a Masonic hymn, whose verses he wrote to the music of "Rock of Ages," and an Odd Fellows hymn to the music of "America."

Not everyone applauded Bill's energetic efforts, however. Carl A. Gieser wrote a letter to *The Lutheran Witness*: "I had seen the ad: 'Masons! It's your Night at St. Mark's." This is the church which makes a 'Food, Faith, and Fun Night' of its weekly prayer meeting and which 'knows how to do things,' if we are to believe its own church bulletin. So I went to the service. I did not expect to be as disgusted as I was with the performance. The Masonic hymn made Masonry an object of adoration. Was there ever anything more blasphemous? But what did Stidger preach? The sermon was divided into five parts: every Mason is a *M*an, is *A*ctive, *S*incere, *O*nward-looking and *N*eighborly. It is impossible to give even a synopsis of the various parts, which, to a great extent, were a higgledy-piggledy enumeration of anecdotes."[7]

Despite some naysayers, a vastly larger number of people raved about Bill's ministry and about St. Mark's. How had he done it? He later decided to record his success for posterity in a book entitled *Standing Room Only*, published in April 1921. He followed up with a second book, three years later, on the same subject, entitled *That God's House May Be Filled*. Within the pages of these two books was the blueprint he followed and that he wished to pass along. Some of the points he made in his two books were these:

Credo: "I believe that a preacher has a right to use any legitimate way under God's sun—as long as it is dignified, and as long as it is reverent—of producing an atmosphere of reverence and worship in the minds and hearts of the people who come to his church."[8]

How should a church reach out to the city's population? "You reach the masses through the medium that talks to the masses in a great city, and that is the newspaper. There is no other way."[9]

Get in the news columns. "You reach the masses better through the news columns than you do through paid advertising. Teddy Roosevelt and 'my fellow townsman' Henry Ford are talked about and written about because they are always doing something that makes good news. That is the way for the modern minister to get publicity. You catch the hearts of the masses not through generalizing but through focusing on a single individual. The Marjorie Allen story gave me an introduction to Detroit. The publicity was a by-product for service. I did what any minister would have done; indeed it was the duty for any minister to have done. It was service and it was news."

Get in the newspapers before the church service, not after. Bill wrote that he once came upon a group of preachers who were discussing publicity. "One of the ministers said, 'I think it's fine to get your sermons in the papers on Monday morning. I like that kind of publicity. It's dignified. It gets your name before the public.'"

"Wrong," Bill said firmly. "What you're talking about is what I call *post-mortem publicity*. It has about as much value as an obituary. The kind of publicity that is worth its weight in gold tells what you are *about* to do, what kind of sermon you are going to preach in the future, preferably, tomorrow morning."

Help the city editors. "The city editor will not allow the same name or the same church to be featured too often in a short time," Bill advised, "so he will cut out one or the other, either the Saturday or the Monday publicity. If this editorial psychology is true—and I know that it is, having been a city editor—concentrate on getting the Saturday publicity. Make it easy for the city editors by sending in a summary of your coming sermon."[10]

Use advertising to attract the crowds. "The first advice I was given when I arrived in Detroit was, 'Don't advertise in any Billy Hearst paper. The folks who read that paper don't go to church anywhere.'

"If that's so," I replied, "that's the crowd I'm after and that is just the reason I'm going to put my advertisements in that paper. Anyone can steal a congregation from someone else; I'm going after the folks who don't go to church anywhere. And I'll get them."[11]

Advertise. "Nobody can expect to get an overflow crowd in a great American city who does not advertise regularly and consistently. We use paid space, double column, every Saturday in the three big Detroit papers; in fact, we started the habit of using double column ads. Now more than ten churches in Detroit are doing so."

Do art ads. "Last Sunday I put a cut of Rodin's 'The Thinker' at the head of my ad. A copy of the statue had been erected near St. Mark's so I decided to focus the attention of Detroiters that 'The Thinker' was 'out our way.' We also have 'out our way' the largest sewer in the world, the largest stove and the largest filtration plant. I have modestly used these vehicles to call attention to the fact that St Mark's is among the colossal institutions 'out our way.' Some preachers might not care to refer to some of the things that I have mentioned. All right, let them leave out all reference to anything save the bronze 'Thinker.'"

Try the one-hour service. "'Can a service be cut to one hour and be successful?', a preacher asked me with skepticism in his voice. I said, 'It can most assuredly. We have tried it out over three month periods in two summers, and I am here to say it is spiritual, interesting and draws the crowds.'

"I advertise that we will have a 'One-Hour Service.' My public believes me because I keep faith with them absolutely. When they see a certain statement in a St. Mark's advertisement they know that they can believe that statement. Sometimes of course we take longer for one thing, than another, but if the time element is watched with care, this service can be run through in some such way as this:

Prelude	2 minutes
Prayer	3 minutes
Scripture	4 minutes
Announcements	2 minutes
Collection	3 minutes
Book talk	5 minutes
Art pictures	5 minutes
Sermon	23 minutes
Total	47 minutes

"I leave six minutes for solos and special music and the reminder of the hour for hymns and the 'Big Sing.' I always leave the sermon to the last thing so that I myself may determine how long it will be and close promptly on time. I stop my sermon three minutes before the hour so that I may have time for a closing hymn and an invitation to join the church, which I give at every service."

Give pulpit editorials. "The pulpit has no right to remain silent on matters of civic welfare that are of vital interest to every person. A pulpit editorial should be written out carefully in manuscript form, with several carbons made, because most of the newspapers of a city will want copies of it. Editors will send their reporters posthaste to the minister who announces that he is going to speak on timely civic themes, especially if this theme is controversial. I do not say that a pulpit editorial should be only done for attracting the attention of the editors, but I do say that its publicity value is great."

Make prayer memorable. "Prayer ought not to be long and tedious, taking in every nation, official and problem of humanity by name, swinging into the old formula that includes every man from the President of the United States down to the janitor of the church."

Erect a lighted cross. "A simply constructed, beautiful white cross is made. Just a little secret between us preachers that mustn't get out: that is, that the wire framework of the cross, which stands about three feet high, I got from an undertaker. This wire framework of a cross which is stiff enough to stand on its own feet is wired with electric lights; and white, frosted bulbs are put in, outlining the entire shape of the cross. The frosted glass makes a beautiful, snow-white light.

"At prayer time, we turn all the lights of the church off gradually, just as they do in the theaters. This causes an effect of twilight with darkness gradually approaching and produces an atmosphere of reverie. Then the choir sings softly any of a score of songs or hymns about the cross. With all the other lights in the church off and only the white form of the beautiful cross itself shining down on the audience, the choir singing softly, the congregation is in a subdued mood for the prayer that follows. Why should we not use color, light, motion and music to produce the atmosphere of reverence?"[12]

Leave no aspect of church practice unchallenged. "The following are chapters [in *Standing Room Only*] I recommend reading: 'New Possibilities in the Church Bulletin,' 'Hints that Will Help for Special Nights,' 'With the Help of the Hymns,' 'The Candlelight Service,' 'Something New in Prayer Meetings,' 'Lifting the Loose Collections With Laughter,' 'Monthly Service Clubs Promote Church Amalgamation.' There are plenty more."

Give them symphonic sermons. "An idea came to me when I read a phrase from Sir Joshua Reynolds: 'A verse may oft catch him whom a sermon flees.' The symphonic sermon method developed from this thought. I would identify a verse or phrase, usually two lines that had a theme and 'that would sing its way into human hearts like great music.'

"At the conclusion of each division of my sermon I will quote those two lines. Following every illustration, these lines leap to my lips and out into the hearts of my waiting congregation. The first sermon that I preached of this kind was almost ten years ago. I went back this summer to the town where I preached it. At least five people referred to that sermon. They had forgotten the text; they had forgotten the illustrations, but they had never forgotten my theme, which was from an Edna St. Vincent Millay poem:

The sun can split the sky in two
And let the face of God shine through!

Sing it! Sing it! Sing it!"

A dramatic book sermon can save the day. "The preacher who thinks he can produce two original first-rate compelling sermons a week is delusional. But take a great book with powerful characters placed in a moral setting and there is a tailor made dramatic book sermon.

"I first tell the story of the book if it is fiction. The folks want and expect that. If they do not get the story they are confused all evening. If they get the story itself, clearly and simply told, just as you would tell it to a child, they are happy. Then when you draw the moral lessons they will have the background of the story clearly in their minds.

"Sometimes you can use a book that does not seem to have any spiritual lesson in the way we of the orthodox church think it ought to have. I cite *Babbitt* as an illustration of this type of novel. What the preacher can do with such a book is to tell its story; paint its life of materialism; set forth its prosaic characters, and, make them live. It all seems so hopeless when you have read the book. This materialistic world of ours seems so selfish, fat-souled and corn-fed. Even the author has no remedy. He admits it. He is in the dark as much as the world. But we, the Church, have the remedy.

"Then I end up with this thought: 'What Sinclair Lewis and what Babbitt did not know was the great truth that *There is a God in Israel!*'

"Then you can go on and make your Christian application of the book. In other words, if what you want to preach to people is not in the book, use the book as a background and use it as a picture of what the world can not give.

"I am asked if I memorize the dialogue. I do when it is short. If it is not short, I often read it. However, the less reading from the book done the better. The minute you start to read you lose the audience to a certain extent.

"I always take the book into the pulpit with me. It gives a note of authority. I use as many illustrations outside of the book as I wish to make clear the point that I am trying to establish. I often compare two or more books that illustrate the same thing. My audiences after some exposure to *dramatic book sermons* are now interested when I compare certain brilliant passages in one book with those of another."[13]

Don't forget food, faith, and fun. "If there is any church institution that needs the shock of new electrical life shot into its nerves it is the Prayer Meeting time. I have solved the Prayer Meeting problem in a conclusive and overwhelming way so that instead of having ten people at Prayer Meeting, St. Mark's has from five to six hundred every Wednesday night.

"At six o'clock supper is served cafeteria style in the gymnasium by the women of the church. There is every appliance available to them, including an electric washing machine for the dishes, fully equipped steam tables and a chef to help. Supper tables are circular to emphasize family spirit. The father comes from his store or office downtown and meets his children and wife. Dinner costs each person thirty five cents which leaves enough over, after all expenses, for the women of the church to pay from ten to fifty dollars each week toward the Church Building Fund. From seven o'clock to eight, everyone goes up to the Prayer Meeting rooms. Because of the great crowds we have graded our groups into Adults, Intermediates, Juniors and Primary. This new idea of big and divided prayer meetings has attracted newspaper reporters and preachers from cities as far away as Boston and San Francisco to see how the programs work out. Each Prayer Meeting is filled with variety: the personal testimony time comes first so that it may be a free and unhindered testimony not influenced by what the leader may say. The people like to testify and they may take all the time there is. The warm, cheery hour at the supper tables has opened their hearts and lips, and thoughts and words flow freely.

"The Fun part of the family night begins at eight o'clock with the whole crowd returning to the gymnasium. The little tots go to a special quiet game room, where under a competent physical director they play until ten o'clock. The Intermediates have their games in another large room. Out on the gymnasium floor, the Adults have volleyball, indoor baseball and mass exercises.

"Food, Faith, and Fun night feeds our people's bodies, it feeds their souls and it satisfies their social and play instincts. It is following the example of Jesus in feeding the bodies of folks first and then their immortal souls. It does not require any special equipment, save a kitchen. The athletic part does not need special equipment for we do not have very much gym apparatus and what we do have could not be used on

Wednesday nights because of the crowds that come. We just play big games in a mass formation, and the people all go away happy."[14]

What are the results? "If someone dropped in for any of our Sunday night services, the first thing he would notice would be an air of happy expectations. He would find our church filling up an hour and a half before time to begin. He would find folks laughing and happy as they crowded into the largest auditorium in Detroit. And usually he would find chairs in behind the altar railing, in the aisles, in every available inch of space with forty or fifty people sitting on the pulpit platform. He would find six hundred extra chairs in use every night. So much for the crowds.

"Second, he would find a program of variety in music, art, color, motion, laughter, orchestra features, and likely a *Dramatic Book Sermon* preached. While he was listening to that sermon being preached he would see a crowd of people listening to the old truths presented in a dramatic human, happy way; and at the close he would, without fail, hear an invitation given to folks to come into the fellowship of Christ. And more than that, he would find them coming. Sometimes he would find four or five responding to that invitation, and sometimes ten or fifteen; but always some.

"If he remained after that service he would find the pastors at the altars of the church talking with people about their souls, their homes and their children for half an hour every morning and evening. When he went away he would say to himself what all who come and see are willing to admit. It is new, but it is the old, old story. It is a new way of preaching—that *Dramatic Book Sermon*—but it is the old, old Gospel after all; presented in an impelling way; a way for today."[15]

Bishop Henderson commented on Bill's first anniversary:

> When the church, in the City of Detroit, of which he is now the Pastor was being built, some modern skeptics pleasantly taunted the administration responsible for erecting a church which would never be filled. With his accustomed vitality, virility and versatility he began his pastorate in this, perhaps the largest church auditorium in Detroit, and in four weeks' time it was overcrowded, and has remained so to this day, night after night, with "Standing Room Only" the rule, with an increase in membership of fifty people a month. . . . Every Sunday in his church, God's house is filled. And not only that; but Christ is the purpose and passion of every program of this unusual, unique and forceful preacher. Every activity centers and culminates in Christ.[16]

Bill was teeming with ideas, and he swept up Iva and Betty in his enthusiasm. They helped him open the church for morning service and closed it with him late in the evening. Betty's favorite time was Sunday night service, with two and three thousand people jammed in, coming an hour early to get seats, with chairs in the Sunday School room for the overflow, and finally the ushers saying, "Standing room only." "Believe it or not," Betty said, "people would willingly stand." Betty recalled her memories of St. Mark's:

> I loved Detroit. We lived on Jefferson Avenue, not far from the largest stove in the world and right across from Waterworks Park. At three in the morning

a train would bring coal to the Waterworks. There was one switch that always caused trouble. The whistle would toot and the men would call and the freight cars would grind around that turn. I knew by the harshness of the sounds what the weather was: the noise was blanketed in the rain; soft and wide-spreading on the hot summer nights; sharp and blasting in the crisp cold air of winter. I always awakened to that sound. It was as comforting as a mother's lullaby.

I also loved Saint Mark's. What singing there was! From "Beulah Land" and "If Your Heart Keeps Right" to "Nellie Gray" and "My Old Kentucky Home." Dad always had a "Big Sing" early in the service with a mix of folk songs, popular evangelistic hymns and famous old hymns such as "Rock of Ages."

Dad was good at taking collections. He'd tell jokes, ad lib a bit and then say, "Well, I've made you laugh, dig down deep past the jingle money and pull out some bills and laugh when you put them in the collection plate." People chuckled even after they put their bills in the plates. The "loose" collection at Saint Mark's paid staff salaries and eventually exceeded ten thousand dollars a year. It was thought to be one of the largest, if not the largest, collections in the country. Dad figured that most ministers hate taking collections; consequently the congregation hates it also, or is indifferent to it. He took it seriously and it paid off.

After the collection the lights in the church would dim and the electric cross would shine, high up behind the altar. Helen Douglas would play softly on the piano and Dad would stand, his head raised a little, and he would speak softly: "Dear Lord . . ."

Not long prayers and not too many thee's and thou's, just a humble man pouring out his heartfelt thanks to his Creator. It was a hushed and sacred moment and I think I love that memory best of all. Dad standing there in the semi-dark, his cutaway a shade on the green side, his hands clasped behind him. He was motionless, his head lifted, eyes closed and the light of that cross shining softly on the "half moon where his hair had once been." You could almost know the angels were smiling when Dad prayed.

The thoughts in Dad's prayers were worth a month of hellfire and damnation preaching. He prayed as his heart dictated. Sometime he had a thought to unload. Picture him standing in the light of the cross, the people hushed and waiting, "Dear Father, thank you for the beauty of a yellow butterfly fluttering to rest in the heart of a full-blown rose—Amen." There was no doubt in my mind, Dad had beauty in his soul.

Yes, church was fun. I expected it to be fun. That my Dad was a top-flight preacher and minister, I took for granted. But I think Dad was at his best when he baptized a little baby. He was not one to stick to an accepted ritual. If he found something he thought was better he wouldn't hesitate to throw aside the old way. So it was with baptism. Dad would cradle the young babe in his arm. He spoke directly to the father and the mother, telling them simply that when they brought a new young human to the altar of the church they were promising to raise that child with loving care. He asked them to promise to instill their child with Christian love.

It was a rare and beautiful ceremony. Any witness knew he was in the presence of the true Kingdom of Heaven.[17]

In 1920, when Bill arrived, Detroit was infatuated with the automobile. Earlier, at the turn of the century, it had been a city obsessed with wheels—bicycle wheels. The use of bicycles had been almost universal, with 80 percent of the city's population riding around town on them. It was pressure from the cyclists, tired of potholed dirt roads, that led to the paving of the streets. This network of superior roads, in turn, facilitated the explosive growth of the automobile, which, for all practical purposes, dated to October 1, 1908, when the Model-T was officially introduced at a price of $825. The mechanical features and its low price gave the Ford Motor Company justification in claiming that "no car under $2,000 offers more, and no car over $2,000 offers more except in trimming."[18]

Horseless Age and *Motor Age* each published photographs or diagrams of the Model-T, along with highly complimentary stories. There was such an outpouring of interest that the company stopped taking orders on May 1, 1909, for nine weeks. By mid-1914 more than 550,000 Model-Ts were on the roads, and beginning in 1920, for six years, annual sales exceeded one million vehicles.

Detroit quickly became the automotive capital of the country and the symbol of America's manufacturing prowess. It grew to fourth from sixteenth in size by 1921, and its population grew commensurately, fed by active recruiting in Europe for new workers for its factories. Detroit's population by 1921 was about a million. Geographically, it was suited for its role. A factory in Detroit could be reached by freighter from any foreign port in the world; raw materials were easy to ship in, and finished vehicles easy to ship out.

If Detroit was in an opportune location, nevertheless there was one man who particularly capitalized on this location and who was the primary impetus behind the cultural revolution of the automobile. His name was Henry Ford. He was born in 1863 in Dearborn, near Detroit, and founded the Ford Motor Company in 1903. Until well into the 1920s, his company captured and held a market share of over 50 percent of the automobiles sold. Besides perfecting the mass-production method for manufacturing cars, Ford aggressively and annually reduced the cost of his Model-T; by 1916 its price had been slashed to $360. Despite the price reductions, which hurt its competitors, the Ford Motor Company was profitable. In addition, with each lowering of the price more and more people around the world could afford to own a Model-T. Moreover, in 1914, with his company profitable and the consumers well served by reduced prices for Ford cars, Henry Ford decided to do something significant for his factory workers. Reporters were called to the Dearborn plant, where they were told that Mr. Ford had doubled the wages of his workers to five dollars a day and shortened their workday from nine to eight hours. It was dramatic news that was flashed around the globe, and it made Henry

Ford an international celebrity virtually overnight, a status that he retained the rest of his life. Even fifty years later, *The Economist* called the Ford five-dollar-wage policy "the most dramatic event in the history of wages."

By 1921 Ford was acknowledged to be the wealthiest man in the world. Despite the publicity that surrounded him, Ford was, however, quintessentially a man of mystery, a shy person who shunned reporters. He threw around himself a barricade of organizational watchdogs. The fiercest of them, Ernest Liebold, his personal secretary, took almost malicious pleasure in denying reporters access to Ford. For his part, Ford knew exactly what Liebold was doing and told an employee, "When you hire a watchdog, you don't hire him to like everybody that comes to the gate. They're [reporters] all a bunch of skunks."[19]

With little or no information coming directly from Henry Ford, the press had to be content with rehashings of Ford's foibles or hearsay passed from reporter to reporter until it seemed to be true by virtue of its continued repetition. Ford's self-imposed exile encouraged the press to dwell on two of his missteps—one a perceived misstep, the other a quite real flaw. In 1914, prior to the entry of the United States into World War I, Ford, an extreme pacifist, leased a ship and, together with a band of believers, sailed to Norway to attempt to persuade the neutral countries to intervene and stop the war. Ford's powerful friends, whom he invited to join him, ultimately all declined to participate in what they regarded as an ill-advised mission. Those who did sail bickered so much on the way over that Ford ducked out on them once they had docked in Norway. In the middle of the night, incognito, Ford boarded a ship headed back to New York; the peace efforts continued without him, although he footed the bill. Ultimately, it became evident that the war could not be stopped, and the peace mission was abandoned. Rather than reward him for his altruistic and humanitarian efforts, the press mocked him as naïve.

The second and highly controversial misstep by Ford was his authorization of a notorious ninety-one-week campaign of anti-Semitism, launched by his wholly owned newspaper, the *Dearborn Independent,* on May 22, 1920. The motivation of the paper's editor was to build circulation: "Find an evil to attack, go after it; and stay after it." No pussyfooting—"One single series may make us known to millions."[20] Ford—and he was not alone in this regard—had grown up in a rural community where prejudice against Jews had been prevalent, even though "the only Jew seen was likely to be a roving peddler." Liebold, Ford's powerful secretary, was "viciously anti-Semitic,"[21] and his thinking found a fertile field in Ford. Though he did not instigate the *Dearborn Independent's* campaign, Ford certainly condoned it, sending copies of the articles to his friends. The fact that so prominent an industrialist, indeed a man known throughout the world, would associate himself with such a campaign against Jews gave it serious weight in the United States and abroad. Adolph Hitler went so far as to include Henry Ford's name as the only American mentioned in the U.S. edition of *Mein Kampf.* Hitler said: "Jews were increasingly the controlling masters" of American labor. "One great man, Ford, to their exasperation still holds out independently."[22]

It was in the midst of the *Dearborn Independent's* anti-Semitic campaign, in late 1920, that Bill entered the picture. The managing editor of the *New York World* had asked Bill to write an article on Henry Ford, which Bill agreed to do, and did without an interview.

Arthur Brisbane, who headed up Hearst's editorial department in New York, liked the article so much that he suggested that George Hargreaves, head of Universal Service, Hearst's syndication company, contact Bill to see if he would agree to do a series of articles on Henry Ford for distribution to its eleven million paid Sunday subscribers. Bill told Hargreaves that he would be willing to undertake this assignment—for pay—on two conditions: that Hearst arrange for access by Bill to Ford and that Ford representatives check Bill's facts for accuracy.[23]

Henry Ford agreed to the interviews, a fact that Bill later modestly called an act of generosity in Ford toward him, a relatively young man and a minister (Bill was thirty-five, and Henry Ford was fifty-seven). "Perhaps he has been kind to me for the same reason that he was kind to the timid boy reporter on a country newspaper after he had refused interviews to the city reporters in Cincinnati. When I asked him about this incident, he smiled a kindly smile and said, 'Oh, I just wanted to help that young man. He was so scared that he couldn't even remember the name of his paper.' "[24]

Precisely at the appointed hour for his first meeting, Bill presented himself at Ford's Dearborn office. "What do you want to find out, Doctor Stidger?" the industrialist inquired with some curiosity but no hostility.

"I want to know just what the average American wants to know: your religion, hobbies, home life and intimate friends, your ideas and ideals, your plans for the immediate and for the far future; what you are going to do with your money when you die; what is really going on down deep in your heart," replied Bill, having thought this all out beforehand.[25]

Ford looked at Bill thoughtfully, sizing him up. He decided to proceed. "Ask your first question, Doctor."

"Mister Ford, what is the real heart of your great industry?"

"I do not understand just what you mean, Doctor Stidger."

"I mean, as the human heart is the center of all life and activity in our bodies, so your great worldwide industrial organization must have a central motive or pulse beat. What is that central idea? I want to know what you think it is, so that I can pass that idea on to the world."

Ford paused before replying. Bill had wondered what kind of answer he would get. He had thought that possibly Ford might use the figure of the engine of a car, money, or some other such symbol, which would tell Bill that power was at the heart of his company.

Instead, Ford said quite simply, "The heart of our organization is spiritual."

It was now Bill's turn to say, "What do you mean?"

"I mean if you do your part honestly and try to serve others, the unseen will make what you are doing spiritual. A business that attempts to serve everybody, from workman to consumer, will prosper," said Mr. Ford.[26]

The chemistry between the two men was immediately positive. Neither presented any threat to the other. Bill had true interest in Ford, his ideas, his business, even the way in which Ford gathered the four natural resources that were the cornerstone of his empire: coal, water power, soil and minerals, and forests. To Bill, Ford was like a grand master at chess: he foresaw every move and had a winning strategy that was leagues ahead of his competition.

At first Bill found it difficult to get Ford to relax enough to give him answers to the personal questions he wanted to write about. Ford had fended off reporters for so long that opening up to one now made him nervous. Bill's tactic was to get Ford to talk about his business, which he was comfortable doing, then innocently hit him with a question about his personal views on some subject. Before each article was published, it was vetted at least twice by Ford's staff, once for factual correctness and once for content, and usually read by Ford himself.

In the days and weeks that followed, Bill and Ford scheduled regular meetings, as many as three per week. From these meetings Bill would gather enough for an article every two weeks in the *Detroit Times,* which was then syndicated across the country by Hearst. Bill was often invited to join Ford at his daily roundtable luncheon with his top executives, which Bill liked to refer to as the modern "King Arthur's Round Table," at Dearborn.

(Even after leaving Detroit, Bill was to maintain his friendship with Ford, usually visiting him at least once a year until Ford's death in 1947. His relationship with Ford was such that it was Bill's opinion that the *New York Times* would seek when rumors circulated that Ford might become a candidate for the presidency in 1924.)[27]

"How did your first car come about?" Bill asked one day when Ford was in an expansive mood. The industrialist leaned back in his chair as he gazed out of the window in his Dearborn office, across the snow-covered fields in the distance and an ice-covered pond nearer at hand.

"Before the car attracted my attention I had wanted to make a tractor. I had worked on my father's farm near Dearborn and knew what farm work meant in all of its drudgery. I was that 'hoe-man' that your friend Edwin Markham talked about in his poem. I guess I've hoed ten thousand miles in my day. But hoeing isn't so bad. I've done a lot of thinking as I hoed. But . . . I made up my mind that I would relieve men of some of that drudgery so that they could have some time to play and think and live."

"Did you think it out that way?" Bill asked.

"No. Not just in those words. . . . Maybe I was lazy and just wanted to get out of work. . . ."

"But you didn't work the tractor out first, did you?"

"No, the automobile had to come first to teach the farmer the use of motor power. He learned power machinery while he was having fun with his motor car. . . . A farmer is a stubborn rascal. He doesn't take up with a new idea very fast."

Ford continued, "One day I was walking to Detroit when I came across a man driving a road engine. I was fascinated with the thing. I begged the man who was running it to let me get up in the seat and drive it. I couldn't get it out of my mind. . . . Of course, I had heard of attempts to build horseless carriages in England[,] . . . but, because they frightened the horses, they passed a law making it a penal offense to drive one on the public highways."[28]

"I've heard that Thomas Edison had something to do with your first car. How did that happen?"

"Well," continued Ford, "he was my boyhood hero, though I had not met him. Although he was called 'The Wizard' of the electrical world and everyone was thinking in terms of electric power, he also foresaw the future of the gas engine. I believed that the gasoline car was the thing of the future without the slightest doubt. My experimenting with engines was going nowhere, however. I was discouraged, listless and very stale.

"Then," Ford said, "I went to a convention of Edison engineers in New York City in 1896—I was myself an Edison engineer. At the dinner table, where Mister Edison was also sitting, someone turned the conversation into a discussion of my ideas of a gas motor car. I didn't expect Mister Edison to approve much of this talk of gas engines, but he asked me to describe what I was working on. When I had finished explaining it to him—and I remember that I drew my plans out for him on a menu card—he banged his fist down on the table and said, 'Young man, that's the thing; you have it! Keep at it! Electric cars must keep close to power stations. The storage battery is too heavy. Steam cars won't do either, for they have to have a boiler and fire. Your car is self-contained, carries its own power plant, no fire, no boiler, no smoke and no steam. You have the thing! Keep at it!' "

Henry Ford looked at Bill with the excitement in his eyes that he had felt at the convention dinner table when Thomas Edison had validated his work: "That bang on the table that night was worth worlds to me. Up until that time I had not been given any encouragement from men who knew what they were talking about. But here, all at once and out of a clear sky, the greatest inventive genius in the world had said that my gas motor was better than any electric motor could be. I could go long distances, he said, and there would be stations to supply the cars with hydrocarbon. That was the first time I had ever heard that term used for liquid fuel, which of course we today call 'gas.' "

"When I got back from that trip I said to Mrs. Ford, 'you are not going to see very much of me until I am through building this car.' "

At this point, Henry Ford became philosophical, "So, you see, there is always somebody along the way to help when one needs it most. Life is like that. If we are willing to learn, there will always be teachers. If we are friendly, there will always be friends. We all need each other."[29] Ford changed the subject, and Bill had to follow his lead.

In June 1923, while Bill's articles were fanning out across the country through Universal Service's syndication, *The American Magazine* published an article to its 1.9 million readers entitled "The Seven Greatest Americans," by James Harvey Robinson, the retired chairman of the history department at Columbia University. Robinson concluded that Abraham Lincoln, Theodore Roosevelt, John D. Rockefeller, Thomas A.

Edison, Mark Twain, William James, and John Dewey were the seven Americans whose lives and contributions would leave "footprints on the sands of time."[30]

Among the industrialists he had considered, Robinson cited Andrew Carnegie, James J. Hill, J. Pierpont Morgan, John D. Rockefeller, and Henry Ford as having been his candidates, having already eliminated Cornelius Vanderbilt and John Jacob Astor as standing for families rather than individuals. Robinson wrote:

> If one must select among these candidates the best known, most persistent, ingenious and overwhelmingly successful handler of our modern facilities for inordinate pecuniary gain I am inclined to think the choice would lie between Rockefeller and Ford. The businessmen with whom I have talked seem to be much divided on this question. Ford is reputed to be richer than Rockefeller is now, and he is not yet sixty years old, whereas Rockefeller is over eighty-three. So there are possibilities ahead for the younger man with which it is impossible to reckon.
>
> The Ford car and tractors and the extraordinary methods used in cheapening their production have greatly influenced the daily lives of millions of people. Then Ford's courage and success in bucking other powerful financial and industrial combinations are exhilarating to the onlooker, as are his bold experiments in paying high wages.
>
> But the sorry fiasco of the "Peace Ship" and, especially, his anti-Semitic mania reflect on Ford's knowledge and judgment when he wanders beyond his own bailiwick. Rockefeller, on the other hand, in spite of all the bitter criticism his business methods have aroused, has devoted half a billion dollars to the promotion of science and learning according to the accepted standards of his age. So on the whole I believe that he should be adjudged the more considerable man and placed . . . on our list as the representative of modern business.[31]

Bill's friendship with Edwin Markham led to annual visits by the poet to stay with the Stidgers, often for as long as a month. On one of these trips to Detroit, Bill arranged that Markham and Ford meet. Henry Ford was properly charmed by Markham, and they immediately became engrossed in serious conversation. They talked earnestly about the responsibilities of society toward its workers. The time slipped by; Ford suddenly realized it was late and that he had forgotten his role as host: "Why, here it is nearly two o'clock and we haven't had any lunch."

While they continued their talk as they ate, Ford sent "a boy across the snowy fields to his own library for some of Markham's books." Then, at Ford's request, Markham stood and, after clearing his throat, majestically delivered his two great poems: "The Man with the Hoe" and "Lincoln, the Man of the People." As Bill later wrote, "It was a dramatic scene."

Of Ford Markham said, "That is the outstanding afternoon of all my life. Ford is Lincoln-like: simple and direct and humble and powerful. Did you notice that he never spoke above a quiet conversational tone? I have never met such a striking persona."[32]

As the months passed, article after article on Henry Ford appeared in the *Detroit Times* and in newspapers across the country. Bill decided that he had enough material to create a book on the industrialist. During the spring of 1923 he assembled the chapters and added new material. To clear the text of his biography with the Ford "censors" (which included the correcting pencil of Henry Ford himself) and yet escape with his style and content intact was a constant and harrowing battle.

June 5, 1923
Tuesday Evening

Dear Mr. Liebold:

I am sending the proofs of my Ford book to you as per our arrangement. You will remember that you and Mister Ford promised to put a proof reader to work on them so that we could get them back to New York quickly. I greatly appreciate that.

I want to tell you several things about these chapters:

First: They have all been gone over by Mister Cameron for checking up facts and matters about Mister Ford.

Second: I want them checked over again.

Third: I hope that whoever reads them will not feel it incumbent to assume the authorship of the book. By that I mean that I hope he will not change the actual style and reading. I merely want a check up on facts. There are two reasons why I mention this matter: The first is that every change in the proofs that is made I have to pay for out of my own pocket. That is a universal custom in publishing circles. Second, I want the style to remain as it is. It may seem rugged and rough and jerky—but it is mine and I find that people like it and—what is better—they READ it.

I greatly appreciate your courtesy in this matter and all that you have done to help in this book and the articles I have written on Mister Ford.

I hope that we can get these proofs back to New York this week. Please send them back to me personally so that I may look them over again and mail them from here.

Thanks!
Fraternally and Faithfully,
Wm. L. Stidger [33]

Though his articles on Ford were "vacuum-cleaned," Bill's stubbornness prevailed. His book emerged from the Ford maw of quality control largely intact and received very good notices when it appeared in late 1923. The *New York Tribune,* in January 1924, wrote:

HENRY FORD: THE MAN AND HIS MOTIVES

By the Rev. William L. Stidger.

The Rev. Mr. Stidger's book is perhaps the most successful of the recent volumes about Mr. Ford. The author's omission of biographical chapters gives him greater leeway for discussing the subject's views on men and affairs. The result is an interesting and illuminating work, uncluttered by inessentials. Regarding "the four great stones" upon which the Ford industry is founded as coal, water power and soil and the forests, the Rev. Mr. Stidger discusses Mr. Ford in relation to each and gives his opinions on many topics of public interest, including religion, politics, automobiles and prohibition. In response to a straight question about the last mentioned, Mr. Ford replied: "Booze never did anybody any good in any place at any time. That's the way I feel about it." His other answers are similarly forthwith and sincere. In the chapter on "Eccentricities," it is stated that Mr. Ford never had a cold, which will seem to many an immunity more to be envied than certain other of his possessions. Those who accuse Mr. Ford of carrying common sense to extremes will be more annoyed than ever to hear him explaining: "I am never sick because I take lots of exercise, eat lightly and get all the fresh air I need."

In 1921, the year after Bill arrived in Detroit, the Hearst newspaper organization purchased the struggling *Detroit Times,* and under Hearst's dynamic leadership the paper's circulation rose in the first year after acquisition from twenty-six thousand to two hundred thousand. James Schermerhorn, a prior owner of the *Detroit Times,* became its editor. For the next four years, while Bill remained in Detroit, he developed a close friendship with Schermerhorn and undertook a series of writing assignments for the *Times,* ranging from the report on the devastation wrought in Japan by the earthquake in 1923; to the recognition by the United States of Mexico, also in 1923; and to a personality piece on Frank R. Murphy, a rising judge in Detroit (and later Supreme Court justice). Bill's most unusual assignment with the *Times* began on August 6, 1922, when a new Sunday edition was launched featuring leading writers covering local, national, and international topics. Bill was asked to be a featured contributor of articles of "exceptional local interest to Detroiters," which he agreed to do, and for two and a half years, every Sunday, his full-page articles appeared. He was in the company of celebrities in the Sunday edition, which included H. G. Wells, Will Rogers, Damon Runyon, Lloyd George, and Babe Ruth.

Bill had to decide how to make stories about Detroit compellingly interesting, even when the subject might not be. There was large influx of European workers, who quite naturally knew little about their new city, and the *Times* believed that familiarizing them with the highlights of Detroit would serve a distinct public good by creating civic pride in the city. But, how, for example, could Bill make a description of the new General Motors Building, the largest office building ever constructed, or the new Belle Isle Bridge, then almost completed, more than a recitation of facts and statistics? His solution to this puzzle, a solution that startled many readers, was to write an imaginary dialogue between himself and the building, bridge, or other inanimate object he chose to describe.

So it was that for the next thirty months, Bill had high profile in the press as the reporter who spoke to museums, libraries, and animals in the Detroit Zoo, fire engines, traffic towers, major streets, and churches. It was relatively easy to portray him as completely loony or shamelessly trying to attract attention. The *Times,* however, found that Bill's articles were extremely popular; they struck a responsive chord with the paper's readership.

His imagination ranged freely: his General Motors Building took on, because of its imposing size, an air of arrogance that the Ford Hospital, nearby, resented. Jefferson

Avenue was shown to be a lithe, young, active avenue that envied Woodward Avenue for
its history and more established position. Bill, of course, took advantage of his article
on Jefferson Avenue to talk about St. Mark's, presenting himself as the reporter talking
to Jefferson Avenue:

> "I'm very busy—can't see you until about two o'clock this morning," said
> Jefferson Avenue when I asked for an interview.
>
> I expected this, for that is what all of the streets in Detroit tell me when
> I go to interview them.
>
> I made an appointment just as I would have made with an automobile
> magnate and kept the tryst to the dot.
>
> "I'm considerable of a street. I've become so gradually. I don't mind
> saying, in confidence to you, that I'm about the busiest street in Detroit. I
> know that Woodward Avenue, my pal, will dispute that, but he's just kidding
> himself."
>
> "At least, your friend Woodward," I commented, "will have to agree that
> you have as much distinction as he with all the famous institutions and land-
> marks that you possess along your way!"

Some of the Things Jefferson Has

> "Yes, I'm some street as far as institutions are concerned. I start off on the jump with
> a college. That gives me intellectual standing. Then I have the Deaconess Hospital and
> that gives me standing as a servant of the sick and afflicted."
>
> "Sure and you have 'The Thinker,' Rodin's great statue right on your highway, and
> the Fine Arts Palace and that gives you standing in cultural groups," I added.
>
> "Yes, and I have the largest stove on earth. Everybody knows about that. Every
> tourist who comes to Detroit goes out my way to see that stove. . . .
>
> "I have many churches, including that great square building with the lighted cross
> revolving on it every night. I hear more talk about that cross than anything on the street."

A "Trouble-Making" Church

> "St. Mark's Methodist Church?"
>
> "Yes. It's out my way. It's a trouble maker for me, too."
>
> "In what way?" I asked the old avenue, a bit embarrassed.
>
> "Why, when the crowds pour out of that church on Sunday nights they congest
> traffic and we have to have a policeman to handle it and the automobiles line up for
> several squares. But still, it's a good thing to have churches. It gives one the right
> atmosphere. I have a great Presbyterian church going up now at the corner of Burns
> and East Jefferson and further out several units of big churches. I am comparatively
> new out that way, so these institutions are in their infancy."
>
> "Are you an old street?"
>
> "I was laid out in 1807."[34]

Not all of the press was favorable to Bill's writing or headline-grabbing abilities. Leonard L. Cline, in an article in *The Nation* on the subject of Michigan, criticized many things about both Detroit and Michigan, including Bill on an unnamed but unmistakable basis: "The new Michiganders go to church dutifully, and listen to panting harangues against rum, by salesmanlike ministers who have carried out the Coney Island idea in religious advertising to remarkable perfection, adorning the house of the Lord with illuminated revolving crosses and other kewpie bangles."[35]

Besides his church responsibilities, his work with Henry Ford, and his reporting for the *Detroit Times,* Bill followed the development of the new technology of radio with keen interest. In the early 1920s radio broadcasting was still in its infancy. Each year was marked by a number of firsts. In 1920, Westinghouse was the first company to apply to the Department of Commerce for a license to begin regular broadcasting service. Jack Dempsey's knockout of Billy Miske at Benton Harbor, Michigan, on September 6, 1920, occurred during the first prize fight to be broadcast on radio. On January 2, 1921, the First Calvary Episcopal Church broadcast the first religious service, over Pittsburgh's KDKA. In 1922, Warren Harding became the first president to use radio when he dedicated the Francis Scott Key Memorial at Fort McHenry, Baltimore, on June 14.

Bill's earliest experiment in radio broadcasting came in 1923, when for two weeks he gave the first series of "evangelistic addresses that has ever been given over this new invention of adventure into the unseen." The broadcasts were sent from the *Detroit News* tower over WWJ, one of Detroit's two major stations, and reached listeners as far as Chicago and a hundred miles into Canada. He made a direct appeal for religion, presenting "the claims of Christ," asking for responses from those listening.

Bill wondered how his talks would be received, and he soon found out; the letters flowed in at the rate of twenty-five a day. Like most people, he was mystified by the strange properties of radio waves. He was startled to learn that they passed through "wood and iron. Nothing seems to stop them." One of the letters he received described this:

Dear Rev. Stidger:

It has been only a few moments ago that your voice came flooding through the night, and as the announcement came, I hastily called my wife to hear you. You seem to be old friends to both of us for we attended St. Mark's many times, and your voice came as clear and strong and distinct as though we were sitting in your church, drinking in one of those marvelous word pictures from your Book Sermons.

The radio that enables us to hear you is of my own make with the exception of the receivers. The aerial is of four wires stretched in the attic and the set is entirely enclosed by the house, so your voice came not only through the night but through the very walls of the house to reach us, and for that and the many other times that your messages have reached us, we both sincerely thank you.[36]

Bill made several discoveries about radio broadcasting. He had to tailor his voice to the medium, since reaching the back pews—a necessity when he was in the pulpit—required no effort when his voice was carried electronically. Perhaps more important, however, was the fact that the message had to be more of a fireside chat than a spellbinding oratorical tour de force. He learned this quickly when he received his first comments from listeners. He found he could adopt a conversational style easily by letting his imagination ride the airwaves and mentally "seeing" the people gathered around their wireless sets listening to him. Response to his adjusted style was immediate and favorable. People applauded his message, his articulation, and his conversational way of speaking. Radio, he realized, had the potential for letting him reach truly amazing numbers of people. He liked it, and he saw how it could make the Church more effective.

Bill also saw practical advantages for the Church in using radio. He wrote the following enthusiastic summary of how, he thought, radio could be beneficial:

> With the proper equipment we could send our entire church services into the homes of old folks and the sick. In my own church we have about two hundred old folks and shut-ins who hunger for the church. It is a real hardship to them that they cannot hear the preaching and the singing of the old hymns. With a mere nominal expenditure the church could install receiving sets in the homes of the old and the sick and they could hear the services just as if they were well. The possibilities of the radio in religion along this line are infinite. . . .
>
> I have frequently been urged to have an overflow meeting but have known that it would not succeed. Now that the wireless is possible when our crowds overflow, as they frequently do, we can have a meeting in the chapel and it will be an exact reproduction of the other meeting with its music and its sermon.
>
> The possibilities of the use of the radio in religion are as boundless as the heart of the God who makes the radio possible, and who from time to time reveals to some careful and prayerful and reverent searchers one of His great secrets—the greatest of which, to date, is the wireless.[37]

No discussion of Detroit in this period of the early 1920s—or of the United States—would be complete without describing the impact of Prohibition, which was particularly severe in Detroit. In the coldest part of the winter, there was heavy traffic on the frozen Detroit River. The action ranged from a single skater towing a sled across the ice to a loaded caravan of as many as seventy-five cars. What was going on constituted the second-biggest business in Detroit, just behind the automotive industry—bootleg liquor operations. The Detroit River was less than a mile wide in some places, and there were thousands of coves and hiding places along its twenty-eight mile length. It was a smuggler's dream. In Ontario, just across the Detroit River, forty-five Canadian government-approved and licensed distilleries and breweries went into high-gear production after January 16, 1920, when the National Prohibition Act and the Eighteenth (Prohibition) Amendment became law. The U.S. government estimated that three-quarters of the liquor supplied to the United States during Prohibition came into the country along the connected waterways of the Detroit River, the St. Clair River, and Lake St. Clair.

Liquor was dragged beneath boats; sunken houseboats hid underwater-cable delivery systems; most brazen of all, a pipeline was built under the river between a distiller in

Windsor and a bottler in Detroit. Soon after the beginning of Prohibition, the number of "blind pigs" (illegal stills) operating within Detroit city limits exceeded twenty-five thousand.[38] The police reported that "more than half of the homes in Detroit are brewing their own beer."[39] People drank openly, and the law of the land was flouted.

Bill was not in any doubt about drinking. It was illegal, according to the U.S. Constitution, and immoral, according to the Methodist Church. What was worse, organized crime and lethal gangs were beginning to have the run of Detroit. Money from the illicit traffic in alcohol went to corrupt city officials at all levels. Many citizens became innocent victims of the gang wars, and the city officials turned blind eyes to their plight.

Enforcing Prohibition became a frequent topic of Bill's "pulpit editorials." Though limited to ten minutes and presented early in the evening service, these comments on topical issues packed a wallop. The texts were distributed in advance to reporters, and the subjects of the pulpit editorials were widely advertised. Some of the issues Bill discussed were of narrow interest, such as the number of traffic tickets (too many) the police were issuing for violation of the new traffic laws, like the newly introduced stop signs. Other subjects, however, like politics and bootleg alcohol, had widespread reverberations throughout Detroit. He even went so far as to "interview" a liquor bottle for the Sunday *Detroit Times*; the piece appeared on February 17, 1924:

I was called into a home a while ago to see a dying man.

"I don't know what is the matter with him," said the woman, who was not a member of my church but one of those hundreds of people who call on the staff of St. Mark's when they are in trouble.

The house was full of an unmistakable odor. The man was unconscious. I saw at once that he had poisoned himself with bootleg.

"What you want is a doctor and not a minister," I said to the woman.

They called the M.D. to take the place of the D.D. and, after a two-hours' fight, pulled the victim through. He looked at me when I called the next day with a shamed face, for he was a pretty good fellow after all, and said:

"I went out on a little party last night and got sick. They brought me home. I don't know what happened. I guess I drank a little too much."

Most preachers in a great city like Detroit are called upon several times a year to bury the victims of this bootleg booze, and we wonder at the sheer stupidity of otherwise sane men who will drink the stuff without ever knowing whence it came and of what it is made. It is like the Biblical verse about the winds: "The wind bloweth, but we know not whence it cometh, nor whither it goeth."

So is it with bootleg booze. We know not whence it cometh and if we did we would as soon jump off the Belle Isle bridge into the river as drink the stuff.

I decided that it would be interesting and educational if I interviewed a bottle of bootleg booze and saw just what it was made of and where it came from—its past history, its social status in life—its creative work—but particularly its past. So I sought out a bottle of bootleg for an interview. Where I found it matters not at this moment.

In the "conversation" with the bottle of Hennessy Cognac, Bill learned how illegal liquor was made:

"Well, I am made out of a white alcoholic substance, as Prohibition officials will tell you, a white alcoholic substance—about 90 percent alcohol—called 'Parisienne Solution.'

"What is that?" I asked.

"It is a foot-washing concoction. Its bottle has a picture of a human foot on it and it says 'RECOMMENDED FOR PERSPIRING FEET.'"

"Do you mean to tell me that that white poison called 'Parisienne,' which is recommended as good for perspiring feet, is the base of all bootleg booze in this city?," I questioned, shocked beyond belief.

"Exactly! They make the finest so-called whiskies which sell from $6 to $22 a quart, with me as the base!"

Bill closed the interview by citing some examples of the tragic circumstances befalling the hapless victims of poisonous bootleg.

"What are you capable of doing in this old world anyhow, Mister Bottle of Booze?"

"Well, the other night a friend of mine, a bottle made in the same room out of that foot-washing lotion, was sold to a taxi driver, and a half hour later, he managed to run into a post, killing a young husband and a young expectant mother. They were on the way to the hospital for the great event. I can do things all right, but not the right kind of things.

"A week ago a fine-looking man came into the hole where I was made, paid $6 for a bottle of stuff that had been made the same as I had, only it was in a prettier bottle, and it was labeled with a fake label 'Maxwell'—and that night he went home and drove his wife and daughter out of the house with a revolver—shooting the child because she begged him not to hurt her mother.

"One bottle of bootleg booze is enough to send a man to the morgue. Go down there and that will give you the best illustration of what I can do in the world. You'll find girls down there with ice at their shoulders to keep them from spoiling; you'll find what was once a young man of tremendous build, blue and bloodless and dead as the ice that he is packed in. I fill that morgue and I keep it filled. I do that well. They pick my victims up and shove them into one of those little vaults with the ice. I'm hot stuff, but I turn them cold and clammy in three hours. That's what I can do."

My blood was cold with the horror of this interview. It was worse than my interview with the morgue itself—but we went on.

"Yes—I can do many things—but all bad things—I can make a fool out of a public official; I can make men traitors to their own national laws when they wouldn't think of breaking any other laws. I can make men who are otherwise good citizens and parents beasts that wallow in the filth of licentiousness and drool at the mouth—and die!"[40]

As Bill wrote his interview with the bottle of booze, he was already embroiled in a major battle, pitting himself against the police commissioner and the mayor of Detroit. Headlines about the police commissioner broke in the newspapers on Monday morning, January 7, 1924, all instigated by Bill. One headline was: "What Did Croul Tell Dr. Stidger About His Views on Drinking?" "I haven't a —— word to say," was Police Commissioner Frank H. Croul's "hot retort" to the pestering reporters' questions.[41]

Croul and the reporters were fully aware of what Bill had said from his pulpit on the prior evening: "A man with his views [Croul's] has no moral, ethical or honorable right to retain the office of police commissioner. And the reason is . . . Well, ask Croul." Bill teased his congregation:

> I challenge him in this pulpit and in the public prints to tell the public what he told me in his office about his own personal attitude toward booze. I told him when I sought the interview that it was for this pulpit editorial. In spite of this my old newspaper training makes me hesitate to reveal what he told me, when he banged his fist down on the table about his private attitude toward Prohibition. I leave that for him to tell the public.[42]

When the reporters were unable to pry any statement out of Croul as to what he had said, they flocked to Bill, who needed little prodding to divulge Croul's conversation. Bill said Croul admitted to him that Prohibition was not enforceable. Such an admission, Bill added, destroyed the morale of the police department and made the work of honest policemen almost impossible. He went on to say that Croul defiantly stated, "I'll have my drink! Nothing will stop me, neither the Volstead Act [enforcing the Eighteenth Amendment], nor anything, nor anybody else!"[43] Croul's words were so inflammatory, especially since they were made by a man high up in the city administration, that the reporters knew that they had something they could sink their teeth into. The fight between Croul and Stidger escalated quickly into a fight involving Croul's boss, the mayor of Detroit. Joseph A. Martin was the new interim mayor, standing in for Frank E. Doremus, the elected mayor, who had become too ill to continue serving. Martin had not had time even to have his first meeting with his council, yet Bill's war with Croul was preempting all other official business. Bill's charge was that Croul's lax attitude contributed to the breakdown in "dry law" enforcement in Detroit.

Bill was relentless, and the following Sunday he continued to hammer away at Croul, much to Martin's annoyance. The *Detroit Times* gave the story front-page treatment and banner headlines—"STIDGER ACCUSES CROUL." The title of Bill's sermon was, "Who is Police Commissioner Croul's Bootlegger Now?" Before 2,700 listeners at St. Mark's Sunday night service, in a sermon read by John Meredith (Bill's assistant—the pastor had fallen victim to tonsillitis), Bill ridiculed Croul. He said Croul had admitted to him that because his own supply of liquor was gone, he was ordering his new rum from the East. If true, Bill told his congregation, shouldn't Croul be arresting his illegal bootlegger?[44]

During the week, Martin met with several ministers, among them, Dr. M. C. Pearson, secretary of the Detroit Council of Churches. Afterward, Pearson said that the council would not press officially for Croul's dismissal. "We have left the matter entirely up to Mr. Martin," he said.[45] Pearson went on to add that *personally* he felt Croul should not be allowed to remain in office, especially after the police commissioner declared that "the police would not interfere with persons carrying hip-flasks."[46]

Bill hit the roof when he read Pearson's remarks in the newspaper. In his sermon that Sunday, January 20, 1924, Bill came out, all guns blazing, against "Talking Mayor" Martin, whose law enforcement conference could be described as a "beautiful assembly of buck passers"; against the Federation of Churches; against Pearson; and against "Mamma-boy" preachers," as he referred to them.[47] What, Bill was asked, did he mean by "Mamma-boy preachers"? "When preachers refuse to take a stand on moral questions and remain silent, they are like toy dolls which don't holler until they are squeezed."

Bill's sermon also contained the extraordinary revelation that he would, under certain circumstances, "take the law into his own hands if the police refused to act."[48] He said this in the context of defending the action of a woman who had appealed to the Ku Klux Klan when the police refused to help her:

> I am known in this city as an inveterate foe of the Ku Klux Klan and their methods of taking the law into their own hands, and yet I would feel neglectful of my duty as a citizen of this city if I did not call the city's attention to the fact that not only theoretically does a man of Commissioner Croul's type drive a city to Ku Klux Klan methods, but he has actually done so in a specific case on the east side of the city.
>
> For nearly a year, a businesswoman in St. Mark's has been tormented night and day by a gang of bootleggers in the flat opposite her living quarters on East Jefferson Avenue. They had their still across from her sleeping room, and she could see them making beer and whiskey any time by raising her window. She complained to the police department times without number. She gave the department the names and the actual address of this bootleg joint. But the police only laughed at her. . . . Then she came to me, her pastor, and asked me to help her close the bootlegging joint that night after night kept her awake by quarrels and drunken carousels. One day she saw an old man go into this bootleg den and after a while they threw him downstairs. He fell and cut his head and lay for a long time in a pool of blood. Nobody paid any attention to him for an hour, and then the bootleggers themselves came and got him and took him back into their rooms. This woman never saw that old man emerge from those rooms and does not know what became of him. He may have been murdered.

One night in a stupid, drunken brawl these bootleggers and their customers, right on East Jefferson, got to throwing bottles of beer at each other.
One of these bottles of beer flew out of the window into this woman's yard.
She brought it to me, her preacher, for analysis. I took it to Dr. Vaughn. The
analysis showed over 4 percent alcohol in that beer. Not a large percent, but
against the law.

She also reported this case to the police department but got no action.

A few weeks later, she told a friend of her predicament, saying that she
was desperate. She did not know what to do. "Why don't you report that case
to the Ku Klux Klan?" suggested her friend. "I don't know any Ku Klux Klan
members," replied the widow. "I do, and I'll report the case for you. . . ."

Whatever the facts in this case may be and whatever conclusions may be
drawn from them, one fact stands out, and that is, that after applying in vain
to the police department for more than a year this woman was finally forced
to make an appeal to the Ku Klux Klan, and she got results.

I am not in favor of Ku Klux Klan methods—but I can assure the
police department that if, as in some cases that my congregation reports, I
had a gang of bootleggers . . . annoying my family . . . and generally terroriz-
ing my home and its peace and quiet; and I could not get any action from the
police department, I would get that bootleg joint cleaned up the quickest and
best way I could. . . . If I found that an appeal to the police was in vain as so
many citizens do—then I would take the law into my own hands.

. . . What Detroit needs now are some preachers, and a Church
Federation, and some newspapers that will stand up and fight for decency
and law enforcement.[49]

To Mayor Martin, to some newspapers and to some citizens, Bill's rhetoric had gone
way too far. He appeared to be advocating vigilante action. Was his cure for Detroit's
malady worse than the sickness itself? Martin now was furious, and he made an excori-
ating statement calling Bill a "paramount liar," sneering that Bill would never have the
"guts" to say to Martin's face what he had said to his St. Mark's congregation.[50] The battle lines were drawn. Bill unhesitatingly picked up the telephone and called Martin's
office to make an appointment to meet him face to face. The time agreed upon was
Wednesday, January 23, 1924, at 3:30, at City Hall.

On the day Bill was to meet Mayor Martin, the *Free Press* printed a front-page arti-
cle, unfriendly to Bill, entitled "Stidger's 'Pig' is Evanescent as Beer Foam." It began:
"The ghost of a bottle of beer is sitting on the revolving cross of Rev. William L.
Stidger's church."[51]

Precisely at 3:30 that Wednesday afternoon and accompanied by Charles Freiberger,
the mayor's secretary, Bill, according to one newspaper report, "smiling and with a jaunty
air walked briskly into the mayor's office. He removed his overcoat and laid it on a table.
Then he walked to Martin who was standing by the mayor's desk. 'Good afternoon,
Mister Mayor, I'm Doctor Stidger,' he said smiling and extending his hand.

"Martin did not remove his hands from his pockets. He eyed Stidger for a moment, and then said: 'I am a native of Detroit. We do not ask quarter here and we do not give it. I don't believe I want to shake hands with a man like you.'

"The minister stiffened: 'That's pretty small. I came here on a friendly mission. In the first place, I came here because you dared me. . . .'

"'No dare was implied,' cut in Martin.

"'And in the second place, because I read in an afternoon paper that you would be glad to see me.'

"'That story was a lie. I am not and never will be glad to see you,' said Martin.[52] "Before we start the interview, I'd like you to sign this statement." Typed on the piece of paper that Martin handed him was a pledge that Bill would not publish under his signature anything that transpired during the meeting. Bill glanced at the paper. "Nonsense," he said and tossed it back on the desk. "I agree not to write anything for the newspapers, but I also won't sign your paper."[53]

"I gave you this paper to sign because I do not want a repetition of the Croul interview in which several unsubstantiated statements are published," the mayor said. "I am not willing to accept your word."[54] With this, Martin, over Bill's objection, invited reporters into his office, "in order that an accurate story might be written. By the way," Martin added, "do you come here as a reporter, a minister or a citizen?"

"As a minister," Bill replied, "responsible to five thousand people in my community." It was now Bill's turn to take the initiative and he began by giving Martin some advice: "I would immediately call in all police inspectors and tell them to clean out the blind pigs in their districts. They know where they are located."

"Your suggestion really comes a little late. I conferred with the inspector Monday morning on that matter."

"That's good," said Bill, unfazed by Martin's efforts to deflate him. "Much good could also be accomplished by following the suggestions made today by Sheriff Walters to establish a large vice squad for the sole purpose of running blind pigs out of Detroit."

"That suggestion did not originate with Sheriff Walters," replied Martin. "Several days ago Reverend Pearson[,] . . . one of the men you attacked, sent me a letter that this squad should be established."

"Well I am pleased to learn that Pearson is doing *something*. And as for Croul, I think you should demand that the commissioner refrain from drinking."

"I don't know that he does drink. He has never told me so," Martin replied.

"He told me so, and it is a matter that the entire public knows," said Bill.

"That is what you charge. I have weighed the *source* of the charge . . . and decided not to ask him whether he drank or not," Martin said.

Bill replied, "I believe Croul is honorable and honest. If you ask him if he told me that he would get his liquor and that no man or law would stop him, I believe he would tell you the same thing. Remember I do not want to have the commissioner removed. He was a good commissioner fourteen years ago. But he is too old. He has admitted to me that he should never have taken the job."

"I am not satisfied that you are altogether honest and sincere in endeavoring to clean up Detroit," Martin flung at Bill. "Were you accurately quoted when you said you do not know of a blind pig in Detroit?"

"Yes," Bill replied, "I know they are in my community. It is not my business to find them. People out my way have to bring up their 'kiddies' under terrible conditions because of the bootleggers. I have a congregation of 2,600, and I know that no one connected with St. Mark's drinks. If I caught any one who did, I would give them a good talking to and possibly even exclude them from the church."

"You know that Henry Ford thinks we should use the Army and Navy to 'dry up' the nation," said Bill.

Martin countered quickly: "Despite what Mister Ford says, I could not agree to any campaign that meant putting Detroit virtually in a state of siege."

At times the conversation became heated, and faces of both men flushed under the direct charges of each other; one time a couple of "damns" were quoted, and on still another occasion the acting mayor warned Dr. Stidger he was dangerously close to being insulting.[55]

Martin went on, "You state that within a month I should have Detroit dried up. How long did it take you to report to the police after one of your parishioners gave you a bottle of beer as evidence?"

Bill got defensive. "Well, I admit it took me about two weeks."

"Did you call this to the attention of the police before the lady complained to you for your laxity?" Martin enjoyed pressing his advantage.

"I guess she did see me two or three times before I sent the beer down. She told almost everybody around town about it, I believe. You see I was conducting a lecture tour and did not get the time," Bill said uneasily.

Martin pounced: "Then you consider a 'lecture tour' more important than reporting a violation of the law to the police, do you?"

Bill tried to brush the issue aside, "Well, let us not discuss that further."

"In other words," persisted Martin, "it took you two weeks to report one case, and you expect me to clear up an entire city in one month."[56]

At this point, both Mayor Martin and Bill realized there was nothing productive left to say. Bill couldn't resist giving some final advice, however: "If I were chief executive of a city I would see to it that every official under me observed every law to the letter. You're a young man. You've got the greatest opportunity in the world before you with chances of reaching unlimitable heights if you will only throw yourself into this war against Prohibition violations."

"Some sixty-five thousand voters believed I would be capable of doing that when they elected me. I'll try to show them they were right. You were wrong to accuse me of passing the buck and lacking courage. The one reason I received you the way I did when you came in here was because you said I lacked courage. That's a charge I won't take from anyone."

Bill said: "You have convinced me you have courage since I met you, and I'm here to tell you that if you go out now and do everything you have said you will, you will find me right behind you. I'm sure you mean it. Go to it."

At the conclusion of the interview Dr. Stidger made no attempt to offer his hand to the acting mayor who plunged into a pile of papers on his desk as his visitor started for his coat.[57]

Subsequent press reports emphasized the differences between the two men. The newspapers set the tone; they wanted a pitched battle between the hot-headed politician and the equally hot-headed minister. Nothing less would do. Even a newspaper reasonably favorable to Bill, the *Detroit Times,* ran a headline declaring "Dr. Stidger Denies Seeking Croul's Job as Police Head" followed by a second, "Dr. Stidger in Denial."[58]

In an official resolution of Saint Mark's dated February 13, 1924, Bill was given a vote of confidence by his board:

> We realize our inability to adequately recognize in a substantial way the incalculable services of our pastor but this Quarterly Conference does hereby pledge itself to back his program with every means in its power pledging to him their full cooperation and support. BE IT ALSO RESOLVED that this Quarterly Conference hereby expresses itself as being behind Dr. Stidger one hundred per cent in his worthy and ceaseless efforts to correct the law enforcement weaknesses of the city government.[59]

Some others in the city were of a different mind, castigating Bill for his aggressive behavior. The following letter was submitted to a Detroit paper:

STIDGER

To the Editor: When did the "Rule Ecclesiastic" for Detroit begin? That seems to be a fair question of the present day. According to best recollection we elected a mayor and council to administer the affairs of the city, and I can not recall any provision being made for over-lordship by either clergyman or kleagle [a Ku Klux Klan official].

To be sure we unloaded a tough job on a younger man, but we made it perfectly plain I think that we held him capable. Then what means this "buttinski" with the pink halo, who is scrambling for the spotlight position in Detroit's affairs? Hasn't he had all the front-page stuff he needs, that he must attempt to use Detroit's City Hall for a Bally-Hoo stand?

"I must see some result by the end of the month."—"I must know your plans for administering your office."—"I will stand behind you if I am satisfied."—That, apparently, is Mr. Stidger, an east side parson, talking to the mayor of all Detroit. One wonders what would happen if, at the end of the month, the reverend gentleman were not satisfied. Will he attempt the role of a local Mussolini, substituting the White Hoods for the Black Shirts? Or is that veiled threat only more "sound and fury," and for advertising purposes only? Were I on visiting terms with Mr. Martin I would advise him to have several trusted friends at his back, should Mr. Stidger carry out his promise to "stand behind him"—either that or wear a mail shirt.

If it were not for the fact that both pulpit and press are contributing generously to the gentleman's support, one would be forced to conclude that only a public job would still the clamor: on the theory that a nose in the trough utters no squeals. No rough, sinner-contact-infested job like Mr. Croul's, but something like Official Interviewer of Monuments (there are some left); these can not talk back, nor, fortunately, perhaps, can they rise up and fall upon the interviewer, no matter what asinine hokum they are made to utter.

Anyway, someone should, gently, but firmly, take this gentleman aside and explain that as a preacher we think he is a whale; and that we admire his boundless energy as well as his literary style; and that we think his advertising methods are "just too cute"—but, down at the City Hall demanding resignations, promises and guarantees, and acting the great Pooh-Bah in general, he is out of focus—he gums up the picture.

Many Detroiters agree with Mr. Stidger's view on the Prohibition Law, and most of them endorse the desire to see enforcement of that law as well as all other laws— but few of them believe that his loose-flung, ill-considered oratory is going to help in any way to accomplish anything—except perhaps the attendance records at his church. There are some who believe that to be the object of all the fuss and fury.

Take down the "Welcome" sign, Mr. Mayor, and hang out "Nothing Doing" for all meddlesome busy-bodies and notoriety seekers. Let them rave if they must, but— outside. The electors look to you, and you alone, for vindication of their confidence expressed at the polls. They don't expect you to take orders from any man, even though he does button his collar at the back.

R. D. COLQUHOUN
1950 Blaine Avenue[60]

The more Bill thought about his stormy meeting with Martin, the more upset he became. So it came as no surprise that his Sunday sermon was like a machine gun directed at Martin, his fellow ministers (whom he now called "pulpit pastry cooks"), the Anti-Saloon League, and the *Free Press*.

"At my conference with him on Wednesday," Bill told his congregation, Martin had made a number of promises, among them that "he would clean up Detroit in a shorter time than General Butler cleaned up Philadelphia and that he would fire any police commissioner who does not live up to his oath of office. He also said he would drink no more while he is in office, a statement that I am afraid may put him in an embarrassing position.

"Martin asked me if I could enforce the laws if I were police commissioner, and I answered that I, or any other man who wanted to do so, could. I did not, as the *Free Press* incorrectly reported, offer to take Commissioner Croul's place, nor did I apologize for my remarks made here at St. Mark's last Sunday.

"And speaking of the *Free Press*, they printed the most disgusting and deliberate sacrilege that I have ever seen. Saying that 'the ghost of a bottle of beer is sitting on the revolving cross of Rev. William L. Stidger's church,' is a low-brow, ruffian, irreligious, sacrilegious insult to the cross and to the church. It is not only an insult to me—I don't care what they say about me—but to every Christian and to every churchman, to every Protestant and Catholic in this city. A paper that has dared to insult the cross of Christ ought to have its circulation ripped into shreds in every Protestant and Catholic home. I stop my subscription tomorrow and challenge every member of this church to do the same."[61]

The congregation, numbering nearly three thousand, applauded Bill heartily after he issued his indictment against the *Free Press*. After the service, the press immediately asked Martin for his reaction to Bill's sermon. "I have nothing to say at this time," he replied. "Will you comment later in the day?" a questioner persisted. "I hardly believe so," said Martin.[62] He did not state anything further on the Croul matter, and he did not fire the police commissioner, either. Bill felt he had done all he could with his protests and dropped any further assaults on Croul. For a time some progress on enforcing the Prohibition laws was made.

Martin bitterly resented Bill's outspoken behavior, and Bill felt Martin was unfit to govern. Moreover, Bill knew that Martin, if he were to continue as mayor, had to be approved by the citizens of Detroit in the elections coming up later in 1924. Bill determined to find the right man, support him, and get him elected; Martin was not his candidate.

Bill's candidate was Detroit postmaster John W. Smith, whom he had met the prior August in Mexico City. The U.S. Commission on Recognition of Mexico had been in Mexico City hammering out the final details of an accord. The Hearst syndicate had asked Bill to cover the events for its readers, and there Smith made an unofficial call on his fellow Detroiter, Charles B. Warren, chairman of the commission. Bill met Smith on that occasion, liked him immediately, and asked to do an interview. As Bill wrote, "Smith is one of these friendly souls, with a great human heart in his prize-fighter chest; a grip like a man who has either milked cows in his boyhood or who has shaken hands with a lot of people like a preacher or a politician; and it was as natural for him to get into politics as it was for him to breathe."[63]

The *Detroit Times* shared Bill's view that Martin should not be elected mayor. By late spring 1924, under Bill's prodding and with support from the *Detroit Times*, Smith had been persuaded that it was his "duty" to run for the mayoralty. His campaign met with an immediate and positive response. It was the kind of battle that Bill relished, a David pitted against Goliath. Martin was, after, all the incumbent mayor and enjoyed the support of the establishment, namely the highly respected Senator James Couzens, who had also been Detroit's mayor. In addition, Martin had the backing of two of the three daily newspapers.

As the campaign reached its final month, Martin lashed out at his opposition. He sensed he was losing ground to Smith and to a write-in candidate, a lawyer named Charles Bowles. Martin denounced the "group of malicious bigots and disgruntled politicians who, though naturally opposed, have joined hands in desperation and will stop at nothing to accomplish my defeat."[64]

Martin publicly analyzed the interests opposing him, concentrating particularly on Bill, a "passionate supporter of Smith." Martin said, "Stidger had an assistant pastor named Calkins. Through Calkins, the Ku Klux Klan was induced to put a candidate in the race with the idea that he, by taking votes from me, would assist 'Stidger's candidate' to go over. In the primary race, the Ku Klux Klan candidate ran third. By every rule of fair play and sportsmanship and the spirit of our primary election laws, the third candidate should thus have been eliminated. But with him out of the race the Stidger group felt I surely would be elected. So, through Calkins and the Ku Klux Klan, the Klan candidate was induced to run for the final election on November 4 on 'stickers' [on a write-in basis.] Both these disgruntled politicians are now working tooth and nail to elect the Stidger candidate for revenge on me."[65]

Martin's flailing was to no avail. Smith won Detroit's mayoralty with 115,772 votes; Bowles, the write-in candidate, placed second with 105,902 votes, and Martin drew only 83,769 votes.[66]

Smith's victory capped Bill's fourth year in Detroit. His congregation at St. Mark's was bursting the huge building. The average morning crowd on Sundays was 2,500, and on Sunday evenings it averaged three thousand. Two policemen were detailed to manage the "throngs that besieged his church every Sunday night." The midweek Food, Faith, and Fun prayer meetings had grown to average eight hundred each Wednesday.

Some people questioned whether the increasing size of St. Mark's membership was solid. "Is his work permanent?" Do his converts hold out? queried the skeptics. An article published on April 1, 1925, written by Rev. Walter Rice Davenport and entitled "The Man Who Did It," attempted to respond to the skeptics:

Doctor Stidger's work will pass this test, as the records will show. To exemplify the thoroughness of his follow-up system let it be said that he has a "Reception Day" for new members one Sunday every month. The week prior to that event, Doctor Stidger writes not a form letter but a personal letter to all the expectant members. The next week he calls upon each of them in person. The Friday of that week they are all at a "Service Club Night" when they are introduced to hundreds of former members and made "at home." The same thing is repeated every Friday night for the rest of the year, when each new member is assigned some definite task of church work. It is the intention to have no drones at St. Mark's.

Davenport summarized Bill's writing and ministerial duties for the year 1924:

Three books written and published.
Three hundred articles written for papers and magazines.
Fifty poems published.
Three hundred twenty-five sermons and addresses.
A thousand pastoral calls.
Fifty funerals.
One hundred fifty babies baptized.
Four hundred people received into church membership.

In concluding, Davenport observed, "Bill advertises his church as 'The Big Church, with the Big Crowds, and the Big Cross, and the Big Heart.' But *his* is the biggest heart of all, and it requires little exercise of the imagination to visualize him standing before his thousands at St. Mark's and preaching to them the unsearchable riches of Jesus with such compelling power that they would heed as well as hear."[67]

"The Man Who Did It" was only one of a number of articles that signaled a growing national awareness of Bill and his activities, the most prominent being a profile in *The American Magazine* by Alison Gray in 1923, entitled "A Man Who Draws a Crowd Because He Knows Human Nature." (*The American Magazine* had published the article on Billy Sunday in 1907 and, monthly, reached a readership of just under two million.) Bill's articles on Henry Ford were syndicated across the United States by a Hearst company, Universal Service, to eleven million subscribers weekly. One of Bill's sermons was selected for publication in *Best Sermons of 1925*. And Edgar DeWitt Jones, in preparing for a book entitled *American Preachers of Today* (published in 1932), selected Bill as one of thirty-two leaders whom he profiled, out of the thousands of American preachers then currently practicing.

The timing of Davenport's article turned out to be curiously appropriate as a summing-up of Bill's accomplishments in Detroit, because Bill had been approached by the Linwood Boulevard Methodist Church in Kansas City to become its minister. It was an opportune time to move on, particularly with the excellent record that he had amassed at St. Mark's, including the reduction of much of the church's debt. In addition, his new assignment was also a step up the ladder; Linwood Boulevard Church had a large and beautiful building and a well-established and wealthy congregation.

The news of his decision leaked out prematurely, requiring Bill to make an announcement to his St. Mark's congregation earlier than he had planned. The following appeared in the weekly bulletin on June 21, 1925:

A WORD FROM THE PASTOR

To the Folks of St. Mark's:

It has been my habit, from time to time, of talking frankly to you in this Bulletin. Last Sunday's newspapers carried a story about my acceptance of the pastorate of the Linwood Boulevard Methodist Church, in Kansas City. I had promised Bishop Nicholson not to say anything about this change for a week, but the news was given out at the Kansas City end. That is the reason why St. Mark's did not hear this news first from its pastor, rather than from the papers.

I came to St. Mark's at the earnest request of Bishop Henderson five years ago. There was considerable of a task, and it could never have been done, if it had not been for the almost phenomenal loyalty and generosity of the people of this church. I never have found, and I never expect to find, any loyalty to surpass it. I have the deepest appreciation of all you have done.

During the past five years we have raised in St. Mark's $500 a week in interest, bonds and permanent improvements in addition to paying our running expenses—a task unequalled in Methodism. During these five years more than 2,000 new members have been received at the church altars and 600 babies baptized.

In addition to this we have had our part in the civic history of Detroit in these five years. The things for which we have stood have come to pass. The final results of our stand in the matter of a Police Commissioner will be vindicated in time.

We have met and made friends we shall hope to keep for life. St. Mark's will always have a sacred place in our memories and our hearts. We have put five of the best years of our lives into St. Mark's. That kind of an investment will be followed up with our interest and our prayers. . . .

This preacher could go away happier if he felt he had done even half enough for the folks of St. Mark's. But it is a small world. This preacher comes and goes a lot throughout the church world, lecturing, and poking his nose into this town and that; and he will visit St. Mark's a lot from time to time; and the doors of our Kansas City home will be nailed back when St. Mark's folks visit the "House of Hospitality," which is the parsonage out there. Everybody come along!

Fraternally and faithfully,
William L. Stidger[69]

The *Detroit News*, which had disagreed with him so often, gave as its headline "Tears Flow as Dr. Stidger Bids Throng Farewell."[69] The tone of the long article reflected the sense of loss everyone was feeling, knowing that an outspoken voice, sometimes difficult but always vital, would soon be gone.

The *Detroit Times* gave him a nostalgic and heartfelt valedictory:

GOOD BYE, DR. STIDGER!
DETROIT WILL NOT SOON FORGET YOU.

Tonight Dr. William L. Stidger will conduct a prayer meeting at St. Mark's Methodist Church, and tomorrow he will leave Detroit for Kansas City, where a big church is waiting for him.

One wonders if the publicans and sinners of Kansas City realize what exciting times are just ahead for them. Dr. Stidger will be chasing them through Kansas and Missouri about forty-eight hours after his arrival, if he is in his best form.

A bitter enemy of hypocrisy—[neither] wealth nor prominence ever daunted his smashing attacks on sanctimonious sham in Detroit.

He has stormed into City Hall and police headquarters, fought judges on the bench, castigated fellow ministers for cowardice, denounced newspapers that were then great and powerful—all this without losing his sense of humor and without bitterness . . .

The *Times* has not always been in complete accord with Dr. Stidger—but his honesty and splendid fearlessness, coupled with an extraordinary capacity for work, make him a man Detroit can ill afford to lose at this time.

Good-bye, and good luck![70]

As a postscript, Police Commissioner Croul resigned on July 15, 1926, following a report by the Rockefeller Foundation into vice conditions in Detroit that classified the city as the worst in the United States "in the matter of social evil."[71] Croul said in his letter of resignation that the vice report made serious charges against the "police higher ups." "Of course, I am the highest up, and as such I accept full and entire responsibility for the work of the department." Croul resigned rather than attend a meeting called to discuss the vice report.[72]

In 1972, St. Mark's was closed. Its membership had declined to fewer than a hundred people, and the building was sold to another church for use as its regional headquarters. In 1981 there was a newspaper report of a reunion of the seventy-five remaining parishioners "of a once mighty Detroit congregation. . . . The parishioners reminisced about the golden years at St. Mark's, days when people brought picnic lunches to eat on the church lawn, so they could be early enough for the evening service." The article concluded: "The former St. Mark's building, with its unique illuminated, rotating cross (now dark and stationary), was a familiar site for motorists on East Jefferson."[73]

But the memories of its vibrant past, its five years of boisterous vitality, echo today through its vast hallways and rooms. One can almost hear the click of a bowling ball as it knocks the pins and the thud of the ball rolling into the gutter; the cheers on the basketball courts as Betty and her friends scream for the home team to win; and Bill's voice as he leads his congregation in prayer, the lights dimmed and the music soft and far away.

Notes

1. *Saint Mark's Methodist Episcopal Church Bulletin,* June 21, 1925, author's collection.

2. Alison Gray, "A Man Who Draws a Crowd Because He Knows Human Nature," *The American Magazine,* June 1923, 128–29.

3. *Saint Mark's Methodist Episcopal Church Bulletin,* June 21, 1925, author's collection.

4. Gray, "A Man Who Draws a Crowd Because He Knows Human Nature," 128–29.

5. Gray, "A Man Who Draws a Crowd Because He Knows Human Nature," 129.

6. "Nursery Cares for Babes during Service," *Detroit Times,* December 20, 1920, author's collection.

7. "Masons! It's Your Night," *The Lutheran Witness,* January 1921, author's collection.

8. William L. Stidger, *That God's House May Be Filled* (New York: George H. Doran, 1924), 110.

9. Stidger, *That God's House May Be Filled,* 110.

10. Stidger, *That God's House May Be Filled,* 124.

11. Walter Rice Davenport, "The Man Who Did It," *Zion's Herald,* April 1, 1925, 396–98.

12. William L. Stidger, *Standing Room Only* (New York: George H. Doran, 1921), 78–79.

13. Stidger, *That God's House May Be Filled,* 28–35.

14. Stidger, *Standing Room Only,* 35–40.

15. Stidger, *Standing Room Only,* 58–59.

16. Article (untitled), unidentified newspaper, author's collection.

17. Betty Stidger Hyland, *Those Heavenly Years,* unpublished manuscript, 1955, 79–85.

18. David L. Lewis, *The Public Image of Henry Ford* (Detroit: Wayne State University Press, 1976), 41.

19. Lewis, *The Public Image of Henry Ford,* 130.

20. Lewis, *The Public Image of Henry Ford,* 137.

21. Lewis, *The Public Image of Henry Ford,* 138.

22. Lewis, *The Public Image of Henry Ford,* 143.

23. William L. Stidger, *Henry Ford: The Man and His Motives* (New York: George H. Doran, 1923), viii–ix.

24. Stidger, *Henry Ford,* x.

25. Stidger, *Henry Ford,* xii.

26. Stidger, *Henry Ford,* 135–36.

27. "Says Ford Will Get Prohibition Nomination; Chairman Summons Party to Washington," *New York Times,* October 18, 1923, 1.

28. Stidger, *Henry Ford,* 120–21.

29. William L. Stidger, *The Human Side of Greatness* (New York: Harper, 1935), 1–11.

30. James Harvey Robinson, "The Seven Greatest Americans," *The American Magazine,* June 1923, 14, 138.

31. Robinson, "The Seven Greatest Americans," 138.

32. Stidger, *Henry Ford,* 42–44.

33. Letter dated June 5, 1923, from William L. Stidger to Ernest Liebold, Henry Ford Museum.

34. William L. Stidger, "Everything from a College to an Amusement Park Makes Its Home along Jefferson Ave.," *Detroit Sunday Times,* August 19, 1923, 5–6.

35. "Swats Brother Bill's Cross," untitled article in unidentified newspaper reporting on story in *The Nation* entitled "These United States," November 1922, author's collection.

36. Stidger, *That God's House May Be Filled,* 149.

37. Stidger, *That God's House May Be Filled,* 152.

38. "Dusting off the Purple Gang," *Detroit Monthly,* December 1992, 69–70.

39. "'Dry Spy Squad' Called Menace," *Free Press,* November 19, 1921.

40. "Bottle of Bootleg Tells Story," *Detroit Sunday Times,* February 17, 1924, 5–7.

41. "What Did Croul Tell Dr. Stidger about His Views on Drinking?" *Detroit Times,* January 7, 1924, 1.

42. "Croul Refuses to Bare His Rum Views," *Detroit Times,* January 7, 1924, 1–2.

43. "Croul Gets Martin's Warning," *Detroit Times,* January 8, 1924.

44. "Stidger Accuses Croul," *Detroit Times,* January 14, 1924, 1.

45. "Pearson Puts Croul Blame Up to Martin," *Detroit Times,* January 15, 1924, 1.

46. "Pearson Puts Croul Blame Up to Martin," 1.

47. "Stidger Flays City Clergy as 'Mamma Boys,'" *Free Press,* January 21, 1924, 1, 12.

48. "Stidger Flays City Clergy as 'Mamma Boys,'" 1.

49. "Stidger Flays City Clergy as 'Mamma Boys,'" 12.

50. "Martin Assails Stidger in Clash over City's Rule," *Free Press,* January 24, 1924, 3.

51. "Stidger's 'Pig' Is Evanescent as Beer Foam," *Free Press,* January 23, 1924, 1.

52. "When They Went to the Mat," *Free Press,* January 24, 1924, 1.

53. "Dr. Stidger Denies Seeking Croul's Job as Police Head," *Detroit Times,* January 24, 1924, 1–2.

54. "Dr. Stidger Denies Seeking Croul's Job as Police Head," 1–2.

55. "Dr. Stidger in Denial," *Detroit Times,* January 24, 1924, 2.

56. "Martin Assails Stidger in Clash over City's Rule," *Free Press,* January 24, 1924, 1, 3.

57. "Dr. Stidger in Denial," 2.

58. "Dr. Stidger Denies Seeking Croul's Job as Police Head," 1.

59. *Official Board of Saint Mark's Resolution,* February 13, 1924, author's collection.

60. "Stidger," undated letter to the editor, author's collection.

61. "Rum Drive Good Start, Says Pastor," *Detroit Times,* January 25, 1924, 1, 4.

62. "Rum Drive Good Start, Says Pastor," 1, 4.

63. William L. Stidger, "John W. Smith," *Detroit Sunday Times,* August 31, 1924, 5–6.

64. "Martin Flays His Opposition," *Detroit News,* October 13, 1924, 1.

65. "Martin Flays His Opposition," 1.

66. "Smith Victor, Bowles Says He Will Fight," *Detroit News,* November 5, 1924, 1.

67. Davenport, "The Man Who Did It," 396–98.

68. *Saint Mark's Methodist Episcopal Church Bulletin,* June 21, 1925, author's collection.

69. "Tears Flow as Dr. Stidger Bids Throng Farewell," *Detroit News,* September 14, 1925.

70. "Good Bye, Dr. Stidger!" *Detroit Times,* September 14, 1925.

71. "Detroit to Clean Up Vice," *New York Times,* July 8, 1926, 18.

72. "Commissioner Resents Criticism in Vice Row," *Detroit Times,* July 15, 1926.

73. Harry Cook, "St. Mark's United Methodist Had 3000 Members," *Free Press,* June 19, 1981, 3A.

Eight

Elmer Gantry: Kansas City

" **E**lmer Gantry was drunk. He was eloquently drunk, lovingly and pugnaciously drunk."[1] These opening sentences of Sinclair Lewis's novel *Elmer Gantry* rocketed across the country with the book's publication in Kansas City on March 10, 1927, and they enraged and humiliated Bill Stidger.

Bill preached an impassioned sermon filled with emotion and fury on that Sunday, March 13, not because he had just read the book (he had seen galley proofs at least a month earlier) but because the publication of *Elmer Gantry* had been an immediate sensation in Kansas City and was moving throughout the country like a forest fire out of control. The character Elmer Gantry—a rogue preacher, a drunk, a womanizer, a nonbeliever, a profiteer—represented everything Bill Stidger was not and stood against. But this fictional "man of the cloth" looked like him and had many of his attributes: he had a small-town, midwestern origin, and he had been a college football player expelled for a prank; he was a charismatic public speaker, a physically powerful and commanding presence, a pioneer in radio preaching, and a preacher who understood that advertising to parishioners did work and that effective ministry had to be entertaining as well as filled with substance. To make certain there was no mistaking the connection, Lewis provided Elmer Gantry's new Wellspring Church with an electrified revolving cross.

To the Kansas City community there was understandable confusion about how much truth existed in the rumor that Elmer Gantry and Bill Stidger were one and the same person. Bill had proclaimed to his congregation and the press that he had invited the noted author to Kansas City and challenged him to write a major book on the ministry. He had presumed that Lewis would use him as a model and that Lewis's preacher would be the kind of compelling character that he had created in *Arrowsmith*. But Sinclair Lewis had very different ideas for his "preacher book." Bill responded from the pulpit in anger at this betrayal of his expectations, and he attacked the author.

William Allen White, editor of the *Emporia Gazette* (Kansas) and a Pulitzer Prize–winning journalist, wrote the following précis of *Elmer Gantry:*

> Briefly, the story is this: Elmer Gantry, a roughneck from a Kansas country town, goes to a freshwater college, a meager football station, with a little academic trimming. He belongs to the crowd that drinks and chases waiter girls, and is a football hero known as "Hell-Cat." The usual revival appears in town and Elmer Gantry is roped in.
>
> He goes to a theological seminary without any conviction, merely because he has a bull-roaring voice and a certain facility for emotional expression. He romps through the theological school, a bounder and a roughneck, until his senior year, drinking, flirting in the big city adjacent, and finally, on a large brown toot, is caught and leaves the theological school without his degree, but not before he has seduced a girl in a neighboring country town where he has gone to fill the pulpit in a temporary vacancy
>
> Being without a degree, Gantry becomes a traveling salesman, a drinking, poker-playing, waitress-chasing, he-harlot. He falls in with a lady evangelist, becomes her assistant, leaves the road, and, after he has lived with her a few months, at her death gets a job as preacher, goes to a small town, marries the merchant's daughter, climbs up and up in the world as an exhorter with all the evangelist's tricks and manners; finally gets into the city, still a woman chaser with a lip for surreptitious liquor, gets tired of his wife, takes up with the woman he had seduced in his boyhood, falls in with another woman who is working a frame-up on him, establishes her as his mistress, is exposed, wriggles out of it.
>
> Lewis closes the book with Gantry in a paroxysm of repentant prayer, looking with a wary eye at an ankle of a girl in the choir. That is the story.
>
> The presumption is that this is the story of the man who commercializes organized religion. The trouble with the book is that it lacks contrast. The only good preacher in the book is a saphead. The only good women are dull. And the thing bears the same relation to life that Punch and Judy bear to life.[2]

Sinclair Lewis and Bill Stidger had first met in the summer of 1922. On arriving in Terre Haute, Indiana, to lecture at a Chautauqua conference, Bill ran into a good friend, Dr. Edgar DeWitt Jones, in the lobby of the hotel. Jones spotted Lewis's name in the hotel registry. "Say, Bill," said Jones, "I'd like to meet Lewis."

"We'll introduce ourselves," replied Bill. "I have a bone to pick with that guy, anyhow." Lewis had become a celebrity with the remarkable success of *Main Street*, the most controversial book of 1920, which "attacked the mores of Middle America and tore apart the hitherto sacred values of the people of its small towns." *Babbitt,* in 1922 his current novel, was also a best-seller.

Lewis readily agreed to meet with them the next morning and then insisted that they all have lunch. Bill opened the conversation with a provocative statement: "I don't like that preacher, Doctor Drew, that you have in *Babbitt!*" Lewis took that protest for a topic, and they argued all morning. At one point, Bill said, "You don't know anything about being a preacher. I wish you would write a real preacher book: a man who lives and walks and has a being, not all good, not all bad—some of both—a human being!"

"By gosh, I'll do it!" said Lewis. "That will be my next book. Let me come to see you in Detroit and live with you and talk with you and meet your people and see what it's all about."

Lewis and Stidger did meet in Detroit, but the author stayed for only a few days. He was not yet ready to write his "preacher book." The two exchanged correspondence over the next three years. Bill sent Lewis a sermon he had written on *Babbitt:*

A DRAMATIC BOOK SERMON STUDY OF BABBITT

Every preacher ought to know *Babbitt,* for several reasons. One reason is that everybody will be talking about it and asking him if he has read it. Another reason is that this book pictures for us our cornfed civilization. Third, it will give preachers a vehicle for teaching a great truth. That is the reason why I have included this book in the list of my "dramatic book sermons."

It is a satire. But it is a true one.

Sinclair Lewis has been made a revolutionist for the same reason that a lot of editors of church papers have been made revolutionists. For instance, I read an editorial a while ago in a great church paper which called attention to the fact that last year we people in America spent:

$750,000,000 for cosmetics.

$50,000,000 for chewing gum.

$350,000,000 for sodas.

$3,000,000,000 for joy rides.

While the rest of the world was starving, we did this. . . . That is the reason we need books like *Babbitt* and that is the reason why preachers may well use it to shake awake our complacent audiences who feel that they have done well enough and given generously enough to missions and to starving humanity. . . .

We may use the book to show what a narrow, sin-blighted life brings one to; and then show what poor Babbitt's life needed; what the desert of his prosaic life needed, to make it "blossom as the rose," was the water of Christ flowing through it. And, if you want a text, I know of none that will fit *Babbitt* better than that found in Matthew 16:26: "For what shall it profit a man if he shall gain the whole world and forfeit his own soul?"

That is Babbitt's spirit. He is fat-bodied, fat-eared, fat-eyed, fat-souled. He has starved his spirit. His chief aim in life is to make money, but in doing so he loses his own eternal soul.[3]

Lewis replied to Bill's letter with appreciation:

25 Belknap Road
Hartford, Connecticut
November 13, 1922
Dear Bill,

That was a great boost—the Babbitt sermon and the program you so thoughtfully gave me. When are you coming this way? We have a bed and a chop always ready for you—and plenty of talk.

> *My best,*
> *Sinclair Lewis*[4]

From the moment they met, Sinclair Lewis and Bill Stidger seemed destined to be great friends. They were the same age, thirty-seven, having both been born in 1885; had grown up in small towns (Lewis in Sauk Centre, Minnesota—a "prairie village," as he characterized it); were brilliant speakers; had graduated from major Eastern colleges (Lewis went to Yale); had worked as journalists and loved to write; and had traveled widely. They shared the attributes of red hair, blue eyes, and fiery tempers, and both knew that they were charismatic. Lewis had even considered going into the ministry and was becoming increasingly fascinated with the ministry as a topic of a novel.

When Lewis visited Bill in Detroit in August 1924, he was interviewed by a reporter from the *Detroit News* who asked about his next project. Lewis replied: "I have had the idea for a long time that I might do a book about a certain type of clergyman, one man in Detroit especially making me want to write it as he fits into my imaginary character so well."

The article went on to observe:

Long, lean, lank and red-headed, Mr. Lewis seems filled with a kind of nervous energy that he works off in his high-pressure conversation. His freely gesturing hands aid his extreme volubility, and it is apparent that if he had not chosen the literary profession for his career he might have gained a measure of fame on the stage.

While Mr. Lewis is primarily a literary man, his grasp of contemporary events is astounding and his rare good judgment in things other than the creation of fiction is no less remarkable, as might be shown in a question he was asked. "What, Mr. Lewis," asked a serious-mined person, "do you think of the economic and political situation in this country today?"

Mr. Lewis fixed the questioner with a large blue gaze and pondered for a moment. He seemed to be searching for a thought. Then suddenly a radiant smile spread over his large and rather scattered features and astutely he made answer, "Yes."[5]

In the fall of 1925, after two months' vacation in Colorado with Iva and Betty (now thirteen years old)—during which Bill wrote his one and only novel, *Mother Man*, a work that was given a swift interment—Bill Stidger began his ministry in Kansas City, Missouri.

His first Sunday at the Linwood Boulevard Methodist Episcopal Church was on September 24, 1925, and, characteristically, Bill made a big splash. In his sermon, he declared, "I am mighty glad to get back to America. For the cities of the East can't be termed American. There the population is from 90 to 95 percent foreign-born. Here it is just the opposite. I expect to find here more of the spirit of fair play, friendliness, neighborliness—qualities that are peculiarly American. The people of Europe, born and bred in an atmosphere of intrigue and threatening eruption, naturally are suspicious of everyone." He went on to attack the fundamentalists, who, he said, "are causing confusion by trying to take the Bible for something it isn't. The Bible is not a book of science, nor literature—although it contains the finest literature in the world—nor history, although it tells the story of the Hebrew people. It is a book of religion, which tells the story of the striving of mankind to find God."[6] Stidger's bluntest words directed at the fundamentalists were, "How ignorant and stupid are those who refuse to listen to the voice of science; who fail to recognize that these stops [scientific discoveries] are only a part of the great organ of the universe that the Great Organist—God—is playing forever and a day."[7] Finally, he plunged into a defense of former president Woodrow Wilson's vain efforts to support the League of Nations, and he did this with full knowledge of how conservative Kansas City and his congregation were.

The next week, the most prominent minister in Kansas City, Dr. Burris Jenkins, complimented Bill on his liberalism and his bravery in brandishing it publicly in so conservative a community:

> Dr. Stidger! Dr. Stidger! Don't you know that this is the blackest spot on the map for Wilsonphobia? How do you dare to come here and declare that Wilson's name will stand high on the rolls of fame and immortality, when those who have opposed him will be forgotten in the dust? Didn't you come here to prophecy smooth things? Didn't you come here to get popular? Or did you by any chance come here to tell the plain truth?
>
> Then how in thunder did you succeed in getting the newspapers here to print what you had to say, and especially the one newspaper that has always hated Wilson worse than a bunch of rattlesnakes to print a column of your sermon? We have heard that you are a magician, and as Studdert-Kennedy would say, "By our holy aunt," we begin to think you are!
>
> Dr. Stidger! Dr. Stidger! However much Wilsonphobia is abroad in this community there is one thing about Kansas City—it likes a man who dares to

tell it what he believes to be the truth, without fear or favor. Strange as it may seem, you will not lose any friends by your last Sunday's sermon. Strength to your elbow. May you be always as fearless as you then showed yourself to be.[8]

The *Journal-Post,* reporting on a speech Bill had made to the Advertising Club on the same weekend as his first church service, described him as a "high-pressure, ink-burning go-getter in the Kansas City pulpit":

"Publicity is the most important requisite for a successful ministry," the Rev. William L. Stidger, new pastor of Linwood Boulevard M.E. Church, said today in an address before the Advertising Club. . . . Mr. Stidger said he challenged any Kansas City theater to produce as entertaining a program as he intends to arrange for his church this winter. He said Sinclair Lewis, Edwin Markham, and Eddie Guest, newspaperman and poet, would be three of the leading attractions.[9]

Betty later gave her own perspective on Kansas City:

Dad's church was over on Linwood Boulevard. It was the most churchy church we had ever had. Not only were there beautiful stained-glass windows but there was also a wonderful pipe organ with echo chimes. The congregation was rich and conservative. Dad conducted his Wednesday services over the radio, and I was allowed to sit in his office and take down all the telephone messages that were called in: "Am sitting by the radio in St. Louis and getting a heartful of religion": P. L. Jones; "Will you please sing 'In the Garden'": R. E. Goodman, etc. After I copied them down, I would self-consciously, but with a sense of the dramatic, take the notes in to Dad and he would read the messages to the listening audience.

All went well until one Wednesday, Dad, carried away by his own fervor at the close of his address, announced the singing of "Rock of Ages" and then proceeded to sing along with the chorus. When I was a child and awakened in the middle of the night frightened by a nightmare, Dad would come into my room, lie beside me with my head cradled on his shoulder, and sing "Jesus Lover of My Soul." He was never in true pitch and always chose the wrong key, but that unmelodious voice soothed me to peaceful slumber. Not so, however, for his radio audience. After his Wednesday night "performance," telephone calls and wires by the hundreds came in, and all week letters flooded his office. They all demanded that "the man who has such a terrible voice please be released from the choir." Dad said that there was at least one good result: he found out how many people were listening.[10]

Barely had Bill been settled in Kansas City than he received, in October 1925, a letter from Lewis: "I am now ready to write that preacher book." He said he planned to spend several weeks in a hotel, and he asked Bill to try to keep his calendar free so they could talk about the ministry. Bill lost absolutely no time in telling his congregation of this good news. In the November 1, 1925, church bulletin, he reported the following: "Sinclair Lewis—He who wrote *Main Street, Babbitt, Arrowsmith*—wrote the pastor last week: 'I'll be with you for a week the second week in February. I'll look in on your Prayer Meeting; I'll talk to your people; I'll be happy with you.' Linwood Boulevard Methodist Church will have many visitors of his kind this year."[11]

A second letter arrived in which Lewis advanced his arrival date and asked if he could stay in the Stidgers' home. He wrote, "Ask your wife if she will have me. Incidentally, I will want to talk over with you the reality of religion and what conversion means, and a lot of things like that."[12] As Bill later told his congregation, "Mrs. Stidger and I decided we would be willing to do that much in the way of hospitality to a famous author, whom, up to that time, we never had had in our home; and whom Mrs. Stidger never even had met. Nor do we have any regrets about having him. He was an easy guest, an interesting one, and everybody in our home liked him."[13]

Harcourt Brace, Lewis's publisher, announced on January 13, 1926, that Lewis was departing for Kansas City to spend ten days with the "Rev. William L. Stidger, the prominent minister."[14] Lewis was at the Stidgers' home for two weeks. Betty's version of the novelist's visit was as follows:

> He was a fascinating guest, very considerate, but not too conscientious. He had the florist deliver huge baskets of flowers to his charming hostess, my Mother, and then charged them to Dad. He raved over our Jessie's cooking and then Jessie would forgo the vacuuming to concoct some special dish for supper and likely as not "Red" Lewis would just eat at the Athletic Club that night. He slept until noon, used innumerable bath towels, wiped his razor blade on Mother's linen face towels, refused to send his shirts to the laundry because Jessie was such a nice ironer, brought a veritable host of friends home late at night and expected sustenance and gaiety.
>
> Jessie, our black cook, allowed Mr. Lewis to trample on her good nature—but just let me suggest having a friend come home for lunch and Jessie would grumble all day. She was a character—wore a wig and false dentures, white uniforms and a chef's white starched cap. She looked fine if she was all there but Jessie had a husband she fought with. She would come to work many mornings without her teeth because "Sam was mad on her and had hidden her teeth." That wasn't as bad as the two times he really became angry. Those days she came without teeth or wig and she was a wonder to behold without her accessories and with the chef's cap perched on her shining brown dome.
>
> Dad was most cooperative while Mr. Lewis was doing his research work. He took him to all the Wednesday morning preachers' meetings, instigated discussion groups so that Mr. Lewis could fully understand preachers and their problems, introduced him to other preachers and generally was errand boy and source of knowledge for all questions that Mr. Lewis could think up through the space of six months.[15]

From Bill's point of view, he and his wife, Iva, had some wonderful conversations with Lewis in the privacy of their living room:

> We used to sit in front of the fireplace and talk of his books, particularly of *Arrowsmith,* and old Dr. Gottlieb, the research character in that masterpiece who, as Lewis used to tell us, "ached a little for research and had a divine curiosity." Dr. Gottlieb was the idol of all the boys in the medical school, and young Arrowsmith wanted his sweetheart, Leora, to admire that old scientist as much as he did. One day on the campus Dr. Gottlieb walked past them, bent and stooped as if moving with pain. Young Arrowsmith longed to run after him.
>   Leora said, "Is that the Professor Gottlieb you're always talking about?"
>   "Yes! and say!" young Arrowsmith eagerly replied to his sweetheart. "How does he strike you?"
>   "I don't know—Sandy, he's the greatest man I've ever seen! I don't know how I know, but he is! He's a great man! I wish—I wish we were going to see him again. He's so—oh, he's like a sword—no, he's like a brain walking. Oh, Sandy, he looked so wretched. I wanted to cry."
>   And as we sat before the open fireplace going over that immortal scene in that great masterpiece, I said to Mr. Lewis, "That's the greatest character you ever painted, and that is the finest scene in any of your books."
>   "Maybe you're right," Lewis said, "I fell pretty hard for Dr. Gottlieb, for he was a truly consecrated scientist."[16]
>   Lewis also talked about his writing of *Main Street.* Initially, he said, he intended calling it *The Village Virus.* It was the story of a man who had returned "to the small town from college with ideals. Then, after a year, that same man would go to his office unshaven. Another year, and he wouldn't care whether his linen was dirty or clean. In three or four years, he had slumped and slouched. He no longer walked erect. He had started out as a lawyer with ideals, and he ended with deals."[17]

The success of the book, both Bill and Lewis agreed, was the "universal picture of us in it—we were curious to see ourselves as we were—and are—God pity us."[18] Bill preached that *Main Street* was a book of regressions, the story of men and women who had lost their ideals; he urged his congregation instead to follow the indomitable spirit of the apostle Paul, who, no matter what he had attained, kept striving, never losing sight of his ideals.

Rumors of Lewis's reasons for being in Kansas City provoked keen interest on the part of the newspapers. In an interview, Lewis tried to disabuse them of the idea that he desired to write a book on the ministry. The *Kansas City Star* of January 18, 1926, reported:

> Kansas City can settle back into being itself again. It is not being considered for the next Sinclair Lewis novel. The author admitted as much today at the home of Dr. William L. Stidger, 6521 Wornall Road. "There is a great deal of talk going around," Mr. Lewis said slyly, "about my writing a book on Kansas

City Methodists and Dr. Stidger in particular. Maybe the Methodists are trying to get some publicity. But I can't truthfully support them in it. I'm staying at Dr. Stidger's because he lets me act nice and comfortable, and not be on my good behavior all the time."[19]

Sinclair Lewis kept his promise to speak at Bill's church. He preached a sermon on January 24, 1926, before "an audience which filled every seat, jammed the aisles and the doors and peered even through the ventilators. Several hundreds were turned away."[20] It was an upbeat talk, directed at the idealism of youth. "I want to tell the youngsters," Lewis said fervently, "those who are dreaming, those who had rather be a research expert or a poet—without hope of reward—to go on in their wickedness. If they are insane, I am insane with them and I find my insanity an incomparably agreeable state."[21]

Virtually the last thing he did in Kansas City was to inscribe in a copy of *The Trail of the Hawk,* one of his early books, the following:

TO THE STIDGERS

Especially to Betty, and Iva and Bill
AND Atta Boy [a stray dog that Betty had adopted], from the fifth member of the family,

Sinclair Lewis
K.C., January 28, 1926

For those in Kansas City and for Bill and his family, Lewis's visit was a great beginning of a wonderful project. On February 3, 1926, just after he left Kansas City, Lewis wrote his publisher, "I got more out of Kansas City for the preacher book than could be imagined; it was not only Bill Stidger—I wrote to Don [Brace] how really excellent his book sermons are, and I hope you send him out all the books he wants—but at least a dozen other ministers of all denominations, who varied from mild sympathy to real friendliness. I am going back there to start planning the book as soon as I can ask any one of these dozen or more preachers for the information I want, stay there a couple of months, and after that[,] . . . God knows! I feel fine and think the adventure is in every way a great success."[22]

Lewis also wrote his friend H. L. Mencken, the famous critic, "I had two weeks there, staying with a Methodist padre who is a hell of a good fellow. I am going to fight bitterly with you about the intelligence of some of the more liberal Methodists, Baptists and Presbyterians, even—or especially—in the corn belt. I met a dozen ministers in Kansas City who form a liberal-preacher group and are as vehemently opposed to fundamentalism as you. It is true that most of them are for prohibition and reforming in general; it is equally true that they have kidded themselves into a belief in Jesus as the Christ; and it is true that they have become sentimental about the value of the communion of souls in a church meeting. But on the whole, I found them no more filled with bunk than any group of writers, doctors, or editors that I know."[23]

On April 4, 1926, Lewis wrote that he was back in Kansas City and about to settle in at the Ambassador Hotel in order to get busy on a definite plan for his novel. He had now found a minister, Dr. Birkhead, on whom he would base some of Gantry's characteristics. Lewis described him as a "Unitarian and generally disillusioned preacher who was for ten years a Methodist preacher whom I'll use as an encyclopedia for data about church organization and the like."[24] In the same letter Lewis began to talk with his publisher about the title for his proposed book. He asked that the titles "The Reverend," "Reverend Bloor" and a third conceivable candidate, "The Salesman of Salvation," all be shown to a group of people to test whether any might work. He went on to say that the "Reverend Bloor" title might grow on his colleagues at Harcourt as it became more distinctive in their minds, "just as we all liked 'Babbitt' better and better as it became more familiar to us."[25]

Lewis added, "Gawd, the new novel goes swell, I have a perfect corker to assist me on it—the Reverend Dr. Birkhead, of whom I wrote you. He has given me exactly the dope I need. Twenty new scenes appear every hour and at the present moment I feel fairly sure it is going to be much the biggest and much the most dramatic thing I have ever done."[26]

Without knowing Lewis's agenda for his novel, Bill continued to court his attention, although he was taken aback by Lewis's growing interest in Birkhead. This seemed odd, on the face of it, because Birkhead had such a checkered religious history. Born into a Baptist family, he had had an adolescent conversion at a Methodist revival meeting, become licensed to preach at eighteen, attended a Methodist college, and conducted revival meetings, all with a fundamentalist bent. (Lewis himself had come from a fundamentalist Congregationalist background.) Birkhead's faith gradually had failed him, and he had become an agnostic, while still preaching Methodism. At last, in 1915, he became a Unitarian and eventually pastor at All Souls' Unitarian Church in Kansas City. He described himself as an "immoralist" who promised Lewis that he "wouldn't try to reform him."[27] What Bill and his fellow ministers misunderstood was that Lewis was slipping away from them, like a man who had let go of the gunwale of the boat and was sinking into the depths. Lewis had no interest in writing about their liberalism and their efforts to bridge the gap between science and religion. He was on a witch hunt to find out what was wrong, not what was right, and Birkhead was made to order for his purpose.

Lewis's book had already evolved beyond either the lines of *Babbitt* or *Arrowsmith*, in which Lewis had been sympathetic toward his main characters. Lewis and Mencken had negative views regarding the ministry and were alarmed at what they regarded as a rising tide of fundamentalism across the country, particularly the evangelistic fundamentalism spreading in rural communities. Lewis believed "that religious fundamentalists and fanatics sought a takeover of the government intending to use the power of the state to coerce behavior in accordance with the beliefs of fundamentalism."[28] Elmer Gantry, the character Lewis was creating, was part Stidger in kinetic energy and physical appearance, and part Birkhead spiritually. But Gantry became a man who, in Lewis's words, "got everything from the church, except, perhaps, any longing whatever for decency and kindness and reason."[29] Through the actions of Elmer Gantry, Lewis hoped to discredit both fundamentalism and evangelism.

Sinclair Lewis's books were elaborate satires designed to illustrate the author's strongly held beliefs about doctors, businessmen, preachers, or the values held by citizens living in small towns across the country. Harrison Smith said of Lewis that he was a "youthful reformer with the illusion that the lot of men and women would be bettered if their faults could be pointed out to them." Lewis made his novels and therefore his ideas seem plausible by providing exhaustive information and detail on his locales and characters. Bill was therefore important to Lewis as a source of vivid impressions that Lewis could hang on his Elmer Gantry creation. Lewis would see nothing wrong with making Gantry like Stidger; in fact, through his writing, Lewis could argue he was giving Stidger a kind of immortality.

Bill later described the process that the novelist employed during his stay at the Ambassador Hotel:

Naturally, since he was writing a preacher book, I wanted him to meet as many of the finest preachers of this city as I could. I took him to the Methodist preachers' meeting. I took him to various churches. I introduced him to a group of so called "liberals" in the city.

It is only fair to say these men, whom Sinclair Lewis dubbed his Sunday school class, had been meeting for a long time.

It is also only fair to say that every man in that class knew what was going on while Lewis was here. We have been dubbed "guinea pigs," on which a writer was experimenting. We cooperated with him to help him get the background for his literary work. When he came to these meetings and hurled his invectives at us and at the Church, there was a general understanding we would be patient with his egotism and with his condition. At other times he talked quietly, entertainingly and cleverly.

He would leave the room a few minutes and when he came back he would talk like a motorcycle going ninety miles an hour. He would stride up and down like a hyena in a cage.

Lewis usually opened with a bombardment: "What the hell right has the Church to exist anyhow? What accounting can you loafers give society? What right have you to draw salaries? What do you believe in anyhow? What have you to give to the world?"

After those opening remarks the preachers had their comeback. Many answers were given, which thoughtful visitors from time to time, like William Allen White and others, agreed were real answers, but as far as we learned none seemed good answers to Mr. Lewis.

The group was aware of just what Mr. Lewis wanted. He was honest with them and they were fair with him. Everyone had a stimulating time. Lewis has a quick mind, even if it is not a profound mind—and he awakened that group of preachers as they never had been awakened before.

A preacher left one of the first of the meetings and exposed the dreadful fact that though it was a group of preachers they did not even say grace before they ate.

"That bird is a crook and I'll prove it to you before I leave this town," declared Lewis.

He did.[30]

Samuel Harkness, a liberal Presbyterian, later wrote his recollections of Lewis's "Sunday School" sessions. He said that Lewis would fling verbal grenades into the theological dugouts. "Why don't you tell your congregations that you are agnostics?" Lewis stormed. "The conventional Christ is sheer myth. Your Jesus is the hat rack on which men have hung their prejudices through the ages. Do you not realize that organized Christianity has had two thousand years to conquer the mind—and has failed? What other idea has ever had a like chance? Don't you see that no man can be a successful preacher unless he is a fundamentalist, because dogmatic denunciation is the intellectual gait of the people in your pews?"[31]

Lewis was invited to speak at the Linwood Forum, a weekly lecture series sponsored by Dr. Burris Jenkins of the Linwood Boulevard Christian Church. The crowd that packed the auditorium on April 18, 1926, heard him flay fundamentalist preachers who had been reported as claiming that God had struck down Luther Burbank because he preached evolution and was a nonbeliever in God. Lewis cried, "Many pastors are seeing in the death of Burbank a divine sign. They say he forgot heaven and hell. I say, somewhat impertinently perhaps, that Burbank gave back to God all that God gave to him. If he had to stop and take care of heaven and hell, they must be puny institutions indeed! Is there no joy, no greatness, in living? Is it the fear of hell that makes us good? If this theory is a part of your Christian religion, then damn your Christian religion."[32]

Lewis, warming to his task, charged on. "Burbank said he was an infidel, and so he was 'struck down.' William Jennings Bryan declared he was a fundamentalist, and he became a 'martyr,' dying in his glory! These *pious* people know Burbank died only because he was an infidel and yet Bryan died at an age fifteen years younger than he. Why didn't God strike Burbank down at the time of his utterances and make things clear?"[33]

At this point, Lewis pulled out his pocket watch and dramatically placed it on the rostrum. "If there is a fundamentalist God, I challenge Him to strike me dead within the next ten minutes." Taking the rapt audience—which filled the church—into his confidence, Lewis commented on his challenge: "Here's a lovely chance for God to show what He can do." He continued lambasting the fundamentalists and then took a swipe at most ministers, saying, "The trouble with the average sermon is that it is so darn dull." The newspapers certainly did not find the famous writer to be dull, and Lewis was described by the *Kansas City Times* as having "flamed"[34] in the Linwood Church. The story, much to Lewis's delight, was sent to newspapers across the country. It was great publicity, including the comparisons that some reporters drew between Lewis's challenge and a similar one that George Bernard Shaw had made on an earlier occasion: "I give God only three minutes to strike me dead," Shaw had cried, "because I'm a very busy man."[35] Lewis also immensely enjoyed the power the pulpit gave him and was doing dry runs for *Elmer Gantry* sermons yet to be created.

Less than one month later, in early May 1926, Lewis orchestrated another controversy, once more designed to attract attention, when he formally turned down the Pulitzer Prize awarded him for *Arrowsmith*. Rumors that he would win the prize had circulated, and Lewis had encouraged them. He rejected the Pulitzer, however, on the grounds that no writer should accept any such honors because doing so implied he had written (and encouraged others to write) according to guidelines established by the prize-awarding juries. There was, perhaps, a better reason for Lewis's action. He had been angry since the *"Main Street* burglary" in 1920, when the Pulitzer selection committee chose Lewis's book but the Board of Trustees of Columbia University, which had the final say, overturned its committee's recommendation and awarded the prize to Edith Wharton's *Age of Innocence*.[36] In 1930, moreover, Lewis was to display no qualms about receiving awards, gladly accepting the Nobel Prize in literature. Besides thumbing his nose at the establishment by turning down "their" Pulitzer Prize, he also surrounded himself and Kansas City with a bright spotlight of national attention, especially useful in the promotion of his forthcoming "preacher book."

In mid-May of 1926, Lewis the whirlwind departed and left behind a Kansas City dizzy and trying to steady itself. At their last meeting he told the ministers to whom Bill had introduced him, "I'm going to give you hell, but I love every one of you."[37] Lewis headed for his father's home in Sauk Centre, Minnesota, where he planned to spend the summer writing his book. Accompanying him were Birkhead, whose help Lewis needed with his research, and Birkhead's wife and son.

Elmer Gantry was written during the summer and fall of 1926. His biographer, Mark Schorer, says that Lewis's life fell to pieces as he came to the end of the book. Late in the summer of 1926, his father died quite suddenly, and Lewis, by the accounts of his friends, became considerably depressed. Later, in Washington, D.C., where he and his wife took a house so that he could complete the novel, just as he had done previously with *Main Street,* his marriage fell apart. H. L. Mencken was later to write that the last thirty thousand words of *Elmer Gantry* were created "in a state of drunkenness. . . . He had hardly delivered the manuscript to his publisher when he was taken off to a rest home to be 'dried out.'"[38] This issue of drunkenness that appears in *Elmer Gantry* may be the author's own contribution to Gantry's character.

By late January 1927, early proofs of Lewis's book had been made available to reviewers and a limited number of others—including Bill. Betty wrote:

> Dad had occasion to travel east. Mr. Lewis was on his way to Europe and found it impossible to see Dad and make an explanation—"Bill," he said, over the phone, "you won't like Elmer; you'll hate him like hell. But he would be written. Someday I'll write your kind of a preacher."
>
> On the way back to Kansas City, Dad had to wait between trains at Chicago, William Allen White was waiting too, so they made a twosome for lunch. After discussing many subjects, they quite naturally got around to the subject of Sinclair Lewis and *Elmer Gantry*. Mr. White expressed his regret that such a book would ever be published. "You know, Bill," he continued, "Lewis asked God to strike him dead in church!"

"Yes, and I was disappointed at the results," said Dad.

"But you shouldn't be," White added. "God works in wondrous ways. He did strike Lewis dead, from the neck up!"[39]

On February 9, 1927, Alfred Harcourt, the publisher, wrote Lewis, who had just arrived in Europe, that he had received a long letter from Bill. "He doesn't like the book, just as you told him he wouldn't, but hopes for its success. Kansas City seems het up by talk about it, and the sale there will start with a rush; in fact, it begins to look as if it will start with a rush everywhere. I had a note from Mencken saying it is magnificent—even better than *Babbitt*, which you know has been his favorite till now. You wrote it; we'll sell it; the public will scrap about it."[40]

On the March 9, 1927, the day before the publication date, Harcourt wrote, "We are printing up another carload [that is, railroad carload] of paper, which will make the actual printing before publication 138,000. The Book-of-the-Month Club will take between 35,000 and 40,000. I expect reorders to come in promptly." On March 11, 1927, the day after *Elmer Gantry* was published, Harcourt cabled Lewis: "News stories everywhere. *Kansas Star* five columns. Reviews violent either way. Clergy hot. . . . Reorders already. Everything lovely."[41]

The *Kansas City Star* ran seven articles on various aspects of *Elmer Gantry* on March 10, 1927, the book's official publishing date. On that morning, bookstore employees arriving for work found customers already waiting outside their doors. Lewis's new book flew off the shelves at a rate that storeowners admitted was unprecedented. The *Star*'s lead article was a review by William Allen White, a known admirer of Lewis's writings. The *Star* prefaced the review with the following note to its readers:

> Since it became known a year ago that Sinclair Lewis's next novel would deal with the clergy and that much of the material had been gathered here, its publication has been awaited eagerly by Kansas City and this vicinity. Today the new book, *Elmer Gantry*, goes on sale. William Allen White has written for the *Star* the first impression of the new novel. His review may be considered the opening volley in the controversy that is bound to rage. But Mr. Lewis, perhaps America's greatest satirist, always arouses controversy. Previous novels, *Main Street, Babbitt* and *Arrowsmith*, were bombs to those who were being satirized, or thought they were.[42]

The opening and concluding paragraphs of White's devastating comments follow:

> Sinclair Lewis stood in the pulpit of a Kansas City church last spring and defied God to strike him dead. So far as Sinclair Lewis, the artist, is concerned, in the book *Elmer Gantry*, God took him at his word.
>
> Sinclair Lewis, the artist, is dead. He may rise again; probably he will. But in this book he got so excited making faces at God that he forgot his craftsmanship.
>
> Nevertheless, this is a book which should be widely read, a book which undoubtedly will be widely read. It is controversial. It is a polemic against

commercialized religion, but Lewis's satire is so deep and cutting as to be broad and unconvincing. . . .

Hate overcast Lewis's eye and his art failed him. It is a fine art that can make a villainous hero and make us pity him while scorning him, but it is poor art that makes a basswood figure on casters that moves through the plot without the reader's sympathy and finally without the reader's interest. The man cannot hate and be an artist. Hate poisons any art. Unless pity which is akin to love softens and reveals the truth about a novelist's villains, they are dull and uninteresting. After all, in art and in life "the greatest of these is love."[43]

The second article was "Does Gantry Live Here?" with the subtitle "Speculation, Begun Before Publication, is Up To the Reader to Answer." The third article was "Not Directly from Life," in which the Reverend Birkhead explained that the characters in the book were composites. The fourth article, entitled "Flaws Seen By Two Pastors," liberally quoted Bill's disappointment in the final product. Bill said, "We were looking for some criticism of the Church—of its capitalistic ways, of its attitude toward peace. Instead we got this story of a little, perverted minister, an altogether impossible picture, entirely unreal, not even a good caricature. I'll tell you what this book is. It's the biological autobiography of Sinclair Lewis. *Elmer Gantry* is a picture of what Lewis would do if he were a preacher. And he thinks others are that way. I say this without any personal animosity against Lewis. I like him. I am only talking about his art."[44] The second pastor referred to in the article was Dr. I. M. Hargett, pastor of Grand Avenue Temple, who commented, "Well, they say I'm Elmer Gantry. But the book is overdrawn. It's preposterous. Lewis doesn't know anything about what we preachers are working for in our churches." Besides himself, Hargett mentioned Bill, Birkhead, and Burris Jenkins as characters alluded to in the book. "They say Stidger kind of expected himself to be the chief character. I guess he isn't disappointed it didn't come out that way now. But I think Lewis is taking a little slam at Bill in some of his prayer meetings."[45]

In the fifth article, "Lewis Came Here By Chance," with the subtitle "Acquaintanceship With Dr. Stidger Inspired His Visit, Which Was Lively," reference was made of Lewis's early contact with Bill. A sixth article was entitled "An Array of Pulpit Types," which contrasted the clergy types found in the novel. The last article concluded with a statement that book dealers were said to believe that more consumer inquiries had been received about *Elmer Gantry* than about any other novel before the day of its release.

Betty said, "Dad was very blue about Mr. Lewis and *Elmer,* for now the reviewers were not only panning the book but hinting quite boldly about Lewis's source of information."[46]

Bill saw himself portrayed in *Elmer Gantry.* He had presided over a great new church in Detroit like Gantry's Wellspring Church, with its "dozens of Sunday School rooms, a gymnasium, a social room with a stage . . . and over it all a revolving electric cross and a debt."[47] St. Mark's Church in Detroit had all the features described and a weekly attendance of five thousand, standing room only. Bill championed the importance of attracting younger people to church to keep them as members as they became adults. Only this, he reasoned, would stave off the decline in church membership then occurring nationally. Lewis has Gantry deliver a Chautauqua lecture entitled "Whoa up, Youth!" exhorting abstinence, chastity, industry and honesty, its "heaven-vaulting poetic passage about Love (the only bow on life's dark cloud, the morning and the evening star)."[48] Lewis writes that Gantry's speech on youth became one of the "classics among Chautauqua masterpieces."[49] Bill had met Lewis at a Chautauqua conference.

Lewis recalled Bill's raid against the brothels on the Barbary Coast in San Francisco and in San Jose and his hounding the acting mayor of Detroit out of office for failing to enforce Prohibition. Newspapers avidly covered Bill's crusading efforts, and he was often on the front page. Lewis has Gantry announcing from the pulpit that the "authorities of Zenith were 'deliberately conniving in protected vice' and that he would give the addresses and ownerships of sixteen brothels. . . . There were front-page newspaper stories, yelping replies by the mayor and chief of police, re-replies from Elmer."[50]

Bill, like Sinclair Lewis, had been a reporter. He understood the importance of publicity and the press. He worked with the Advertising Council in Kansas City and introduced Lewis to the group. Lewis says of Elmer: "But of all the clerics, none was so hearty, so friendly, to the reporters as the Reverend Elmer Gantry. His rival parsons were merely cordial to the sources of publicity when they called. Elmer did his own calling."[51]

Bill was given honorary doctor of divinity degrees by Allegheny College and Kansas Wesleyan. Gantry is called on by the president of Abernathy College, an institution of Methodist learning. The book continues:

> "Hm," Elmer mused. "I bet he's out raising money. Nothing doing! What the devil does he think we are!" and aloud: "Go out and bring Dr. Dodd right in, Miss Bundle. A great man! A wonderful educator! You know—President of Abernathy College!"[52]

To the request by President Dodd to seek funds from Gantry's congregation, Elmer says,

> "Can't do it, doctor. Impossible. We haven't begun to pay for this church. . . . But possibly two years from now—Though frankly," and Elmer laughed brightly, "I don't know why the people of Wellspring should contribute to a college which hasn't thought enough of Wellspring's pastor to give him a Doctor of Divinity degree!"[53]

The degree Elmer sought was promised and delivered.

Lewis not only appropriated incidents from Bill's life for *Elmer Gantry* but went on to create a cynical, calculating, mercenary, hypocritical motivation behind these actions. Bill's Stidger's own public persona had been built by himself, like a great building, brick by brick. He had started from nothing and produced a public personality and a national reputation through his writing and speaking, as well as through what was written about him. Lewis seized Bill's public persona and twisted it to his own ends. Bill had no one to blame for this misdeed but himself; he had gone out of his way to cultivate his relationship with Lewis and to encourage him in his latest task. No one who knew Bill well could confuse him, a liberal thinker, with Gantry the fundamentalist. But regarding the insinuations of greed, or cynicism, in Gantry's character, might not a reader who did not know Bill well wonder whether Lewis was describing what the real Bill Stidger was like?

In the three days that separated the publication date from his next Sunday service, Bill's temper had time to rise to a fever pitch. His sermon played to a packed church, filled with people loyal to him who were on the edge of their seats to see what he would have to say. His text was "And Ben-hadad Was Drunk," which gave him license to lavish attention on Lewis's serious drinking problem. He said Lewis would often arrive at meetings with ministers Bill had introduced him to "red-faced, nervous and much the worse for drink."[54] He declared publicly, "Sinclair Lewis was drunk when he wrote *Elmer Gantry*."[55] He added, "Elmer Gantry came out of a mind whose standards of conduct and morals are such that if they were universally adopted or condoned would destroy the institution of marriage, the home, the American constitution and the Church itself."[56] The newspapers reported that Stidger "spoke with intense feeling in his denunciation of the book as utterly untrue and a 'big shell' on the way over but a 'dud' when it landed; the work of an 'inflamed mind.'"[57]

Bill continued:

Now, as to the book itself, it is untrue. It is dishonest. It is not even a good caricature. Dr. Harry Rogers, who has been in Kansas City twenty years, told me he had never known a man like that in the ministry or anything like him. Dr. B. A. Jenkins, who has been here twenty years, says the same thing. They cannot remember a single man, in the very city in which Lewis did his laboratory work, who has been untrue morally and survived. The book is written to sell. Everybody who knows "Red" Lewis knows that.

Elmer Gantry is not typical. He is not even an isolated case. Lewis has drawn an impossible character, and he did not do it with a worthy purpose, and there is no defense left for him, even from his best friends. If Lewis really had handled some of the big problems and faults of the church, we would have hailed him as liberator instead of castigator. If he had said the Church was capitalistic; if he had said we did not live up to the Christ teachings of poverty and peace; if he had attacked Christian ministers for living in luxury while pretending to be followers of a Christ who had nowhere to lay his head; we should have been glad. If he even had handled the great and dominant problem of fundamentalism and liberalism in a real way we could have forgiven him. We who read *Main Street, Babbitt,* and *Arrowsmith* felt Lewis was capable of doing the big thing in this preacher book. That was the real reason we wanted to help him.

Lewis didn't remember four or five of the finest preachers in America. Before I came to this city I knew of its ministers. I knew of them as wholesome family men. I saw to it that Lewis met them. He forgot he had heard several of these men give their personal testimony to the efficacy of religion and the Church. He forgot that these men, without fear from his hectic onslaughts, gave him such personal testimonies as a man like [William] James in *The Varieties of Religious Experience* admits are true and valid.

I remember one dear old lady on whom I called. Lewis asked to go with me. She was dying. I prayed with her. She turned to Mr. Lewis and said, "I am the richest woman in the world. I have my children about me. I have my church. I have my religion. You are a rich man and you are a great man. I only hope that, when you die, you will be as rich and as happy as I." Mr. Lewis seemed greatly impressed.

Lewis conducted the laboratory experiments and then refused to abide by the results, and his scientific friends, whom he met in writing *Arrowsmith,* would despise him for that.[58]

That Sunday and Monday, March 13 and 14, 1927, were unique in Kansas City. On Sunday at churches across the city, pastors railed against Lewis and his evil creation, *Elmer Gantry.* On Monday the newspapers enthusiastically reported the churches' abuse to Lewis and fanned the controversy. One church even advertised in the *Star* to attract those who wished to avoid the debate: "If you prefer to hear about Jesus Christ instead of *Elmer Gantry.*"

Lewis's spokesman, Birkhead, sprang to the novelist's defense. He answered Bill's charges against Lewis point by point. He claimed Bill could not know Lewis's "condition" when he wrote the book since only he, Birkhead, was present: "I will say that it was a base falsehood to charge that Mr. Lewis wrote the book while he was intoxicated." He also denied Bill's claim that Lewis's motivation in writing *Elmer Gantry* was commercial: "He was compelled by this inner urge to express himself in *Elmer Gantry* and not by financial considerations." Birkhead continued, "Mr. Lewis's personal habits are not concerned. He is not on trial, the preachers are. . . . [T]he preachers feel the sting of being portrayed realistically. . . . When they are criticized they usually reply by hurling epithets and by abusing their critics."[59]

This attack by Birkhead further incensed the clergy. Dr. Hargett of the Grand Avenue Temple in Kansas City said,

This preacher book of Sinclair Lewis's will provoke a great jubilee in hell . . . and be very pleasing here on earth to boozers, cynics, agnostics, atheists, louts, and all the underworld crowd. If you ever questioned the reality of the devil and devil possession, read this book. I doubt if the devil has a more clever propagandist and promoter than Sinclair Lewis. He must be very proud of him and extremely fond of him. The very name of the book, *Elmer Gantry,* has a sort of swinish swagger that fits its contents admirably. The yellow binding also is significant. Mr. Lewis came to Kansas City, got into the good graces and confidences of many of the preachers, formed what he called a Sunday school class out of them and pumped them dry. Now in this book he betrays them like a yellow dog.

For twenty-five years I have been in the ministry, and I have met many, many ministers, but I have not yet met Elmer Gantry, the drunkard, the blasphemer, the brazen hypocrite, the corrupter. Did you ever meet such a preacher? I never did. Elmer Gantry is a gross caricature of the Protestant churches and ministry. Unfair and written without any knowledge of the facts, it will do little harm and no good. The picture is so much overdrawn it will defeat its own purpose. He says so much, he does not say anything. The descendants of Judas are not all extinct.[60]

Again and again, Birkhead defended the book and its author: "Don't take the judgment of the preachers about *Elmer Gantry*. Naturally they'll yelp; they're hit. . . . I will speak two weeks from this morning about the book as a work of art and three weeks from this morning about '*Elmer Gantry*, and What's Wrong With the Preachers?' "[61]

Sinclair Lewis, in Venice, wrote Alfred Harcourt: "Bill Stidger in his comments on my book must have been hit hard from the way he squeals! I shan't answer him; Birkhead will do that!"[62]

Most reviewers, except Mencken, were negative about *Elmer Gantry*. In his sophisticated effort to destroy fundamentalism, Lewis was seen by most readers to be criticizing the entire church establishment, whether liberal or conservative. This was an unpopular message, and many libraries across the country banned *Elmer Gantry*. Others criticized Lewis on literary grounds. Rebecca West, for example, wrote a review in the *New York Herald Tribune Books* in which she stated that *Elmer Gantry* "is probably one of the most disappointing books that a man of genius has ever produced. It is full of willful abnegations of fine qualities. . . . Elmer Gantry, this snorting cringing creature, this offspring of the hippopotamus and the skunk, between whose coarse lips the texts sound as if he were munching sappy vegetation, under whose coarse hands sex becomes a series of gross acts of the body ending in grosser acts of the spirit, such as deceit and cruelty. . . . [Lewis] falls into these tricks of flat writing and lethargic handling of incidents. . . . He does not fulfill that necessary condition of the satirist: he has not entered into imaginative possession of those qualities that each of which he derides in others. . . . The result is that this book will not start any great movement towards enhanced sensitiveness of life, which might make people reject fake religion. It will start a purely factual controversy as to whether parsons do in any large numbers get drunk and toy with their stenographers, which is really a matter of very little importance."[63]

Charles W. Ferguson noted in the *Bookman*, "To say that the man has not fairly represented the ministry is to be unfair to him—obviously he never intended to."[64] Elmer Davis in the *New York Times Book Review* pointed to Lewis as preaching the gospel according to the prophet Mencken, who in *American Mercury* praised the book's design, shrewd observations, gargantuan humor, and main character, Elmer Gantry, as the "gaudy and glorious" crusading rogue.[65]

As for the Stidger–Lewis battle royal, a curious incident occurred almost a year later, in mid-1928. Betty describes it:

Bill Stidger, age nine, in 1894. He was the oldest of five children.

Roy Stidger, Bill's father, in 1894. His grocery was nearly ruined by his partner's embezzling. Roy worked for years to repay the outstanding debts.

Bill played tight end on the Central football team.

Iva, a senior at Allegheny College.

The Methodist bishops visited Allegheny College in the Spring of 1907.

Star baseball player turned evangelist, Billy Sunday.

Bill and Iva married in 1910. Betty, their daughter, was born in 1912 just as Bill, ready to be a preacher, graduated from Brown University.

Do Not Be Startled

Sunday Night
About 9 O'Clock

At the Strange Light

IN THE SKY

Not a Comet!
Not a New Planet!
BUT

An Electric Revolving Cross
❧—ON—❧
CALVARY CHURCH

Come to the Dedication Service and
See It Lighted for the First Time.
SPECIAL SERVICE at 7:45
Corner 19th Avenue and Judah Street

Calvary Church, built on a sand dune, needed a congregation. Bill invented an illuminated revolving cross that created a sensation and "packed 'em in."

Calvary Church, Sunset District, San Francisco: the first illuminated revolving cross—ever.

The Sunset District, home of Calvary Church, had little more than scattered houses and sand dunes in 1913.

There is a frightened look in Bill's eyes as he anticipates the dangers ahead at the "Center of Immensities."

"My best picture," wrote Bill. Too soon, he needed the gas mask to survive on the front lines in France as he drove a truck amid constant shelling, rain, snow, and mud.

Bill and missionary Oscar Huddleston in the jungles of Luzon, north of Manila, with members of the Negrito tribe. Bill's straw hat did not protect him and he suffered heat prostration.

Iva and Betty

Chinese rascals; Bill's graflex is slung over his shoulder.

Bill admired the missionaries and their commitment to help their fellow man—even at their own great personal sacrifice.

Bill at Baguio before heading for Java in March 1920.

Photo by J. Wells Chilson

St. Mark's, a "white elephant" of a burden for Methodists, was a church that Bill readily filled with "Standing Room Only" congregations. (*Standing Room Only* was also the title of a book that he wrote describing for other preachers the tactics that he used to keep his churches full.)

Food, faith and fun night at St. Mark's.

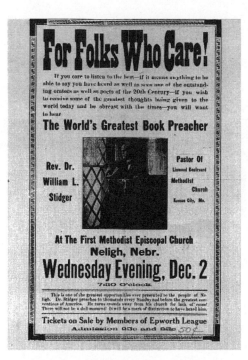

Promotion . . . promotion . . . promotion.

The illuminated revolving cross atop the Linwood Boulevard Church in Kansas City.

FRIENDSHIP BROKEN—AND HOW!

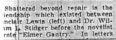

Shattered beyond repair is the friendship which existed between Sinclair Lewis (left) and Dr. William L. Stidger before the novelist wrote "Elmer Gantry." In letters made public here yesterday, Dr. Stidger tried to weld the broken friendship, but Lewis said "nothing doing."

DR. STIDGER STILL READY TO GREET LEWIS AS BUDDY

Rebuff Has Not Aroused Any 'Hard Feelings,' Says Clergyman.

Dr. William L. Stidger wants it distinctly understood there are no hard feelings on his part because Sinclair Lewis, author of "Elmer Gantry" and other novels, has spurned his offers for a renewal of friendship.

The former Kansas City pastor, furthermore, has no regrets that he wrote a letter apologizing to Lewis for assertions he made three years ago, charging the novelist was drunk when he wrote "Elmer Gantry."

That letter and a reply, written by Lewis severely censuring the minister and coldly rejecting his offer of friendship, were made public yesterday by the Rev. L. M. Birkhead at All Souls' Unitarian church. Dr. Stidger, however, is unperturbed.

Heard Lewis Missed Him.

"I wrote that letter of apology," Dr. Stidger said today at the home of Mr. and Mrs. William G. Zimmerman, 418 West Sixty-eighth street terrace, where he is visiting, "because a friend of mine told me Mr. Lewis desired to renew our friendship.

"Eight months ago Mr. Lewis told a friend of mine that the thing he regretted the most about writing 'Elmer Gantry' was the loss of my

as if a mountain had no right to be or publicly. It was just wasn't tricking you have been dangerous and I honor you no matter what I said, of a terrible thing which naturally followed because you had so much preceding its You will be your usual self, sure, and forgive and that injustice

I am writing this to let you know that be fair. Second, to feeling that I may justice. Third, because I feel lonely without your because I do not want you to think that I remember it when it is done etc. I valued you cause you were and are a great writer, but because I valued "Red" Lewis, one of the cals I ever knew him to be.

And, also, because I believe that that book was written because I felt that you were the very type that justifies anything about being written. I have done nothing about my profession—because I have been disgusted at the investigation of my worse characters in painting him.

Such an apology would be useless, old man, as a us personally, to myself publicly in the review of the public statement for the last of March in public saying the things I have to say, nor have nothing said of the Young Matron's way, meet in Birmingham cancel my engagement chance to do it deeply and I want to be completely happy in my

May 5

This may seem cheap Betty calls "bologna" never, more abject in my life. It is not because I am filled with what scorn for the church world will you but I mean to go on you are satisfied

ABARET DANCERS | LOCAL GIRL FLIER
RY FINGERNAILS | WRIGGLES OUT OF

Novelist Sinclair Lewis not only rebuffed Bill's apology for calling him drunk while he was writing *Elmer Gantry*, but also leaked it to the press to embarrass Bill, who was on a speaking tour in Kansas City in March 1930.

The author and his grandfather just before Bill's nervous breakdown in March 1940.

Bill Stidger was an unconventional preacher from his first day until his last in August 1949.

As far as we were concerned, we were through with Mr. Lewis—he had been our friend but betrayed us from the florist bill to the book, but—Mr. Lewis wasn't through with us—and it was all my fault.

Dad had a wonderful library in our house with thousands of books. He received new books all the time—reviewer's copies from the publishing houses, gift copies from all his friends—and when there were books he wanted to read that he couldn't acquire through these sources, he would beg them from the Methodist Book Concern, or, as a last resort, buy them. About once a year, Dad would weed out his books and send for the second-hand man. Dad had certain shelves on which he kept his first editions and autographed copies, and these were never culled. One time I was dipping into the wealth of Dad's library and ran across an early novel of Sinclair Lewis, called *Free Air*. It really wasn't up to his later books. Nothing at all like *Babbitt* or *Main Street* or *Cass Timberlain*, but it was a first edition and auto-graphed, so it resided on Dad's select shelves. I took it to my own room, read it and put it back, but not where it should have been placed.

Then the book dealer came and took the discarded piles of books.

The phone rang one evening a few weeks later. It was a newspaper ask-ing Dad for a statement: *Free Air* by Sinclair Lewis, an autographed first edi-tion, had sold at an auction that day for $150! Had Dr. Stidger discarded the book because of his new dislike for Mr. Lewis?

Of course Dad was speechless. He didn't know a thing about it. He couldn't believe it was his copy and, if it was, he was entirely unaware of its loss.

The next day came the fireworks. Mr. Lewis made a scathing retort to the press and I having confessed my part in the incident was in disgrace. Dad was noncommittal to the press about the whole affair and if the Republican Convention hadn't come to Kansas City, wiping the feud off the front page of the *Star,* no one knows what might have happened.[66]

Just two weeks after the Republican Convention met in the blazing heat of mid-June 1928 and nominated Herbert Hoover as its presidential candidate, Bill received a call to go to Boston University's School of Theology to teach. Though there had been many positive aspects of his ministry in Kansas City, there was also the overlay of his tempes-tuous experiences, both positive and negative, with Sinclair Lewis, which stretched from Bill's arrival in Kansas City through the moment of his decision to leave. The Boston offer came at a opportune time and was also fitting, as Bill's statement demonstrates:

I hereby tender my resignation as the pastor of this church, to take effect at the termination of my pre-sent annual conference appointment. A call has come to me to take the chair of preaching and pastoral science in the theological school of Boston University, our largest American theological school. In con-junction with this I am to preach once a Sunday in the Copley Plaza Methodist Episcopal Church. I shall accept this honor subject to the approval of Bishop Waldorf.

No man has an ethical right to resign from a pastorate of this importance without having good reasons for that resignation and without feeling that he has a call to service of very great and unusual importance and possibilities. That I feel. During the last three or four years there has been a decided movement on the part of theological seminaries to get into their teaching chairs younger men who have been successful in the actual ministry. The new movement is in the direction of a practical more than a theological pedagogy. In response to that new movement a number of men have left successful and outstanding churches to go to our theological schools to teach young men how to preach. Among these rather startling changes have been Dr. Harry Emerson Fosdick, who accepted the chair of homiletics in Union Theological Seminary in New York City in conjunction with his pastorate of the John D. Rockefeller church [Riverside Church]. Dr. Reinhold Niebuhr recently left a successful pastorate in Detroit to go to another chair in Union seminary. Dr. Gaius Glen Atkins, said to be one of the ten most brilliant preachers in America, left the largest Detroit Congregational church to take the chair of homiletics in Auburn Seminary. Dr. Alva Taylor within the past month has accepted a teaching chair in the Union Theological School of the South in Nashville, Tennessee. Dr. Halford Lucock, formerly contributing editor to all Methodist publications, two months ago accepted the chair of homiletics in Yale University Theological School, filling the chair occupied for a long time by Dr. Charles Brown.

These men have all felt, as I have come to feel, that the opportunity of influencing the young ministers of the church as they go out to become the leaders of the churches of America is not to be turned aside under any circumstances. I have long been interested in this particular field. I have written more than a dozen books of sermons and church methods. I have experimented in the practical laboratory of four great city churches. I feel that I have something definite to contribute to this new field—even more than I have to the ministry itself.

Freedom to lecture, write, travel and teach appeals to me. The privilege of influencing the future leadership of the Church in the seminary with the largest enrollment in Protestant circles is not to be turned aside. Therefore I go.

William L. Stidger[67]

Bill Stidger and Sinclair Lewis went on about their lives. Lewis was angry at Bill and no longer considered him a friend or a person worthy of comment. Bill was also no longer useful to him. For his part, Bill was sorry for the way he had handled the incident, no matter what the personal slight he might have suffered. On January 14, 1930, he wrote Lewis a long letter of apology, admitting he had "defamed" Lewis in Kansas City, requesting forgiveness "for that weakness and that injustice to you," and offering to retract publicly the statements he had made about Lewis. Forthwith Lewis flatly declined this apology, writing a letter that Bill felt was condescending, bitter, and inaccurate. Lewis vindictively arranged for Birkhead to release a copy of Bill's letter and of Lewis's reply so that publication of these two letters in Kansas City while Bill was speaking there would maximize the embarrassment that the correspondence might cause. The *Kansas City Journal-Post* printed the letters on Monday, March 31, 1930, but provided Bill with ample opportunity to comment. The headline and article follow:

DR. STIDGER STILL READY TO GREET LEWIS AS BUDDY;
REBUFF HAS NOT AROUSED ANY 'HARD FEELINGS,' SAYS CLERGYMAN.

Dr. William L. Stidger wants it distinctly understood there are no hard feelings on his part because Sinclair Lewis, author of *Elmer Gantry* and other novels, has spurned his offers for a renewal of friendship. The former Kansas City pastor, furthermore, has no regrets that he wrote a letter apologizing to Lewis for assertions he made three years ago charging the novelist was drunk when he wrote *Elmer Gantry*.

That letter and a reply written by Lewis severely censuring the minister and coldly rejecting his office or friendship, were made public yesterday by the Rev. L. M. Birkhead at All Souls Unitarian Church. Dr. Stidger, however, is unperturbed. "I wrote that letter of apology," Dr. Stidger said today at the home of Mr. and Mrs. William G. Zimmerman, 418 West Sixty-eighth Street Terrace, where he is visiting, "because a friend of mine told me Mr. Lewis desired to renew our friendship.

"Eight months ago Mr. Lewis told a friend of mine that the thing he regretted the most about writing *Elmer Gantry* was the loss of my friendship. When I learned of that feeling on the part of the novelist, there was nothing for me to do but to make apologies for the things I had said about him. I had intended to make public that letter myself, but when I received Mr. Lewis's ungracious reply, I assumed he did not want any publicity on the matter.

"I have no condemnation whatever for Mr. Birkhead in making public my letter and Mr. Lewis's answer. If he thought that was the proper thing to do, it is perfectly all right with me. I think I made myself clear in my letter and if 'Red' Lewis wants to stay mad, that is his undeniable privilege."[68]

Dr. Stidger's letter to Lewis reads as follows:

January 14, 1930

Dear "Red" Lewis:

I want to do what I should have done long, long ago—and have always known that my sense of fair play would compel me to do—and that is, to apologize to you for saying that you were drunk all the time you were writing Elmer Gantry.

Now that that is off my chest, I feel as if a mountain has been removed. I had no right to say that either privately or publicly. It was poor sportsmanship. It just wasn't cricket. You know it and you have been damned decent about it and I honor you for your attitude toward what I said. I said it in the midst of a terrible disappointment about that book and in the heat of a public pressure which naturally focused directly on me because you had been in my home so much preceding its outlining and writing. You will be your usual liberal self, I am sure, and forgive me for that weakness and that injustice to you.

I am writing this letter first of all to be fair. Second, to relieve my mind of a feeling that I may have done you an injustice. Third, because I like you and feel lonely without your friendship. Fourth, because I do not want you to think that Bill Stidger would do an unjust thing and not remedy it when he saw that he had done so. I valued our friendship, not because you were and are Sinclair Lewis the writer, but because you were and are "Red" Lewis, one of the most likable rascals I ever knew in all my life.

And, also, because I have come to believe that that book had its place, and that you were feeling toward an evil and a type that justified an Elmer Gantry *being written. I do not claim to know anything about the book as a work of art, nor do I believe that Elmer is typical of my profession—but since you wrote that book I have been doing a little honest investigation of my own and I have found worse characters in the ministry than you painted in him.*

Such an apology as I am making would be useless, old man, if it was just between us personally, so I am going to make it publicly in the very city where I made the public statement. I am to speak there the last of March and I shall make a public apology there. I would prefer to have nothing said of my intentions until I do that: for I am afraid that if it leaked out that I intend to do that, the women of the Young Matrons' club, who, by the way, meet in Birkhead's church, might cancel my engagement before I got a chance to do it. I feel this all very deeply and I want to do it. I shall not be completely happy until I do.

This may seem like so much of what Betty calls "baloney" to you, but I was never more abject or more humble in my life. It is not easy to do, and I know with what scorn a large part of the church world will hold me for doing it—but I mean to go through with it until you are satisfied that I have been fair and true and square. You are the one I want to feel satisfied.

I love you, and I am happy in your new books. I particularly like Dodsworth—*and I am happy with you in your new home-making.*

I do not expect you to enter the ministry yourself—nor do I expect you to sprout wings for a few aeons, but I do know that you are a good scout—that you and I feel so much alike in our hatred of "bunk" and a lot of things for which my profession stands. And, incidentally, so far as I can feel around the shoulders where wings ought to begin to sprout, I cannot feel any coming out of me, either.

I want to see you and have a good talk some day—and do my part at least—if that is possible, to wipe out this "strange interlude" in our friendship. Don't expect me to come to you chewing tobacco, or even smoking cubebs, or drinking highballs. They would make me sick at the tummy if I tried—but I come as a true friend if I get a chance, and—as of old—I'll not come judging or condemning, or with a "holier than thou" attitude—God knows I don't feel that way, ever.

Here's my hand and here's my heart.

Fraternally and faithfully,
Bill[69]

Sinclair Lewis's reply to Dr. Stidger reads as follows:

January 18, 1930

Dear Mr. Stidger,

Your letter of January 14 shows such persistence that I must answer it, though I have never answered the numerous attacks you have made on me, and though I have thrown into the wastebasket the several letters by which, in the past year, you have endeavored to regain my friendship.

Your apology for having said, noisily and publicly, that I was "drunk all the time I was writing Elmer Gantry*" is of no value for four reasons:*

First, it comes nearly three years too late.

Second, it is insincere. This I judge from the fact that you follow it by saying "I do not want you to think that Bill Stidger would do an unjust thing and not remedy it when he saw that he had done so." You really can't expect any credit for nobility when you have taken over two years to "see that you have done so."

Third: at the time when you were in an orgy of vilifying me, you presented me as drunk all the time, yet said that Elmer Gantry *was written in three months—or it may have been in two months; I forget which. Now aside from the fact that you knew perfectly well that the writing of the book took me nearly a year, it was obvious even to the semi-literate that no one could write a carefully documented, carefully revised book of 200,000 words in three months and be drunk all the time. So these two lies cancelled each other, and there is no need of apologizing for either of them.*

Fourth: you made so many other false accusations about me and my book that this one alone isn't really important.

How many of these there were, I don't know. I was abroad, and heard of them only from letters and clippings; and, after nearly three years, I have forgotten many of those that did reach me. But even so, I know of an astonishing number—of which I shall give examples.

You said—and if I remember rightly you said in your own sacred pulpit—that when I first came to Kansas City, you were loath to invite me to your house to stay, but that I insisted on your doing so, and you consented regretfully.

As you know, the opposite is the truth. I had planned to stay at a hotel, but you insisted on my staying with you, and while I was there, you got every ounce of publicity for yourself that you could out of the fact.

This particular lie was far meaner and pettier than an accusation of drunkenness, because it pictured me as a thick-skinned blackguard.

Next, you went about telling people that you had found a large number of errors in matters of fact in Elmer Gantry; *particularly misquotations from the Methodist Discipline. When the Rev. Mr. Birkhead, himself an ex-Methodist clergyman, denied this, and challenged you to produce specific errors, you evaded the challenge, but went right on with the lie.*

Next, at Brown University—and I imagine at other places—you obtained interesting publicity by asserting that it was you who first suggested to me that I write a novel about preachers. You know, and knew, of course, that I had planned it years before I ever heard of you.

Next, I am informed that you whispered about that my father had died in circumstances of great scandal. But apparently you never used this peculiarly atrocious lie publicly, and you may never have said this at all, so I leave it to you yourself to remember whether you were guilty of this also.

Next, in a speech you took William Allen White's remark that "When Sinclair Lewis challenged God to strike him dead, God took him at his word by killing his sense of artistry," and you got publicity for yourself by quoting it without credit to White.

Next, on many occasions you asserted that I deceived you as to the general nature of my plans for the book; whereas often and definitely I warned you that you would not like it.

These are but a few out of the lies and misrepresentations that I remember. There were many more. And don't try to tell me that you were misquoted, because some of the worst libels—such as your false picture of our "Sunday School Class"—were in your own writing.

I hope that now, finally, you will understand how impossible it will be for you ever to "see me and have a good talk some day." And do not go out to Kansas City and pose again as my friend, or pretend that you have regained my respect.

I see no reason why we should ever have further correspondence. If you have any more apologies to make, don't make them to me but to the God in whom you so loudly proclaim a belief.

Yours sincerely,
Sinclair Lewis[70]

While Bill was still in Kansas City—but after the above correspondence had been released to the public—he was asked about his fight with Sinclair Lewis. In his reply he quoted a bit of doggerel which he said "applied nicely" to Lewis's attack on preachers and the church:

A red-headed woodpecker tried to tackle
The tin roof of the tabernacle
The noise was great; the damage small,
And that's "Red" Lewis after all.[71]

By coincidence, or perhaps in retaliation, Lewis visited Kansas City during the following month, in April 1930, and stayed with the Birkheads. He granted an interview to a newspaper reporter and was asked: "Do you remember Dr. William L. Stidger?" It was reported that Lewis popped to attention and put on his gold-rimmed spectacles. He asked to borrow Birkhead's typewriter and then he typed out:

Kansas City
April 15, 1930

I feel that by himself the Reverend Mr. Stidger has already been able to obtain sufficient publicity out of his slight acquaintanceship with me, and I am disinclined to give him any more.

Sinclair Lewis"[72]

Later the same year, Lewis became the first American to win the Nobel Prize for Literature. In the presentation ceremonies in December 1930, his background and achievements were summarized by the permanent secretary of the Swedish Academy, who made the following reference to Lewis's "preacher book":

His big novel *Elmer Gantry* (1927) is like a surgical operation on one of the most delicate parts of the social body. Presumably it would not pay to search anywhere in the world for the old Puritanical virtues, but possibly one might find in some of the oldest corners of America a remnant of the sect which regarded it as a sin to remarry, once it had pleased God to make one a widower or widow, and wicked to lend money at interest. But otherwise America has no doubt had to moderate its religious rigidity. To what extent a pulpiteer like Elmer Gantry is common over there, we cannot here have the slightest idea. Neither his slapdash style of preaching with his cocky pugilistic manners ("Hello, Mr. Devil"), nor his successful collecting of money and men inside the gates of the church can hide the sad fact that he is an unusually foul fish. Mr. Lewis has been neither willing nor able to give him any attractive traits. But as description the book is a feat of strength, genuine and powerful, and its full-flavored, somber satire has a devastating effect. It is unnecessary to point out that hypocrisy thrives a little everywhere and that anyone who attacks it at such a close range places himself before a hydra with many dangerous heads.[73]

Sinclair Lewis and Bill Stidger had wounded egos, each by assaults on their characters inflicted by the other. Lewis would never forgive Stidger, nor would he apologize. Bill did apologize and buried the hurt to his ego by henceforth referring only to the pleasant memories that he had in his relationship with Lewis. In 1936, Bill wrote an article about a visit to William Allen White's home and office in Emporia, Kansas, a decade earlier, during which he introduced Lewis to White. He made no reference in that article to *Elmer Gantry*, to his fight with Lewis, or William Allen White's taking Bill's side of the issue.

Notes

1. Sinclair Lewis, *Elmer Gantry* (New York: Harcourt Brace, 1927), 1.

2. William Allen White, "*Elmer Gantry* Reviewed," *The Kansas City Star,* March 10, 1927.

3. William L. Stidger, *That God's House May Be Filled* (New York: George H. Doran, 1924), 239–41.

4. Letter dated November 13, 1922, from Sinclair Lewis to William L. Stidger, Stidger Papers at Brown University Library, Providence, Rhode Island.

5. "Seeks Another Babbitt; America's Arch-Satirist Hunts Idol to Shatter," *Detroit News,* August 15, 1924.

6. "Famous Minister, Dr. Stidger Preaches First Sermon in Linwood Blvd. Church," *The Church at Work,* Kansas City, September 25, 1925, 1.

7. "God Is Organist of Universe, Is Stidger Theme," *Rocky Mountain Day,* November 24, 1925, 1.

8. Dr. Burris Jenkins, "Drift of the Day," *The Church at Work,* Kansas City, October 2, 1925, 1.

9. *Kansas City Journal-Post,* September 26, 1925.

10. Betty Stidger Hyland, *Those Heavenly Years,* unpublished manuscript, 1955, 96.

11. *Linwood Boulevard Methodist Church Bulletin,* November 1, 1925, 3.

12. William L. Stidger, "A Preacher Tells the Inside Story of Sinclair Lewis and His Preacher Book," *Dearborn Independent,* March 19, 1927, 1.

13. "*Elmer Gantry,* Denounced by Rev. W. L. Stidger," *Kansas City Star,* March 14, 1927.

14. Mark Schorer, *Sinclair Lewis, An American Life* (Minneapolis: University of Minnesota Press, 1963), 440.

15. Hyland, *Those Heavenly Years,* 102.

16. William L. Stidger, *There Are Sermons in Stories* (New York: Abingdon-Cokesbury, 1942), 98–99.

17. William L. Stidger, *Personal Power* (Garden City: Doubleday, Doran, 1929), 65–66.

18. Stidger, *Personal Power*.

19. "Sinclair Lewis Visit to K.C.," *Kansas City Star,* January 18, 1926.

20. "Linwood Boulevard Church Talk," *Kansas City Times,* January 25, 1926.

21. "Linwood Boulevard Church Talk."

22. Harrison Smith, *From Main Street to Stockholm: Letters of Sinclair Lewis, 1919–1930* (New York: Harcourt, Brace, 1952), 193.

23. Schorer, *Sinclair Lewis,* 441.

24. Smith, *From Main Street to Stockholm,* 202.

25. Smith, *From Main Street to Stockholm,* 206.

26. Smith, *From Main Street to Stockholm,* 206.

27. Schorer, *Sinclair Lewis,* 442.

28. Richard Lawrence Miller, "Elmer Gantry's Kansas City Connections," *Star Magazine,* March 29, 1987, 8.

29. Lewis, *Elmer Gantry,* 1.

30. "*Elmer Gantry*, Comments by Dr. Stidger of K.C.," *Kansas City Star,* March 16, 1927.

31. Schorer, *Sinclair Lewis,* 449.

32. "And Author Gives Views on Youth, Religion and Other Things," *Kansas City Times,* April 19, 1926.

33. "And Author Gives Views on Youth, Religion and Other Things."

34. "And Author Gives Views on Youth, Religion and Other Things."

35. Schorer, *Sinclair Lewis,* 448.

36. D. J. Dooley, *The Art of Sinclair Lewis* (Lincoln: University of Nebraska Press, 1967), 123.

37. Dooley, *The Art of Sinclair Lewis,* 122.

38. Mark Schorer, "Afterword," in *Elmer Gantry* (New York: Signet Classic, 1967), 429.

39. Hyland, *Those Heavenly Years,* 103.

40. Smith, *From Main Street to Stockholm,* 234.

41. Smith, *From Main Street to Stockholm,* 235.

42. *Kansas City Star,* March 10, 1927.

43. White, *"Elmer Gantry* Reviewed."

44. "Flaws Seen by Two Pastors," *Kansas City Star,* March 10, 1927.

45. "Flaws Seen by Two Pastors."

46. Hyland, *Those Heavenly Years,* 103.

47. Lewis, *Elmer Gantry,* 396.

48. Lewis, *Elmer Gantry,* 365.

49. Lewis, *Elmer Gantry,* 365.

50. Lewis, *Elmer Gantry,* 351.

51. Lewis, *Elmer Gantry,* 342.

52. Lewis, *Elmer Gantry,* 396.

53. Lewis, *Elmer Gantry,* 397.

54. "*Elmer Gantry*, Denounced by Rev. W. L. Stidger," *Kansas City Star,* March 14, 1927.

55. John Creecy, "'Gantry' Riled Detroit Pastor," *Detroit Sunday Times,* August 14, 1960, 4.

56. "'Gantry' Product of Inflamed Mind, Stidger Charges," unidentified Rhode Island newspaper, November 28, 1927, Brown University Archive, Providence, Stidger File.

57. "*Elmer Gantry*, Denounced by Rev. W. L. Stidger."

58. "*Elmer Gantry*, Denounced by Rev. W. L. Stidger."

59. *"Elmer Gantry*, Upheld by Rev. L. M. Birkhead," *Kansas City Star,* March 14, 1927.

60. *"Elmer Gantry*, Denounced by Rev. W. L. Stidger."

61. *"Elmer Gantry*, Upheld by Rev. L. M. Birkhead."

62. Smith, *From Main Street to Stockholm*, 238.

63. Rebecca West, *The Strange Necessity* (New York: Doubleday, Doran, 1928), 295–307.

64. Martin Bucco, *Critical Essays on Sinclair Lewis* (Boston: G. K. Hall, 1986), 6.

65. Bucco, *Critical Essays on Sinclair Lewis,* 6.

66. Hyland, *Those Heavenly Years,* 104.

67. *Kansas City Journal-Post,* June 27, 1927.

68. *Kansas City Journal-Post,* Monday, March 31, 1930.

69. *Kansas City Journal-Post,* Monday, March 31, 1930.

70. *Kansas City Journal-Post,* Monday, March 31, 1930.

71. "The D.A.R. Fading Out. Recent Clash Is Explained by Former Pastor Here Today, and Sinclair Lewis and *Elmer Gantry* Are Mentioned," *Kansas City Star*, March 31, 1930, 10.

72. "Sinclair Lewis—*Elmer Gantry*, Criticized by Dr. William L. Stidger, Visits K.C.," *Kansas City Star,* April 15, 1930.

73. "Presentation by Erik Axel Karlfeldt, Permanent Secretary of the Swedish Academy," in *Literature 1901–1967*, Nobel Lectures (Amsterdam: Elsevier, 1969), 275.

Nine

Preaching Out of the Overflow:
Boston

I t was late afternoon in mid-December 1928: Tremont Street in Boston, near the Ritz Hotel. The bum bent over the tall wire basket, reached inside, and began to rustle through the contents for something of value—a bit of discarded food perhaps, an article of clothing to protect against the cold, or a magazine with pictures to be read around the fire. He found a magazine, glanced through it, and then curled it into a tight roll that would fit in his jacket pocket. The bum shuffled on, crossing the Boston Common, checking out other homeless men who were making the Common their shelter. Some had fashioned beds out of paper cartons or had covered themselves with newspapers. "Can you spare a dime for a cup of coffee, brother?" The litany was directed at anyone passing by who looked like he might have some extra money.

Besides being a haven for the homeless, the Boston Common was an area for the exercise of free speech. The bum, if he had been listening, could have heard many voices, each offering a cure for the national malaise. There was a small group of socialist firebrands in one spot, while across the way a clutch of communist speakers held forth.

But the bum wasn't listening. He seemed intent on making his way as quickly as possible across the Common toward Louisberg Square, the most fashionable address in Boston. He presented a sharp contrast to the finely dressed men and women hurrying along Mount Vernon Street, anxious to be wherever they were headed so they could be out of the penetrating winter cold. He had three days' growth of beard—a red scraggly beard. An old battered hat was pulled down over his eyes. He did not have an overcoat, and his light jacket, drawn up close about his neck, was fastened with a heavy safety pin.

A distinguished-looking elderly gentleman drove up to the curb at 72 Mount Vernon Street, the home of the Boston University School of Theology. The gray-whiskered man was Dr. Marcus Buell, retired professor of New Testament studies. Mrs. Buell was in the back seat of the Ford. Just as Dr. Buell removed the car keys and was preparing to get out, the tramp opened the front door of the car, and slipped onto the front seat beside the professor. Mrs. Buell stiffened in horror; the alarmed professor straightened up, not at all sure what harm this desperate man might bring him.

"What do you want, sir?" Dr. Buell asked.

"Old man, I'm hungry. I gotta have money for food. I haven't had a bite to eat for two days—I'm starving and desperate. You gotta give me money to eat!"

Somehow, Dr. Buell felt that he and his wife would be better off if they engaged this man in conversation. "What is your name?"

"My name's Kahn, sir. What of it?"

"Where did you come from?" The old doctor was sparring for time, looking for a police officer as he talked.

"I came from Pittsburgh. I've been workin' in the steel mills. They've shut down. I was told that I could get work in Boston and I can't. I'm starving."

"What is your nationality?"

"I'm German, and I have five children, and I gotta have money to get a bite to eat—and you gotta give it to me."

The kindly old professor pulled out a worn purse, reached down into it and handed the tramp a quarter—the price of a meal in those days. With a smile, Dr. Buell said: "I believe you. You look tired and hungry. Go and get something to eat, and God bless you."

Then the tramp looked directly into the face of his old teacher and said, removing his hat, "Dr. Buell, you really are generous, aren't you?" Dr. Buell's eyes opened wide with astonishment. Then, as he recognized the mischief maker, he smiled with amusement. "Why, Bill Stidger! What will you be doing next?"

As he sat in Dr. Buell's warm car that cold afternoon, Bill told him that he had been out since dawn dressed as a tramp, walking the streets of Boston to discover just how much Christmas spirit Bostonians had and what a man out of work, hungry and desperate, was really up against. It had been Bill's own idea. He had proposed the plan to the *Boston Evening American,* and they sent him out for twenty-four hours on this adventure.

By the time he parted company with his old professor, it was growing dark. According to his agreement with the newspaper, he had to find a place to sleep in one of the charity organizations of the city, the choice being left to him. It occurred to Bill that he might find a place to stay and at the same time fulfill a long-standing invitation to speak. The request had come from Dr. E. J. Helms, a fellow Methodist minister who ran a group of institutions for the "down and outs." Helms had been doing missionary work in Boston's poor East End and had created Goodwill Industries, which collected old clothes and then patched, mended, and sold them, using otherwise unemployed men and women to do the work, and paying them from proceeds. He had asked Bill to come down and lead his early morning chapel service at Morgan Memorial, the church serving the Goodwill Industries' workers as well as the outcasts. Bill described what happened next:

With one of two nickels I had left from my begging that day, I telephoned Dr. Helms from a fruit stand booth. I told him that I would be down the next morning and would be glad to lead the morning devotions at Morgan Memorial. He was excited and happy and said: "Fine, Doctor Stidger! I'll call all the workers and tell them the good news! Come along promptly at eight! I'll be there to welcome you."

About midnight I went humbly into the Seavey Hotel, which is a part of Morgan Memorial's welfare work. Fred H. Seavey had been sheriff of Suffolk County for years, while Helms had been chaplain of the Suffolk County jail for twenty years. Seavey noticed that Dr. Helms was making good, decent, self-respecting citizens out of the prisoners. He told Helms that one day he would do something for Helms's work.

The Seavey Hotel was the result of that wealthy businessman's respect for Dr. Helms. It is a hotel for destitute men. If a man is without money and without friends he is especially welcome in the Seavey Hotel, which is next door to the five-story Goodwill Industry building.

I wanted to test the sincerity of the institution. Often, this type of institution demeans the personalities of the outcasts. I walked in, asked for a bed, registered, was given a ticket, sent to the warm baths, handed a blue gingham nightshirt and courteously taken to the dormitory upstairs to sleep with 200 other homeless men who, like myself, were friendless and penniless. Rather than being demeaning, they were kindly in their necessary questions, considerate and Christian. I found that they wanted to help me.

I went through the regular routine, slept fitfully because of the harsh coughing of those poor men around me, one of whom slept above me in a double-deck bed arrangement. When I too began to cough, one of the men insisted upon my taking some of his medicine. He was so kind about it and so insistent that I finally swallowed a dose. It nearly strangled me. I have never fully recovered from the shock of that comrade's medicine. But it was given in love.

I ate breakfast at five A.M. with the gang, after which I prepared to go to the eight o'clock chapel service as its morning speaker—dressed, however, just as I was after twenty-four hours tramping the streets in my old clothes and with three days' of scraggly red beard.

When I ran into Dr. Helms in the lobby of the chapel, he talked with me, informing me that "Doctor Stidger" was about to speak and "could I please remain for it was to be an especially interesting chapel." In fact, Dr. Helms seemed afraid that the man who stood before him, whom he thought to be a tramp, might fail to remain for the service and miss this glorious opportunity of hearing the renowned clergyman. Finally the tramp could stand the humor of the situation no longer and said:

"Yes, I think I will remain, Doctor Helms, and hear that guy. I understand he is good. You can never tell what he will either do or say, so I've been told. In fact, that's what Doctor Buell said to me yesterday afternoon: 'Bill Stidger, what will you be doing next?' So, if you're ready, we'll go right into the service."

Dr. Helms looked at me as bewildered as had Dr. Buell. He looked into my face, deep into my eyes, at my beard, my clothes. Then he smiled a sickly, surprised smile, looked again at my clothes and said: "But not in those awful clothes?"

I replied: "They may be awful but I got them in your Morgan Memorial store, so we'll go into the chapel just as I am."

"But," he protested, "we have a formal service here. Our speaker wears a robe. We try to make it a dignified service—just like a stately church service."

I sympathized with his efforts to give that crowd a dignified service but insisted upon going into the pulpit that morning just as I was so that I could tell that audience the story of my adventure in humanity; so that I could bear testimony to the actual goodwill and friendliness of his institution; so that I could tell them that I had put the whole institution to the test when it was not on parade and that I had not found it wanting.

And I did speak, just as I was dressed, in my Morgan Memorial clothes, and I have never had such an attentive audience, nor such a glowing hour of fellowship in any of the great, rich churches of America.[1]

Bill's story and four photographs of him appeared in the *Boston Evening American,* and it is likely that a majority of Bostonians read or heard about the eccentric pastor in their midst. The story of his Christmas experience as a bum not only made the newspapers but became a legend at Boston University School of Theology. One student, Walter G. Muelder, who later became dean of the Theology School, saved the news clipping and retrieved it for me in 1996, sixty-eight years later.

A man's life is built on opportunities and coincidences, and this was particularly true for Bill in 1927. The storm surrounding the publication of *Elmer Gantry* had only begun to subside when Bill received an invitation to be a guest lecturer at the Boston University School of Theology. He welcomed the opportunity for a change of scene and was pleased to be returning, if only briefly, to the one place where he had always wanted to wind up—the School of Theology.

G. Bromley Oxnam was the head of the Department of Practical Theology (that is, preaching), and it was he who asked Bill to speak to his students. Bill lectured on how he was able to keep his large city churches filled to capacity, a subject that he figured would inspire the students and give them some insight. He also lectured on how to construct symphonic and dramatic book sermons, two popular innovations of his that had been written about and imitated.

All went well until a student shot this question at Bill in an open forum following one of his lectures: "Just what are your goals in preaching; what are you getting at; and what do you want to accomplish?" Bill described his reaction:

It was a startling question, and it almost took me off my feet. I asked for a few minutes to answer that question. I had not, up to that time, stopped long enough to formulate my goals in this sacred calling. But I did, then and there. Up out of my subconscious swept these goals, just as if they had been there awaiting my call.

First, my goal in preaching is to be educational. I must inform people. Jesus looked upon Himself as a teacher, first of all.

Second, my goal is inspirational. I must take tired men and rest them. I must take men who have been beaten about in the competitive world and relax them. I must take weary women and bring them quiet and repose. In a word, I must take men out of time and make them feel eternal. I must make them know that they are made but a little lower than the angels and crowned with life everlasting.

Third, I must make men realize the best that is in them, and I must do that in every sermon. That must be one of the goals of the sermon.

Fourth, I must bring a sense of peace to their souls, peace with their own warring natures, peace with their neighbors, peace with their God.

Fifth, I must bring to them in every way I know how that Jesus said that He came to give the abundant life.

Sixth, I must aim to bring them to God and to bring God to them through Jesus our Savior.

These, I take it, are the fundamental goals toward which a minister ought to be aiming in every sermon. There may be other things, but these are the primal [sic] goals.

But perhaps the most important result that came to me out of that student's question was the facing of my goals in my own mind, the necessity he brought to me of formulating these goals.[2]

At Boston University word spread of Bill's positive impact on the students, of his unusual ability to think on his feet, and of his willingness to engage in personal exchanges with the students, as exhibited by the student's challenging question on Bill's philosophy of preaching.

In the spring of 1928, Bromley Oxnam was elected president of DePauw University, an important Methodist institution, leaving vacant at Boston University the chairmanship of the Department of Practical Theology. The decision on who would replace Oxnam was made by Boston University's president, Daniel L. Marsh, and the dean of the School of Theology, Dr. Alfred C. Knudson. Marsh had been elected two years earlier, and one of his first appointments was to elevate Knudson, the senior member of the faculty of the School of Theology, to the deanship. The two men now decided to use the appointment of Oxnam's replacement as a way to effect a reorganization of the Department of Practical Theology, whose core course was on the theory of preaching. They wanted to inject new life into the department and concluded that they needed a dynamic, younger man, full of energy, inspiration, and emotion to be its head. They also wanted to find other practicing ministers of diverse skills to assist him as adjunct professors. Bill's growing reputation as an innovative, controversial, even flamboyant preacher and his recent success in his guest lectures at the school made him their prime candidate.

The executive committee of the Board of Trustees of Boston University on Monday, July 17, 1928, adopted President Marsh's "challenging plan" for the Department of Practical Theology, electing Bill head of the department and naming four of the "most successful" preachers in the greater Boston area as his assistants. These ministers were: Dr. Henry Hitt Crane, pastor of Centre Methodist Episcopal Church, Malden; Dr. Henry Knox Sherrill, rector of Trinity Episcopal Church, Boston; Dr. Samuel Macaulay Lindsay, pastor of First Baptist Church, Brookline; and Dr. Raymond Calkins, pastor of First Congregational Church, Cambridge. As one newspaper said, "These leaders from four strong denominations will supplement the work of Dr. Stidger with a course on 'The Minister and His Task,' each of the assistants teaching two hours a week through one quarter of the school year." The *Zion's Herald* added:

> Many church leaders with growing approval have been watching the development of this successful preacher [Stidger]. Bishop F. J. McConnell declares, "Dr. Stidger is one of the most thoroughly alive men in the ministry today," and Dr. J. Fort Newton notes that "no man among us has come nearer mastering the art of preaching to the mind in a world on wheels, which asks for a method of approach of which our fathers never so much as dreamed." Dr. Ozora S. Davis, president of Chicago Theological Seminary, declares that "Dr. Stidger in the dramatic 'book sermon' has made one of the most distinctive contributions of the last twenty-five years to the work of preaching."[3]

As a further inducement to come to Boston to stay, President Marsh arranged for Bill to become pastor of an important church that the Methodists had acquired two years earlier from the Unitarians. It was located at the corner of Exeter and Newbury Streets; although officially renamed Copley Methodist Episcopal, it was universally referred to as the "Old Edward Everett Hale" Church. The Episcopalians' flagship, Trinity Church, was nearby, as was the Congregationalists' Old South Church. The Methodists wished to have an important city church, and Bill was thought the perfect choice to be its minister.

Iva and Betty preceded Bill to Boston, as Betty describes:

> It's a long way from Kansas City, Missouri, to Boston, Massachusetts. Not only by mileage! Mother and I drove east ahead of Dad because the new school year started before the Church Conference and Mother wanted to get us located and settle me in my junior year at high school.

Mother and I took a room at the Kenmore Hotel on Commonwealth Avenue. While we lived there, Mother drove me to school mornings and then hunted houses the rest of the day. Mother and Dad finally decided to live near Newton High School at 99 Atwood Street, Newtonville. It had a fine reputation and seemed a most promising place to live.

We were no longer plain preacher folk. True, Dad was to preach, but his main job now was to be a professor of homiletics at Boston University. Mother felt that she could relax a little. She wouldn't have a big house, just an apartment within a two-family house. There would be less entertaining and fewer church meetings. Dad was no longer the pastor. [As, officially, the "morning preacher" at Copley Church, Bill's primary responsibility was to preach at 11 A.M. every Sunday morning. Day-to-day pastoral care of the parishioners was in the hands of another minister, Guy Wayne.] All he had to do was appear in his robe, march down the aisle behind the choir and climb up into his "Crow's Nest" at the appropriate time and pronounce words of wisdom.[4]

Bill wound up his affairs in Kansas City in late July 1928 and headed to Boston by train. He anticipated that the coming year would be extremely demanding, because he was slated to be teaching two courses throughout the academic year, for which he had no syllabus or library of notes to rely on. If he was building a factory like his old friend Henry Ford had done, then he stood now at the earliest stage, with only a green field facing him where the factory was to go.

As he absentmindedly watched the landscape fly by, his practical and organized mind seized on a solution to this major problem. He would write a book on the content and style of preaching: each chapter could be finished in time to use as the basis for a class or series of classes, and he would be able to test its appropriateness by his students' reactions.

Bill began to outline the opening chapter of his book as the train was passing through an oil field on its way eastward. Lining the tracks on both sides were forests of oil derricks, which sent the heavy odor of oil through the walls of the Pullman car. It had, as Bill recalled, a pleasant tang. As he studied the derricks, which stretched out miles in all directions, he remembered that oilmen classified wells into three types: dry—with no oil at all; those that have to be pumped to retrieve their oil; and wells that gush oil and "overflow." Those that overflow do so, he thought, out of the abundance that is stored away down deep "in the earth's subconscious-self, as it were."

It was while crossing these oil fields that Bill saw the analogy between the types of wells and types of preaching, and from this analogy came the book's title, *Preaching Out of the Overflow*. Preaching that corresponded to the dry hole was so well known to congregations that the phrase "as dry as a sermon" had been coined. Then there was the type of preacher who had to pump himself, to strain, to battle, sweat, and worry both himself and his family each week into misery over a sermon. Finally, there was the man who had such an abundance of ideas that he preached out of the overflow, effortlessly.

Bill reflected on his own experience: for him, joy in preaching consisted of having more ideas and suggestions than one could ever use; and this distinctive joy, akin to elation, occurred only when his mind and notebook were crammed full. The best preaching, Bill believed, was the natural overflow of a receptive mind and the expression of an ever-growing storehouse of experiences. He said more than once, "A good sermon is never worked up; it is worked out."

As the train rocketed eastward into the night, he concluded that *Preaching Out of the Overflow* should be looked upon not as a pure textbook but as a work of enthusiasm about the business and pleasure of preaching. (It would be published in 1929 at the conclusion of his first year of teaching and would turn out to be his most popular book on preaching.)[5]

In the fall term of 1928, when Bill joined its faculty, Boston University was justifiably proud of the reputation of its School of Theology and of its contribution to education and the Church. Since its founding in 1839, four thousand of its students had graduated to serve nineteen different denominations, and a large number had become missionaries in non-Christian lands. Sixteen graduates had been elected bishops; thirty-four were serving as presidents, deans, or principals of universities, colleges, or schools; and eighty-one were professors in theological schools and colleges.

Bill became one of twenty-six professors serving an enrollment of almost four hundred students, approximately seventy in each class (junior, middle, and senior); 130 additional students were candidates for advanced degrees, and another fifty were special students, taking courses without being part of specific programs. There was a concentration of students (106) from Massachusetts, and there were fairly large contingents from Ohio, New York, Pennsylvania, Indiana, Iowa, and Michigan (almost twenty-five students each), as well as a smattering from thirty other states and eleven foreign countries.

The school's curriculum was divided into nine departments, one of which was Practical Theology (with Bill as chairman). Bill's department taught, principally, homiletics (the study of preaching), as well as courses on speaking, evangelism, and church music. Practical Theology was the most important department for students who were preparing for "typical pastoral service"—that is, to become ministers, with churches. Students who wished instead to make teaching their career were required to take only one-third of the hours in Practical Theology that those who planned to become ministers did.

In Practical Theology, the professors, like Bill, were more likely to have been practicing ministers than academics. Professors in other disciplines, however—men like Dr. Edgar J. Brightman, professor of the philosophy of religion—were recognized scholars, known as much for their published work as for their classroom skills. It was entirely natural, therefore, that students whose prospective careers lay in academia might regard professors like Bill as intellectual lightweights and their courses as "fluff." Furthermore, Bill's sensationalist methods, his pioneering use of advertising to enhance church attendance, his championing of radio as a medium for preaching, his friendships with celebrities, and his incredible popularity only tended to confirm their view. On the other hand, the majority of the students were headed for pulpits across the country, and for them Bill Stidger's classes were a revelation.

When he looked carefully at it, Bill was aghast at the stodgy description in the school catalog of the course on Homiletical Theory he was about to teach: "A study of sermonic materials. The fundamental principles of sermon construction. A critical consideration of sermons of pulpit masters, past and present, in the light of modern pedagogy."

He quickly rewrote the course description. As revised with his personal stamp, the description of his course on homiletical theory differed substantially from what it had been: "A study of sermonic materials; the basic principles of sermon construction; a critical consideration of the great sermons of past and present with particular emphasis on the preachers who are doing the task in this day and age. A study of the sources of sermonic material in the Bible, literature, the drama, art and life. This course will also aim to make the ministry 'a thing apart' as well as a profession 'linked with life.' One great objective of the course will be to make the student love the task he has taken up, as well as teach him the practical background of that task. Questionnaires following each period bring out the problems of the student."[6]

For his second-semester course, "Advanced Homiletics and the Pastoral Office," he amplified the description from "The psychology of preaching, qualities of the effective sermon, the art of illustration" to 'Discussion in open forum of great preachers of today and their production. Lectures on pastoral work, ministerial etiquette, executive leadership, new types of preaching such as the dramatic book sermon, the symphonic sermon, the drama sermon, art sermons, etc."

Bill immediately introduced a framework for students to get experience in a controlled classroom setting: "Preaching clubs. The classes are divided into groups of eight or ten each. They meet once a week and at each meeting two members preach under assignment of the leader. After the sermon both students and teacher offer suggestions and criticisms."[7]

It was generally agreed among the faculty at the school that despite his lack of academic experience, Bill fitted in well as professor of homiletics, because, as the school historian later put it, "he so obviously loved preaching and the students who aspired to be preachers. The fitting word for William L. Stidger was 'exuberance.' Never did the title of a man's book represent its author better than Bill's *Preaching Out of the Overflow*. If he had a fault as a teacher of homiletics, it was that he was sometimes impatient that his students couldn't tap springs as free-flowing as his own. But usually he exercised admirable restraint in dealing with his budding preachers."[8] Dr. Sam Hedrick, a colleague in preaching, described Bill: "As a teacher, he was both ruthless and tender. Let some brash junior deliver a sermon in Preaching Club which that junior obviously regarded as the standard by which all other student sermons were to be judged, and Bill would pace the floor with his hands on his hips. His first utterance would be, 'I am at a loss to know what to say. That was by all odds the worst sermon I have ever heard. I can't give a grade lower than F because the School makes no provision for a Z, which is the way I rate it.' On the other hand, many a timid, uncertain student whose gifts were unequal to his graces has felt that strong, firm hand upon his shoulder and heard Bill's resonant voice say, 'We can do something with a lad like you. You may never be a great preacher, but we will see to it that you are a good one.'"[9]

Bill considered himself friend and ally of the student. Many came from the hinterlands of the country, out of the Methodist colleges of Indiana, Iowa, Illinois, Nebraska, and Missouri, and they arrived with "unreconstructed" theological minds. In many of these rural areas, the idea of evolution was still an unresolved issue (the Scopes trial, addressing the legality of teaching Darwinian theory, had concluded in 1925, only three years earlier). The strong liberal position taken by the school, and the dense intellectual reasoning put forward especially by leading philosophers like Edgar Brightman, could figuratively "knock the legs out from under" these young students. They would be intimidated by the most powerful professors and would feel defeated—"I'll never make it, I just can't get this in my head." Bill would take these students, pick them up, and say, "Yes, you've got the stuff, you can preach. You don't have to be an expert theologian to be a fine pastor and teacher."[10]

Sometimes a student who was aiming to become a pastor would rebel against the academic thrust of the school. This rebellious spirit struck a responsive chord in Bill, who firmly believed that undue emphasis from the pulpit on social service or on abstract religious doctrine drove people from the churches. One of his students, J. Kenneth Cornwell, was particularly troubled, so much so that he felt that his dilemma was of crisis proportions.

Bill invited the young man to his house in Newtonville, and over dinner, he and Iva talked with Cornwell about the essence of preaching. The dialogue became heated—not at all in anger but in fervent agreement about how wrong the teaching was in theological schools in general. Preachers, they agreed, should show their congregations how to find personal redemption, thus making the church relevant again to each individual. Bill leaned forward at one point with such excitement that blood vessels stood out on his neck, and Iva touched him on the arm to calm him down, saying, "Now, Daddy . . ." He continued, however, declaring with real feeling, "Methodism was built around preaching and evangelism, but, now, we're always apologizing for our emotions. The Lord knows we need to break down into tears on occasion."[11]

In November 1930, Cornwell would write in *The Essentialist* of his own struggle:

I shall never be able adequately to express my appreciation of one professor, Dr. William L. Stidger. He is laboring with unwearied effort to make men Christian ministers. It is commonly conceded that students at Boston are being trained for teachers and professors rather than preachers; but in his class room, chapel, sermon and personal conversation Dr. Stidger stresses conversion, a definite Christian experience, and the absolute necessity of the "ministerial call." Just a few weeks ago as I sat at his dinner table he told me that if he did not believe in conversion and a definite change of life he would quit preaching immediately. Two quotations follow:

"I don't care what these theologians say; there must be a feeling of utter futility; and then a feeling of joy as God comes in."

"A definite sudden experience is necessary to every minister. If you don't have it you lose nine-tenths of your power; I mean an experience apart from religious growing."

At the end of my year I faced a crisis. If there had been any reality in my conversion, if I had any call from God, it was in line with Dr. Stidger's emphasis. I was called to preach Christ, not criticism. Thus I faced a crisis. A school that exalts criticism, neglects the evangelical point of view, and presents to men a reduced Christ could give me no equipment for a Christian ministry, this was my crisis.[12]

As for his new church duties, Bill had not needed much romancing to be interested in Copley Church. The association with Edward Everett Hale, one of the brilliant

Boston preachers of the nineteenth century, nephew of the American patriot Nathan Hale, was very appealing to him.

Dr. Stidger Fills Dr. Hale's Pulpit
Begins Ministry in Copley Church Tomorrow

A new voice speaks from a famous pulpit. The Rev. Dr. William L. Stidger, a great modern preacher, begins his ministry tomorrow at the church, the pulpit of which was made famous by Edward Everett Hale, the illustrious prophet of a former generation.[13]

So read the *Boston Herald* on Saturday, October 6, 1928. Hale had been a dynamic orator and prolific writer, publishing over fifty books, including novels and poetry, during a long and productive life. He had become famous for his widely acclaimed novel *The Man without a Country,* a story that had seemed so real to many readers that Hale had repeatedly had to state that it was a product of his imagination and not a true account. By comparison, Bill, who was only forty-three, was already acknowledged to be an outstanding orator, preacher, and writer. Bill had twenty published books to his name and hundreds of articles (a stillborn novel, *Mother Man,* lay unpublished in a box in his attic) by the time he arrived in Boston. Still, he appreciated the connection with Hale so much that his new letterhead read:

Copley Methodist Episcopal Church
"The Methodist Religious Society in Boston"
Exeter and Newbury Streets
"Old Edward Everett Hale Church"
William L. Stidger, D.D., Morning Preacher

A newspaper, *The Christian Leader (Universalist),* welcomed Bill:

Bill Stidger in Boston

Something will be doing this fall on our corner in old Boston. Here stands the Edward Everett Hale church, taken over by the Methodists a year or so ago. . . .

Where Bill Stidger comes the crowds come, and standing-room-only signs speedily are hung out. . . . Honest, outspoken, unusual in his methods, always earnest and eloquent, Bill Stidger, as he is affectionately called, has carried everything before him in the West. Can he do as well in Boston? Will the self-contained, cold, reserved New Englanders flock to hear him? Will he pack a Boston church where even the very janitor gives an icy stare to one who speaks to him without a proper introduction?

. . . Perhaps he will be tamed. We hope not. A little shirt-sleeve hustle would make an impression anywhere in what used to be the Hub.

We must not give the wrong impression. Dr. Stidger is an ex–truck driver in the war zone of France, but he is also a poet of insight and the author of some twenty serious books. We wish Dr. Stidger the greatest success, both as a preacher and a teacher. We are glad to have such a virile, charming personality as a neighbor.[14]

In addition to Sunday morning services, Bill also conducted Sunday evening events and midweek services. For him it was an ideal arrangement; he could pursue his teaching responsibilities as well as his writing and outside speaking engagements.

Bill's primary objective at Copley was to "save souls," which meant giving sermons that dealt realistically with people's problems, providing them with hope and guidance. But he knew he had to be an impresario and entertainer to succeed. He needed advertising to attract the public's attention and get them in the door, and he needed lively services to keep them coming back as steady customers each Sunday. Church attendance across the country was on a noticeable decline, and Bill had to fight this trend. His competition included movies, theater, and, increasingly, radio. But inertia, simply not caring enough to go to church, was his biggest enemy.

As would be expected of a good advertising man, Bill knew his market. His biggest population base was students attending the numerous colleges and universities based in Boston. For them, lively current topics would appeal, such as the heated arguments surrounding the presidential campaign then being fought out between Herbert Hoover and Democratic New York governor Al Smith. Smith was a Catholic, and while his candidacy gave evidence of the emergence of the Catholics as a political force, there were suggestions, held to be fact by some, that if Smith won there would be papal interference in the federal government. Students found the presidential race not only fascinating but relevant, since many were old enough to vote for the first time. Bill therefore addressed the national election in each of his first three Sundays, advertising his sermons as offering a comparison and contrast between Woodrow Wilson and Al Smith, followed by Theodore Roosevelt contrasted with Al Smith, and culminating on the Sunday before the election in Herbert Hoover contrasted with Al Smith. Knowing also that access to a student's mind is often through his stomach, Bill announced a series of Sunday evening meetings called "Fireside Forums," which were to begin at 7 P.M. and would be followed by free dinners for college students. Edwin Markham appeared at the first of the Fireside Forums, where he read his "immortal masterpiece" "The Man With the Hoe" and others of his poems, as well as answered questions on the topic "Life Problems and Poetry" posed to him by the several hundred students from more than fifteen colleges and universities who attended.[15]

Bill knew many celebrities, and he also knew how to use these celebrities to attract people to church. In the first hundred days, Edwin Markham appeared on four Sundays, reading his famous poems as well as "Our Israfel," his most recent prize-winning poem, on Edgar Allan Poe. Edna St. Vincent Millay, another highly regarded poet, visited Copley to read her signature poem, "Renascence." Bill's real coup, however, was inviting Ethel Barrymore to be his special guest when, on December 2, 1928, he gave a sermon on her new play, *The Kingdom of God*, which had opened in Boston. Miss Barrymore was not only beautiful and talented but widely acknowledged as the reigning first lady of the American stage. The Shubert Organization had just named one of its Broadway theaters after her. The *Boston Herald* reported:

> Ethel Barrymore, the actress, was the magnet responsible for one of the largest church attendances in Boston yesterday, when she appeared at the Copley

Methodist Episcopal Church to hear the sermon on her new play, *The Kingdom of God*, delivered by Dr. William L. Stidger, Pastor. Every available seat was taken and a large number remained standing throughout the service.

Miss Barrymore was lauded by the Pastor as belonging to the imperial royalty of her great profession, and he praised her "as the outstanding woman of the stage." At the close of the service, hundreds flocked around to shake her hand.[16]

A photograph in the newspaper showed Miss Barrymore and Bill in front of Copley Church, and both benefited from the publicity. But there was more to the story, as Bill later made clear:

> I was speaking on her play and had thought that it would be a very interesting thing for her to hear and for my audience to have her there. She promised to attend, and sure enough, that morning she was sitting in the front row of my church. But she looked deathly pale and ill.
>
> After the church service was over I went to her and said: "Now may I take you to your hotel, Ethel?"
>
> She replied: "No, you cannot take me to my hotel, but you can take me to the Massachusetts General Hospital if you have time."
>
> I thought she was joking and said: "Why, what's the matter?"
>
> "I have a temperature of 104 degrees and the doctor forbade me to come to your church service, and wanted to take me to the hospital two hours ago. But I had promised you, and you had advertised that I would be there, and I didn't want to disappoint either you or the people. Besides I wanted to hear the sermon," she smiled.
>
> When she finally convinced me that she was not joking, I took her to the hospital and there she remained for two weeks with a serious attack of influenza. But that Sunday morning she had the spirit of "the game must go on!" and came to my church, even though she did have a temperature of 104.[17]

When she was recovered from her flu, Ethel arranged for 150 of Bill's theology students to see *The Kingdom of God,* in a specially reserved section of the theater. Bill's popularity at the School of Theology soared because of connections like these.

Crowds of people, especially students at Boston University, the Massachusetts Institute of Technology, and Harvard, began to surge to Copley Church on Sundays, making the church a new habit. Bill's strategy worked. He did not overlook any aspect of church life that attracted people. Excellent music was important, and to this end he secured the help of Jim Houghton, his colleague at the School of Theology, who was professor in charge of music. Houghton was a physically large man, with big hands and a huge, resonant bass voice. With him as soloist and director of music, Copley's music was quickly among the best in the churches of Boston. On the same Sunday that Ethel Barrymore visited Copley, Bill announced that he would have as soloist Harriet Clarke Price, the winner of the second prize among contraltos in the nationwide Atwater-Kent contest. Jim Houghton had won first prize among men. Together Houghton and Bill persuaded Harriet to become a part of Copley's music team, though many other ministers were striving to capture her for their churches.

Shortly after the turn of the year, a huge revolving cross arrived on Copley's front lawn. It remained (just as it had come from San Francisco) in its wooden case, leaning up against the tower wall. The pageant of the revolving cross attracted much attention, particularly when Bill announced that it would not be erected until it was entirely paid for and could be dedicated free of debt. Bill had ordered it from his manufacturer as soon as he arrived at Copley Church. He made certain the newspaper reporters knew that he had invented the first electrified revolving cross for his church in San Francisco in 1913, had patented the idea, and was earning royalties from the two hundred other crosses that had been ordered and installed in churches around the country.

So it was that Bill completed the whirlwind of his first hundred days, satisfied that he had a thriving and even overflowing congregation, that the line of succession from Edward Everett Hale to himself had been accomplished fittingly and that Boston knew that he and Copley Church were there. The *Boston Herald* summarized Bill's strategy: "To the Copley Methodist Episcopal Church, proclaimed to the world as the Edward Everett Hale Church, has come within the year the Rev. William L. Stidger. Methodism has here placed one of its most successful preachers, a man with a record of popularity. His methods are unusual, in fact his pulpit technique is quite individualistic. He is being energetically backed by his congregation and by the leading officials of Methodism. If organization, expenditure, energy and pulpit style that has been proven effective elsewhere can conspire to make of this church a kind of cathedral of Methodism for the Boston area, this combination certainly will be tried with enthusiasm."[18]

The second phase of Bill's development of the congregation at Copley was a month-long series of sermons on human psychology, which he began on the first Sunday of January 1929. He focused almost exclusively on a series of drama or dramatic book sermons dealing with and answering individuals' personal questions regarding fear, power, and success. These sermons addressed the burgeoning interest in psychology, reflecting the popularization of Freudian analysis. He wrote about this project in his book *Personal Power,* published in 1929:

> I had been working toward this type of sermon [on psychology] for ten years. In late 1928 I started off with [a sermon on] John Rathbone Oliver's book entitled, *Fear.* It proved so popular, caused so much discussion, brought such a crowd to my church, overflowing it into the street, that I suddenly realized that I had struck something in which people are vitally interested. Then I decided to give a month's series of dramatic book sermons on books dealing with practical, everyday psychology; something that the people could feel was meeting a need in their lives.
>
> A man is subject to fits of anger. If he understands the reason for such excesses; if he understands inhibitions, complexes, repressions, and explosions from the viewpoint of the psychologist, he will be better able to control these moments of weakness.

The preacher may not be a psychologist, but he can read the findings of psychology, link them up with the observations of that greatest of all psychologists, Jesus Christ, and hand them on to his people, thus giving his people real help in their human problems.

The series of Dramatic Book Sermons ran into four months: January, February, March and April. They grew in popularity, and the whole city in which they were preached got to talking about them. I did for that town what the average professional lecturing psychologist does, only I didn't charge fifty dollars for the series. In addition to that I gave them a scientific background for the series, instead of sucking my information out of my thumb. I was merely interpreter for men who had spent a lifetime in this field.

I say, without a shadow of hesitation, that this is the most popular and helpful field for sermonizing into which I have entered. It works. It helps. It inspires. It sends people forth from a church with clear minds and braver hearts.[19]

The sermons on psychology were filled with illustrations, many of which were drawn from Bill's own life. He was able to talk about his shortcomings and foibles, which helped his congregations grasp the points he was making but also made him a more real person to them. Bill told of two recurring dreams, one of which reflected his wish to return to his hometown, Moundsville, West Virginia, where he wanted to be appreciated for what he had accomplished. It was also possible that the dream was about Bill's wish for recognition among the intellectual giants at the School of Theology. Of his dreams he said:

I am a daydreamer. I would like to loll all day long on a mountainside under a tree with the sun pouring on me. But, long since, I have disciplined those daydreams and I am known as a doer and not a dreamer.

Night dreams have the same effect. I have several favorite and recurring dreams. I dream that I can fly. I always fly back to the little hometown, and when I arrive I am the focus of admiration and the hero-worship of my old friends. I light on the spire of the church and give a talk. Then I give several shrugs of my shoulder muscles and show them how it is done. I am aware of the fact that this is an "ego dream!" Therefore, I have disciplined that dream. I am not fooled over why that flying dream comes; I, at least, know myself.[20]

The second dream Bill recounted to his congregation is remarkable for its candor. He said:

One of my regularly recurring dreams is that I am in the pulpit, preaching, with nothing on but a white shirt. I have a hard time of it keeping the audience from discovering my naked legs. I snuggle up close to the pulpit; I squirm and twist and turn so that those on each side in the first seats will not see me. It is always a trying ordeal. I also dream that I am in the pulpit with nothing to say, or with my sermon ill-prepared.

But I know what these dreams mean. They are both symbols of unpreparedness. Every preacher has them. I have disciplined them by understanding what they mean. They have taught me the lesson of preparedness. I never allow myself to get into a position of unpreparedness in my life task.[21]

Bill's series of sermons covered the broad topics of the sources of human psychological power, fear and faith, discipline and goals. He advertised them widely as follows:

FIRST SERIES
"LIFTING YOURSELF UP BY YOUR BOOTSTRAPS"

Take up your journey to the stars! Be a person! Get out of that physical and mental slump and live! Probe your own powers and possibilities in this sermon series!

All of us have powers of personality, charm, talent and poise which lie unused and untouched. We have sources of charm and genius which may lie dormant forever if something does not awaken them.

Most of us get into the dumps and fall into ruts; we beset our paths with what I call the fear of failure. We do this when we have powers within which would conquer the earth. This series is calculated to link practical everyday living, bread-earning, money-making life with religion. It is to bring to you what Jesus said He came to bring: "The Abundant Life."

SECOND SERIES
"THE ABUNDANT LIFE SERIES OF SERMONS!"

Sermons to set the soul singing and soaring! A frank, scientific study of personality and power!

THIRD SERIES
"LIFTING LIFE TO THE HAPPY HEIGHTS!"

The new way for the new day! Science and the old gospel! How to let your own powers loose from the chains of habit and inhibition![22]

This extraordinary series of sermons exemplified Bill's constant efforts to be innovative. He integrated the latest thinking on psychology into his views on religion in an effort to provide help to each member of his audience. He also incorporated the idea of self-help into his sermons, which emerged as a philosophy of thinking positively, all of which struck an extremely responsive chord among the members of his congregation.

What Bill was doing at Copley was being discussed in the halls and classes at the School of Theology. Pat McConnell wrote an article summarizing the impact Bill had had on Boston after six months:

Before William L. Stidger came to Boston, the Copley Methodist Church was commonly known as "Edward Everett Hale's Old Church." Now it is known as "Doctor Stidger's Church" by a host of youth who attend every Sunday morning. The young people who attend this historic church are not mere sermon tasters who flit from place to place, but serious-minded youth. . . .

Let no one think that this preacher escapes criticism. Preachers whose pews are never dusted by a crowd scoff at crowds in the churches of others. Colonial dames whose feathers have not been ruffled since their ancestors "first fell upon their knees and then on the aborigines" take exception to his rugged utterances. Big Wig churchmen worry about the sacred traditions of the past. Sensationalism is decried by folks who shout themselves hoarse at the Yale-Harvard game. All of this helps to fill the pews of Copley. Young people follow the crowd and the criticism.

Copley Church is filled every Sunday morning with people—young, old, rich, poor, wise and not so wise. They come from the Back Bay and the waterfront, from the student dormitories and from the taxi drivers' rooming section. I have watched them leave often enough to believe they get something. At any rate they return for more of the same.[23]

Of course, as McConnell said, Bill drew criticism as well as praise, the most outspoken of which appeared in January 1930, at the end of his first year. The criticism appeared as a letter to the editor in the leading Methodist newspaper, the *Christian Advocate*. The letter was written by a senior member of the Methodist Church, Bishop Wilbur P. Thirkield. He did not name Bill in his letter, but there was no doubt in anyone's mind, especially Bill's, as to whom the bishop was referring.

"THE SERMON AS SENSATION OR SACRAMENT?"

Editor, The Christian Advocate:

Sir:

There is a great city church that is advertised as the "students' church." It is central to the university life of over 10,000 students. At great cost it was purchased and for its support urgent appeal was made to the Methodist Episcopal people of the city in behalf of the religious life of the university. This church is set for the high task of ministering to the larger spiritual life of an unusual student community, and a great, eager group of a city university, with its intellectual claims, its doubts, its temptations and its claimant distractions, surely needs the opportunity for worship and the spiritual culture that such a church may offer.

It is fitting that the noble tower should bear aloft a flaming cross, the central symbol of our Christian faith; the cross, which still stands in the straits of the soul and makes appeal for cleansing, grace and guidance. But my heart and mind are burdened for this church in my old university town. Last year the themes for the opening ministry of the new professor-preacher as the university year began were, in the midst of a hot political campaign, Al Smith, et al. This for four Sundays. Surely the student group through seven days of the week had first-page and startling headline insistence on such contraverted themes. Did they not yearn for a spirit of worship and devout contemplation on Sunday that would make the sense of the presence of God a reality in the midst of a turbulent and noisy cam-

paign? And what about the observance of the holy communion during that first month? Surely, with the pulpit turned into a platform with such secular and controversial themes, the administration of the holy sacrament would be a profanation. But was there any student need so urgent as to have life kindled afresh at the Table of our Lord to flame with divine light and power!

Although burdened for the student group and for the status of my church, I held my peace, with the confident expectation that such secular themes would give way to a ministry that would bring to the students fresh spiritual strength and the way of eternal life. What is my sorrow this year to read as the first themes of our student preacher:

"H. L. Mencken"

Elmer Gantry

The Strange Interlude, *Eugene O'Neill [The mayor of Boston banned the production of this play on moral grounds in 1929.]*

"What Is Back of the New Morality?"

Mencken, more blatant and vulgar than Voltaire; Elmer Gantry, *a novel that should be let lie and die in its own filth;* The Strange Interlude, *over which an excited controversy was raging on account of certain obscene passages! What themes for a minister who, as [the British poet and critic] Matthew Arnold said of [Ralph Waldo] Emerson, should be the friend and helper of all those who would live the spiritual life!*

And now over the nation is flashed the sensational news that the themes for the two succeeding Sundays have involved an attack on the teachings and ideals of a nation-wide organization of women [the Daughters of the American Revolution]. While perhaps justified in his attitude, yet why turn the pulpit into a controversial platform for such themes? What a sermonic example to several hundred theological students who look to this pulpit for homiletic models and intellectual and spiritual guidance!

Silvester Horne [prominent English Congregational minister] sounds a note of warning in the word: "The only thing that can kill preaching is that we shall lose the sense of its majesty and unique authority." This means that the preacher is a prophet of Almighty God with a message of life and truth inspired by the word of God. The pulpit now has rivals. But neither the printed page nor the radio can ever supplant the preacher with a living, burning message uttered in the power of the Spirit. Protestantism must never lose its prophetic voice. The lecturer or the entertainer in the pulpit cannot match the radio. But the preacher to whom, as Dr. Cadman says, "the sermon is a sacrament," can. The radio can talk, but it cannot bring the atmosphere of worship with its sense of the presence of the divine, and the realization of the immediacy of God, which reverent worship in the house of God may bring, to the devout worshiper.

May I add that this student-preacher has such ability and power of attraction that these sensational themes are not required to draw the people, for I am assured that in the chapel of the School of Theology he has uniformly given as deeply spiritual and uplifting addresses as any that have been heard there. "Who go to hear Phillips Brooks preach?" was once asked. The answer, "Hungry people," is pertinent today. The people are hungry for the Bread of Life. The same principles of spiritual insight and interpretation applied to the Word of God would bring such illumination and spiritual power as to draw the people and give to students the example and inspiration that in olden days hundreds of us got at Trinity Church, where the sermon was a sacrament.

Wilbur P. Thirkield
New York City[24]

Criticism like Thirkield's was made to order for Bill to address. The bishop had not personally witnessed one of Bill's services but, rather, drew his conclusions from published reporting of the events. Criticism by a bishop cried out for a reply, and Bill immediately supplied one. The *Christian Advocate* printed both Bill's reply and a letter in his defense written by George Truman Carl, a student at Boston University School of Theology:

"TWO LETTERS ON BISHOP THIRKIELD'S CRITICISM"

I.

From a Student in Boston

Editor, The Christian Advocate:

Sir:

Bishop Wilbur P. Thirkield has seen fit to launch what I regard as an unfair inquisition against Dr. W. L. Stidger of the Copley Methodist Church and the Boston University School of Theology. I dislike to regard it as an irate or vicious attack, for one of my fondest recollections is the very beautiful spirit of the bishop as he presided over the Illinois Conference at Mattoon, when first I entered the Methodist Church. And in this article of the 9th of January he graciously recognizes the inherent genius that has made Dr. Stidger such a magnetic attraction in the church world.

Nevertheless, it is inevitable that such an article should have a most unfortunate influence. A shallow clergy and laity, unaware of the salient facts of the case, and simply drawing their conclusions from the specific indictments, will harbor in their minds a prickling prejudice against one who is rendering a most unique service in revitalizing a Methodist ministry.

In the first place, let me say that Dr. Stidger unhesitatingly affirms his positive belief in the power of a definite personal conversion experience through Christ. He deplores the present tendency of the Church to smother its God-tuned voice in heralding the most potential factor in the history of the institution. This conviction sweeps in cyclonic fashion across his entire ministry. . . .

To be sure, the people are clamoring for the "Bread of Life." But there may be no bread if the earth is robbed of the fertility that is conducive to the production of "Bread." The future security of our beloved nation depends upon the prophets of the Church of the living Christ, who dare to stand in their pulpits, dauntless and unafraid, defying those insidious forces that are sucking the very life-blood of her sacred ideals and institutions.

What security did Al Smith and his program offer the sanctity of our youth? We needed someone to bombard and blast the strangling influences of the "Strange Interlude" on our American homes, if the highway is to be safe for our questioning, searching, daring youth. H. L. Mencken, devoured everywhere, needed to have his blatant conceit exposed for what it really is.

It is my honest experience and [that of] hundreds of other students in the city of Boston, finding their way into the silences of old Copley—once the entrenched citadel of Unitarianism—now packed with the power of the cross, that they come away with a mystical sense of peace. And more than that, gleaming from their eyes is the aroused spirit to fight to the last ditch against the encroachment of devilish intrigues, whether they be in the disguise of respectability or not.

Copley is now synonymous with God and Christ. She welcomes hundreds of students in the name of His love. Dr. Stidger has opened the doors to this Christ. We see Him in all His wondrous beauty. We feel Him in an unforgettable devotional atmosphere. And as we tarry we sense a strange newness. The baying hounds of sin have been stilled within our hearts.

Respectfully,
George Truman Carl [25]
Boston University School of Theology

II.
Professor Stidger Speaks for Himself

Editor, The Christian Advocate:

Sir:

I am doing a thing I have done but once or twice in my life. I am answering, publicly, an accusation that has been made publicly, even though Bishop Wilbur P. Thirkield did not name me by name in his letter to The Christian Advocate *of January 9.*

    The personal picture was so clearly drawn that no man could mistake it. It was so clearly drawn that many letters have come to me urging many things. An attorney friend has advised a suit for libel, because what Bishop Thirkield says is untrue. I never in my life preached a sermon on H. L. Mencken, nor did I defend The Strange Interlude, *as his letter implies. The fact is that I did exactly what Bishop Thirkield himself indignantly suggests: I condemned not only this play but the whole movement that is back of it. I felt then and still feel that the prophetic implications of my ministry compel me and all other ministers of God to concern myself with politics, with life, and with social evils of all types. Bishop Thirkield has never heard me preach. It seems to me unfair to condemn any man in my position until he had either talked with him or had heard him preach: and knew his spirit and what he was after in his ministry and in his teaching.*

    What Bishop Thirkield does not know and does not seem to care to find out is that I have never preached a sermon without giving the call to the altars of the Church, and that throughout my entire ministry I have seen men and women and children kneeling at those altars at the rate of one a day on an average.

    I have always had a deep sense for a sane ritualism, and have a most profound reverence for the communion service. I have always tried to develop a deep spiritual atmosphere in my churches, and am even now in the midst of an observance of Pentecost running throughout the year. I believe with Dr. E. P. Dennett and many other wise leaders that Methodism is not a ritualistic church; that we are a preaching church; that if people are enamored of ritualism they ought to go to the Roman Catholic Church, or to the Protestant Episcopal Church, where they do it right.

    This vital matter I am willing to debate with Bishop Thirkield at any time or place. I stand at the opposite pole from him in that respect, and I believe that the Salvation of Methodism lies not in ritualism but in preaching[,] which has been the very genius of Methodism from the beginning. . . .

    I respect Bishop Thirkield for the martyrdom he suffered in the cause of racial justice long ago, and for his little book of prayers, which I use every year in my services. It is one of the most worn and used books I have.

    So what I wish to say is that maybe he is right. At least there must be some right in his criticisms. Surely I am not infallible. My family would testify to that. I admit it to save argument. I love Bishop

Thirkield. I thank him for what he has said to me—thinly disguised—in public print. I shall profit by it. As "Father Taylor," on whom I am preaching this very week, once said when he got into an involved paragraph of sermonic utterance and couldn't straighten it out, he stopped dead still, looked his audience in the eye, and said: "Brethren, I've lost the subjunctive mode, but I'm on the way to glory!"

I shall take whatever is of worth in his letter and profit by it. In the meantime I invite Bishop Thirkield to visit us some Sunday morning in Copley Methodist Church, unannounced, and I confidently believe that he will find several things—rain or shine, winter or summer—a crowded auditorium, a reverent atmosphere, a spiritual hope, and a contented people.

I suggest that, in the light of the poise, the calm, the good judgment and the kindliness that we have a right to expect of ripe and mellow old age especially of the sunset years of a bishop of our great Church, that he, at least in the future, before he makes an open and public attack on a young man in an official position in the Church, write him personally, or at least talk with him, or visit his church and hear him preach, try to find out what the spirit of that man is. Be fair and kindly in all judgments and criticisms. What is the loving thing to do, Bishop Thirkield?

> *Fraternally and faithfully,*
> *Wm. L. Stidger*
> *Boston University School of Theology*
> *Boston, Massachusetts* [26]

Bill's open letter to Bishop Thirkield broke the ice between them and one year later, in 1931, when Bill's book *Men of the Great Redemption* was published, Thirkield wrote the following words of praise, to be used by the publisher in promoting the book— "Chapters that are vivid, moving and fairly glowing with life, taken right out of human experience[;] . . . illustrations out of the deep heart life of men who have been touched by Christ and lifted to higher levels by the powers of the world to come."[27]

For twenty years, Bill Stidger had what he regarded as the best job in the world. Each fall, he was greeted by a new crop of students, 150 in number, over whom he was given responsibility—and the privilege—to inspire and instruct. Each aspiring young preacher could be expected to reach the hearts and minds of 20–25,000 people over his career, which meant that all of Bill's students over the span of his teaching career would reach somewhere in the neighborhood of 50 million people. And, like the "smile" that Bill wrote about when he followed it one morning from a cheerful newsboy to an austere businessman, the smile, as it passed from one person to the next, fanned out, infecting others along the way; so, too, Bill's stories of inspiration and hope spread outward from his students to people in their congregations and to those people's friends.

Bill has moved on and so have most of his students. A twenty-five year old in Bill's first class in 1928 would be almost 100 today and a student in his last class in 1948 would be in his seventies. With no more than one notice in the School of Theology's alumni magazine asking "Do you remember William Leroy Stidger?," 50 replies from his former students appeared almost immediately. No better proof of his lasting contribution to his fellow man could exist than these testimonials which describe what he was like in the classroom and as a friend and mentor. What follows is what his students have to say about him.

"It was out in the West on a lonely road, dusty and gray and long, When suddenly into the schoolhouse strode a sorcerer of song." [Edwin Markham]

These words were delivered by Bill Stidger, the guest preacher at a Sunday morning service in the large Wesley Methodist Church in downtown Worcester. It was our first time to hear Bill and today, sixty-five years later, I still remember the symphonic theme of that sermon, so appropriate for the day before the opening of the public schools and especially meaningful to weary travelers like we who had arrived from the mid-west. My own grade school years had been spent in a one-room school in north Missouri on a dusty road about a mile from our home. I could immediately relate to his theme.

I grew up in northern Missouri and graduated from Baker University in Kansas in 1931. My wife and I were married about a year before we decided to leave a good Missouri pastorate and go to Boston University for my divinity degree. Bill had been pastor at the Linwood Boulevard Church in Kansas City while I was in college, but I had never met him or heard him speak. I had heard, however, older ministers comment about him, many of them critical of his so-called "egotism" and his "sensationalism." I think now that these comments came from ministers who were jealous of his successes, but there were enough of these comments to make me think seriously of not going to the School of Theology at Boston University. In fact, some of my advisers put the matter quite forcefully to me.

But I continued to be drawn to Boston, and I have been forever thankful that I went. What's more, Bill proved to be a good friend, a respected teacher and an inspiration to me. My wife and I drove from Savannah, Missouri, to Boston in an old secondhand Chevy, and we were lucky to get there. On a Saturday night just before Labor Day weekend we stopped in Worcester, Massachusetts on the last leg of our journey to Boston. It was there we first heard him speak.

All in all, it was a wonderful introduction to the man who would be my professor of preaching. I have kept my notes and many of the hand-out programs from his churches that he gave to us, and I have often turned to them through the years because they were invaluable.

All the way from Iowa to Boston I wondered what the School of Theology would be like. When a friend and I pulled up Beacon Hill and I saw those famed big numbers, "72," in gold upon the lunette over the towering heavy doors with their highly polished brass appointments, my friend said, "This is it, Ralph. This is your new home." As I climbed out of our laden automobile onto the old cobblestone street and looked at the smoke-smudged, blackened building covered with the grime of decades, my apprehension must have been evident. He quickly countered, "It may not be new but you are going to love and appreciate it."

We climbed the steps through the entrance and were greeted royally by a personable young woman in an enclosed glass office-cage—a woman who was the wife of one of my new-to-be friends and a theolog. Then my traveling companion gave me a Cook's tour, starting with the Richards room. It was a large room with a black and white checkered tile floor. It was the heart of the School, a place where everyone gathered or passed through on their way to or from class. Even today I can still see that famous bearded poet Edwin Markham stationing himself in the Richards room in a centrally located wingchair so he could hold forth to the passing population. He would await Bill's call to join him in his classroom to give a poetry reading.

To the left of the Richards room was the Salon, a formal room facing Mount Vernon Street. We quickly learned that this was no student lounge; it was strictly to be kept a place of quiet. Its windows were tall and the ceiling was high, made still higher by a raised plaster cove. On opposite walls in the Salon were massive gilded mirrors that spoke of the elegance of former days on Beacon Hill. The positioning of the mirrors gave endless reflections of the walls and of a lovely cut-glass chandelier that hung from the center of the ceiling. "Formal Teas" were held here on a regular basis so we might learn to be comfortable with our more affluent parishioners. It was in the Salon where I first met Mrs. Stidger. She presided with great dignity over a faculty reception for Bishop and Mrs. Herbert Welch. On that occasion, the Salon was filled with flowers and the coffee table was spread with delicious food, which was a great treat for all of us students.

Sets of stairways rose to the second floor on either side of the Richards room, the one on the right led to the Library. Our elderly librarian ruled with an iron hand over a handsome mahogany room with an elaborate plaster ceiling decorated by four beautifully carved wooden owls. Opposite the library on the second floor at the top of the other stairway was a waiting room leading to the Dean's Office, which was richly appointed and lined with books.

Near the Richards room, but on the Chestnut Street side, was the Registrar's office as well as several professors' cubby-hole offices. Beyond these offices, there was the new building, which had a wide corridor leading to Robinson Chapel, which was the crown jewel of the School. There were more small faculty offices along this corridor, Bill's among them. More than once I would go into his office to get a new book to read or to seek some advice and, always, a word of encouragement. Walking past Bill's faculty office, you came to a few stairs, climbed them and entered into the back of the chapel. It was gothic in design with a most lovely chancel area and organ. The stained-glass windows had been designed by the Connick Studio in Boston and, in my opinion, were priceless works of art depicting the "basic" Saints, Old Testament characters and Apostles. It was in that luminous setting we heard some of the finest messages brought by visiting church leaders as well as from our mentors.

Likewise in that setting we found ourselves reaching for the stars in our humble efforts toward homiletical preaching and also getting worked over by Bill following our trial sermons in Advanced Preaching Classes. It was there we heard Edwin Markham, Robert Frost and other literary greats as well as fine musicians, who visited us in some of our regular required Chapel meetings.

Under both the old and new structures there was a basement used for classrooms, offices, the laundry area and the heating plant. There our wonderful older friend, Sanders Wilkins, held forth. Sanders was an unschooled black man who had an apartment in the bowels of "72." He did the janitorial work as well as keep the heating system going for us. But he also did a lot more. A visit with Sanders was a religious experience. He was a man of rich faith who took pride in keeping the place clean and polished. He viewed all of us as his charges and did not hesitate to shower us with advice if we got out of line, but he would have defended us to the death against any outsider. After all, we were a part of the School of Theology family. The faculty saw themselves in the same light. They might have internal disputes and disagreements, but to the world at large they were totally protective of each other.

Students entering Bill's class in homiletics saw facing them a man of generous frame with a large round head and strong chin. Mostly bald, his short-trimmed hair was light in color and might have been red but was now showing gray. He was dressed in conventional suits not always newly pressed but with a slight rumple that seemed to fit his frame, which tended toward being a little paunchy. His usual expression was open and friendly, and when he smiled his eyes wrinkled at the corners with humor. His manner of speaking was direct with no suggestion of any pious overlay. Overall, he was kindly and even tender. He had no trace of pretension, arrogance or false piety.

We all knew him as "Bill" but of course never called him that to his face. I remember that when the bell rang for class, Bill would be seated in the chair behind the lecture desk with a newspaper in his hands which he continued to read as we filed in. When the class had assembled, he would put the paper down and begin in a friendly, relaxed manner. One day I arrived very soon after he had begun, but I was definitely late. He looked up at me, interrupting his line of thought to say, "Good evening, sir, you are just in time for the benediction."

To this day, what I replied to this famous minister surprises me for its brazenness. I can only guess that Bill Stidger's openness and lack of pretension somehow gave me the nerve to say, "Then, I suppose I should just as well leave." Upon that I walked out of the room, waited a few minutes and returned, quietly, taking a back-row seat. From that moment, Bill seemed to take a personal interest in me and began greeting me in a very friendly fashion whenever or wherever we happened to meet.

In preaching, Bill stood frequently with his hands clasped on top of his head, with his eyes closed, although he usually insisted that we avoid oddities in our pulpit stance. Much of his time was involved in our "preaching clubs," to which we were assigned at the beginning of our first year, meeting weekly for that year. We took turns in preaching—either a sermon preached at a fellow student charged with listening, or one prepared specifically for the evaluation of the entire class. Comments by our fellow classmates were not too critical; after all, each of us knew we would be up front getting judged by our peers, maybe even at the next session.

One member of my preaching club (I'll call him Alfred), a sorry soul if ever there was one, finished his sermon and sat down. Instead of kind, encouraging, words, he heard Bill say, "Young man, you ought to think of some profession other than the ministry," giving chapter and verse for his judgment. Alfred jumped to his feet protesting, "But I have saved souls," and stomped out of the room. Bill's judgment was shown to be absolutely correct. Alfred graduated but quickly left the ministry, sincerely unhappy at the responsibilities he had as a preacher. Bill had extremely sound instincts and his practice was to encourage those who needed help but to be honest with those who needed to hear the truth.

The earliest recollection I have of Bill was his charge to us in our first class with him: "Go down to the Boston docks and learn about life!" This was an eye-opening experience for me, coming from a small mid-Western town: to see, learn and evaluate how others lived their lives.

To me it is axiomatic of life that leadership will always have its detractors who make snide remarks about truly great personalities. One such totally unmerited, uncalled-for comment of certain members of our student body came to the surface when Bill Stidger was called "the Idaho potato," implying—because he used the first-person pronoun "I" almost constantly—that he, like the potato, was filled with "eyes."

In our first year, Bill Stidger's class instruction was directed toward public speaking and sermon organization. Bill continuously emphasized clear enunciation and projection of words. He made us think of projecting our voices as if we had coins on our lips being hurled to the back of the room. In the second year, we studied sermon content and the search for materials to illustrate and to make the message compelling. Here we discovered some ideas quite new to contemporary preaching.

We were, let us be assured, studying in Methodism's most liberal school of theology. This meant a rejection of biblical fundamentalism and an openness to using the Bible as a resource for many things: history, devotion, morality, but not as a book of law to be accepted without question. The School's position opened up the realm of creative writing as a source for preaching materials. Bill wanted us to base sermons on themes we would find in great books. And he developed a technique that he called the "Symphonic Sermon" with a recurring theme, usually two lines from well-known poems, such as:

> Boatswain Bill was an atheist still
> Except sometimes in the dark.
> —Joaquin Miller

He made a practice of offering a book to any who would read and prepare a written review of it. When the review was submitted to him, Bill
would give the student still another book to read, review and keep. He
received the books himself from several publishing houses which sent him
new works to review. We students benefited from this largesse.

He drove us to read, read, read. He did not deny the claim made of him
that he himself read a book a day, but he also wrote and published at least
one new book a year. He told us that right after he returned from France at
the end of his stint in the First World War, he took a room in a hotel in New
York City and produced a book in a twenty-four-hour period entitled *Soldier
Silhouettes,* which was published in 1919.

Preaching Out of the Overflow, 1929, became his best-known book, in my
opinion. (Some students called it "Preaching Out of the Overblow," but they
were very mistaken.) It proposed wide reading as the best sermon preparation,
so that the result was a sermon that gushed forth like an oil well tapping into a
large underground oil field under natural pressure. The book drew a number
of critical comments, mostly based on what people thought, superficially,
about Bill. In my judgment, it was the best insight available into the "how" of
preaching—and today, more than sixty-five years later, it still is.

Ten years after leaving the School, I did a paper for a group of preachers entitled, "The Books Every Young Preacher Ought to Own," getting
help from many noted intellects around the country. On preaching, I asked
Bill to name four books he thought important. I also asked Harry Emerson
Fosdick, the foremost Baptist liberal theologian of the period. Fosdick was
the preacher at Riverside Church in New York City as well as Bill's counter-
part in practical theology at Union Theological Seminary. Fosdick wrote
back saying a preacher should read everything in print, which sounded to me
like the same advice Bill gave in *Preaching Out of the Overflow.* Bill, however,
listed a number of books such as *The Idiot* and *Crime and Punishment* in his
response. Then he added four of his own titles, saying that only his innate
modesty kept him from putting them first.

I had wanted to sit at Bill Stidger's feet in a classroom experience but I met
with the counsel that his courses were too easy, soft and not profound. I
waited until my third year before enrolling in his classes but I am eternally
grateful for the work I had with him. The exposure I gained into his mind
and spirit played a heavy role in my years of ministry. He prepared me for
the practical tasks of being a servant in the church as well as growing my
own soul. Tertullian spoke of how he could not see a rose or a feather from

a bird's wing and not think of God. Bill Stidger helped to set my spirit free in a world where all about me I found vibrant forms of the Eternal far beyond the most intricate theological statements of the learned. It remains amazing to me how he found God in so many varied forms.

The most memorable experience of my whole time at the School of Theology was Edwin Markham's visit to Bill's class. He stood before the class with his long white hair, full white beard and flashing brown eyes. With emotion and a flair for the dramatic, he recited this quatrain:

> They drew a circle that shut me out:
> Heretic, rebel, a thing to flout
> But love and I had the wit to win;
> We drew a circle that took them in.

I knew what it was to read poetry after hearing Markham.

Bill also loved to push us into being witnesses to the faith by making us preach on the Boston Common. Or, we would attend his preaching at the Church of All Nations. We watched him address a sanctuary filled with grateful workers at Goodwill Industries. It was an inspiration to see the handicapped come in, their gnarled and broken forms enthusiastically responding to his inspirational message to them. On another occasion he ran across some Jehovah's Witness leaders with their phonograph player and invited them to our class. We were eager to engage them in a dialogue—if not argument—but they took refuge from our questions by playing us their record.

Bill's own ministry used techniques that were so out of the ordinary they were sometimes hard to believe. His donning the garb of a bum and begging from the wealthy was part of the legend about him. He was also reputed to having conducted a service for the "dead" church. He had the congregation file past a coffin that showed the reflection of the observer in a mirror. These were grandstanding tactics, but they made valid and timely points. Out of these exploits, however, grew a cruel and unfair saying:

> Boston, dear Boston
> The city of baked beans and cod,
> Where the Cabots speak just to the Lodges
> And Stidger plays vaudeville for God.

Bill never seemed to mind this type of criticism. In some respects he thrived on the public report of his activities, whether bad or good. He wanted us to understand what he did, but he also pushed us to explore other ministerial styles, even more out of the ordinary than his. Evangelist Aimee Semple McPherson visited Boston in the winter of 1933–34 and Bill urged us to hear her speak at Boston Garden. We all knew she was the model for Sister Sharon Falconer in Sinclair Lewis's *Elmer Gantry*, and there was quite a lot of talk about Bill's being the minister Lewis had studied and twisted into his fictional character. Bill never commented negatively about Lewis, but the novel was known to be "sensitive ground" for him. This knowledge made Aimee Semple McPherson's appearance all the more interesting. Dressed in a voluminous flowery white dress, Aimee preached from the large stage that she shared with a huge motorcycle, the kind used by the police. From time to time she would go over to the vehicle and sound the siren, "Sinners, Beware!" She preached compellingly and a number of the audience stepped forward, signaling their conversion to her brand of Christianity.

Bill prided himself on his ability to outline his sermons and would show us how to do this effectively. I benefited from his instruction all through my ministry. My roommate turned in the following outline and Bill liked it so much that he incorporated it henceforth into his lectures on outlining:

> Text: "I Went Down to the Garden of Nuts." Song of Solomon 6:11
> 1. Nuts in the Old Testament
> 2. Nuts in the New Testament
> 3. Nuts in contemporary life
> Conclusion: Nuts to you

Bill Stidger and Pat McConnell not only were great friends, they both had a passion for baseball and, as clergy, they routinely received passes for both the Red Sox and the [then Boston] Braves games. It was not unusual for either of them to ask, at after-lunch classes, "How many of you fellows have passes to the ball game?" Since student theologs were able to get passes, a kind of majority rule, in which the Stidger and McConnell votes always assured a majority, adjourned the class to Fenway Park or Braves Field.

One beautiful spring day Bill and Pat, with afternoon classes at the same hour, announced that the two classes would meet in the bleacher section of Fenway Park, "because it is such a pretty day and the Yankees are in town. Those not interested in this kind of educational pursuit will find a long reading assignment on which they will be expected to write a report."

Pat said, "You know, Bill, the Lord has been awfully good to us. He built our School near Fenway Park and He has provided us with a side door to slip out to a game without being spotted by the dean."

World War II was making a big impact on the east coast. Rationing was in force and food stuffs scarce. My folks on the Iowa farm knew of our very limited resources and also scarcity of food supplies. Meat, dairy products, potatoes, and eggs were hard to come by. Bill one day remarked in an off-the-cuff manner how he missed good fresh eggs and bacon. By coincidence that afternoon when I arrived home I found a double egg case in the foyer of our residence with my name on it. Dad and Mother had packed an egg case, one side with fresh eggs and the other with some home-baked goods, cheese, butter and sugar. Rationing had not yet started in Iowa on foodstuffs. We also found a note stating if we could share a dozen Iowa eggs with his friend, Dr. Stidger, my father would be pleased.

I fixed up a package but just identified the donor as an "Iowa farmer who loved his produce." The good Professor did his sleuthing and at the close of the next day's class called out: "Ralph, I want to see you after class." When I presented myself to him, he tipped his head forward and looked at me rather sternly. He said, "There could only be one of my students who would do this, and you're it. Confess." I had to confess and told him it was from my Dad. I did not want any credit for the crime. Then he broke into a big grin and shook my hand, expressing his gratitude.

Bill asked for my Dad's name and address and then he wrote the folks. The letter was nothing short of "way-out."

February 6, 1943

My dear Brother Kitterman:

Your son, than whom there is no finer; one of my favorites in this school as, indeed, he is of all faculty and students—handed me with your compliments—a box of Iowa eggs. He didn't tell me exactly that YOU had laid them—but that was the impression I got from him; at least that you had hand raised the hens that DID lay them; had fed them a special type of Iowa tallcorn (perhaps [Henry] Wallace's [vice president 1941–45 and a plant geneticist] type). In any case I have them—ate two of them this morning for breakfast—but alas with no bacon. I said to him when he handed them to me: "What, Ralph boy —no bacon?" For, after all, Iowa DOES grow hogs also doesn't it? At least it seems to me last June when I went out to Iowa to make that talk at Cornell that I saw hogs in the fields about as big as elephants. But, at least I'm grateful for the eggs even if you didn't send any bacon with them.

And as I write I am reminded that Iowa lays something besides eggs for there was Herbert Hoover—and now we have Henry Wallace, and a good boy he is—about our biggest Internationalist—no matter what some of you out in his home state think of him. He has us fooled—and how!

Then there was Grant Wood; you Iowan boys laid a good and great artist egg in him—and Ruth Suckow—what a girl she turned out to be. I read everything she writes and Sinclair Lewis once told me that he considered her the finest writer of fiction we have in America.

And you lay another type of egg out there that is helping to win this war for I spoke for Bill Smith (one of my students) in Burlington and I went through that huge Ordinance Plant there and saw the big blockbuster bombs in the making. I'd say that those are some eggs for Hitler and Hirohito. You are quite an egg-laying state.

Seriously—you were mighty thoughtful to think of me and to send those eggs to me. I shall think of you as long as they last and of your kindness long after.

> *Fraternally and Faithfully,*
> *William L. Stidger*

In short order another shipment came from Iowa and this time there was some choice bacon along with some double-yolked eggs. We theologs had a feast and I took some to Bill with glee. He was moved by the response and asked what he could do for Dad. I told him if he would just write out his poem of "I Saw God Wash the World" in his own handwriting that would be a treasured gift. Dad received such and another wild fun epistle. Dad loved that possession. When sorting things after his death I found the envelope it had been mailed in and Mother had written on the exterior: "Stidger-for-Ralph."

Saturday, February 20, 1943

Dear Friend Kitterman:

Now I retain my faith in Iowa. It just didn't seem right to have eggs without bacon—even though they were the finest eggs I ever ate.

Now I KNOW that I was not drunk and seeing things last June when I watched those hogs as big as water buffalo or elephants in your Iowa fields. For that fine old Ralph of yours, with a grin, handed me a pound of bacon to go with my eggs yesterday. Last night because we haven't had bacon for so long (two months) we just ate bacon sandwiches to our heart's content; and man alive; that was the finest bacon we ever set teeth to. You must have personally trained that hog, taught it to lead a moral life, taken it to Sunday School and given it a college education—the way it tasted. No hog could taste like that or produce bacon like that and not have been a gentle, cultured hog, loved sunsets, music and poetry. I'll wager that that Iowa hog could play a violin, at least as well as Jack Benny, one of our major prophets of this day.

All of which is my feeble and stumble-bum way of thanking you for that additional courtesy and kindness.

> *Fraternally and Faithfully,*
> *William L. Stidger*

I believe that most of us who attended his classes would agree that he was different from the other members of the faculty. Virtually all the other professors were distinctly intellectual in their approach. Bill did not have a scholarly or intellectual approach but rather what we might call a popular approach to encouraging us and teaching us to be preachers.

He stressed the importance of our developing "homiletical minds," urging us to be alert to people and circumstances around us which we might include in sermons, to increase their interest and appeal to ordinary people. He was extremely influential in this respect and "Stidgerisms" found their way into the preaching of most of his former students.

In class he would often tell us stories which totally captured our attention even if, sometimes, they were stories on himself. I remember one in particular. Bill was a good friend of Dr. Fred Winslow Adams, a professor of worship. Dr. Adams was a very small man, only a little over five feet tall. (We referred to him as the "Jockey" behind his back because of his small size.) Bill, who was a big, powerful man about twice the size of Dr. Adams, told us about an occasion when the two of them and their wives were trying to look at the special Christmas displays in the windows of the big Boston department stores. Because of the crowds, Dr. Adams was not able to see over the heads of the other people. Bill bent over, picked up Dr. Adams, without his consent, and holding him over the heads of the people, advanced into the crowd saying, "Will you folks please let my little boy see into the windows?" He said to us that the Jockey kicked and struggled to get down and "He wouldn't speak to me for a week afterward."

When Dr. Adams died in 1945 Bill was asked to write a tribute for his good friend by *Zion's Herald*. Though he could play practical jokes on those colleagues he most admired and liked, Bill would always retain their friendships since he acted playfully and totally without malice. As Bill wrote:

> The editor said: "I want you to write an obituary for Freddy Adams. Write it in your own way."
>
> This is my way, and I think it will please Freddy. I am truly getting a kick out of writing it and you will see why, immediately.
>
> Freddy Adams had as keen a sense of humor as any man I have ever known, and it did not desert him in the last week of his full, busy, eventful life. One day I said to Freddy: "You are going to get over there before I do, and I want you to reserve a nice, single, humble, sunny room for me, will you Freddy?"
>
> "Yes, Bill, I will, and I'll have a harp for you to play when you get there."
>
> Then I said to him: "I also want you to prepare the way for me: speak a good word for me. I'm not a bad sort, and I love people; so speak up for me, Fred."
>
> "Sure I will, and I'll also be down to the docks to meet you when your ship comes in, Bill."

There were many tall tales of Bill Stidger's ministry, but they all fit his larger-than-life persona. I remember one story about him that went the rounds, which was said to have occurred on Easter Sunday at his St. Mark's Methodist Church in Detroit. The service had begun but Bill was nowhere to be seen. Whispers coursed through the ranks of the congregation, and many people had twisted around in their seats to see if they could find him.

Some, located toward the rear of the church, saw a funeral hearse pull up to the front steps. The undertaker and his assistants drew a casket out of the hearse, carried it up the steps and into the church and down the center aisle, setting the casket up in front of the pulpit. All eyes in the church became focused on that dark brown casket. The organist had shifted from the joyful music of Easter to quiet subdued music.

When the suspense had built to an almost overwhelming point, the casket cover flew open and The Reverend "Bill" Stidger sat up from his prone position in the white linen interior, climbed down from the coffin, agilely, and faced the congregation, spreading his arms to them, saying in a strong, exultant voice that carried to the back of the highest balcony, "I am the Resurrection and the Life! Hallelujah!" With the congregation in a dumbfounded state, the organist launched into the traditional hymn "Christ Our Lord is Risen Today" at full power and the Easter service was underway.

I had heard this story in many versions, and, while most of my colleagues doubted that it had happened as the legend was told, all believed Bill was capable of feats like this. He coached us as aspiring ministers to be dramatic because our congregations would more readily remember our lessons. And, after all, was not the story of the resurrection itself incredibly dramatic?

Then, in May 1949, after my commencement from Boston University, I had lunch (at the New England Kitchen on Charles Street, I think) with Bill, Iva and my wife. I asked him if the Easter Service story in Detroit were true and he smiled, saying it hadn't happened quite that way. But he sensed I was troubled about something and asked what was on my mind. The truth was that I had one more Sunday to preach at Peoples Methodist Church in Newburyport before moving to my new post at East Natick–Wellesley Falls Community Methodist church. The prior Sunday I had made a serious gaffe in my sermon, and I dreaded facing the congregation again.

Bill gave me his complete attention and asked me to fill him in. I said that I had preached on the family and the problems parents create when they spend more time at meetings of organizations than they do with their children.

"One man I talked to recently," I said in my sermon, "stated that he belonged to over twenty clubs and was never at home." Then, continuing, I meant to say: "Too many husbands and fathers are coming home from work, changing clothes, grabbing a snack and rushing out to their meetings without spending time with their children." What I actually said was: "Too many husbands and fathers are coming home from work, changing clothes, grabbing a snatch." Whereupon the organist, an excitable and rather uninhibited lady, remarked in a stentorian whisper that carried throughout the church: "That's exactly what they all come home for." The congregation spread her comment from pew to pew, erupting in gales of laughter. Of course I corrected myself and battled on through the rest of my sermon, but all I could think about for the rest of the service was my glaring blunder. Then when I stood at the door of the church and shook hands with my people, they would try to keep a straight face but many couldn't and would dissolve into paroxysms of mirth. I was devastated.

Bill, however, on hearing my tale of woe broke into a huge grin: "Ronnie Boy, that's great! The people will always remember you for that, and that's good. That's something like what happened to me when I was pastor of Linwood Boulevard Church. I had been reading about the immensity of our universe: that our sun was but a star in our galaxy and our galaxy but one of millions of galaxies in our universe. How small we are, I thought, like a grain of sand amid all the beaches in the world, how great God is and, yet, still He loves and cares for us.

"But in my sermon I said, 'Why, compared to God, we are nothing but a pea in the ocean.' Well, you know I meant a pea, like a green pea. The congregation became convulsed with laughter, and, even to this day, I can't go back to Kansas City without someone saying, 'Hey Bill, how about that pea in the ocean?'"

Armed by his reassuring reaction to my predicament, I learned how to put my mistake into proper perspective and, better yet, to realize that there was even some good that would come from a major blunder.

I wish I could take you back in time so you could sit in on one of Bill's classes. They were tremendous, and I am still benefiting from them to this day, more than fifty years later. Bill filled me with confidence and pride that, as a minister trained and educated at Boston University School of Theology, I could speak to and interview anyone at any time. He gave us resources, suggestions and honest appraisals that meant something the rest of my life.

I had a difficult time at first with the physical facilities of "72" but they grew on me and in the end they were as comfortable and easy for me as an old shoe. I learned to appreciate the culture of Beacon Hill and Boston proper. It is with great nostalgia that I now return to Boston. I did seminary visitation in the mid 1960s, some time after the move from the Hill. [In 1949, the School of Theology left its quarters on Beacon Hill to become a part of Boston University's new campus on the Charles River.] Longingly I tarried in front of "72" as I saw workmen shoveling plaster and debris from the upper windows down long chutes into waiting dump trucks. Our old school and home was being remodeled into high price apartments. Barricades were up all around "72" so I could not venture near enough to take a souvenir.

Still later, in 1993, I made the trip to Boston for my fiftieth reunion and once again climbed Beacon Hill to pay homage, finding it to be much steeper than the hill I remember running up from work to make it to Bill Stidger's afternoon class on time. It was a hot May day. The shuttered windows were open which had been tightly closed when I was a student there. Around Louisberg Square, people were grooming their dogs and washing their cars. I sat on a wall on the edge of the Square and gave myself over to memories. It was pleasant and sad at the same time. I missed the feeling of exuberance which I had as a student, and the excitement of all the experiences that lay ahead both for me and my wife. Now, the experiences lay behind me as treasures, and a sadness overcame me, how I missed my mate.

After a time, I walked to Charles Street to an ice cream parlor that is still there and bought an ice cream cone, though it no longer cost ten cents. That night I learned that the theater across from my hotel was presenting the last ballet of the season. The man at the ticket booth was reading a book on philosophy. He looked up when I stood at the window. Then he handed me a ticket, saying, "It is just about one third over. Go in and enjoy it." The seating was in an area where there were plenty of empty seats around me and I was glad. The tears ran down my cheeks, and I found the special healing, the kind Bill would write and preach about.

I won't probably be able to go back again, though I have longed to tramp the old haunts and feast my soul on things eternal. But my warm feelings remain vibrantly alive for the School. What a rich heritage has been mine because of men like Bill and his great colleagues.

Notes

1. William L. Stidger, "Pastor Tells Quest of Christmas Spirit," *Boston Evening American,* December 20, 1928, 1, 12.

2. William L. Stidger, *Personal Power* (Garden City: Doubleday, Doran, 1929), 177–78.

3. "A New Departure," *Zion's Herald,* July 25, 1928, 949.

4. Betty Stidger Hyland, *Those Heavenly Years*, unpublished manuscript, 1955, 135.

5. William L. Stidger, *Preaching Out of the Overflow* (Nashville, Tenn.: Cokesbury, 1929), 1–14.

6. "Practical Theology," *Boston University Bulletin, School of Theology,* 1929–30, 37.

7. "Homiletics and Pastoral Theology," *Boston University Bulletin, School of Theology,* 1929–30, 39.

8. Richard Morgan Cameron, *Boston University School of Theology 1839–1968* (Boston: Boston University School of Theology, 1968), 85.

9. Cameron, *Boston University School of Theology 1839–1968,* 85.

10. Interview with former dean Walter G. Muelder, Boston University, School of Theology.

11. J. Kenneth Cornwell, "A Review and an Appreciation," review of *Men of the Great Redemption,* by William L. Stidger, unidentified publication.

12. J. Kenneth Cornwell, "I Press On," *The Essentialist,* December, 1930, 223, 224, 259.

13. "Dr. Stidger Fills Dr. Hale's Pulpit," *Boston Herald,* October 6, 1928.

14. "A Shirt-Sleeve Hustle at the Hub," *Christian Advocate,* September 13, 1928, 1112.

15. "Edwin Markham, Poet, at Copley Methodist," *Boston Herald,* November 3, 1928.

16. "Ethel Barrymore Hears Sermon on Her New Play," *Boston Herald,* December 3, 1928.

17. Stidger, *Preaching Out of the Overflow,* 162.

18. "Achievements and Changes in Greater Boston Pulpits," *Boston Herald,* December 22, 1928.

19. Stidger, *Personal Power,* ix–x.

20. Stidger, *Personal Power,* 139–40.

21. Stidger, *Personal Power,* 140.

22. Stidger, *Personal Power,* xii–xiii.

23. C. M. McConnell, "'Bill' Stidger Preaches to Youth," unidentified publication, 1919, author's collection.

24. William P. Thirkield, "The Sermon as Sensation or Sacrament," *Christian Advocate,* January 23, 1930, 113.

25. George Truman Carl, "From a Student in Boston," *Christian Advocate,* January 23, 1930, 113.

26. William L. Stidger, "Professor Stidger Speaks for Himself," *Christian Advocate,* January 23, 1930, 113.

27. William L. Stidger, *Men of the Great Redemption* (Nashville, Tenn.: Cokesbury, 1931), publisher's promotion material.

Ten

The Depression: Boston

O n October 29, 1929, the stock market crashed and brought a long era of prosperity and optimism to a close. On this Black Tuesday, at times, there were no
buyers of stocks at any price on the major stock exchanges. The high that the *New York
Times* Index of Industrial Stocks recorded on September 3 fell 50 percent over the following ten weeks.[1] While the stock market crash caused widespread concern, the country did not initially realize that a catastrophic event had occurred. Political and business
leaders came forward with statements meant to bolster public confidence. Henry Ford
announced he would do his part by raising daily wages in his factories to seven dollars
and by launching a $25 million expansion of his facilities.[2]

For the time being, all seemed to be well. But it wasn't. The longer-term effects of
the stock market decline, coupled with consumer caution and a slowing down of investment by companies, spread across the country. Business investment in the American
economy began to drop dramatically; it went from $16.2 billion in 1929 to $10.5 billion
in 1930, a decline of 35 percent. It fell another 60 percent in 1931 and by another 88 percent in 1932, virtually vanishing in 1933, when it was $800 million—a decline of 95 per-
cent from 1929. This precipitous change in business investment translated directly into
huge losses of jobs. By 1933, 25 percent of the nation's workforce was unemployed.[3]

President Herbert Hoover referred to the deteriorating economy as a "depression,"
so as to avoid using what he regarded as more alarming terms, such as "panic" or "crisis."[4]

Bill was occupied with his teaching at Boston University, with his preaching at the
Copley Church, and with the momentous occasion of his daughter Betty leaving home for

her freshman year at Smith College in Northampton, Massachusetts. Betty's absence was wrenching for him, but he dealt with this loss by sending her a hail of letters filled with good cheer, friendly advice, and pep talks—as the occasion warranted. Though it was he who was relentless in wishing to communicate frequently, he wrote her, "I was just thinking as I shaved this morning and looked forward to writing to you as I do every Monday, Wednesday and Saturday morning how you have tied me to your heart with hoops of steel."[5]

By the end of 1930, economic conditions had worsened so much that Boston University and Copley Church both had to take action. Enrollments at Boston University were down, and its president, Daniel Marsh, initiated a 5 percent faculty pay cut university wide. This unusual action shook the faculty. At Copley the collection plates were increasingly bare, reducing what the church could afford to pay its two ministers. Families everywhere, however, were suffering cuts in their income, students were dropping out of college, and it was not surprising that money was a concern to Betty. An early letter gave her Bill's philosophy on this matter:

I like the tone of your letter. Mother and I want you to have just the happiest time of your life in college and you will. I don't want you to feel cramped. I want you to have what you want but not to be extravagant, and I know that you will not be. I am willing to work my head off so that you can have all of the things that you need and as many of the extras as will make you sanely happy. You do not need everything that everybody has for that, however—as you well know. The harder you work this year the happier the last three years will be. You will then be able to feel relaxation and have more time to enjoy the social and cultural life of the college.

Having his salary cut at Boston University might have made Bill anxious, but he revealed nothing of this to Betty. To offset the reduction of his income, he poured his energy into the two activities he knew could earn him extra money: writing and speaking. He reassured Betty, "Things are picking up with us financially and I am getting a lot of new speaking engagements. I must have gotten five or six this past week—also a letter from Stan High [editor of the *Christian Herald*], saying that he was going to send me a check this coming week for a serial he bought from me three months ago or more. That doesn't mean that we are rolling in wealth but it does mean that the tightness has loosened up a bit."

Being away from home and alone in a large college atmosphere, Betty was frightened and uncertain of herself. Bill sensed Betty's distress and kept up a steady stream of letters and communications as his lifeline to her, assuring her, implicitly and explicitly, that he and Iva stood squarely behind her, no matter what:

I am glad that you have the feelings about Smith that you told me about, when you looked up at the observatory and at the lighted windows coming back to your dormitory in the twilight. I remember having had those same feelings when I was in my first year at college. I could take you to the exact spot in Meadville where it suddenly flashed over me one beautiful twilight hour that I was on my own, my own "Boss," that

I was a part of a great institution, that I had the making of my own life and future in my own hands. I felt like jumping up and down and shouting out to the stars. I felt as if I had the world by the tail and was swinging it around over my own head. So you catch the idea that I know just how you felt that night you walked home by the astronomical observatory.

Betty had yet to learn study habits that helped rather than hindered her efforts. She later wrote, "I studied all the time. I learned so much that I knew too much and I began failing in French and history." Bill told her:

I don't care if you do get a flunk card on that French. Your Mother says that your French teacher talked beautifully about you——and said that since it was a full year's course that they would not think of sending you home on that—even though you do have a "warning" in history. Therefore this semester you can make up both your French flunk (if you get it) and by the end of the year you can make up both your French and your History. In any case they will NOT send you home. I am convinced of that—so just forget that concern, kid!

Don't worry if you get that French warning. Thousands of others get them. I always had at least two warnings in college—and it was only by the skin of my teeth that I got through at all. The same is true of your Mother. She and I talked about it—I had just exactly the same trouble that you are having. I didn't like history and I had a helluva time in getting it straightened out. It didn't seem to have head or tail to me. However, it is easy for me NOW. I wish I had a chance to take European history all over again. It would have some meaning to me which it did not have in my college days.

I am telling you this so that you will understand that you are just like other people. They would never have let me stay in college if it had not been for my football and athletics. They were always struggling to get me out of two warnings so I could play football. They used to send tutors to me before the big games to get at least one warning off so I could play on the team. AND I AM NOT DUMB. It isn't a matter of dumbness. It is a matter of interest. I could get those things in which I was interested. I DID GET THEM. So can you. But in your case—you will just have to concentrate on that history and get it—since you are not playing football on the Smith team.

If, at the end of the year, you are not happy at Smith and do not want to return, you can go to Rollins, Allegheny or Wellesley or one of a half dozen schools. I am not going to have you unhappy in your college years. But my guess is that, when this year is through, you will want to go back and finish at Smith—and, if you do, you can.

When Betty called to say that she had been invited to her first college football game, between Yale and Dartmouth, Bill, almost as excited as if he were going, shot off the following "advice" to her:

I am hoping and praying that you will have a good weekend—without rain for the game. Have a good time, for it's really going to be a great game. I can't think of a single bit of advice to give you. Mother is just full of that stuff and she'll probably send you a carload of it. However, I feel that, as a careful parent, I ought to add some things that she may never think of:

Don't get drunk—too drunk. You might get just a trifle piffled, just enough to make you funny,
and foolish—but not dead drunk. It isn't being done these days.
Don't swear in the exciting parts of the game for it may shock your roommate's pious parents.
Besides it doesn't sound right for a Methodist parson's daughter to cuss too much. Be mod-
erate in all things. Don't swear any more than I would.
Don't run off and get married—just yet. It's too hard work, as Mother will testify.
Don't chew tobacco. If you must chew, "chew the rag" (since talking is your specialty) or take
along some spearmint gum. Tobacco makes a big bulge in the cheek and it stains the lips.
Don't gamble on the game. You might lose what little money you have and then have to pawn
your belongings.

Mother will tell you the minor things not to do. Evidently she has already been about that, judg-
ing from a bill of complaint that you sent in a letter of a few days ago. I gave her hell for scolding
you—but I don't think it will do her any good. That woman just has to scold somebody—and keep
them on the job—and while she's at you she lets me alone—so, for my sake, take it and profit by it.
Both of us—as I have said heretofore—need a good taskmaster to keep us on the job. I know that I
do, and since you are so much like me—I guess you do, too. So take it with a smile—and pick out the
nuggets of gold here and there and throw the rest away.
There is a pile of dishes to wash—as high as the Bunker Hill Monument—and your Mother
gave me my choice of writing to you or helping her wipe them there dishes. It didn't take me long to
decide. If I get through writing this letter before she gets the dishes washed I am to help finish the wip-
ing, so this is going to be a darned long letter even if I have to look up some new words in the dictio-
nary or copy off a chapter from some book. I feel a long period of creative work coming for me. I made
a mistake this morning, because I felt sorry for her, and helped her wipe the morning dishes, and, as a
result, she suggested that I keep up the good work this evening. If you give a woman an inch she'll take
a mile—I've learned by bitter experience.

Directly following the game, Bill wrote:

We listened in on the Yale-Dartmouth game yesterday afternoon and it was certainly about the most
exciting game I ever heard. In the middle of it Graham McMemee interpolated into his report the
story of a battle that was going on below him. He said: "There's a private fight down here in the Bowl,
and it is attracting more attention than the game. It's a woman fighting." I turned to Mother and said:
"I'll bet it's Betty." We are anxious to hear from you all about your weekend—what you did and
what sort of a time you had in New Haven. Did you go to chapel? You are no doubt back in
Northampton by this time and are having a good talk-fest telling the other girls all about it. I'd like to
hear your report.

Several weeks before Thanksgiving, Betty developed the conviction that she was
pregnant. The following narrative, in the first person, is taken from her book, *Those*
Heavenly Years:

And suddenly a terrifying realization occurred, which came out of nowhere. One night in early November I awoke with a start. I was going to have a baby! I was perspiring over every inch of my body, my heart pounded in my throat and I could hear its throbbing in my head. This idea was too real to be wrong! As fast as I had heated up, chills swept over me and left me trembling. I tried to plan what I could do. I could save my allowance, sell all my clothes and books and disappear. I'd go to New York City—no one could find me there.

I waited restlessly for the dawn, thinking about packing an overnight bag and planning my escape. I couldn't leave right away, however. Mid-term exams were the next week and Carmen Hart, a freshman I had met and whom I admired, had asked me for dinner on Tuesday. But I resolved I would be prepared to leave when it became necessary. Every night from then on I would awaken with the certainty of my approaching motherhood. I decided that Parry was the father because he was the only person who had really kissed me. Yes, logically I knew that kisses didn't make babies but logic hid its head and imagination ruled.

My days were haunted, butterflies flew at random in my tummy and an obstinate lump in my throat deprived me of the desire to eat. I couldn't study, and I began losing weight. I failed my exams. I was jittery. I talked to no one. Oh, was I miserable. Thanksgiving weekend approached and I was worse than ever. Mother had written telling me that Dad and she expected me to come home for the holiday but I didn't want to face them.[6]

Betty finally confided her (unfounded) fear to Iva, who in turn passed it along to Bill, who immediately wrote:

Now listen young lady—here's a scold: Cut out that darned fool talk about your "fear." If you don't watch yourself you'll think yourself into a real "fear complex" and we'll have to send you to the "Dumber Academy" or to some Nut House for the feeble minded. Keep that bunk to yourself when you think it. Mother worried about it, and I don't see any reason, first of all, why you should fuss around about an impossibility. A broken leg is a broken leg. You know how you get broken legs— and when you have one you can well remember how and where you got it. There is no doubt in your mind about such an event—as to the exact spot and day and hour you broke it.

Now—as to this damned fool notion you have which you call your "fear"—you can't have one of those, young lady, unless you know exactly where and how and when you got it—just like a broken leg. Do you get me? Now wake up and use your bean and cut that kind of talk out, now and forever. If you don't quit talking the way you do I'll begin to suspect that you are doing things you ought not to be doing. That's the only conclusion I can draw—and up to this time I've drawn nothing along that line but my breath.

Betty's story continues:

Never had I been so emotionally low. I think I would have left this world gladly but even at my lowest point such a thought never entered my mind. I was too

afraid I'd miss something. On the Tuesday morning before the dreaded
Thanksgiving holiday I stumbled from my bed and started dressing. Mary
Gilbert wandered in to borrow a pin, and she shattered the dark spell that I had
been under. "Betty," she said, "What a swell figure you're getting—I'll bet
you've lost forty pounds since fall!"

As suddenly as I had decided I was pregnant, I was cured of the problem—
the whole idea had passed. For the first time in six weeks I became aware of
logic again. I looked at myself, my face was thin, the bones showed on my
shoulders, my slip hung loose and my bulges had disappeared. I was thin! I was
young! I was free, and I was not going to have a baby![7]

As the Depression wore on, each ray of hope—whether it was an upbeat speech
from Washington or a momentary rise in the stock market—was dashed by further bad
news. The underlying trends of production, wages, prices were all down, and the clear
direction of unemployment was up. Institutions, like churches, that depended on the
generosity of others to survive suffered terribly. In education, students withdrew from
schools and returned to their parents' homes, where it was cheaper to live. However, it
was the lower end of society's economic scale, generally the blacks and the new immigrants, that suffered most.

During this period of anxiety and unhappiness, Bill initiated a monthly feature
in the *Christian Herald* that he called "The Column of Conrad the Cobbler." As Bill
explained, "Conrad has a little radio beside his bench, and as he cobbles he listens
in on what he calls the 'driftwood of the day.' He doesn't care much for the jazz
[depressing talk] that comes flooding in over the radio these days, but he does enjoy
the driftwood of fun, frolic and philosophy that lodges in the eddies of his memory, like driftwood tossed up by the tides. Most of it is made up of small bits, but
when gathered together it makes a beautiful fire and provides a glowing light and
warmth."[8]

A cheerful voice in a world of gloom, Bill's column became popular, and it ran
every month for over two years. His stories were the perfect antidote for an atmosphere
filled with despair. He showed that men and women anywhere could rise above their
troubles and achieve great things, making the world a better place for themselves and for
others. He wrote articles which were published in *True Story* magazine: profiles on Henry
Ford; Frank Murphy, the mayor of Detroit and later a justice of the Supreme Court;
Cecil B. De Mille, filmmaker; Roland Hayes, tenor (born of slave parents and asked to
perform before the king and queen of the United Kingdom in Buckingham Palace);
Charles Connick, artist and craftsman, who designed the stained-glass windows in the
Cathedral of St. John the Divine; Edgar Guest, newspaperman and poet; Martha Berry,
founder of a system of schools to educate children living in poverty in the mountains
of Georgia; Angela Morgan, journalist and poet; Fred Stone, actor and comedian; and
William Allen White, editor of the *Emporia Gazette* and novelist. Bill found that stories
of well-known people who had had to overcome the same problems as anyone else were
popular with all his readers.

Most of Bill's interviewees became friends for life once he had had a chance to get to know them, hear their story, and enjoy their company—and they his. He found that meeting one celebrity invariably led to being introduced to another. He told Betty about this:

> *I have had an adventurous day. I always manage to bump into some sort of worthwhile adventure and today it happened in the Connick studio. Charles Connick had a studio showing of "The Rose Window," which is to go into the American Church in Paris. I was an invited guest.*
>
> *In came Mr. Ralph Adams Cram, the [famous church] architect, and I had a visit with him. Then in walked a little man with a white goatee. I asked Mr. Connick: "Who is the little old fellow with the white whiskers?"*
>
> *Connick replied: "That is Cyrus Dallin, the sculptor of "The Appeal to the Great Spirit," which is in front of the Boston Museum.*
>
> *I said with a good deal of enthusiasm: "I want to meet that man."*
>
> *It didn't take long to go through that formality, and when I told Mr. Dallin that I knew his "The Scout" in Kansas City, "The Appeal to the Great Spirit" in Boston, "The Signal of Peace" in Chicago, "The Medicine Man" in Philadelphia and "Massassoit" in Plymouth; that I had lectured about his work, written about him and preached about him for years, he invited me to visit him in his studio tomorrow evening at four o'clock. So I am to have the joy of an interview with him and am to get to know one other truly great artist.*

In 1930, Stanley High, editor of the *Christian Herald,* and Daniel A. Poling, a contributor, coauthored an editorial that informed its readership of one million subscribers that the "evidence accumulates of a great and unsatisfied hunger among Church people—preachers and laymen—for the rediscovery, in their personal lives, of a vital religion."[9] Church attendance had been on the decline, a fact that men like Bill, Poling, and High believed to be the result of neglecting the individual. The Church, for the better part of two decades, had been championing its social mission—universal suffrage, fair wages, and reasonable working conditions—at the expense of concentrating on the specific problems of the individual.

Stanley High commissioned Bill to investigate and write up the stories of "redeemed" men from all walks of life. It was Bill's thesis, and in this he was fully supported by High, that the awakening of one's soul came more often from a quiet internal revelation than from the noisy, public stage of a revival meeting or a church service.

Out of a series of interviews published in the *Christian Herald* Bill fashioned a book he called *Men of the Great Redemption,* which was published in 1931. It was Bill at his best, as an investigative reporter and as a skillful writer of stories of men and women who had found inspiration in their lives. By focusing on the problems of the individual, Bill reasoned, the problems of society and ultimately of the economy would be solved. As he wrote, "If we any longer expect to have a redeemed society, a regenerated industry, a prophetic pulpit, and a Church which has recovered its lost beauty and its ancient attractiveness, we shall have to go back to preaching of redeemed men."[10]

President Marsh of Boston University thought enough of Bill's message and presentation to write the introduction to his book. He lauded Bill for bringing attention back to the individual: "Christ's method of transforming society was not the devising of a social system but the quickening of single lives and the thrusting of these lives out to transform social institutions."[11]

Between the Christmas of 1930 and New Year's, Bill criticized the "vulgar rich" for throwing lavish debutante parties over the holidays, in cynical disregard of the widespread suffering of others. His words were picked up by many newspapers, including the *New York Times*. When he chastised profligate spending, he had in mind, among other things, the contrast with the tough financial straits of his own students. He knew intimately the details of many of their lives. One of his students described his life at the School of Theology:

> I arrived in Boston supposing I might quickly find a restaurant job to provide my meals. Many and perhaps most of the "theologs" had been able to get jobs in restaurants in downtown Boston and our class schedule was arranged for a two hour break at noon each day to allow students to rush out, hurry across Boston Common, don a white jacket and "bus" restaurant dishes after quickly downing a meal. Toward two o'clock in the afternoon, we hurried back to the classroom and battled with fatigue in the often vain effort to remain awake. If a professor could succeed in stimulating us enough to shake off drowsiness, he was a star teacher. These same students would head back to their restaurants for a "free" supper, but generally would not need to work the evening shift.
>
> My roommate, who was in his senior year, had a job in a restaurant and he told me that one "stood in line" until an opening occurred. Only occasional substitutions came to me during that entire first year in Boston. Accordingly I made do by purchasing cheap items at the market (three loaves of sandwich bread for ten cents; a quart of milk for ten cents and canned beans). These had provided my food until I and one other first year student were invited by Bill Stidger to spend Thanksgiving day at his home. When we arrived we were introduced to their daughter Betty, who had come down from Smith College to be with her parents. The editor of a Detroit newspaper was also a guest in their pleasant home.
>
> To be recipients of such an invitation was not surprising as other faculty members did the same, especially for those newer students who had come some distance to Boston. The table conversation was principally between

Dr. Stidger and his guest from Detroit on political and other matters which were nevertheless of interest to us. Mrs. Stidger, who was a warm and strong appearing person with an easy manner which made us feel comfortable, served us the full Thanksgiving menu with ample turkey, sweet potatoes, rich dressing with gravy and pumpkin pie. I ate heartily. . . .

I soon learned that the selling of one's blood for transfusions was a well-established money earning procedure. The School of Theology was about a fifteen minute walk from Massachusetts General Hospital where one could register as a potential donor. I registered and left the School's phone number as my reference. When needing a donor the Hospital would call the School. All such calls were directed to our janitor, Sanders Wilkins, who would consult his list to determine the next-in-line. He would then locate his class, knock gently on the closed door of the lecture hall and say "Mr. So and So" is wanted. That student would leave the class and hurry down the hill north to the hospital where he would announce his presence and wait until summoned by a physician.

The blood donor would have a rubber tube inserted into one of his opened arteries with the tube's other end being inserted directly into the vein of the patient. This was no easy undertaking, even if it paid us well. One of my class-mates had arteries in both arms cut before an acceptable flow was established.

I was summoned once to the hospital and sat for two hours waiting my turn to give blood. My turn never came; the patient had rallied. I was dis-missed but received a check for five dollars. Unfortunately there were so many donors registering to give blood that the Hospital reduced the pay for each donation to $25. Oh, the Depression—even blood was cheap.[12]

Despite Bill's letters of enthusiasm and recipes for diligence, Betty continued to flounder in French and history. She was certain that she would be asked to leave Smith. Bill sent her a long letter to cheer her up. He said that with hard work he was certain she would be able to make up her grades by the end of the year. In his letter Bill referred to the desperate financial position in which many people found themselves. "Think of the poor girls who have had to leave school because of finances. You say there are more than three hundred of them. YOU DO NOT HAVE TO LEAVE! With this abnormal rate of exit they are going to be mighty slow to send a girl away unless she has broken the laws and is no good. You are not in that class."

In May 1931, Bill sent her a birthday greeting and this pep talk:

Dear Betts,

I love you! That's good news, isn't it?

My, how well we did enjoy our visit with you last Saturday, that day when you got to be an old woman—when nineteen years of age crept upon you unawares and bowled you over. That was a terrible experience, wasn't it? To come to an advanced age of NINETEEN? You felt the same way that I did in Detroit when my fortieth birthday came—but I have never felt that way since. Birthdays don't bother me any more. They are not important. What IS important is to live largely as you go along—getting as much out of life as it has for you; making other people happy, doing the work that is set before you the day and hour that it is supposed to be done; reading, loving a few people devotedly—and laughing with life all the time. That makes for happy living, I have found. Never to lose the spirit of play; never to forget that, after all, life is a game to be played just like any other game; according to the rules, and to win if possible; if not possible, to get fun out of the game itself.

Now your classes are over—and you have a full, free week to get ready for those exams. This is NOT play week, or show week but work week, kid—and USE IT as such. I don't want you to worry. If you get through, you get through. And if you don't, we'll not send you to the penitentiary. So do the best you can, walk up to those exams like a man, and knock them for a goal. I'm confident that you will get through, and that's all I ask. The most successful and happiest people on earth are not necessarily the honor students. In fact my experience teaches me that the average human beings who do average work in college—get through—and know how to meet and adjust themselves to other human beings are the happiest and the most successful after all. That's what I want you to do and be.

It will be lovely to have you at home, and between the time you are here and camp, we'll plan a lot of fun—maybe Detroit and New York just for a lark—and then you can go to camp. I want you to have a real rest this summer and get in good condition for next year's work.

All my love,
Dad.

In fact, Betty surprised herself and achieved passing grades for her freshman year, which she thought was nothing short of a miracle:

Fate intervened and with its help, I somehow made it through final exams. The freshman year was now over; my grades scraped along at the bottom of the barrel. That I just passed Zoology, was on the borderline in French, and was only saved from failing in History by my term paper, no longer fazed me. What of it! I was still in college and next year would be different.

Dad played an incredible role for me, behind the scenes. So I later discovered. Smith College believed they could get along without me, and so they wrote Dad a fine letter explaining that, although I had not completely failed, they would advise Dad to save his money and send me to a smaller school with less strict standards. Dad didn't even show the letter to Mother. He sat down and wrote directly to President Neilson:

Dear Dr. Neilson:

Enclosed please find my check for the tuition of my daughter Betty's sophomore year at Smith College.

We Stidgers are sometimes slow at catching our second wind. Perhaps I am wasting my money but, if so, it is in a cause of which there is no better. I have absolute faith that Betty will earn my trust in her ability.

Faithfully and fraternally,
William L. Stidger

Smith College never said another word on this subject, and I am forever grateful to Dad for his confidence in me and his forthrightness with President Neilson.[13]

By the end of 1931, after two years of the Depression, President Hoover, desperate to restore public confidence, presented a balanced government budget to Congress, eliminating the deficit, which had risen to 60 percent of government spending due to the disastrous decline in tax revenues. In order to accomplish this, the 1932 tax bill enacted the largest peacetime percentage increase in taxes in the nation's history. With a balanced budget, there was no stimulus to the economy from government spending. Since private investment was virtually at a standstill, the tax bill was colossally antiexpansionary.[14] It became evident almost immediately that the new measures would not work. Hoover even went so far as to predict, privately, a further economic collapse rather than the restoration of confidence that he had sought. The public by now had grown angry with the president's overly optimistic statements, in which he would declare that the Depression was over—at a time when more and more workers were without jobs. Chicago mayor Anton Cermak told a House committee that Washington had a choice: it could send relief, or it could send troops.[15] William Allen White saw hopelessness ahead and warned that effective relief would be "the only way to keep down the barricades in the streets this winter."[16]

With presidential elections coming in 1932, Hoover's chances to get reelected were increasing problematic. Onto this chaotic national scene, filled with despair and the threat of violence, came Franklin Delano Roosevelt, governor of New York, as the front-runner among the Democratic candidates. Roosevelt's compelling attributes were his buoyant optimism, his unfailing cheerfulness, and the impression he gave that he knew how to make things better for everyone. He had great personal charm, as well as a patrician bearing that also attracted people to him. Roosevelt had assembled a group of advisers, later referred to as the "Brain Trust." One of the significant positions he took in his campaign was presented in a radio address in April 1932, in which he talked about the "Forgotten Man." In this broadcast Roosevelt committed himself to a much larger role for the federal government than it had ever before assumed in peacetime. The root cause of the Depression, Roosevelt said, lay in the problems of farmers and the resulting lack of individual purchasing power in rural America, which then represented one-half of the country's population. He argued that income had to be redistributed. This proactive and interventionist theme set the tone for his campaign, making him an instant friend to the common man and immediate enemy of those who wielded control over the large blocs of power and wealth.[17]

Bill could scarcely be oblivious to the impact of the Depression everywhere around him. He preached and wrote of optimism and self-help, and on a personal level he gave whatever he could to those less fortunate than he. One of his students wrote:

> Bill gave help to under-privileged students, and there were many in those
> Depression years. I know about the money he gave or lent, with no expecta-
> tion of being repaid, to needy students, especially black students in the semi-
> nary, because one of them, the late Reverend James R. Cannon, was my best
> friend in my class of 1935. He told me of loans and gifts which Bill gave him
> in those days when he was trying to work as a barber part-time while going
> to the School.[18]

The Depression put an additional financial burden on Bill, and in an unusual way. He was involved in the plight of Edwin Markham, who, as a result of a series of disas-trous investment decisions, had to depend on an exhausting schedule of lectures, read-ings, and talks to earn enough money to survive. With budgets everywhere pared back, Markham was having trouble finding enough places to speak. He threw himself on Bill's doorstep, literally, once a year for an entire month, counting on Bill to line up engage-ment after engagement. Markham also expected royal treatment while he was at the Stidgers'; Iva was understandably annoyed at having the eccentric poet in her house, with his peculiar eating habits, his humming of hymns in the middle of the night, and his using the water pitcher in his bedroom for a urinal. When not giving talks in Boston, he would cut a wide swath through bookstore after bookstore, taking for himself any book that caught his fancy and leaving Bill to pay. Having Markham arrive in Boston was time-consuming and expensive for Bill, who increasingly struggled to keep the poet gainfully occupied. To deal with his "Markham" problem, Bill conceived of a gala celebration for the poet's eightieth birthday, to take place at Carnegie Hall, in New York City. Bill's idea met with an enthusiastic response from Markham and the poet's close friends. The cel-ebration occurred on April 24, 1932, and attracted over two thousand guests from thirty-two nations, as well as extensive media coverage.

President Hoover sent a telegram of congratulations, which Bill, as master of cere-monies and featured speaker, read to the enthusiastic audience. Bill had been requested by the head of the organizing committee to keep his remarks lauding the poet to four min-utes, but he could not comply. As he wrote afterward to Markham, "I hope that my con-duct of the evening and my small tribute (crammed into ten minutes) pleased you. I felt that it was inadequate but what better could a man do in that limited time?"[19] The Carnegie Hall event helped to keep the poet in the spotlight of publicity; that increased the number of his speaking invitations and made good sense for Bill on a different level, because he was about ready to tackle a project he had long intended: writing a biography on Markham.

By 1932 black unemployment reached approximately 50 percent nationwide, and lynchings were on the increase. The *New Republic* wrote that Ku Klux Klan practices "were being resumed in the certainty that dead men not only tell no tales but create vacancies."[20] The few women who could find jobs were underpaid; farmers suffered not only from the collapsed economy but from worn out, misused land that in turn created the dustbowl conditions described in John Steinbeck's *Grapes of Wrath*. Among laborers, there were two mass actions in 1932: one was between workers who were presenting their demands to management and police at the Ford plant in Dearborn, Michigan; the second was between the federal government and World War I veterans from Portland, Oregon, who marched on Washington to demand payments that had been promised by Congress but deferred until 1945. Unrest and unhappiness were everywhere. As if to mark the dire conditions, "Hoovervilles" sprang up on the edges of the larger cities— shacks of discarded packing boxes and advertising signs, of odd pieces of rusted corrugated iron and broken fence slots. Hoover by mid-1932 had few friends and millions of detractors, all of which spelled opportunity for the Democrats.

On the fourth roll call at the Democratic Convention, which began on June 27, 1932, in Chicago, the delegations of Texas and then California shifted their votes to Roosevelt, giving him the two-thirds majority he needed to win the party's nomination. In his acceptance speech, long and rambling so as to cover all the bases, Roosevelt called for an experimental program that would be aimed at achieving an economic recovery benefiting all the people. He concluded, "I pledge you, I pledge myself, to a *new deal* for the American people."[21] The next morning, Rollin Kirby, the cartoonist of the *New York World Telegram,* depicted Edwin Markham's oppressed "The Man With the Hoe" looking up, puzzled but hopeful, at an airplane labeled "New Deal." The public embraced Roosevelt's platform as the "New Deal," and this phrase came to overshadow all other descriptions of his administration.

In June 1932, the end of her sophomore year, Betty wrote: "Astonishingly enough, when I received my final grades, there seemed to be room for hope that I might pull up and finally graduate from college with decent grades. I had studied less than ever but I was better adjusted to college life and, what's more, I couldn't believe my good luck: it was July 1932, and I was going to Europe! Dad would be giving talks at the shrines of the great Methodist fathers: Wesley, Calvin and Whitfield. The *Christian Herald* and American Express were running the tour and invited Mother to accompany Dad. This, Mother decided, was my great opportunity. She had "been" to Europe and there might never be such a chance for me again. It was the Depression and money for everyone was a scarce commodity. Mother gathered together my new wardrobe, gave me some secret spending money and plenty of shrewd advice."[22]

Bill and Betty were given first-class treatment on board the MS *Georgic,* with, as Betty put it, "a lovely cabin, big and airy, on A Deck." On the third day, Betty was introduced to Dick Thomas, to whom at first she only paid scant attention, since he was thirty years old to her twenty—"much older, too old probably." They went dancing and had a good time, especially on the last night, when suddenly Dick looked much more appealing than he had. Betty had presumed that their relationship was over, but Dick surprised her:

> The next morning when everyone was saying their good-byes, Dick came up
> to Dad and me and asked if he might join our group for the next few days. I
> thought that this was a great idea; Dad said it was fine with him, though I could

tell he was less than wildly enthusiastic. We landed in Liverpool, spent the night, and headed off before dawn, northward, on a train, then a bus through the Lake District of England. When we crossed into Scotland we were again on a train. Coming back from the dining car, Dick gave me my first kiss in Scotland and nearly took my breath away—in fact he kissed me twice. I adored it because it was so romantic. Dick was wonderful; I only wished he were a bit younger.

Scotland was cold and rainy. We also attempted too much, which was my Dad's doing because he had boundless energy. I'll never forget the days when we were up before dawn and not finished before eight or nine at night. Dad would give brief lectures which were interesting but his listeners were too exhausted to remember. When Dick left us, I was devastated. Even Dad's excellent talk on Wesley, a spellbinding evangelist and founder of Methodism, failed to cheer me up. Dad didn't help matters at all. He said he doubted if we'd see Dick Thomas again. I was frustrated, exhausted and depressed. I was good for nothing but collapsing in bed. Then, in the middle of the night I felt this tap on my shoulder and it was Dad, rousing me. He made me dress and took me out in the late twilight to see the mill of George Eliot's *The Mill on the Floss* by moonlight. I could have killed him—still I'm glad I saw it. Years later I realized it was a subtle gesture on his part to distract me from Dick Thomas's leaving, and I loved Dad all the more for it.[23]

The tour group traveled down through Shakespeare country, stopping at Oxford University, where Bill gave a brief lecture in John Wesley's former room, then on to London. To Betty's relief, Thomas rejoined them, and in the evenings Bill, Dick, and Betty explored London together. Before Bill and Betty headed off for the continent, Betty arranged to meet Dick at the end of the stay in Paris. This was all under the watchful and wary eye of her father, who had been given strict instructions before leaving by Iva to make certain that Betty returned home safe, sound, and unattached. Betty later wrote:

We visited The Netherlands, Germany (on the eve of elections in which Hitler's Nazi Party gained significantly), Switzerland, winding up in France. Dad's lectures were given up along the way: no one wanted to spend time listening to long spiels on the sainted Methodists and Dad soothed his conscience by announcing that his talks were all written out and available for anyone to read. At last Paris, the City of Lights. One night we sneaked out— Dad and I—to go to the Follies Bergères. It was my idea and I had to persuade Dad who was reluctant; he felt it would be wrong for him, the leader of a religious tour, to be seen at such a very risqué show. I was determined and eventually won out. So we went. I guess the jokes were pretty raw, the French dancers were like nothing you could imagine: grace and beauty so intermingled that I soon forgot to think about their lack of clothing. Just before intermission an English speaking team of comedians held the stage. Dad's face reddened and reddened with each succeeding joke.

"Betty," he whispered, "This is too crude. Let's get out of here now, before the lights go on. If anyone knew I'd brought my own daughter to a filthy show like this!"

"Daddy—don't be so straight-laced. This show won't last forever and I want to see the other dancing acts. Besides, there is no one to report on you." Just then the lights went up and people started rising to go to the lobby for intermission. Dad plunged his face into his program and pretended to be in deep contemplation of the words in it. The intermission dragged on and on, and finally people straggled back to their seats and the lights were lowered and Dad breathed a sigh of relief.

The show ended in a whirlwind of naked dancing figures, the clashing of cymbals and varicolored floodlights. We stood up and turned to make our way up the aisle when suddenly above the hubbub of crackling French, we heard:

"Betty, Doctor Stidger—fancy seeing you here!—What a small world!"

What a small world is right—there were two of Dad's students from the School of Theology and, behind them, a couple from our group, who gamely waved at us, looking perhaps as sheepish as Dad felt. He had little hope that his explanation that our visit to the Follies was purely educational would hold water. To give his "educational" gambit some substance, he took me to the opera the following night and I frankly was bored to tears. After the ballet sequence, I timidly suggested that we go home, and Dad, to my surprise, readily agreed.

Dick Thomas re-joined us, and he, Dad and I spent our free time sightseeing. When Dick bid me farewell, he hinted that he had a most important proposition "when you're dry behind the ears. Go home. Have plenty of fun with Joe College—love 'em all. Then you'll be ready for what I want to ask." And as he made this last statement, he put a small box in my hand which I jammed into my purse, which I later found to be a lapis lazuli ring. His final words were: "There, wear it and remember Dick Thomas who loves you."[24]

With that melodramatic farewell barely a memory, Bill and Betty headed home. The boat train to Le Havre, on that afternoon of August 12, 1932, was as hot as Kansas City in the middle of the summer. The pier was hot and dirty, and the ship was four hours late in docking. It was dark when they finally went aboard:

We found our cabin, and what a cabin it was! D deck, right over the propellers, whose vibrations shook your very bones, made your teeth clatter and gave you the same feeling as the reducing machine Mother had bought in one of her thinning streaks. The come-down from traveling deluxe all over Europe was too much. At Dad's suggestion, we climbed to the top deck to cool off and gain extra stamina for the night. We stood watching the last of the cargo being carried from the deck to the hold by a giant crane. One last crate was being lifted; it loomed up over the deck and silently dipped down into the hold, and we saw that it was marked: "Handle with great care—coffin and body enclosed." What a setback to our already abysmal morale!

Dawn came and Dad went to work. By mid-morning he had our cabin changed to A deck. The fresh breeze washed by; the sparkling Atlantic blew over us; the sun was bright; the day was clear and our spirits rose with every passing minute. Dad rented deck chairs and I made a firm resolution that I would read all the books I had acquired on my trip—Kenilworth, *Lady of the Lake*, Shakespeare, and three Edgar Wallace mysteries—and I would devote myself to Dad. On the way home I would become reacquainted with my father. I said to him, "Dad, I am going to be quiet, rest up, read, take walks around the deck with you."

Dad was overjoyed. He had, unconsciously or consciously, worried about me the entire trip. He worried because I danced late on the *Georgic*; because Dick followed us on our tour; he worried that dangers might befall me—that the elevator in the *Georgic* would stop in between floors, that the door in the "W.C." in Munich would not unlock; that the Italian express from Geneva to Paris would derail; that the engines would collapse while we were at sea, and he alone would be to blame! He did not want to face my mother with bad news of any kind concerning me.[25]

Betty's resolve to be "Dad's pal" evaporated quickly when she was introduced to a dashing "Turk with green eyes" who called himself "Mustafa Kemal, just 'Musty' to my friends." His words emanated from a deck chair facing away from Betty. What follows was later related by Betty in *Those Heavenly Years*:

One white leg and then another untangled themselves from the foot-rest and suddenly, standing before me was a man whose striking good looks took my breath away.

His hair, which was thinning out on top, was a soft curly fuzz, almost a gold color. He had green, laughing eyes, a humped nose, a wart on his cheek and a gently mocking smile. His white linen suit was rumpled but clean, his shoes and white shirt were clean. His skin was clean; in fact, everything about him was immaculate, except his canary yellow tie, and it had a large wet spot on the flair part. In his hand, held loosely but lovingly, was a perspiring stein of beer.

But I had never heard of a blonde, green-eyed Turk. My eyebrows raised in surprise. I pronounced his name carefully: "Mustafa Kemal?"

A nod, a serious nod. He added: "Incognito, of course [Mustafa Kemal, now known as Kemal Attaturk, was the president of Turkey], but I also answer to the name: Jack Hyland of Philadelphia. You must be Miss Stidger, and I understand you intend reading your way home across the Atlantic because you left your love in Paris, and no one on the boat inspires you. Won't you sit down?"

"I'm traveling with my father. He's old and tired and needs me constantly," I desperately sputtered. "You will have to excuse me, Mister Hyland
or Kemal, or whatever your name is, as I must get back to Father." As I said
the last, I attempted to arise as gracefully as possible from the low, slanted
deck chair. It was wobbly to begin with and my attempted grace proved fatal:
the deck chair collapsed spilling me awkwardly on the deck.

Mr. Hyland looked down at my plight, saw that there was no harm done,
except to my ego, and burst out laughing. I scrambled up as quickly as I
could and took my leave, certain that I would never see him again.

After dinner that night Dad and I were well on to our fourth lap around
the deck when out of the corner of my eye I saw Mr. Hyland approaching
us. My chin went up in the air, and I tried to sail right on past him.

"Good evening, Miss Stidger, and Doctor Stidger, I believe. Miss
Stidger, I hope you aren't suffering from your fall?"

"Fall, Betty, at deck tennis? I didn't know you had a game with Mister. . . ."

"Yes, Daddy, deck tennis." My eyes dared Mr. Hyland to refute my statement. "This is Mister Hyland."

"How do you do, Mister Hyland. Have you been in Europe on a trip?"

"No, I've been working in Spain, France and Turkey for Commercial
Credit Company for the past several years. I've had the job of checking up on
the whereabouts of hundreds of cars and trucks financed by us whose owners
have defaulted because of the Depression. Now I'm on my way home."

"How interesting. We must have a talk about European affairs—this
new man, Hitler."

"Any time, Doctor Stidger. Right now, I wonder if you could spare
your daughter. There is a good orchestra down in tourist class. I'll bring her
back early."

"Go ahead, Betty, I'll turn in. Salt air makes me sleepy the first couple of
nights. Don't be too late," Dad said.[26]

Thus began Betty's shipboard romance and an elaborate subterfuge on her part—
to keep Bill from finding out that his daughter was falling in love.

On the next afternoon, I was alone on a deck chair since Dad had a poetry
inspiration and had gone to the cabin to set it down.

"Want to go where it's quiet and read with me?" a voice inquired over
my shoulder.

I was startled and said, "Why, Mister Hyland, as far as I'm concerned,
nowhere you are is quiet." I assumed a dignified air, then relented: "But, lead
the way."

It was a lovely afternoon. We went up on the sun deck in front of the
bridge. How Jack (he was Jack, suddenly and naturally) got permission to go
there was a mystery but it was fun. We talked: I learned a lot about him. He

was only twenty-six, had a father and two married sisters in Philadelphia, had been a Phi Gamma Delta at Lehigh and at the University of Pennsylvania, did post graduate work at Harvard Business and was unattached. This was his twelfth Atlantic crossing, and he loved the ocean, loved to watch the wake of a ship and the phosphorous at night.

It was hot on the sun deck. We were lying side by side on two mats. I was staring out at the greenish water and the pale blue sky as I talked and then as my chatter died away I felt a new silence, a peaceful warm silence that permeated into my very heart. I knew Jack was looking at me, and slowly I turned my head until our eyes met.

There were no words, but time stood still.

A gong shattered our peace and warned us of approaching dinner. Jack stood up and offered his hand to help me up: "We will come and watch the phosphorous here tonight," he said quietly.

I showered and started to dress with that calm of the afternoon still upon me. I stood at my mirror to comb my hair, and, suddenly, as I looked at my image in the mirror, my eyes began to shine and the blood pounded in my ears. I saw some new person staring back at me. My skin seemed to glow. My dress curved softly, molding my new being. My lips seemed warm with desire. I wanted to be beautiful and scintillating and desirable.

Dad muttered something about me being slow about dressing just like Mother, and that he was hungry and when I got ready I could join him for supper in the dining room. I was so happy to be alone, to feel the anticipation of just . . . why, just seeing Jack! Of course, how sublime, I loved that "Turk." Suddenly I had butterflies in my tummy. How could I feel this way about a man I scarcely knew? Why should I dare dream he loved me? How could I be sure of anything?

I stumbled breathlessly into the dining room, and there he was sitting at his table. I pulled myself together to sail past. I would have steered a perfect course, only I saw him half-rise to greet me and I collided with a waiter carrying a very full tray. Dishes, tray, waiter and Betty collapsed in a clatter. Dad and Jack reached me at the same time, but Dad ruined any vestige of dignity I could have mustered: "If you had worn your glasses and not stuck your chin up in the air, all this would have been avoided." I said nothing. I groped my way out of the debris and fled from the dining room.

My flight stopped at a stretch of railing between two life boats. The cool sea breeze soothed my burning cheeks and I let the bitter salt tears of embarrassment mingle with the spray. I felt someone's hands gently grip my shoulders: "You find the craziest places to watch the moon, and the phosphorus balls only can be seen from the bow—remember we had a date?" Then Jack turned me around. He was smiling and I knew he was going to kiss me and I knew I wanted him to kiss me. He leaned down toward me and just as his lips were touching mine, I turned my cheek!

"The phosphorous balls, Jack. Do you still want to see them?" I gushed out.

"That can wait. How about a drink?"

So we spent the evening on a funny little bench outside the bar. Jack brought his portable Victrola and we listened to "Parlez-Moi d'Amour" and "Song of India" from 9:00 until 11:45 P.M. After closing time, the waiter said: "Same as usual, Mister Hyland?"

Jack nodded, and the waiter brought four large steins filled with beer and placed them carefully in a row beneath the bench. "The bar closes at midnight, so I get four steins every night. Then when the lights go out I sit here in the twilight, play the Victrola, and watch the stars and enjoy my beer."

We swam together, played bridge together and watched the sea together. I still walked with Dad and read and talked with him. Each day Dad would say "Well, another day and nearer home. I have brought you through safely and soundly and boy, oh boy, will I be glad to see land and the end of my tribulations!" Then we'd both chuckle.

I would chuckle because I was in love and was so very happy, and Dad would chuckle because (much, much later he told me) he was so relieved that I had found no eligible male. Dad knew of course that I went around with that Hyland man. But we were so opposite: I was so naïve, he so worldly, that there was little—no, no danger there.

Betty's story concluded as follows:

So Jack and I spent our days and evenings talking some, but more often spent hours in silence, watching the ocean or the sky. Every evening we ended up at the little bench outside the bar: Jack with his beer and I with a recording of "Parlez-Moi d'Amour." Jack never attempted to kiss me or even hold my hand, but every once in awhile our eyes would meet and he would nod his head slowly.

Jack took me to see the phosphorus balls that last night. It was damp and foggy and the phosphorus didn't shine, but we pretended to be looking for it, and we stood at the rail, mist clinging to our hair, that cool fresh feeling of salty air in our nostrils. Jack leaned over the rail: "See how fast the ship is going: too, too fast. Slow down, old girl. New York is coming too soon."

I made no answering comment. I was calm and serene, just content to stand close to Jack and feel the weight of his shoulder as he leaned over me.

"It will be midnight and then noon before we know it, Betty, so I will say now what I need to say. Words aren't necessary, are they? You know what I want to say. You have felt how much I love you. I want to marry you. I have to get settled here in the States again, and you must finish school. Your parents want that, so I'll have time to make good in my business. I want the world for you. I'll have two years to court you and make you love me, too."

He gave me a silver chain to wear on my wrist in lieu of a ring or a fraternity pin. (I still had the lapis lazuli ring from Dick Thomas—did I even remember him now?)

Jack had put into words what we had gradually understood our peace with each other meant. Love is magic. It isn't as I read in stories: It doesn't gallop over you. It comes in quietly like a London fog, a simple sudden awareness. When Jack spoke, a peaceful warmth curled around my heart, but I said nothing. It wasn't necessary. Salt spray and mist merged and faded, Jack cupped my face in his hands. "I won't kiss your cheek this time, Betty."

Our ship was two hours late when it finally let down the gangplanks. The customs house was stifling hot and Mother had been waiting for three hours in the tin-roof oven. As the boat was docked, I stood at the rail with Dad, who was heavily perspiring in the furious heat. Earlier, Jack had come into the ship's dining room for breakfast just as we were leaving. Dad was planning our strategy: finish packing, get our landing cards, tip the steward and get on deck where we could see Mother when we landed.

I half-listened to Dad as we wended our way past the late breakfasters. When we reached Jack's table I forgot to listen to Dad, and when Jack said, "Want another cup of coffee with me?," I just slipped into a chair and let Dad wander out alone.

"You did mean 'yes' last night, Betty?"

"Oh, yes."

"In 1934, then?"

"I'll see you and write to you and we'll have plenty of time for plans."

When I spotted Mother and my uncle on the dock, I waved my arms. Dad and I were enthusiastically greeting them when Jack walked over to say hello. His hands were filled with paper cups. He said: "Hello there. This custom wharf is hotter than Calcutta. I brought some cool orangeade for everyone."

"Jack, how nice, thanks, and I want you to meet my Mother." I smiled as I accepted my cup. Jack said graciously: "I have wanted to meet you, Mrs. Stidger. Will you have an orangeade?" He bowed just slightly, and I went to hand Mother the sticky drink; just as Mother reached to take it, it slipped and sprayed and splattered Mother's stockings, my skirt and Jack's white linens! I had done it again, I thought to myself: Betty, you clumsy idiot.

After I had said goodbye to Jack, Dad, Mother and I drove home to Boston and it was a full week before I heard from him. One morning Mother called to me: "Betty, here is a letter from Cleveland. Whom do you know in Cleveland?"

"I don't know anyone from Clev . . . Oh, Mother . . ." I grabbed the letter, ripped it open and hastily glanced through it. There it was: ". . . and you know we have a date in 1934, and the time will pass, my dearest."

My head was on Mother's shoulder: "Mother, Mother, it's true, it is, it is. He does love me and he meant every word he said."

"Young lady, you settle down—what is true—who means what?"

"Why, Jack, of course. We love each other and we are going to be married in 1934!"

"Jack, Who? Bill, get in here! Who is this Jack that Betty is crying about?"

"Jack, Jack . . . why there was a Jack Hyland . . . , Betty, what is all this about? You can't be serious . . . why Jack Hyland . . ."

My Mother suddenly added up all the parts: "You mean that man reeking of beer who dropped the orangeade? Elizabeth Stidger, you are out of your mind!"

Dad took my letter and quickly glanced through it: "What does he mean 'you know we have a date in 1934?'"

That brought me to say: "That's my letter. I am in love and so is Jack, and he asked me to marry him and marry him I will, right after I graduate in 1934."

On November 2, 1932, just before the presidential elections, *Zion's Herald* printed a list of ministers supporting Hoover, and Bill's name was included, along with those of the president of Boston University, the dean of the School of Theology, and a number of prominent Methodist bishops. Their endorsement concluded with this statement: "Therefore, we confidently believe, and are constrained to express the opinion, that it will be far better, in these crucial times, to retain Mr. Hoover than to risk Mr. Roosevelt."[27]

There was no endorsement in *Zion's Herald* by any group of ministers for Franklin Roosevelt. Although Bill voted for Hoover in 1928 and did so again in 1932, he had misgivings, which he voiced in a sermon entitled "America's Lost Leadership and Herbert Hoover" on the last Sunday before the election. On election night, November 8, the returns showed no ambivalence on the part of the electorate; there was a landslide for change. Roosevelt carried forty-two of the forty-eight states, with only the six northeast states voting Republican; the Senate was now sixty to thirty-five Democratic, and the House was 310 to 117 Democratic.[28] Bill never commented on his having cast his ballot for Hoover, probably because it was difficult breaking from his own Republican tradition and from a president he had previously backed enthusiastically but now had grave doubts about.

Despite the prospect of better times that Roosevelt repeatedly preached were coming, the Depression continued to worsen, reaching rock bottom in the winter of 1932–33. During the lame-duck period between the election and the inauguration on March 4, Roosevelt could take no action whatsoever, and Hoover felt powerless to act. Farm prices slid badly from the prior summer; factory production, retail trade, and stock and bond markets were all down; unemployment rose to fifteen million. "Farmers were using shotguns to keep their homes from being foreclosed. In the cities, unemployed white-collar people were suddenly on every corner, selling apples."[29]

The crisis, moreover, had become worldwide and was political as well as economic. Britain asked for a suspension of its scheduled debt payments to the United States; Italy, under Benito Mussolini, was shipping weapons into Austria to arm

Fascists there; and, on January 30, 1933, President Paul von Hindenburg was forced to make Adolf Hitler, as leader of the Nazis, chancellor of Germany. Hitler dissolved the Reichstag—but only after it voted to give the cabinet, of which Hitler was the head, power to govern by decree for four years. Hitler then broke up all other political parties and arrested opposition leaders. The League of Nations censured the Japanese government for its aggression in Manchuria; Japan, in anger, withdrew its representatives from the League.[30]

In the first few months of 1933 people began to wonder if times would ever improve. There was a growing fear that that the country might even collapse. People stood in lines to withdraw their deposits, and the banks were unable to deliver the requisite cash. State after state took measures to close banks or put limits on withdrawals. Once bank closures started, panic set in. The news in the papers on March 1, 1933, the morning the president-elect left Hyde Park for Washington and the inauguration, was that more than twelve states had closed their banks or limited withdrawals of funds. In New York City it was announced that several thousand relief workers would be laid off because funds were running low. Newark defaulted on its payroll.

On March 2, the next day, the Federal Reserve Board reported that a quarter of a billion dollars' worth of gold had been withdrawn from the financial system over the past week. It was rumored that the New York banks would have to be closed. Roosevelt, now in a suite at the Mayflower Hotel in Washington, received an urgent request from President Hoover to join in a national emergency proclamation, but Roosevelt declined. He wanted to make a clean break between his incoming and Hoover's outgoing administrations.

The ceremony took place outside the Capitol rotunda on Saturday morning, March 4, 1933; Franklin Delano Roosevelt became the nation's thirty-second president. By that morning virtually all the banks in the country had been closed. The new president addressed a large crowd as well as millions of citizens gathered around their radios. He delivered his remarks in a high, singsong voice that became his trademark. His words rang out across a troubled and frightened country:

> So, first of all, let me assert my firm belief that the only thing we have to fear is fear itself—nameless, unreasoning, unjustified terror which paralyzes needed efforts to convert retreat into advance. In every dark hour of our national life a leadership of frankness and vigor has met with that understanding and support of the people themselves, which is essential to victory. I am convinced that you will again give that support to leadership in these critical days. . . .
>   If I read the temper of our people correctly we now realize as we have never realized before our interdependence on each other; that we cannot merely take but give as well. . . . The Nation asks for action, and action now.[31]

Roosevelt made good on that pledge by calling Congress into an extraordinary session, to begin in five days, and by proclaiming that all banks in the nation would be closed until steps had been taken to restore public confidence in the financial system.

As important as the text of his message was, the new president's use of radio to get his message across to the nation was probably more critical. Over sixteen million families, about half of the American population, owned radios in 1933. The president was able to talk to a large part of the country, telling the people that he was unafraid and that they should not be afraid either. He gave another radio address at the end of his first week in office, on Sunday evening, March 12. He reached an estimated 30 percent of the total radio audience: "I want to talk for a few minutes with the people of the United States about banking," he said in his soothing, fatherly voice. So began the first of twenty-eight "fireside chats."[32]

The president patiently explained banking in everyday terms that everyone could understand ("even bankers," Will Rogers said). He assured his audience that banks allowed to open the next morning would be financially sound. The country believed him, and the next day deposits exceeded withdrawals; the stock market rose 15 percent, its largest one-day increase in history. One man, the new president, had faced down the crisis brought on by the darkest hours of the Depression and for a time, at least, had held the destructive forces at bay. One of his aides later commented, "Capitalism was saved in eight days."[33]

No cure had been found for the crippled economy or for the problem of millions of men and women out of work. But a new voice had come forward to express confidence and hope. The president had been invited into each radio home and, in a friendly, nonoratorical way, asked for their support; Americans gave it to him. Roosevelt understood that radio gave him the means to go over the heads of the establishment, the newspapers, magazines, and the corporations (most of which were aligned against him) to make his covenant directly with the people. His New Deal was a handshake and a wink shared with every person who listened to his fireside chats, and it gave him the moral authority to make big changes.

Bill cheered the president's actions and understood very well the power now resting in Roosevelt's hands, given to him through the use of radio. He had experienced the thrill and power of it himself about a decade earlier, when broadcasting was far more experimental. He had said of his own first Detroit broadcasts: "As you sit there in the radio room talking, you send your imagination hurtling out across the winter-clad earth, over the roofs of city buildings, out over covered fields, leaping rivers and lakes—as your words literally do—speeding above forests of bare trees, down into the homes of human beings, and into the hearts and souls of your fellow men sitting in their homes by their own firesides; and you picture them sitting with a great eagerness in their souls, waiting, listening, for your message; and the thing takes hold of your soul. It is a thrilling adventure every time I talk over the radio!"[34]

Bill found himself increasingly drawn to the new president, and he began to defend his policies. He was in sympathy with Roosevelt's objectives and enthusiastic about his willingness to act to relieve the effects of the Depression. Bill even had to make an excuse for Roosevelt when, among his first actions, the new president put an end to Prohibition. The convoluted logic Bill used to excuse the president's action was reported in the press:

G.O.P. vs. Democrats

Dr. Stidger has a curiously antagonizing technique for stirring the interest of his audience. He warned the churches that they could not lay all the fault of repeal upon the present administration. The administrations of Harding, Coolidge and Hoover were to blame for failing to enforce the clearly expressed will of the people for Prohibition, he asserted.[35]

No matter how quickly the government acted, however, even in the whirlwind of President Roosevelt's first hundred days, neither the economy nor the dire state of large segments of the population was much affected. Getting the juggernaut of an economy to change direction could not be done quickly, and the pain inflicted on the people continued.

In view of the circumstances facing Boston University in 1933, President Marsh felt that he had no recourse but to institute a second salary cut for faculty; this time it was a 10 percent reduction. The minutes of the New England Conference of April 1933, covering Methodist activities in Boston, told the bleak story: "Unfortunately the continual decrease in the benevolence of the Church has annually given a diminishing amount to Boston University School of Theology until now donations from this source have almost reached the vanishing point. The university is operating the school this year at a considerable deficit." The salary cuts instituted by President Marsh obviously helped, as the report indicated: "Boston University has up to date successfully weathered the economic storm, which is testing the strength of many institutions. Decreased returns from investments, diminished gifts, and reduced enrollments made unusually rigorous economy imperative during the last year. The president of the university took hold of the problem with courage and decisiveness. He secured the hearty cooperation of all members of the university family. The result was that the university closed its last fiscal year without a deficit."[36]

To make matters worse for Bill, however, Copley Church was also in trouble. Churches that could not make their interest and debt payments were being closed or their operations drastically curtailed; Copley was one of these. The minutes had this to say: "All of these men [the pastors at Copley Church and Tremont Street] have been doing the work of the ministry with complete satisfaction to those whom they have served. Our problem today is one of finance. With falling markets decreasing the revenue and the value of property, and increasing taxes, we are confronted with a problem that only time can solve if it can be solved at all. The income from invested funds is not sufficient to pay mortgages, taxes and property upkeep. The two churches have been informed that they must reduce their expenses to their level of their income."[37]

The quality of Bill's contribution to the Copley Church was not in question: "A word concerning Dr. Stidger's work. He is doing the thing he was brought to Copley to do. In many respects he is the most outstanding preacher in Boston today. He is not the executive at Copley but the morning preacher. This, the fourth year, has seen a gradual growth [in attendance] until most of the time the church is taxed to its capacity, showing what can be accomplished in downtown Boston."[38]

But all that he could do to build attendance was not enough to bring revenues up to expenses or to hold his salary at prior levels. During 1932, Bill and Guy H. Wayne, the ministers at Copley Church, shared $2,400 in income, down 61 percent from the $6,200 they had shared the year before. The outlook for 1933 was worse.

Bill had been teaching for five years and preaching at Copley for the same length of time. He had now had two pay cuts at Boston University and a serious reduction in income from Copley. Where could matters be going? Enrollments were likely to continue downward at Boston University, and Copley, being a Boston city church, depended heavily on students for its congregation. Speaking engagements, moreover, which had helped him offset the pay reductions, were more sparse in 1933, and the articles that he submitted paid less.

Bill tried to make light of his concerns in a letter to Betty in which he maintained that he enjoyed "saving money":

Bright, sunny Saturday! "And ain't that something!" as that Old Testament prophet Amos of "Amos and Andy" would say. It's enough to make a fellow want to sit up and kick his heels together.

I had a chance to go to the Yale-Harvard game today—but turned it down because it would have cost me ten or fifteen dollars for the trip—and I am trying to save. Even Mother admits it—I am having a great and glorious time doing it. I am not whining, and I do not feel that I am sacrificing one bit. I am doing just what I want to do, as she says I usually do. I really like to save, and I do without so that you can have, and so that Mother can have things.

I enjoy the games over the Radio, and I'll bet I'll have just as much excitement and know more about the game this afternoon by getting it over the Radio than those who actually see it. I'm satisfied, for I can get two or three other games at the same time I get the Yale game. I am anxious to hear the Notre Dame and Northwestern game as well as some others, and I can do that over the Radio. So—I should worry!

Despite his brave talk, Bill felt that there were now good reasons for bringing his job as morning preacher at Copley to a close. He already had in hand an invitation to join the Church of All Nations as its Sunday morning preacher, but its founder, Dr. Edgar J. Helms, took no salary and expected that his fellow ministers would contribute their services gratis as well. The tradeoff for Bill, in giving up a salary, was that he would be joining a strong, solvent institution that was demonstrably doing important work, particularly among society's least well-off people. The Church of All Nations was a part of Morgan Memorial, which also controlled Goodwill Industries, serving the handicapped and out-of-work in Boston, by giving them jobs repairing discarded clothes, furniture, books, and shoes. Selling the refurbished goods for cash paid the wages of the five hundred men and women working for Goodwill Industries. Goodwill Industries' branches were flourishing in thirty-two states and nearly a hundred cities and towns.

The funds not paid out as wages went to build a financially sound institution that could expand its services nationally as well as undertake new initiatives, at a time when churches and schools everywhere were curtailing their activities.

Two of the initiatives that Bill found particularly intriguing were the fully staffed printing plant maintained by Goodwill Industries, which could provide him with attractive weekly church bulletins with which no other church could compete, and the willingness of a group of people close to Helms to embark upon a program of radio broadcasting. Having these resources would give him a unique platform, compensating in part for the lack of salary.

Any reservation he had about joining the Church of All Nations flowed directly from its close connection with Goodwill Industries. It was seen as a peculiar church serving the down-and-outers and the immigrants. Bill knew that some might question his leaving a mainstream church—which Copley, the "Old Edward Everett Hale Church," certainly was. He knew, however, that the Church of All Nations was doing heroic, if unsung, things, all of which he championed. Also, the Church of All Nations was perfectly positioned to survive in the perilous times, and it was in consonance with the programs that President Roosevelt espoused. He did decide, though, to test the waters farther afield to see if there might be a paying position in some major church in another city. He wrote his longtime family friend Bishop Edwin H. Hughes, whose area of responsibility was Washington, D.C., and received almost immediately a warm but unhopeful reply:

March 25, 1933

Dear Will:

I read with interest and sympathy your letter of March 23. I do not need to assure you that I will do anything that I possibly can to assist in getting you properly placed. In strict confidence, it now looks as if Dr. Montgomery would continue next year as pastor of Metropolitan. If he does not do so, judging by what the committee says to me, I think they will turn to one of the strong men in the Baltimore Conference. The spirit of the New England Conference in its attempt to build high fences for transfers in, and low fences for ministers who go out, is not wholly confined to that one body!!! The Baltimore Conference is exceedingly conservative with reference to transfers. I do not know that the men here are putting any special pressure on the Metropolitan Committee, but I do know that the feeling that the church ought to be filled by a Conference man is intense, and that this little Bishop would not add to his popularity if he should strongly counsel putting in an outside party even so good a man as W.L.S., D.D.!! But be assured, dear Will, that I shall have your name constantly in mind, and that I shall be happy to help in any conceivable way. Write or wire me day or night.

Do not let anybody hurry you into a decision toward work that is not congenial. I believe that things are going to pick up directly, and that after that it will be much easier to place some of our men. This morning's mail brings me three importunate letters from well known evangelists in our Church who find that their evangelistic campaigns are no longer possible, due to the economic situation. These men are eagerly beseeching that they be given pastorates. George Wood Anderson, for example, is one of the three.

> *Love to you always.*
> *Yours ever,*
> *Edwin H. Hughes[39]*

With no church apparently available to him outside Boston, Bill's way was clear—he decided to move to the Church of All Nations. The *Boston Globe* reported on April 1, 1933, that "in anticipation of necessary economies at Copley," Bill would begin "tomorrow morning" at the Church of All Nations.[40] To his chagrin but not to his surprise, Bill received immediately a letter from Elwood Rowsey, an old friend, who was minister of the First Westminster Presbyterian Church in Toledo ("The Civic Church With the Civic Heart in the Civic Center"). Rowsey wrote:

Dear Bill,

What kind of a Mission is that you are going to preach in now—The Church of All Nations—or something? I have long believed that when your forty-eighth birthday came, it would be necessary for you to take a church that could pay you no salary. Since you arrived at that state on your forty-sixth birthday—two years ago, I think you would at least stay in a church that had a name and, before you became pastor of it, had some fame. I read about this Church of All Nations stuff in some patent medicine book. The congregation must be composed almost entirely of morons when a patent medicine journal announces the coming of their new Morning Preacher. I will come into Boston some day and see you dolled up in a Salvation Army uniform. That is about where you will alight last. [41]

Rowsey's letter was written in playful jest, but it had a bite to it. Bill knew that other leading ministers, who were his competitors, would be secretly rejoicing about his new appointment even if not calling or writing him directly. Bill was spared further embarrassment, however, by the publication of his new book, *Edwin Markham*; its appearance occurred at precisely the moment he moved to the Church of All Nations. It literally came to his rescue; he found himself mentioned in newspapers and on the radio in a torrent of favorable comment.

The publicity surrounding Bill's book did not happen by chance. He had drawn up a list of the most influential ministers across the country to receive advance copies so that they could "talk up" *Edwin Markham* from their pulpits and in their radio broadcasts. Bill's publisher sparred with him to keep the number of free copies to a reasonable limit. He lectured Bill: "You know we have in mind the idea of *selling* this book in order that you may receive a few cents occasionally by way of royalty. We do not want to *give* away copies to any possible customers."[42]

Both men knew, however, that the key to the book's ultimate distribution lay in avid promotion. Bill's network of friends paid off. As the May 4, 1933, edition of the *Christian Advocate* reported,

DR. WILLIAM L. STIDGER and the Methodist Book Concern are greatly pleased by what they consider the finest radio reception one of their books has ever received. Doctor Stidger's *Edwin Markham* was broadcast nationwide on Sunday, April 16, by both Dr. S. Parkes Cadman and Dr. Dan A. Poling. On the following Sunday, April 23, the poet's eighty-first birthday, Dr. Paul Scherer, substituting for Dr. Harry Emerson Fosdick on the *Vesper Hour* of NBC, broadcast the new book. The *Pittsburgh Sun-Telegraph* book editor gave two broadcasts. Dr. Elwood Rowsey of Toledo, Ohio, broadcast a book sermon on it, as did Dr. Frederick F. Shannon in Chicago, and Dr. Burris Jenkins in Kansas City, Mo. The *San Francisco Call* and *San Francisco Examiner* announced the book over the radio. On Monday morning, April 24, "Cheerio" of the NBC devoted his entire broadcast to the book. Four national hookups and seven local stations within a week sent this publishing news around the nation. This is the first time that a book of the Methodist Book Concern has been heard at least half way round the world within twenty days of its publication.[43]

Press critiques of his book were extremely positive. A well reviewed, authorized biography of so famous a character as Edwin Markham was a feather in Bill's cap. The *Christian Herald* chose Bill's book as their Book of the Month, giving as reasons: "First, because it deserves the distinction; second, because Dr. Stidger and Mr. Markham are both so well known to our readers; and, third, because it is an exceptionally interesting book—as it would have to be, with such a pair to produce it."[44]

Finally, on June 11, 1933, a full, glowing review appeared in the *New York Times*. Its headline stated: "Mr. Stidger's Biography of the Author of 'The Man With the Hoe' Gives an Excellent Account of His Poetic Development."[45]

The more Bill delved into the nature of the Church of All Nations and its sister institutions, the deeper he found the resources of this unique group to be in manpower, the human spirit, money, and know-how. In his new responsibilities, he led the Sunday morning services as well as some of the Sunday evening services, which were followed by rescue mission meetings in Seavey Hall for "men who have lost their way." There were also "Italian, Syrian and Negro" services held in the church at various times. It was both ironic and fitting that when Dr. Helms had found the money to have the "rich, old English gothic style" church built, it had been made out of the bricks of demolished houses of prostitution, torn down to make way for realizing his dream—the rebuilding of men's and women's lives.

Morning chapel was held each working day and was attended by about 250 "old and handicapped men and women who have been defeated in the struggle of life and need the inspiration of religion and a chance to work." It was to this morning chapel group that Bill had appeared five years earlier to lead his first service, dressed as a tramp, having walked the streets of Boston for twenty-four hours looking for handouts.

Betty and Jack's engagement announcement was made by Bill and Iva on Saturday, September 9, 1933. After that the wedding machinery, run by Iva and Betty (but mostly Iva), cranked into high gear, creating a momentum that carried everyone along until the ceremony fifteen months later, on the morning of December 7, 1934.

Bill, spared the wedding labors and worries, concentrated on a pet project that had been on his mind for a long time—publishing a book of his own poetry. His desk drawers and books were jammed with poems he had dashed off over the years. When inspiration came to him, which it did with great frequency, he would scribble his verses on the inside blank pages of any book he happened to be reading. If he particularly liked what he had written he would type the poem out and use it, together with a suitable photograph, on the cover of his weekly church programs. He wrote poetry like he wrote stories or books, quickly and with a reporter's eye for the use of colorful images, as well as a reporter's sense for making a deadline.

No foray of his into the world of published poetry, however, would be complete without an endorsement of some kind from Edwin Markham. With this in mind, Bill began to bombard the poet with examples of his work. In some instances Bill received stern comments, and in others he received praise. "A pleasant fancy" is how the poet described Mrs. Markham's reaction to "Mother's Dust Rag." In another, "Christ Was the Outdoor Son of God," Bill had written: "His hair and heart were washed by showers," of which the poet asked: "Can you put hair and heart together—one is outside, the other is inside? Is the idea harmonious?" But, in the same poem, opposite the line "To Him there were no sweeter tones than water washing over stones," Markham wrote "Good" in the margin.

Markham's meticulous eye and firm pencil corrected Bill's grammar and rhyme schemes, and challenged words that seemed repetitious or overused. He would grade the poems "One of your best," or, as with "Girded With Gladness," he would offer specific criticisms—"Perhaps there are too many 'glads' here. Too much sameness, too monotonous. So it seems to both of us. Not one of your best."

Two of Bill's poems—"A Book and a Child" and "I Saw God Wash the World"— were received enthusiastically by Markham and were among Bill's readers' favorite poems as well. Markham paid Bill the highest compliment in his comment on "A Book and a Child": "This little lyric is worthy of any poet's pen." Later, in a letter to Bill dated April 7, 1934, he put an even stronger stamp of approval on the poem:

My dear Stidger:

Your enclosed poem, "A Book and a Child," is one of your ten best. It must go into your forthcoming volume. I hope to insert it into the revised version of my anthology, The Book of Poetry. *Please send a copy of it to Wm. H. Wise, 47 West 50th Street, and say in a note that I asked you to send the copy as I wish to insert it into* The Book of Poetry *in the revised edition.*

    Perhaps your lines,

> *"Anchored in*
> *The love of Him,"*

could be improved. For one thing, the rhyme is not good—in and Him do not rhyme. Perhaps you could say,

> *"Anchored in*
> *Their mighty spin."*

The idea that the stars spin seems to me to be good sense and good poetry. I somewhere use spin in this sense, yet this fact need not deter your use of the word in your delightful lyric.

Your comrade,
Edwin Markham[46]

Bill half-took the poet's advice, by removing "Anchored in Their mighty spin," but he replaced this with "Clear and white Through the night."

A BOOK AND A CHILD

He who gives a child a book
Gives that child a sweeping look
Through its pages
Down the ages;
Gives that child a ship to sail
Where the far adventures hail
Down the sea
Of destiny;
Gives that child a vision, wide
As the skies where stars abide;
Clear and white
Through the night;
Gives that child great dreams to dream,
Sunlit ways that flash and gleam
Where the sages
Tramp the ages.[47]

Markham liked "I Saw God Wash the World" but had some reservations about Bill's images. Markham felt that Bill made God too much like a "wash woman." In the poem, Bill had written that God took the wet earth and "He hung it out to dry." Markham suggested instead, "I saw His warm winds blow it dry." The poet also quarreled with the line "And put them all to bed," saying that he felt that the phrase was not dignified enough for God: "What you say must always dignify or uplift your subject." Bill appreciated Markham's suggestion but liked the poem better the way he had written it and made no changes. Bill may have been right. Sixty-five years after it first appeared, requests for copies of "I Saw God Wash the World" are still being received by the library at Boston University.

I SAW GOD WASH THE WORLD

I saw God wash the world last night
    With his sweet showers on high;
And then when morning came
    I saw him hang it out to dry.

He washed each tiny blade of grass
    And every trembling tree;
He flung his showers against the hills
    And swept the billowy sea.
The white rose is a cleaner white;
    The red rose is more red.
Since God washed every fragrant face
    And put them all to bed.
There's not a bird, there's not a bee
    That wings along the way,
But is a cleaner bird and bee
    Than it was yesterday.
I saw God wash the world last night;
    Ah, would he had washed me
As clean of all my dust and dirt
    As that old white birch tree![48]

Notwithstanding any changes he may have suggested, Edwin Markham approved of Bill's project and took a fatherly pride in Bill's first book of verses. He wrote a warm and encouraging introduction:

> For twenty years, William L. Stidger has been rousing religious America with prose volumes, alive with ideas and unconventional energy of expression. Among other things, he has put the Book Sermon into the armament of the young preachers of the country. He has helped to make preaching more attractive, to make sermons more crisp and cogent. In my travels over the states I find his volumes in many private libraries.
>
> All those pages from his pen are in a free, flowing and spontaneous prose. But in this new volume, he comes making his first adventures in verse. Here he is entering boldly into the realm of the Lyric Muse. This new book will be a pleasure to his multitude of friends.
>
> Dr. Stidger has facility and felicity of poetic expression. I find in his verses a feeling for nature and a persistent sense of the moral values; but these moral values do not push him into crude and colorless didacticisms. These swinging and ringing lines have a message of cheer and courage—something to help us to carry on when life grows dark.[49]

For a man who was not "worthy" of the great poet (Bill had autographed a copy of his biography *Edwin Markham* and given it to Betty, saying: "Here is a poet the latches of whose shoes I am not worthy to stoop down and unloose,") these fine words from Markham were the most wonderful possible praise. Were he asked, he would have counted this endorsement of his poetry by Markham as the poet's greatest gift to him.

Of all the things Bill felt he might give Betty on her forthcoming graduation from Smith College, the present he settled on as providing him the greatest satisfaction was dedicating to her his book *I Saw God Wash the World*:

> I dedicate this, my first volume of verses, to
> ELIZABETH ROBINSON STIDGER
> My ever understanding fellow-verse-writer as
> My Commencement Gift to her on her graduation
> From Smith College[50]

For Bill, Betty's graduation ceremonies on Monday, June 18, 1934, symbolized his daughter's coming of age and readiness to leave home for good:

> I stood on Smith College campus watching a parade of young girls, including my own daughter; and with my usual discipline and brave control I stood there and wept. Trying to hide my tears, I turned to make a casual remark: "It is the wind." Then I saw another silly old male about six feet tall who looked like he might have played football on a Yale team, and he was weeping too. When we looked at each other he said to me, "Mine's in there too—that one with the blond hair, the big tall beautiful one marching beside the little one with the glasses—and I guess a guy has a right to weep a little today. I haven't shed a tear in ten years."[51]

With the School of Theology closed for the summer and the Church of All Nations on its summer schedule, Bill had accepted speaking engagements in San Francisco in late July, returning through Ligonier to spend a week with Iva and Betty in mid-August. He was at the Hotel Sutter in San Francisco when he learned of the senior Mr. Hyland's death in an automobile accident, and he immediately wrote Jack:

Wednesday, August 1, 1934

Dear Jack:

I have just received word through Mrs. Stidger of your father's passing. I wish I could have been there to have helped you in this tragedy—but as it is I reach my hand and heart and my prayers across the continent.

I have always liked the fine comradeship that you had with your father. One of the first things I liked about you was Betty's telling me that your father always kissed you upon greeting you after an absence. So few families do that. We always did in our family—and do—because we love each other as men. Therefore I was quite used to that family tradition of affection.

I also liked the way your father dropped in on you for a visit since you have been in Pittsburgh.

You will have rich and comforting memories of your long comradeship with him. I wish that I had known him for I was prepared to understand and like him just through Betty's reports on him.

But I thought that there would be plenty of time for that. I am glad, however, that Betty came to know and like him. That is one part of your community of interest worth having.

Mrs. Stidger writes me that Betty went to you at once and that is as I would have wished it. I am glad that you had her there for she is a sympathetic and understanding person. I do not know of anybody I personally would rather have near me than she in time of trouble and sorrow. She always comes through with an understanding companionship in a crisis—and I have gone through several with her.

I hope I shall see you on my way back when I pick my girls up at Ligonier. In the meantime, here is my hand and heart and my sympathy, Jack old boy.

Fraternally and Faithfully,
Wm. L. Stidger [52]

Two days later, with the sad words he had written Jack fresh in his mind, and realizing how fragile life can be, Bill sent the first copy of *I Saw God Wash the World* to Betty, with the following inscription:

Dearest Betty: This book is dedicated to you and this first copy comes to you for your library with your Dad's deepest love. May it ever remind you when you read it that there are songs in my heart whenever I think of you—my best poem to date.

Love,
Dad [53]
San Francisco-Cal.
August 3, 1934

Notes

1. Robert S. McElvaine, *The Great Depression* (New York: Times Books, 1984), 48.

2. McElvaine, *The Great Depression,* 73.

3. McElvaine, *The Great Depression,* 73–75.

4. McElvaine, *The Great Depression,* 72.

5. The several quotations in this chapter not otherwise cited are from letters, William Leroy Stidger to Betty Stidger, author's collection. The letters, all undated, were sent to Bill's daughter while she was at Smith College, beginning in the fall of 1930.

6. Betty Stidger Hyland, *Those Heavenly Years,* unpublished manuscript, 1955, 163–64.

7. Hyland, *Those Heavenly Years,* 165.

8. William L. Stidger, *Planning Your Preaching* (New York: Harper and Brothers, 1932), 77–78.

9. William L. Stidger, *Men of the Great Redemption* (Nashville, Tenn.: Cokesbury, 1931), 16.

10. Stidger, *Men of the Great Redemption,* 10.

11. Stidger, *Men of the Great Redemption,* 28.

12. Letter from one of Bill Stidger's former students to the author.

13. Hyland, *Those Heavenly Years,* 173–75.

14. McElvaine, *The Great Depression,* 86–87.

15. McElvaine, *The Great Depression,* 122.

16. McElvaine, *The Great Depression,* 90.

17. Kenneth S. Davis, *FDR: The New York Years, 1928–1933* (New York: Random House, 1994), 272–73.

18. Letter dated April 5, 1995, from Arthur West to author, author's collection.

19. Letter, undated (although written shortly after April 24, 1932), from William L. Stidger to Edwin Markham, Horrmann Library, Wagner College, Staten Island.

20. McElvaine, *The Great Depression,* 187.

21. McElvaine, *The Great Depression,* 130.

22. Hyland, *Those Heavenly Years,* 186–87.

23. Hyland, *Those Heavenly Years,* 187.

24. Hyland, *Those Heavenly Years,* 188–91.

25. Hyland, *Those Heavenly Years,* 197.

26. Hyland, *Those Heavenly Years,* 201–20.

27. "Methodist Ministers Endorse Presidential Candidates," *Zion's Herald,* November 2, 1932, 1391.

28. Davis, *FDR,* 375.

29. McElvaine, *The Great Depression,* 135.

30. McElvaine, *The Great Depression,* 84–85.

31. McElvaine, *The Great Depression,* 139–40.

32. McElvaine, *The Great Depression,* 140–41.

33. McElvaine, *The Great Depression,* 141.

34. William L. Stidger, *That God's House May Be Filled* (New York: George H. Doran, 1924), 145–46.

35. "G.O.P. vs. Democrats," undated article, unidentified newspaper, author's collection.

36. "Reports of District Superintendents," *Minutes of the New England Conference,* Methodist Episcopal Church, April 5–10, 1933, 208.

37. "Reports of District Superintendents," *Minutes of the New England Conference,* Methodist Episcopal Church, April 5–10, 1933, 208–209.

38. "Reports of District Superintendents," *Minutes of the New England Conference,* Methodist Episcopal Church, April 6–11, 1932, 39.

39. Letter dated March 25, 1933, from Bishop Edward H. Hughes to William L. Stidger, author's collection.

40. "Methodist Changes," *Boston Globe,* April 1, 1933.

41. Letter dated March 28, 1933, from Edward Rowsey to William L. Stidger, author's collection.

42. Letter dated March 8, 1933, from Arthur F. Stevens, executive manager, Methodist Book Concern, to William L. Stidger, author's collection.

43. "Personal," *Christian Advocate,* May 4, 1933, 419.

44. Albert Linn Lawson, "Shall We . . . Read American?" *Boston Herald,* May 1933, 21.

45. Percy Hutchinson, "Edwin Markham, Child of Nature," *New York Times,* June 11, 1933, 2.

46. Letter dated April 7, 1934, from Edwin Markham to William L. Stidger, author's collection.

47. William L. Stidger, "I Saw God Wash the World," in *I Saw God Wash the World* (Chicago: Rodeheaver-Hall Mack, 1934), 50.

48. William L. Stidger, "A Book and a Child," in *I Saw God Wash the World,* 11.

49. Edwin Markham, "Introduction," in Stidger, *I Saw God Wash the World,* 7.

50. William L. Stidger, dedication to *I Saw God Wash the World,* 5.

51. William L. Stidger, "Every Clod," in *There Are Sermons in Stories* (New York: Abingdon-Cokesbury, 1942), 120.

52. Letter dated August 1, 1934, from William L. Stidger to Jack Hyland, author's collection.

53. William L. Stidger, inscription to Betty Stidger, *I Saw God Wash the World,* overleaf.

Eleven

Radio Days: New York

O n October 8, 1934, Bill began a new era in his life, where he was never far from a
radio microphone and where he reached larger and larger audiences electronically—it was an era launched by a radio broadcast called the *Goodwill Radio Chapel Service*.
Each morning the chapel service of the Church of All Nations would be broadcast over
station WHDH, reaching most of the New England area. It turned out to be an ideal
collaboration between Morgan Memorial, which was financially strong enough to cover
the expenses; Bill, an energetic and enthusiastic advocate of radio's ability to give
preachers much larger audiences; and WHDH, a Boston radio station eager to build its
market leadership.

With Bill's characteristic ebullience, the weekly church bulletin described the impact
of the Goodwill broadcasts:

> In they come! Every mail brings these letters thanking us for our Radio
> Broadcast of the Morning Chapel Service. Never has it been our privilege
> to extend the service of this Institution all over New England as we have
> been doing for three weeks. The ultimate success of this type of service
> will be to the extent that more and more people are informed about this
> privilege of listening in on our 8:15 A.M. to 8:45 A.M. Devotional Service.
> Here is one place where all of our members and friends can do a definite
> piece of service for the church. Tell everybody you meet about our Radio
> Broadcast.[1]

The radio broadcasts quickly became an integral feature of Morgan Memorial programs. An editorial in the *Times–Minute Man,* in Lexington, praised the *Goodwill Radio Chapel Service,* comparing it to the content typically found in newspapers:

A MORNING ANTIDOTE

If you are weighed down, and low in spirit each morning upon reading the headlines in your daily paper, if the world seems given over entirely to murders, burglaries and happenings of a depressing nature, turn on your radio at 8:15 A.M. to a short morning program of the Morgan Memorial. Keep right on with your work but let the music and talk be loud enough to give you the relief that such worthwhile things can. The background of service, of mighty helpfulness, of cheer and encouragement will be an excellent antidote for what you've seen in the paper.[2]

October was also a month preoccupying Iva and Betty, as Betty's wedding to Jack Hyland on December 7 quickly approached. Bill received the following letter from his son-in-law to be:

October 23, 1934

Dear Dr. Stidger:

Thank you very much for your fine letter expressing your feelings toward me and the minor parts that we both are apparently playing in this momentous event of December 7th. Fortunately we both are having our desires fulfilled, in that we are being left alone to wearily trudge forward and upward, towards that ever existent—but shadowy, nebulous prize—a woman's happiness. But seriously I appreciate the way you and Mrs. Stidger have let Betty and me solve our own problems and outline our own course. We always hope that it will be correct and we shall appreciate your opinions. Now that is "off our chests" and we can settle down to facts.

The first and most important one is that we are actually going to be married—in other words things have reached the point where I just have to get married. If Betty backs out at the last minute it will have to be with someone. I have rented a house and a maid, signed leases and agreements, purchased a wedding ring, a car, a dog, more insurance, actually made a will, saved thousands of letters, lived a good Christian life, taken physical examinations, read books on marriage, accepted wedding gifts and lastly this letter.

If Betty leaves me at the altar I am counting on you to have someone else ready.

> *With love to you and Mrs. Stidger,*
> *Jack*

P.S. Thanks very much for your book of poems. They are fine. "Mother's Old Dust Rag" is different than all the others—have you written any more in this vein? One of them was written on the boat coming back from Europe because I saw it—or part of it—in a flyleaf of a book you were reading—also enjoyed the radio address.[3]

Betty wrote in her diary, "On this Friday, December 7th, Jack and I were married at Robinson Chapel at Boston University. Bishop Burns read the betrothal and my father pronounced us man and wife. We were to take my new car to New York, so at three o'clock, after the reception, we started out. But, we had to return because Jack had forgotten his wallet. We finally made it to New York by train and stayed at the Waldorf-Astoria in a suite."[4]

On the day after the wedding, Bill sent the following telegram to Jack and Betty, which awaited them in their cabin:

December 8, 1934
Mr. and Mrs. Jack Hyland
S.S. Queen of Bermuda Furness
Bermuda Line
Pier 95, 57th Street, NYC

Dear Kids,

We have nothing but the loveliest memories of your beautiful wedding. Mother and I were proud of your actions. We start you off with the deepest of confidence in Jack and in your future happiness. Our love goes with you on this voyage and on the greater voyage of life.

Dad and Mother.[5]

One week later, Bill and Iva met Betty and Jack at the Waldorf-Astoria. This time the Stidgers were headed to Germany for a month, as guests of a Kansas City friend and oilman, W. R. Davis. The Hylands, just returned from Bermuda, were headed for their new home in Pittsburgh.

Bill and Iva set sail on the express liner SS *Bremen* at midnight on December 16, 1934. Iva wrote:

My dear Family,

It must seem funny to you, it's surely a dream to me, but here I am nearly 1,000 miles from New York on my way to Berlin. I would like to tell you all over again about every step of the wedding, but already you have probably heard about that three times.

We drove to New York in Betty's and Jack's car, and met them at the Waldorf-Astoria. I was overwhelmed at seeing them. Betty is so precious to me, and now, since I have annexed Jack, he's pretty precious too. They seemed happy and very much in love with each other—and that was my greatest desire for them. I can't tell you how I pray that they will be happy. I do want Betty to be a good wife to Jack, and make for him a happy comfortable home. She is a little young, but I see signs of a real woman if it develops. She has changed so much in the last year.

This boat is one of the deluxe boats of the seas. We have a commodious cabin [originally, Iva had written "stateroom," then, thinking better of it in front of her family, she wrote "cabin"] and bath on the A Deck. There are only about one hundred first class passengers, and the Bremen's capacity is probably eight hundred or more in the first class, but we have some very famous folks aboard. Fritz Kreisler [the violinist] and Mrs. Kreisler have the cabin next to ours and Prof. [Carl] Bosch who won the Nobel Prize in chemistry three years ago is on board.

The third class is overcrowded; all the bakers and candlestick makers are on their way home (transportation free) to vote on the Saar Valley question on January 13 [1935, when the residents of Saarland voted in a plebiscite to reunite with Germany, after having been administered by France since World War I]. I suppose every boat will be crowded until that event is over, both French and German boats.

We sleep, walk, read, write, and play around and have a good time here.

We land at Bremerhaven on December 21 and go immediately (a couple of hours) to Berlin where we will be staying at the Adlon Hotel—the best. We meet Mr. and Mrs. Davis in Berlin. I am in hopes I can go to Italy as well as see some of Germany, but will be content to see only Berlin if that's the plan.

> *My best love to all of you,*
> *Always,*
> *Iva*
> *Monday, Dec. 17* [6]

The prospect of meeting Fritz Kreisler was too good for Bill to resist. He sent the famous violinist a note asking for an interview but added that if he were too tired from his long concert tour or if he just wanted to be left alone, "I shall continue to be one of your 'seven best listeners.'" Bill's last phrase piqued Kreisler's interest, and ten minutes later Bill was seated in the Kreislers' living room.

Bill and Iva wound up spending considerable time with the Kreislers on the *Bremen* and later were invited for lunch with them at their home in Grunewald, a suburb of Berlin. Out of these meetings Bill later crafted a lengthy biographical essay on Fritz Kreisler; it was to be published in *True Story* magazine, then reprinted in Bill's *The Human Side of Greatness*. It would also appear, in shortened versions, in two other of Bill's published works as well as on his radio broadcasts.

One afternoon, Bill, Iva, and the Davises had a remarkable experience that Bill wrote up and submitted to *Liberty* magazine for its May 20, 1936, issue. The title of the story was "Hitler Planning to Be Kind to the Jews?"; its subtitle was "A Revelation from Berlin—A Change is Coming, Says 'the Brains Behind Der Fuehrer' in the First Interview Ever Given to an American Magazine." The article follows:

We were a group of four Americans on a recent Sunday afternoon, taking tea at the Kaiserhof Hotel in Berlin. In addition to our party there were only five others in that Kaiserhof tearoom, and they were evidently Germans. We finished our tea and had called for the check when the little German waiter bent over me and said, "If you will stay for another half-hour, Chancellor Hitler will be here."

With typical American curiosity, we stayed.

Promptly on schedule Herr Hitler appeared, almost by magic, in the room. There was a sudden scurry, a sense of electrical excitement, a sudden hush, waiters moving about swiftly, and in stepped a group of young Germans dressed in their Sunday best—black suits, black ties, white collars. They quickly walked over the entire tearoom, examining every curtain, table, and window. Then came Hitler and his entire cabinet.

As Hitler entered, he raised his hand in a lazy half-hearted Nazi salute, walked over to a table, sat down, surrounded by every single member of his cabinet. All of them ordered tea and sandwiches except Herr Hitler himself, who ate nothing during the hour that they remained in the Kaiserhof tearoom. The others ate heartily, talked, told stories, laughed, and seemed to be in a generally hilarious mood.

Hitler himself smiled but did not laugh. He seemed to have come merely to listen to the music of a small group of musicians playing for the guests. Now and then he smiled. Once he included our table of Americans in his smile, and it made quite an impression on the women in our party. We had heard the usual rumors about his physical and mental ill-health—that he was incapacitated; that he had gone crazy.

We sat for an hour watching Hitler's every move and facial expression. He seemed to be in a normal condition, alert mentally, with a rather pleasing smile; not bad to look at; with rather a kindly look in his eyes; quite unlike the man who was said to have taken a personal part in the terrible Purge of 1934 [the "Night of the Long Knives," June 30, in which four hundred leaders of the Nazi SA *(Sturmabteilungen)* were killed in a consolidation of Hitler's power as chancellor].

After an hour of sitting quietly in that tearoom several of the guards suddenly arose and went outside. I was told later that that entire hotel was surrounded by Storm Troopers all the time Herr Hitler and his cabinet had been having their tea. When the guards came back Herr Hitler arose with a quick movement and departed. Each member of the cabinet departed from that room by a different route. It was evident that precautions were necessary and their movements, both in entering that tearoom and in departing, were what might be called cautious.

But on all sides, the day following our chance contact with Herr Hitler, I was told that the real man behind the scenes, more powerful even than those cabinet members, was Herr Joachim von Ribbentrop, and he was not present at that public appearance of the Chancellor. Quietly, modestly, but surely he has been in the ascendancy among the intimate personal friends and advisers of Herr Hitler. I must see him if I wanted to see the real Bismarck of the present regime in Germany. In recent months that general rumor in Germany has been confirmed, for it was Von Ribbentrop who negotiated the French naval agreement; it was he who was sent on a secret mission to Italy; it was he who more recently negotiated in London what was called the First Phases of the Rhine Battle.

Exactly one week after my chance encounter with Hitler and his cabinet in the Kaiserhof I was a guest in the Von Ribbentrop home for lunch and the afternoon.

As we sat at a long family table in that simple German home on the out-
skirts of Berlin, I sat at the left of Frau von Ribbentrop, a young and attractive
German woman who had been educated in England and spoke perfect
English, as did her distinguished husband. It was a typical family gathering,
Herr von Ribbentrop's father and mother were there, a few friends, two chil-
dren of the family, and myself.

As we chatted I told Frau von Ribbentrop of my chance encounter with
Herr Hitler and his cabinet in the Kaiserhof tearoom the Sunday before. She
smiled and said, "Yes, the Chancellor ate lunch with us last Sunday, sat in the chair
you are now occupying, and left here for that Kaiserhof engagement at four. You
see, there have been so many rumors of the physical and mental incapacity of the
Realm Leader that it was thought wise for him to make a personal appearance so
that people could see for themselves that he is well and mentally alert."

Following our luncheon in the Von Ribbentrop home there was an informal afternoon of talk about the affairs of the Reich. There was talk of
Germany's desire to get her colonies back. That seemed to be the chief question in Von Ribbentrop's mind. What did the United States think of that pos-
sibility? What did the United States think of the Jewish question?

When told that the United States could never befriend Germany with
Jewish atrocities going on, I was told that there would be a decided modifica-
tion of those atrocities in a short time; and that even the United States would
be satisfied. I was told by this power behind Herr Hitler that the two of three
leaders in the Jewish persecutions would lose their power in the Reich. I could
count on that definitely.

Then there was talk of the Purge in which Herr Hitler, according to
American newspapers, had taken a personal hand. I asked about that.

Von Ribbentrop replied, without precaution or embarrassment, "On the
day of the so-called Purge, when the Chancellor flew down to Munchen and
back, I met him at Tempelhof [Airport] with my car and brought him back to
stay all night here in our home. When he climbed down from the airplane and
got into the car, I said to him, 'Chancellor, you look very tired. You must have
had a hard day.' The Chancellor replied, 'I am very weary. You see, my comrade, I created all of those party leaders. I took them when they were nothing,
and I gave them places of leadership. They betrayed that trust and that leadership in their degeneracy and in their disloyalty. I was chiefly responsible for
their power. I dared not ask anybody else to do what had to be done today. Yes,
I am very tired and disheartened.'"

Personally I did not dare ask what he meant by that phrase. I had read in
the American newspapers that Herr Hitler had commanded [Ernst] Roehm
[head of the SA] to kill himself, and when he refused, that Herr Hitler had shot
him with his own gun. I did not press the matter, but I shall never forget that
Von Ribbentrop quoted Herr Hitler as saying, "I dared not ask anybody else
to do what had to be done today."

There was talk of the United States and Boston. Herr von Ribbentrop in his youth had spent several years in our country. He had been in Boston one winter. He remembered a certain woman in Boston with whom he had skated on the Charles River. Her name was Eleanor Sears. He had liked her vivacity. He would like me to carry a message back to her with his greetings when I returned to Boston. He had always liked America and American ways. He would like to have American friendship for the new German regime.

I told him that there was one way to win that friendship: to see to it that Jewish persecutions were modified. It was then that he assured me that that was the intention of the present regime in Germany and that I could be assured the power of the chief Jewish baiters was even then on the wane and could watch confidently for it; that Germany was more interested in getting back her lost colonies than anything else; and they realized that to do that they must have the good will of the world, especially that of the United States.

Herr von Ribbentrop is of medium build, decidedly blond, blue eyes; friendly, hospitable, easy, gracious; a perfect host; of a decidedly conciliatory make-up. Nobody in Germany who knows what is going on behind the scenes doubts his power and influence. He is the man who in the next phase of German Nazi history will wield the most personal influence with the Chancellor, and that influence will be a modifying one.

He assured me that he was anxious for the United States to know that the German people cherished the good will of the American people, and that his government would do all in its power to win that good will.

As I was leaving, later that afternoon, something happened that made me know I had been talking in a historic room. Before I left I walked over to a small alcove in the living room to say good-bye to Frau von Ribbentrop and the women guests. Her husband walked to the door with me, and, as the servant was helping me on with my overcoat, said to me, "You will be amused (he evidently meant "interested") to know that in that alcove where you said good-by to the women, the present German government was actually formed, after months of secret meetings and discussions in this house." And then I remembered that it was Von Ribbentrop who had gone to Hindenburg and had persuaded that old war horse that Herr Hitler was the one man who could unify the German people.

We shall hear more and more of this Herr von Ribbentrop in the crucial months and years ahead, for Hitler is depending upon his advice and his modifying views.[7]

When published, Bill's article on Hitler provoked an almost hysterical response from columnist Walter Winchell and from a group of Hollywood actors, writers, and producers, who signed and sent a telegram to *Liberty* magazine. *Liberty* reprinted both the telegram and Bill's response:

Row on Hitler Planning to Be Kind to Jews

We protest the insidious pro-Nazi propaganda contained in your current issue entitled "Hitler Planning to Be Kind to Jews." The record of Hitler's broken promises indicates the complete untruth of the implications made by your William Stidger. There can be no compromises with the American principles of religious and political freedom.

(Signed)Hollywood League Against Nazism
Donald Ogden Stewart
Edwin Justus Mayer
Dorothy Parker
Gloria Stuart
Samson Raphaelson
Frank Tuttle
Edith Evans
Alan Campbell
Viola Brothers Shore, etc.

Boston, Mass.—In reply to the telegram protest for the Hollywood League Against Nazism, I would like to say that the article which I wrote for *Liberty* and which appeared in the May 30 issue is an honest piece of reporting and has nothing to do with propaganda.

The truth of the matter is that events which have happened since I got my interview have proved that the Hitler regime is greatly modifying the Jewish persecution. I honestly believe this is the intention of the Nazi government.

I, too, believe that there can be no compromise with the American principles of religious and political freedom. I agree absolutely with the Hollywood League Against Nazism. I do not condone Jewish persecution by Hitler.

I was simply reporting the facts of the interview for *Liberty,* and not in any sense condoning the unfair or unjust treatment of any race.

—William Leroy Stidger[8]

Events that subsequently unfolded showed that Bill had been taken in by the urbane von Ribbentrop, who was to be convicted at the war crimes trials in Nuremberg and hanged in 1946.

The results of the U.S. congressional elections held in late 1934 favored the Democrats, who increased the number of their seats from 313 to 322 in the House and from fifty-nine to sixty-nine in the Senate. Democratic governorships also increased. With the unusually strong political wind blowing in Roosevelt's favor, the stage was set to propose to Congress a burst of new legislation aimed at providing further help to those hurt by the Depression. By the end of the hot summer of 1935, the president and Congress had acted. The blockbuster piece of legislation was the $4.9 billion Emergency Relief Appropriation, the largest allocation of funds to date in American history. It was meant to consolidate and expand earlier relief programs as well as to fund the newly created Works Progress Administration with $1.5 billion for work programs directed at the unemployed.

Congress also passed the Social Security Act, which provided for workers' retirement and was seen by some as a step down the path toward a welfare state. The National Labor Relations Act gave employees the right to join unions and gave unions the legal machinery to gain recognition as valid partners in negotiations with corporations. This was seen as Roosevelt enfranchising the workers and unions, raising their power vis-à-vis their employers. With the passage of the Banking Act, the Federal Reserve was granted control over all credit in the market. Finally, Roosevelt proposed the "Wealth Tax," mandating higher taxes on the wealthy, though Congress watered down this proposal.

Taken together, the legislation of 1935, which became known as the "Second New Deal," was seen by conservatives as a shift by Roosevelt and his captive Congress to the left politically, concentrating power in the federal government, creating a welfare state, and strengthening labor and unions, at the expense of the heads of business and the wealthy. To the rich, it was a declaration of war against them, while the most liberal fringe of society considered the Second New Deal too mild, ineffective.

During the early months of 1935, Bill was engrossed in the establishment of a second radio venture, much more ambitious than Morgan Memorial's morning chapel service broadcast; this one, a full hour long, consisted of biographical sketches of prominent individuals. Bill agreed to interview each person, write the material, arrange for the music, and narrate the program. Once again the program was presented by WHDH, and it began on March 30, 1935.

The initial broadcasts highlighted the lives of outstanding men and women of different nationalities, drawing on the constituent groups in the Church of All Nations and their contributions to American life. "The theme was selected because Morgan Memorial and our Church of All Nations was made up of a Cosmopolitan Group such as is not found in any other institution in America." Bill added, "I wanted these broadcasts to have three goals: they were to be informing, inspirational and interesting. Those goals were essential if this series was to survive in the Radio World."

The broadcast received "an immediate and overwhelming response from our listeners," Bill said, "and it became evident that we must select a general plan which could run over a long period of time and not run out." From his articles in *True Story,* Bill knew that the reading public was "intensely interested in both great and obscure personalities; that several American magazines with immense circulation had founded their success on stories about personalities." He continued: "I had noticed also that books of biography in the publishing world had been the most consistent sellers over a period of ten years, that people are interested in wholesale gossip, in talk about people, either their own neighbors or personalities who had attained success in life. I had also noticed that, up to that time, Radio had not made a great deal of this universal and popular interest in personalities. Therefore, I felt that a broadcast based on this idea might be acceptable."⁹

Bill named his broadcast *Great American Personalities* and quickly made it clear that he intended to interview anyone who interested him. He was well equipped for this wider venue, since he had a rich supply of material from his years of interviewing contemporary figures for his sermons and magazine articles. The difference between his new program and his preaching was that because his radio show concentrated exclusively on personalities, he was able to deemphasize or eliminate church dogma and unnecessary religious trappings. Radio freed Bill to do what he liked best—interview intriguing people and tell others what he had learned. Bill the consummate reporter moved to stage center in his new radio program, while Bill the preacher took second place but was by no means forgotten—the program was filled with uplifting stories.

WHDH estimated that Bill's audience grew from a few thousand listeners at the outset to over half a million, out of a possible audience of four million in New England, two years later. Bill presented these broadcasts week after week, with no break, continuing for fifteen months until the late summer of 1936.

The effort required to produce each broadcast was prodigious. His radio show on Dr. Edgar J. Helms, for example, was based on a manuscript twenty-three double-spaced typewritten pages long, which Bill dramatized over the air. The broadcast was broken in two places to permit musical interludes—a chorus singing a hymn in the first, and a soloist singing with piano accompaniment in the second.

Bill took extreme care that each script was accurate, fully researched, completely checked, and above all, compelling and dramatic enough to keep his listeners tuned in. He added this workload to his existing teaching responsibilities at Boston University, his preaching duties at Church of All Nations, the occasional broadcast of the morning chapel service, his extensive writing for periodicals, and his speaking engagements. Bill did not publish any books in the 1935–1940 period, and the extraordinary demands of his radio obligations were the primary reason.

Late in the summer of 1935, Stanley High—whom Bill knew well as editor of the *Christian Herald,* for which Bill had written many articles—was invited to join the Roosevelt administration. Commentators described the president's team that had been assembled for Roosevelt's reelection campaign as an "oddly assorted little company," but High was singled out as being unusual even in this group: "And there was the former clergyman turned politician, the mysterious Stanley High, who had slipped into White House favor by a back door opened by Steven Early [assistant secretary to the president]." High was intelligent, driven, and by virtue of his history with the *Christian Herald,* well connected with leaders in the religious world. In this respect he was useful to the president. Also, High wielded a "mean pen," meaning that he was articulate and willing to write with a cutting edge.[10]

High's first job for Roosevelt was to scout through the western part of the country to gauge the extent of the opposition to the president. In deciding how to combat opposition arising on the left as well as the right that High and other Roosevelt "scouts" reported, the president chose to run for reelection on his strongest platform, himself— his popularity and his accomplishments in reducing unemployment and getting the country going again. Out of conversations between High and Roosevelt there emerged the idea of creating an umbrella organization financed by the Democratic National

Committee, to be called the Good Neighbor League. The mission of the Good Neighbor League, of which High would be president, was to secure endorsements for Roosevelt from as many religious, women's, black, and labor organizations as possible.

The league fooled none of Roosevelt's enemies or opponents. Senator [Arthur H.] Vandenberg [R-Mich.] attacked it as a "smoke screen for the Democratic National Committee. If I may use a pun, this creates a new *High* in political boondoggling."[11] It is doubtful if the Good Neighbor League fooled any of Roosevelt's friends either, but with High's energetic organizing skills, it gathered an impressive number of groups that spoke out for the president. Recruiting drives in eight states, for example, yielded a million members; an "Issues Manifesto" signed by thirty-nine professors urged Roosevelt's reelection; public school educators endorsed the president; and three thousand clergymen joined in support.

Approve of High's methods or not—and most of Roosevelt's advisers did not, nor did they much like High, either—no one could argue with his results. Overall, the Good Neighbor League dovetailed perfectly with Roosevelt's strategy to make his campaign appear to be a nonpartisan undertaking. Democratic propaganda was kept out of all campaign literature. As High wrote, "I do not believe that the president, himself, mentioned the party by name more than three times in the entire campaign. He did not mention the Republican Party at all or refer, even indirectly, to the Republican candidate. He did his campaigning, not as a Democrat, but as a New Deal liberal fighting not for party success but for a cause."[12]

Both High and Roosevelt knew that radio would be an extremely important part of the campaign but also that any use of it must also adhere to Roosevelt's bipartisan strategy. High wrote: "When it came to the costly business of radio campaigning, the most frequently featured speakers were not the well-known party orators."[13]

So it was that High chose Bill to head up the 1936 radio campaign, asking him to act as host and narrator of a radio program called *Happy Days,* sponsored by the Good Neighbor League and paid for by the Democratic National Committee. The show was to be broadcast from New York City by CBS; time had been booked for Tuesday evenings from 10:45 P.M. to 11 P.M., immediately following the *March of Time. Happy Days* was scheduled to begin at the end of July 1936 and continue through the end of October, just before the presidential elections. It would be carried on sixty stations across the country and would be Bill's first experience at national broadcasting.

If his agenda was to talk about Roosevelt not as a politician but as a man and father, Bill had to get to know the president, interview him, and find out the details of his life and the answers to questions that any American would have about Roosevelt and his family. For this purpose High arranged Bill's first direct meeting with the president in the late spring of 1936 at Hyde Park, the Roosevelt estate on the Hudson River, north of Poughkeepsie, New York.

Bill, Iva, and High arrived by car at Hyde Park on the appointed day. This is Bill's description of what he saw:

> My car was parked in front of the wide portico, guarded by the massive white
> pillars which stand on each side of the entrance to the house. It was fairly early
> in the morning. The Roosevelt breakfast, a meal that is eaten serially by the var-

ious members of the family, was evidently just completed. At any rate, while I waited in front of the entrance, one after another, practically all the members of the family, save the president, put in an appearance. The president was already in a conference in his tiny office that looks out on the portico where I was sitting, and I could hear his voice through the open window. . . .

John, the youngest of the president's children, appeared with a sweat-shirt thrown over his shoulder and a tennis racket in his hand. He was followed by Franklin, Jr., loaded down with golf clubs which he tossed into a roadster that took him off in a cloud of dust. Then came Eleanor Roosevelt, in riding habit. And she was scarcely around the corner, en route to the stables, when a final figure, the most commanding of them all, moved majestically through the doorway, and Mrs. James Roosevelt, the president's mother, with a somewhat distant smile in our direction, walked slowly to the edge of the steps, looked approvingly across the wide expanse of lawn in front of her, glanced appraisingly at the sky, smiled briefly at me again and turned, with equally deliberate majesty, and moved back into the house.[14]

Bill's assignment was tailor-made for him. He believed in Roosevelt and in what he was trying to accomplish with the New Deal. It was, after all, a national set of programs doing what Morgan Memorial had carved out for itself and had been doing, successfully, for more than thirty years. There was also an opportunity to convey over the radio, on a national hookup, personal vignettes of Roosevelt and his family, work similar to what he had done in writing for Henry Ford ten years earlier and what he was currently doing with his *Great American Personalities* broadcast. Bill believed that there was a great thirst on the part of most Americans to learn more about these illustrious Roosevelts:

> There has never been a White House family like the present one. . . . They have broken more precedents, ignored more conventions, made themselves loved or hated in more unexpected places, done more talking, been more talked about, gallivanted hither and yon with greater abandon; in short, got more attention, good, bad and indifferent, than has ever before been the lot of a presidential family. The result is that, today, it is not the New Deal that's the most discussed issue before the country. It's the Roosevelts.[15]

During the late spring and early summer of 1936 Bill was to meet the president in Hyde Park and in Washington on a number of occasions, each time gaining further insight and valuable detail for his forthcoming broadcasts. He was later able to describe to the American people what it had been like to visit the president:

> Just within the imposing front entrance [of the White House], to the right, there is a hat rack; just an ordinary, undecorated hat rack such as you'd find outside the lunch room at a Kiwanis Club meeting. The hats that hang on that rack may belong to a secretary of state, a foreign ambassador or a senator. Or they may

belong merely to average citizens. Farther on, to the left of the entrance, there is a little office, the door of which is always open. That office holds the White House ushers and the Secret Service men who happen to be on duty.

Every person who gets by the butler at the front door is immediately met by an usher. The usher's business is to keep track of the day's White House engagements, find out how many people are to stay for dinner, notify the cook, announce visitors, and do a variety of the things required in so large an establishment. It is not necessary to explain the job of the Secret Service men.[16]

A guest, as Bill explained, might be deposited in one of the larger main-floor rooms to await his appointment:

Then, when the time arrives, the guest is ushered into the White House elevator, an exceedingly slow means of transportation, taken to the second floor and ushered into the president's large study.

The study is a large oval room, which opens out on the White House gardens in the rear, and looks toward the Washington Monument. The visitor, generally, is hardly inside the door, his name barely announced by the usher before the president calls out a hearty greeting from behind his large and much cluttered desk. That is probably followed with an offer of a cigarette. A chair is drawn alongside the president's chair and the conversation begins.

It always takes Mr. Roosevelt, in conversation, some time to get down to business. He likes people. He likes to talk. If the visitor is an old friend, there are reminiscences to bring up; if he comes from out in the country, the president always has some pertinent question about conditions; if he is a government official the president probably has some gossipy talk about the affairs of the department.[17]

Even if Bill's listeners were generally familiar with the White House procedures and the Roosevelt family, they were certain to be fascinated by the descriptions of events and practices they could never know of unless told to them by an "insider." Bill brandished such information with great relish:

The choicest of all White House invitations are not those which take the guests to the so-called state dinners. They are, rather, the invitations to the family dinners. There the Roosevelts are at their best. And of all family meals, the most informal are those on Sunday night. For many years, the Roosevelt Sunday night supper has been an institution. Almost anyone comes, the menu is informal, and so are the rest of the proceedings. In the White House, invitations to Sunday night supper are reserved for members of the family, or for very close friends.

The guests all gather in the president's study. There is a great deal of banter across the president's desk, with the family and friends ranged in a semicircle in front of it. That period may run from about six-forty-five to seven-fifteen. At seven-fifteen, the very black butler comes to the door and announces that supper is served. Everybody stands aside, and the president precedes the guests through the door and to the elevator. The younger members of the party generally use the stairs, in a race to see who can get to the dining room first. At the door, however, every one waits again until the president [who, confined to his wheelchair, would have come up in the elevator], leads the way.

The meal is served in the paneled, small family dining room. The president does not sit at the end of the table, if the party is a small one, but at the middle with Mrs. Roosevelt immediately opposite him. Very little attention is paid to diplomatic precedence on these occasions, and after the president and Mrs. Roosevelt are seated the guests find their places, as they would in an ordinary home, "wherever you can get a seat."

The big dish at these Sunday night suppers is scrambled eggs. The president has two favorite dishes: scrambled eggs and fish. He can eat both any day in the week. He has a few dislikes also, chief among them being fried oysters. But the servants bring in great plates of scrambled eggs. Meanwhile, a chafing dish, a battered chafing dish which he has long prized, is set up in front of Mrs. Roosevelt. In that she proceeds to scramble more eggs, standing while she stirs them. Then, when the guest has finished all the scrambled eggs on his plate which was brought in from the kitchen, Mrs. Roosevelt picks up her chafing dish and walks around to each place, serving more scrambled eggs. All this, of course, proceeds with a great deal of hilarity. But a Sunday night supper with the Roosevelt family is a poor place for one averse to scrambled eggs.

Very often, to top off the day with relaxation, a first-run movie is brought to the White House for a special presidential showing. It is difficult for the president to go to the theater, although he loves it. Early in his administration he did go on a couple of occasions, but the formality and the attention he received discouraged him, and he has not been at a theater for several years.

He does enjoy the movies, however. They are shown in the long hall on the second floor. The chairs are arranged half-way down the aisle and the president sits in the front row, with the guests choosing their own seats after the president is seated. This picture theater has some advantages. It is possible to make comments aloud. It is, however, a remarkable experience to sit with the president of the United States while a newsreel is being shown which pictures the man sitting near you on the screen or with the crowds cheering his appearance. His comments on such occasions are always jocular. And the family loves to razz him when they think any picture is particularly poor, or when he looks particularly pleased or particularly irritated.[18]

Bill broached with Stanley High the idea of having Edwin Markham read to the Democratic Convention in late June an unpublished poem he had written about Roosevelt. Markham's meeting Roosevelt, especially on a national hookup, would give the public's awareness of the old poet an enormous boost; Roosevelt's greeting a distinguished eighty-five-year-old would be a politically astute act—particularly since the poem read by Markham would urge Americans to vote the president back into office. Finally, Bill, having arranged the introduction, would gain as well.

As the month of June 1936 drew on, Bill's idea took root. High sent a wire asking Bill to arrange to have Markham at the convention in Philadelphia and to read his poem just before Roosevelt delivered his acceptance speech on Saturday night. Bill received in the mail three tickets to the convention—one for himself, one for the increasingly frail (and mentally declining) Markham, and one for Markham's secretary, Mrs. Florence Hamilton. Bill, however, was not prepared for what happened on the evening of the convention:

> That night brought a most exciting experience to us three plebeians. The weather was warm. When we arrived at Franklin Field [the convention hall] we were duly escorted to the official platform up the ramp prepared for the president himself. Mr. Markham, a stately figure with his long white hair, proudly walked past the Secret Service guard. Mrs. Hamilton came next. But when I followed and presented our three tickets, a Secret Service man, a big belligerent-looking fellow, with a protruding chin and cauliflower ears that hinted of a pugilistic past, rammed his chest against me, grabbed me by the shoulders in a none too gentle manner and said: "What are you doing here?"
>
> I said: "I'm with Mister Markham. I was invited to bring him here by Mister High and Mister Morgan."
>
> "All right, we'll see. Here's Mister Morgan."
>
> Then he called Mr. Morgan over and said, "Do you know this man? He says he's a preacher from Boston, a Doctor Stidger."
>
> Mr. Morgan looked me over and quickly replied: "I never saw or heard of him before."
>
> This in spite of the fact that I had talked with him in his Washington office at least a half dozen times. But I have no complaint about his failure to recognize me. He was an excited man that night and the whole affair was like a Roman Circus and in almost complete chaos.
>
> And there was I, responsible for Mr. Markham's safety in that mammoth crowd. He had already been seated on the platform and there I stood at the top of the ramp, and the president was due in ten minutes. I didn't know where to go or what to do. I carried a light overcoat over my arm, in spite of the fact that it was a hot, sultry night. I suppose that I was the only man in that immense crowd who was foolish enough to be carrying an overcoat and that was my undoing. For what I did not remember was that [Leon] Czolgosz, who assassinated President [William] McKinley [in 1901], had an overcoat over his arm which covered up his pistol.
>
> Not knowing what to do, I stood on the ramp for another five minutes. I still hoped that they would come to their senses and let me on the platform. However, instead of letting me on that platform, in a few minutes up came

four husky Secret Service men, all of them surrounding me, and one of them snatching my overcoat, and two others doing what I later learned was technically called 'frisking' me. And they did it thoroughly.

Naturally I had no intention of assassinating the president. I might have been persuaded to assassinate Mr. Morgan, High, or Farley, who had evidently fallen down on their arrangements, but I rather liked the president and at that time was working for him in The Good Neighbor League and had no intention of doing him any bodily harm. But I could not persuade that group of four husky Secret Service men that I did not have evil intentions. That overcoat over my arm on a hot June night had them worried. And, in addition to that, my best friends say that I look like an ex-pug anyhow, so they just laughed at me when I told them I was a minister and a teacher in a theological seminary.

One particularly tough looking officer said to me in language which did not sound at all friendly: "Oh yeah, and do you know any more funny stories?"

Then he added: "You had better come along with us and be nice and quiet about it, or you'll get into trouble."

Naturally I went, for they were four to one. They took me under the Franklin Field grandstand and once again frisked me.

"You'd better beat it now, friend, and get out of here," said one of my captors. "We can't take any chances; and by God, you certainly don't look like a preacher!"

In perfect keeping with the chaos that prevailed that night, Edwin Markham, the eighty-five-year-old poet, who will be remembered long after most of the participants in that night's circus are forgotten, did not get to read his poem, in spite of the fact that he had been officially invited to do so. Two times he was escorted to the microphone in the midst of that turmoil, and each time, just as he got his manuscript out, the band began to play and drowned him out. Then the president himself arrived. Pandemonium broke loose and Edwin Markham never did read his poem.

Several months later Stanley High told the president of this episode, and Mr. High said: "The president roared with laughter."[19]

Bill knew that his success in broadcasting would be to come up with a "scoop," something he knew that no one else did and that both interested his listeners and confirmed for them that he knew his subject intimately. One of these scoops occurred while the president made his way, stiffly and slowly, to the convention podium to give his acceptance speech. Bill wrote in 1938:

It is possible, now, to tell another heretofore unpublished incident, an incident that happened on that thundering night in Philadelphia when Mr. Roosevelt made his address accepting, for the second time, his party's nomination for the presidency.

As the president walked up the ramp to the platform, on his son Jimmy's arm, he lost his balance and dropped the manuscript of his speech, which he was carrying in his hand. There was a great crowd surging around him. Jim's arm was at his side, but the manuscript was about to be trampled under-foot and lost. Jimmy, however, used his head. The president's arm slipped into that of a Secret Service man standing nearby. Jimmy dropped to his hands and knees, in the midst of that crowd, retrieved the manuscript, and the president continued on his triumphal entrance.[20]

Bill, because of his "inside" status, could tell this kind of story even though it violated the press norms. There was an unspoken rule of not discussing the fact that Roosevelt, who had been stricken by polio in 1921, was an invalid who could stand only when he was wearing uncomfortable body braces, and who walked haltingly, usually leaning on someone's arm for support.

Bill's mission was to humanize Franklin Roosevelt, who seemed to all to be an invincible bulwark of optimism and a source of good cheer for a country in need of both commodities. Humanizing him had the advantage of making the president seem like another member of everyone's family. Bill showed the country that Roosevelt, the man and father, suffered like everyone else, yet stood tall as a giant when the occasion warranted. Seen this way, Roosevelt, both man and myth, could not be beaten by any opposition. Bill told the following story in one of his broadcasts:

A friend of mine happened to be visiting a certain famous historical house not far from Washington, overlooking the Potomac.

As my friend sat on the porch with the host, that host said to him one afternoon, "Mr. Roosevelt sat in that chair where you are sitting a week ago. He came out to see our flowers. I saw the White House car drive up and recognized it. Mrs. Roosevelt got out. She said the president could not get out, for he had not brought his canes; they had just come for a ride. However, I went out to the car and invited him in to have tea. He said that he could not come in because he hadn't brought his canes. I begged him to come in and have tea with us, and called some men, who carried him to the porch.

"As he was sitting in that chair, I made a terrible break. I said to him, 'Mister President, I well remember when you were in the Navy [FDR had been secretary of the navy in World War I] that you came to see my place, and walked through those trees.'

"I saw a look of pain go over his face, and was chagrined that I had awakened that memory. I apologized at once.

"He was quiet for a few minutes and then put me at ease by admitting that he had been thinking about the same visit.

"Another period of silence, and the president then said that he would give up everything that had happened between then and now, if he could once again walk through those trees as he had on that visit.

"That was all that was said. After that, he was his old buoyant, laughing self and seemed to enjoy sitting there, having tea with me. He watched the flowers and trees as he sat in that chair where you are sitting. Then we carried him back to his automobile, and they drove off."[21]

Though Bill and most of the voters had decided that Roosevelt was "their man," there was a polarization of views—precipitated mostly by Roosevelt himself, who blamed the country's problems on the entrenched rich, who had exploited the poor. Consequently, organized opposition to Roosevelt and the New Deal was virtually along "class lines," one of the most vocal groups being the Liberty League, composed of financiers, industrialists, corporation lawyers, and conservative Democrats. It actively fought the New Deal as a dangerous departure from the Constitution and attacked measures like the National Labor Relations Act. The league especially scorned the wealth tax.

The Republican presidential candidate was Alf Landon, a successful businessman turned politician from Kansas, who had been the only Republican to win a governorship in the 1934 election. Landon appealed to people who tended to be conservative thinkers. Iva, for example, found much to admire in Landon and said so in a letter to her parents in Ligonier: "What did you think of the [Republican] nomination? I believe I am a vacillating soul. I am against this regime in so many things and yet to me the 'Acceptance Speech' sounded promising. Which way is right? Bill is for Mr. Roosevelt. Mr. Landon sounds simple and more like our kind. Dr. Coughlin [Fr. Charles E. Coughlin, Roman Catholic priest and radio commentator] says Landon is dumb. I am too dumb to know."

From the Democratic Convention at the end of June until the elections in November, Bill was working flat out writing, editing, and presenting his *Happy Days* radio broadcast. There was not enough time for him to do *Great American Personalities* as well as *Happy Days*, so he discontinued his Boston broadcast for the four-month period.

Interspersed with guest speakers that High and Bill rounded up were vignettes of the lives of the president and his family, which Bill presented. "It was," Bill said, "the first intimate, nonpolitical and *completely frank* account of the Roosevelt presidential clan."[22]

Bill dealt with a number of sensitive issues on the program. For one, the public had difficulty understanding how the president's son, Franklin Roosevelt Jr., could have married Ethel DuPont, whose family was so openly hostile to the president. The DuPont evening newspapers in Wilmington carried such headlines and editorials as "More Millions to Be Spent on Worthless Projects" and "The president showed his lack of understanding of finances." "Also the DuPont family," Bill said, "probably has contributed more than any other to defeat not only President Roosevelt but the whole New Deal." Bill indicated that Lammot DuPont, according to a Senate Committee report, contributed to thirty-four organizations that were opposed to the president.[23]

Bill lauded Franklin and Eleanor for "letting the young people [their children] work out their own destinies" and said that as parents they had voiced no opposition to Franklin Jr.'s decision to marry Ethel, despite the politically embarrassing connection. If the Roosevelt–DuPont marriage was puzzling, the fact that Elliott and Anna, two of the president's five children, worked for the Hearst newspaper group was baffling. The president had no deadlier or more powerful enemy than William Randolph Hearst, who plainly detested the president and caused his paper, the *Washington Herald,* to declare in

September 1936: "Beyond a question of doubt the country will be bankrupt if
Roosevelt is elected." Hearst railed at Roosevelt repeatedly, with front-page, two-column
editorials in large black type, asserting such views as: "The Roosevelt administration has
the endorsement of every natural and avowed enemy of the American social order, and
every adversary of the prevailing American economic plan."[24]

Bill's willingness to repeat these criticisms of Roosevelt on the radio showed audacity,
even foolhardiness, on his part but also a conviction that the president was able to surmount
the harmful and vicious harangues of his enemies. Bill noted that there was evidence that
Hearst had finally called off his "mudslingers" probably because "the more Mr. Hearst
shouted vituperations, the greater grew the president's popularity." Still, and here he was
speaking for the average American, Bill found it impossible to understand how Elliott and
Anna could live with themselves, working as they did for the enemy: "One cannot help wondering what the members of the president's immediate family who are in the employ of Mr.
Hearst think of that gentleman's attacks on the president. Perhaps they just think what Mr.
Hearst thinks is his business. A strange land, these United States—and a wonderful one!"

Happy Days was a lively radio show, one that helped to focus the national radio audience
on the only issues that Roosevelt wanted before the people—that their president was embat-
tled on their behalf in a war against the forces of entrenched power, and that if the masses
supported him, the country would win and widespread prosperity would be reclaimed.

The president's campaign tactics worked magnificently. Roosevelt won over
Landon by a landslide, carrying every state but Maine and Vermont, achieving the
biggest popular plurality in history. The number of Democrats in the House moved to
334 versus 89 Republicans (compared with 321 and 104 previously); in the Senate the
number of Democrats moved to seventy-five versus seventeen Republicans (compared
with seventy and twenty-three previously). Roosevelt seemed invincible. Dorothy
Thompson, the newspaperwoman and wife of Sinclair Lewis, remarked, "If Landon
had given one more speech, Roosevelt would have carried Canada, too."

Roosevelt's second inauguration took place on Wednesday, January 20, 1937, a day
of cold rain that left flags sodden and inaugural decorations soaked but spirits undamp-
ened. The president talked of the progress made during his first four years then turned
to the unfulfilled tasks that lay ahead:

Have we reached the goal of our vision of that fourth day of March 1933?
Have we found our happy valley? . . .

I see a great nation, upon a great continent blessed with a great wealth
of natural resources. Its hundred and thirty million people are at peace
among themselves; they are making their country a good neighbor among
nations. . . .

But here is the challenge to our democracy: In this nation I see tens of
millions of its citizens—a substantial part of its whole population—who at
this very moment are denied the greater part of what the very lowest standards of today call the necessities of life. . . .

I see one-third of a nation ill-housed, ill-clad, ill-nourished. . . .

> In our personal ambitions we are individualists. But in our seeking for
> economic and political progress as a nation, we all go up, or else we all go
> down, as one people. . . .
> I assume the solemn obligation of leading the American people forward
> along the road over which they have chosen to advance.[25]

The president, because of the body braces he had to wear if he was to stand at a
public gathering, did not attend his own inaugural reception. Bill said that the newspapers reported that the president went to "play with his stamps instead." Iva and Bill were
at the reception, and Bill wrote:

> I looked forward to it with some awe and misgiving. However, from the
> minute we got into that long line of visitors we felt as well acquainted as if
> we had been in some small-town church reception for the new pastor. It was
> all as simple and democratic as that and, indeed, somewhat in the same spirit.
> There were soft shirts and stiff ones, white collars and blue ones. It was a
> homely everyday American crowd and everybody felt at home.
> When we finally found our way up the stairs into the reception room,
> there was Mrs. Eleanor Roosevelt with her usual smile shaking hands with an
> interminable procession.
> Over in another corner of the room was James Farley [a businessman
> active in the Roosevelt campaign], and he, too, had his own reception line and a
> group of curious citizens clustered around him. In another corner was Madame
> Roosevelt with the largest crowd of all in her line and surrounding her. A curi-
> ous woman friend of mine [Iva] stopped to have a chat with her about her son.
> This woman friend said, a bit complainingly, "I'm sorry the president isn't here."
> The president's mother said, "He's had a hard day, and I guess he has a
> right to play a little bit this evening." There was no argument about it and no
> rancor; just a dignified statement of fact, which appealed to my woman
> friend and settled for her the important matter of the president's absence
> from that particular function. And then that American mother added, "I'm
> more concerned about his catching cold from today's rain than I am about
> his not being at this reception. We can take care of that."[26]

For anyone who had participated in a winning political presidential campaign there
were earnest "thank you's," and for a select few, like Bill and Iva, invitations to the White
House on January 17, 1937, followed by the inauguration ceremony and festivities. But
after that the excitement was over, the political machine rolled on, and Bill returned to
his life, which was centered on the School of Theology, the Church of All Nations, and
the resumption, on November 8, 1936, of his radio program *Great American Personalities*.
High's own political base crumbled and finally collapsed when he published
"Whose Party Is It?" in the February 6, 1937, *Saturday Evening Post*.[27] High spoke the
truth about the dissension that existed in the Democratic Party and named those who

sided with Roosevelt and those who opposed him. It was a classic but colossal mistake, made by a man who enjoyed being in the inner circle of power but who forgot that he owed his position to the magnanimity of the president. The article provoked fury throughout the Democratic ranks—precisely because it was true—as a result of which Roosevelt threw High to the wolves and had a White House spokesman announce that "High had never been seen around the place."[28]

In late 1936, C. D. Morris, a talent scout for the J. Walter Thompson Company, the leading advertising agency, was driving through New England when, quite by accident, he tuned in to one of Bill's broadcasts. Morris realized at once that Bill's radio voice and delivery would be perfect for a program that the Thompson firm had been planning with its client, the Fleischmann Yeast Company.[29] Morris did some background checks on Bill and had a conversation with Bill Rapp, the editor of *True Story,* for whom Bill had written many articles. Agreement quickly developed on a five-day-a-week program that would be fifteen minutes long and contain four-minute sermon "nuggets," as Bill called them. The theme of the program would be upbeat and inspirational, but there would not be much religious talk. On the other hand, there would be music, which Bill believed was very important. There would be an opening piece of music, instrumental or vocal, and a closing piece.

Regarding the Fleischmann's Yeast program (as it was more popularly called), there were sensitive issues that Bill needed to address, such as his being part of a religious program that was sponsored by a commercial company, or his comfort at becoming a promoter of a product, or his earning a salary—a big salary—for his work. Bill treated these points in his own very practical manner.

Bill was not overly sensitive or ashamed about having a sponsor; his forthright statement was, "I'm *grateful* to The Fleischmann Yeast Company, which has made it possible for me to speak to millions every day about the things that are near and dear to my heart." On the question of the money and the product, he said: "I have been bewildered that they pay me to do something which I would willingly do for nothing. I had been taking the yeast I advertise for ten years before I ever signed this contract and my father had been taking it for ten years before me. I began taking it on the advice of a Detroit physician, and, therefore, I felt that I was advertising a product in which I believed and which had for years, and still does, help me."[30]

Bill decided that he would name his broadcast *Getting the Most Out of Life,* and he was clear in his own mind that the simple message he wished to send to as many people as possible was that "we get the most *out* of life by putting the most *into* life." He chose as his daily greeting for the program, "Good day, my friends, and all things glad and beautiful! Are you getting the most out of life?"[31]

Overall, Bill planned to observe certain rules in broadcasting that had paid off for him already in other media. In his earlier books for preachers, he had demonstrated how his methods, if followed, would make churches "standing room only." Bill now set down the tenets for successful radio shows, calling them his Ten Radio Commandments. *Time* magazine later published them in an article about Bill entitled "Neglect the Needless," in its December 6, 1937, issue.

Speak in a conversational tone;
Take your sermons not from the Bible but from life;
Leave out the word "I";
Neglect the needless;
No bunk;
No sob stuff;
Make the web of your sermon optimistic, cheerful;
Check and recheck your script before delivering . . . for absolute factual accuracy;
Keep the word "not" out of your sermon script;
Use no introduction. Plunge right into the middle of the sermon.[32]

The target date set for beginning his new program was Monday, September 27, 1937. Just prior to this, Bill let his *Great American Personalities* show come to a graceful end, informing his audience that his new show was about to begin.

The timing for a program like *Getting the Most Out of Life* could not have been more opportune. In August 1937, the country suffered a relapse back into Depression. It was the most precipitous economic decline in history, owing to a conjunction of factors including reluctance on the part of corporations to spend, the first balanced federal budget in years (which meant that government was providing no stimulus to the economy), two increases in cash-on-hand requirements for Federal Reserve member banks (which meant tightened credit), a drastic curtailment of relief expenditures, and the beginning of the collection of Social Security taxes. Unemployment levels, which had been at six to seven million people in early 1937, soared to eleven million by 1938. "A lag in resuming relief created almost as much dire suffering as in 1932. Yet the decline was not as shocking as in the early thirties. A nation inured to Depression half-expected another."[33]

The return to a depression mentality was a tough additional burden for Roosevelt to bear, because it had occurred despite his New Deal programs. The lines of the unemployed, looking for work, lengthened in front of Morgan Memorial. Supporting the president as strongly as ever and trusting in his commitment to a prosperous economy, Bill believed that now more than ever people needed to find strength from within.

At the first of Bill's new broadcasts, in the WNAC studios in Boston, he stood behind a microphone holding the script in his hand. Before starting he waited to be cued by the music:

ORGAN MUSIC (Saint Anne) in full . . . Fades to

DR. STIDGER:
Are you getting the most out of life?

ANNOUNCER:
Dr. William L. Stidger presents his question and challenge.
Are you getting the most out of life?
This program of hope and inspiration, coming to you each morning at this time, features the famous preacher, lecturer and author, Dr. William L. Stidger.
It is a presentation of the makers of Fleischmann's Yeast.

ORGAN MUSIC OUT:

ANNOUNCER:
Dr. Stidger has become the friend of men and women in all walks of life. He knows them, and his aim in life is to help them all get more out of living.

Through his talks and his books, he has offered wider interests and fuller understanding to all who have heard or read him. A citizen of the world at large, his experience is great and full. He comes now through this program with a thought and a word of encouragement for you.

Before Dr. Stidger speaks to you, the New England Singers, directed by Dr. James R. Houghton, offer for your enjoyment one of the greatest choral compositions of all time . . . Martin Luther's triumphant hymn . . . "A Mighty Fortress Is Our God."

1. A MIGHTY FORTRESS IS OUR GOD (2 VERSES)
THE CHOIR
ANNOUNCER:
We introduce to you now . . . Dr. Stidger.

DR. STIDGER:
The Chinese have a saying that "We are all beggars sitting on bags of gold."

The Chinese legend is that once upon a time a Chinese beggar had been up in the mountains and he had seen bright and sparkling rocks lying on the ground beside a stream where he had camped for several weeks on his way down into the lowlands.

He liked the color of these bright, sparkling rocks, so he gathered a bag full of them and carried them on his back to give to children. He knew that Chinese children liked bright-colored stones.

When he got down into the valley it was cold, and he was hungry, but he did not have any money with which to buy food, and finally one day fell exhausted to the ground with his bag of rocks under him.

Another Chinese Coolie came along and wakened him. The beggar was blue and discouraged but the man who wakened him said: "Look in your bag. As I came up to you I saw some of the rocks that had fallen from your bag. Look at them!" The beggar looked, but said as he opened his bag: "It is not worth looking into. There is nothing in the bag but rubbish and rocks which I have gathered up in the mountains to give to children to play with—just a few sparkling stones."

"It is not rubbish. It is a bag full of gold!" insisted his friend.

The beggar looked and lo! It WAS a bag of gold. And thus, the Chinese have their legend: "We are all beggars sitting on bags of gold."

I sometimes wonder if that is not true with all of us, particularly here in the United States of America where opportunities are so much greater than any other place in the world.

Less than a quarter of a century ago there was a young man who lived in Detroit, Michigan. I have written a life of that young man and I know his history fairly well.

He was poor, but he had ideas. As Victor Hugo said once: "Stronger than armies is an idea whose hour has arrived!"

This boy was so poor that he didn't have enough money to buy the rough materials to use in working out his idea. He was so poor that he had to work in an old outcast barn, which he rented for a few dollars a month. He was so poor that he could not afford to get some greatly needed dental work done.

In fact a Detroit dentist has told me that that young fellow came into his office about this time to have his teeth examined. The dentist told him what ought to be done, and that it would cost about one hundred and fifty dollars. This young man did not come back for months. One day the dentist met this young fellow on the street and asked him why he had not come back to get his dental work done. The young fellow admitted that he did not have any money at all. The dentist said: "If you can get together enough money to pay for the material that I will have to use I'll do the work for you, and you can pay me when you get the money." Another delay of a month before that young fellow could get together enough money even to pay for the material that had to be used in that dental work. Then it took him three months to get that small dental bill paid for.

"But" adds this dentist as he tells me the story: "I have never been underpaid by that man since that day. He pays me generously now. He can afford to and he does it."

This little boy was so poor that he had a hard time to get a helper in his little experimental shop[,] so his young wife helped him all she could.

Nobody believed him. He was laughed at by all of his friends. They called him a fool.

His own father told him that he had better get a job and do something that was useful. The newspaper ridiculed him and called him a fool. He was a beggar sitting on a bag of gold: the bag of a new and great idea. But he KNEW it. In spite of his poverty he stuck to his plan. He begged, borrowed, worked all night and day and finally worked his idea out; and that idea was that he could make a cheap car that all American people could afford to buy.

A friend said to him: "If you can drive that thing from Detroit to Lansing, which is forty miles, I will give you some money to manufacture it."

The young man started out but he didn't get far at first. Something happened but he knew what the trouble was, took it home and fixed it; started another day and drove the thing in triumph from Detroit to Lansing; got five thousand dollars from his doubtful friend to start manufacturing it. That was less than a quarter of a century ago. That boy is now the richest man in the world. His name is Henry Ford.

ORGAN PLAYS INTRODUCTION:

ANNOUNCER: (over music) Henry Ford's favorite hymn "Lead Kindly Light" is sung by the New England Singers.

2. LEAD KINDLY LIGHT
NEW ENGLAND SINGERS
DR. STIDGER:
A moment ago, I cited for you an old Chinese proverb. It said, "We are all beggars sitting on bags of gold."

One bag of gold upon which we all sit is Health. That we should cherish and guard above all things, and if we have the misfortune of losing it, then every effort should be made to regain it.

With me here this morning is (Announcer) who has a word to say in that connection. I believe that what he has to say may be of great value to you.

(INSERT COMMERCIAL)

COMMERCIAL

ANNOUNCER:
Many men and women get a new lease on life—after the driving, hard-working thirties are over. You can be more vital, more interesting and more successful after 40 than you ever were before.

The digestive system is one of the first parts of the body to slow down and grow old.

Around the age of 40, the gastric juices start to flow less freely and have a weaker digestive action.

This gradual slowing down is a natural thing, and there is no need to get nervous over it—for you can check it by giving the system special help.

For stimulating the amount of these secretions and strengthening their digestive power, you will get an active effect from Fleischmann's fresh yeast.

This stimulating action is accompanied by the tonic action of 4 vitamins in Fleischmann's Yeast—each one important in keeping the body fit and healthy.

Almost anyone over 40 will feel better and be capable of better work—if he gives his digestive system this extra help.

Eat 3 cakes of Fleischmann's Yeast a day—one cake about ½ hour before each meal—plain or in a little water. See how it brings you new health and energy.

3. AWAKE MY SOUL
THE CHOIR
ORGAN SEGUES TO SAINT ANNE

ANNOUNCER: (Over Organ Music)
And so, ladies and gentlemen, we conclude this quarter hour with Dr. William L. Stidger and the New England Singers . . . a presentation to you from the makers of Fleischmann's Yeast. Dr. Stidger will return tomorrow to talk with you once again, as he plans to do each weekday morning at this same hour. The hymns on today's program were selected by the Reverend Gordon Gilkey of the First Congregational Church of Springfield, Massachusetts. Tomorrow's selections will be made by Governor Cross of Connecticut.

DR. STIDGER:
Good day, my friends, and, until we meet again, may you get the most out of life, in happiness, in peace, in health.

MUSIC UP BIG AND OUT[34]

The reaction to *Getting the Most Out of Life* was immediate and extremely positive. Letters of appreciation began to flow in. Bill would read portions of them over the air, which would lead to an even heavier flow of mail. One example was:

Dear Dr. Stidger:

I am a grateful mother today. Two weeks ago I scolded my sixteen year old daughter for something she had done and she was angry. She went upstairs, packed her bag, climbed out a window, down the porch and ran away. She was gone nearly two weeks and we were frantic. I phoned the police and they kept up a secret search for her all of this time while I went nearly crazy with grief. Then one day Mary walked in, weeping, threw down her bag, literally jumped into my arms and, between sobs, said: "Mother, you were right and I was wrong. I ran away and went to a girlfriend's home. Yesterday we were listening to the radio; to a program called 'Getting the Most Out of Life.' The man who was talking, Dr. Stidger was his name, I think, talked about the responsibility that we young people have to our parents. I started to cry; looked at Jane; and she said: 'Mary, that man is right. You'd better go home to your Mother.' And I packed up, and here I am, Mother; and I'm so sorry; and from now on, I want to do my part if you'll forgive me!" And Dr. Stidger, you can imagine what a happy Mother I am today, for your talk brought my daughter back to me. I can never tell you how grateful I am to you for that. [35]

One of the most moving letters Bill received was from "Jimmy" Darou, who owned the Cheerio Service Station ("Service With a Smile") in Montreal:

My dear Sir:

Your story today, Dr. Stidger, was, without a doubt, splendid. I enjoyed every minute of it. "The Blanket and the Boy," about the boy who had both his legs cut off and within a few years was able to drive his own car.

Dr. Stidger you are driving that fact home every day. The fact that "It can be done," and with faith and perseverance you can beat any ailment. We are masters of our own body. No matter how bad off a person thinks he is, always remember there is someone worse off than you are and they aren't belly aching about it.

I've been able to stand up for a scant few seconds every day. Some one told me, "Gosh, Jimmie, what's standing for a few seconds?" I would never be contented with that, I'd sooner be dead! Now, Dr. Stidger, how 'bout that guy . . . little does he know, a few seconds this year, means a few minutes next year, and a few minutes next year means a few hours the year after.

And don't forget, in the meantime you've grabbed "Fate" by the neck and choked the devil out of him. I intend to catch a hold of Fate and put him to work for me . . . greasing cars. . . . I don't care what anyone says, no man is ever laid on a shelf by Fate. It is entirely up to him whether he stays there or moves on.

I've learned that good service wins a good reputation and a good reputation warms up goodwill, goodwill gains confidence, and confidence creates customers for the good service.

Dr. Stidger, many thanks for all your fine talks. I listen to every one of 'em, and I can always find something that helps me. My regards to "Pat" Kelly and I'll close with words from [Edward] Benson [archbishop of Canterbury, 1882–96]: "The essence of courage is not that your heart should not quake, but that no one should know that it does."

Faithfully yours,
Jimmy Darou[36]

That Jimmy Darou would send his regards to Pat Kelly should be no surprise. Kelly was the announcer who introduced Bill each day and gave the Fleischmann commercial. To regular listeners who invited Bill into his living room each noon, Bill and Pat became as familiar as old friends.

Bill found himself drawn into, even immersed in, the lives and problems of complete strangers. Moreover, Bill's friendly voice and helpful stories made him seem the natural person for listeners to turn to for advice, and in whom to confide their problems. This connection became for Bill a responsibility to uphold. It was both exhilarating and a burden, the weight of which grew heavier by the day. One satisfied listener after another spread the word among friends to tune into *Getting the Most Out of Life*, and Bill's audience grew exponentially. He sometimes felt overwhelmed:

Each month as I enter into a new period of broadcasting and public speaking, with its daily chores; answering of a voluminous mail, even though I enjoy the work, it often looks like a mountain to climb, and, as I look forward to it, it seems almost insurmountable. But I have long learned to take my work hour by hour, and day by day, and pretty soon a week's work is behind me and then a month's work; and the thing is done.[37]

Thus, the radio broadcast became an extension of Bill's very being. Figuratively, he reached out his arms over the airwaves, summoning his friends to listen. No part of the broadcast escaped his attention. He inspired his organist, Frank R. White, to write his own music instead of just playing the music of others. White had been reading one of Bill's poems and decided he'd set it to music. The result was a hymn called "I Want to Know More About Jesus," which Bill and Frank worked on together and then performed on the air. This collaboration produced a number of hymns, which they called "realistic hymns," because they caught the mood of the times. One of these, "Judean Hills Are Holy," became so popular that over thirty-eight thousand requests for printed scores came in from listeners.

Prior to the first broadcast, Bill held a competition to choose a choral group to perform on his program. A Boston quartet, the New England Singers (mentioned in the broadcast script above), won the competition and became regulars. Also, to involve as many people as possible, Bill formed a committee of a thousand ministers in New England to take turns selecting the "old hymns" that were sung each day on *Getting the Most Out of Life*. Bill invited his old friend and School of Theology colleague James R. Houghton to supervise and lead the music.

Broadcasting during the month of January 1938 did not divert Bill from domestic concerns. It was a month of anxious waiting, because Betty was pregnant and due to deliver at the end of the month. She had already had one child, a boy, who had been born in August 1936 but, tragically, had died almost immediately. Iva took the train to Detroit to be with Betty and Jack, and on January 29, 1938, your author was born, at 9:07 A.M. A caesarean operation was performed by Dr. Milton A. Darling at the Grace Hospital. The process was not smooth, and Iva had to give blood to provide Betty a transfusion. But, as Betty said, "Where there is a will, there is a way."

Bill was in Boston nervously waiting to learn what had happened and feeling left out of these important activities. It reminded him of his waiting in East Providence, Rhode Island, when Betty had been born in Ligonier twenty-six years earlier. When the good news came, he let out a war whoop of relief and sent off this telegram:

Dearest Betty,

I am the happiest grandfather who ever lived and want you to know that I am proud of you. Have told everybody in Boston, and the whole city is excited. Am coming to see you and the athlete soon. Have already ordered a razor for him.

Love,
Dad[38]

Then, irrepressibly, Bill dashed off the following letter:

AN OFFICIAL AND FINAL ANNOUNCEMENT OF
THE BIRTH OF A GRANDSON TO A FRIEND OF YOURS

To a Few Selected and Understanding Souls:

Through the efforts of Mr. and Mrs. John Hyland (Betty and Jack to you) and with Mrs. Stidger's able assistance (Iva to you) I have been made a GRANDFATHER.

It is an event of some importance to me and my guess is that nothing quite as important has happened in American life since Lincoln's birthday. And speaking of that, young Jack Wentroth Hyland with due consideration for both Lincoln and Washington advanced his arrival to Saturday, January 29th instead of waiting until February, a month already overcrowded with great birthdays.

Heretofore it has been the custom for the parents alone to send out announcement but not in this family. The Grandfather has something to say for he has suffered many anxieties over this affair. He stayed at home in Boston while Iva, Jack and Betty were right on the scene of action—Iva even going so far as to horn in with a Blood Transfusion for Betty, just to make a hero out of herself. That left me to bear the bulk of the burden waiting on the sidelines and I'm going to get in on this affair in some way even if it's only with this announcement. A Grandfather has some rights.

Jacky weighed 18 pounds at birth, was three feet tall, and was wearing a pair of Boxing Gloves his Grandfather sent him. He was born by Caesarian Section and landed on his feet running. When the doctor paddled him, where they usually paddle, to encourage the first "Yap" he punched him on the chin for paddling him. Then he winked at the Nurse. They say this is the most remarkable boy ever born in Detroit or anywhere else, and I am prepared to believe it although my usual modesty causes me to discount some of the things I hear. In three days he was eating steak, and the first words he uttered were to ask for the address of Joe Lewis in Detroit. He has red hair, and, as my friend Stanley High wired me when his first son was born, he has his "mother's features and father's fixtures." One of my conservative women friends says I am exaggerating about that 18 pounds, but if you don't believe it I can show you the scales. He has a two cylinder engine; his carburetor is mixing well (a little too much air now and then but on the whole mixing well); and his exhaust is functioning properly. His eyes are blue and his "jump seat" is red at this writing—but that, I am told, will get better. He is streamlined—most of the time and so is his nurse.

Fraternally and Faithfully,
Grandfather "Bill" Stidger[39]

There were some who wondered who actually had had the child, Betty or Bill. Bill, who was excited enough for several parents combined, sent this telegram to Betty:

Mrs. John Hyland
Grace Memorial Hospital, Detroit

Dearest Betty,

Your mother is a pill for she has not written me in a week nor told me anything about the athlete, whether he gets his dinner out of them cute little containers or a bottle. Just bought him a jackknife. Where shall I send it? How is his exhaust working?

Love,
Dad[40]

Despite the pleasant interlude caused by the author's arrival, pressure was gradually building on Bill. *Getting the Most Out of Life* had sparked so much interest that other stations in the New England area had signed on to carry his program. It looked to NBC as if there was sufficient demand for a national hookup—broadcasting over WJZ and fifty-five affiliated stations in the United States and Canada. It would be, in every respect, the big time. But Bill would have to spend his weekdays in Rockefeller Center in New York City, in the studios of WJZ. Bill was offered by Fleischmann's a long-term contract with a thirteen-week option clause, and his pay was set at a thousand dollars a week. He realized that he would be earning in a three-week period what many of his fellow ministers took an entire year to make. What's more, he would be earning this astronomical figure in an economically perilous time.

Bill was now confronted with the realization that if he had to operate during the week from New York, he would not be able to continue all his other activities. He decided that he must resign as morning preacher of Church of All Nations. With Helms's advice, Bill wrote the following formal letter:

Friday, March 4, 1938

Dear Dr. Helms:

I am writing this letter of resignation from the Sunday Morning Preaching at the Church of All Nations so that you may have it to present to the Fourth Quarterly Conference, this resignation to take effect according to the laws of the Church at the end of this Conference Year.

I have had a wonderful four years with you and in many ways count it the happiest four years I have had in any ministry. Morgan Memorial and the Church of All Nations have contributed to me much more than I have contributed to them. Here I have learned the art of broadcasting, and here I had my training in this new medium of preaching and it is because of this experience that I have had opportunities of getting into a wider field of broadcasting than I otherwise would have had and I credit it all to the experience I had in the "Great American Personalities" broadcast for two years from Morgan Memorial.

Grateful for all that has been done for me here and for the friendly co-operation I have had, I reluctantly lay down this pleasant task because I feel that I must have at last one free day in a week for rest.

Fraternally and Faithfully,
William L. Stidger[41]

Traveling to New York each week for his broadcast was initially a grand adventure for Bill. Years afterward, at home in Newton Center, hearing the drone overhead of the daily plane to New York at noon, he would vividly recall the excitement he felt each time he headed to Rockefeller Center, at least in the beginning. His hotel of choice was the Roosevelt, and from his window there he could look out and see the incredible spire of the Chrysler Building sparkling in the sun.

Bill enjoyed being on the radio. The NBC staff called him the "minute man," because he was so unruffled by broadcasting that he could stay outside the studio casually talking to technicians and visitors until barely a minute before going on the air, and then excuse himself and enter the broadcast area booth. The newspapers reported a bizarre occurrence when an unauthorized stranger walked into the studio while Bill was broadcasting and leaned over Bill's shoulder to look at the script. Before a production man could rush in from the control room, the intruder left. Bill kept talking throughout the incident.

Bill visited the churches, restaurants, museums, and theaters of New York and found a stream of stories that he could pass on to his listeners:

> My friend, Stanley High, the well-known journalist, and his wife came in to New York City for an afternoon and evening. We visited the Metropolitan Museum and looked upon its history, sculpture and paintings and yet my heart was not satisfied. Then we went to dinner and dined much better than was my usual custom, for Mr. High was paying for it. Yet I was not entirely satisfied. Then we went to an amusing comedy and we laughed until we wept and yet my heart was not entirely filled. We had fine fellowship together such as understanding friends who have grown into each others' lives for a quarter of a century can have, talking of books, world events, people; and yet there was something, as yet incomplete.
>
> Then I took them to their train which left at midnight from Grand Central Station and, as we stepped into that great Grand Canyon of a building, suddenly we stood entranced, astonished, hushed, subdued; for, out into that grand concourse from a great organ came the strains of "Just a Song at Twilight." We stopped; everybody else stopped. It was a beautiful experience. I felt a lump in my throat and tears in my eyes. I turned away to hide them, and Stanley High said: "You don't need to turn away for I'm weeping a bit myself. Who wouldn't?" Then I learned that the heart needs to be fed with music and memories from time to time. "Man does not live by bread alone." The sweet strains of that lovely song had satisfied the hunger in my heart.[42]

The music played in Grand Central Station interested him, and he looked into the story behind it. He discovered that the organist was a woman named Mary Lee Reed. Bill wrote a few years later:

> She plays a silver-toned organ loaned to her by a large organ company. Her peaceful, hope-inspired music has filled the majority of the stations in the country. She devoted her entire life to helping others by her splendid and inspiring music. For the past nine years she has been playing in Grand Central Station, New York City. Besides her station work she travels around the country organizing community singers, giving organ lessons, and training quartets and vocal groups. She is one of the happiest women I know. She has surely learned how to get the most out of life by helping others.[43]

Being in New York made it easy for Bill to answer a call from Edwin Markham to visit him. The poet's mental health had been failing for some time and had been noticeable at the Democratic National Convention. Physically, the poet remained fit; it was his mind that was slipping away. His son Virgil had had to obtain from the courts custody of his father's finances and general well-being, because complete strangers would turn up at the front porch of Markham's house on Staten Island to ask favors of him. If Markham was not in one of his "brighter" moods he could easily have been persuaded to sign away his remaining possessions. Virgil had even given up his own apartment to be with his father in order to protect him.

Markham, at times, knew he was failing. He wrote Bill, "I am not altogether well, I presume, although I don't feel any illness. I still read my books." He added "I am think-ing of you. Indeed I think of you for hours every day. I am swinging onto the brink of death; and I am comforted by the thought of you as my steadfast friend—don't come just to see me; but step into my door if you happen to be passing. There are many things to say, since I am feeling the wind of the next world on my face. But if I fail to see you here again, I will surely see you over there. So goodbye. May God be good to you. Remember that I am yours for this world and for all worlds."[44]

Markham was speaking from the heart, and Bill was deeply touched. Since they had first met at the San Francisco Exposition twenty-three years earlier, they had been close friends, and now it looked like Markham's death was imminent. At their first meeting Bill had been the young upstart, just thirty years old, and Markham had been the venerated father figure, having turned sixty. In the late summer of 1938, however, Bill was fifty-three and at the peak of his career, while Markham, at eighty-six, was much more the child, caught in the downswing of his life. Bill made the trip to Staten Island. It was a disheartening one:

> In answer to his call to step into his door I went to Staten Island and spent a
> day with him in fellowship. Now and then his mind would wander because of
> his illness, in somewhat the same way that [Ralph Waldo] Emerson's did in the
> later years of his great life, and then he would turn to me and ask me who I
> was; and that was a tragic thing. Then he would have flashes of his old self and
> would rise to beautiful heights in his conversation. But just before I was to
> leave him to go back to New York City he went into another room and got his
> latest book, entitled *The Star of Araby*, sat down in a chair and spent the next fif-
> teen minutes autographing that book for me. As he wrote in that book, slowly,
> thoughtfully—he would look up at me with a penetrating eye and then with his
> pen poised over the book a far away look would come into his eyes; and as
> he wrote he hummed to himself the melody of "Rock of Ages."
>
> Markham always did this: wrote his poems to the tunes of the great
> hymns of the church. Many a night when all the rest of us were asleep we
> have heard him in our home in his own room humming the music of some
> great hymn. I remember the first time we ever had this experience was about
> three o'clock in the morning and my daughter Betty, ten years of age, was
> frightened as she heard the refrain of "Rock of Ages" hummed in the poet's
> room as he sat at his writing table.

But that day the poet seemed farther away from me than usual although we sat in the same room. He seemed like old Conrad the Cobbler, one of his own favorite characters of whom he wrote in "How the Great Guest Came":

His eyes peered out, intent and far,
As looking beyond the things that are.
He walked as one who is done with fear,
Knowing at last that God was near.
Only the half of him cobbled the shoes;
The rest was away for the Heavenly news.

The Heavenly news he was evidently putting into that autograph for me; and once again as he looked up he hummed "Rock of Ages, Cleft for me. Let me hide myself in Thee" as he wrote. And as I sat there watching those strange eyes of his I thought of other lines which he used to describe Conrad the Cobbler:

Indeed so thin was the mystic screen
That parted the Unseen from the Seen
You could not tell, from the Poet's theme
If his dream were truth, or his truth were dream.

But I knew when he handed that autograph to me that his dream was truth for this is what I read and still treasure in my book:

To William L. Stidger, friend of many years with whom I have shared my joys and tears. It is good to see you again. I have traveled with you this shore of time. I will wait for you on the higher shore of eternity. You have brightened for me this lower road of existence. I shall wait for you to come on to find me in the new road that waits us all in the wonderful existence in that world beyond; the world that sets this world right.

Edwin Markham[45]

This was the last time Bill saw his friend Edwin Markham, who died of pneumonia, with only a nurse present, at his home at 92 Waters Avenue, Westerleigh, Staten Island, on March 7, 1940.

Throughout 1938 and 1939, Bill's workload in connection with *Getting the Most Out of Life* had become preemptive of almost any other activity, such as visiting friends like Markham, speaking, writing, or teaching. He asked for a leave of absence from the School of Theology and to be excused from his teaching commitments for the school year beginning September 1938. The dean, Earl Marlatt, granted Bill leave, appointing a younger member of the faculty, Francis Gerald Ensley, to teach Bill's courses in homiletics.

Bill was relieved; he was now able to spend his energy on his broadcast without major distractions. He discovered, however, that even with the additional time, responding to people who poured out their problems in letters to him was endless. Putting on a major broadcast was just plain hard work, he concluded; it created a maelstrom of details and entanglements. Only gradually did he realize that he truly missed the intense human contact of teaching and interacting with his students, and of conducting church services, where he saw actual human faces and could experience their reactions to him. Ironically, while facing a microphone and speaking to an unseen audience was depersonalizing for Bill, some listeners presumed a personal relationship with him, with his radio voice, a perception that in extreme cases led to "psychologist/patient" links that drew Bill into entrapping webs.

A letter from Betty (who had attended a service at St. Mark's) arrived, recalling for him the unusual peace of mind he had had as minister of his former Detroit congregation:

We went to St. Mark's yesterday, and I felt it was like old home week. As we walked down the aisle, we heard on all sides, "Why there's Betty Stidger." Dr. Edwards spoke terribly but he had a wonderful idea which more than likely originated in you. He got so excited he bumped into the bench and cracked his knee, then jumped away so fast he almost fell off the platform onto the altar on the rebound.

He talks with his hands and then seems to think better of it and holds his hands still by placing them low on his hips. Jack was not impressed. Dr. Edwards baptized children and had about six poorly dressed girls up there to follow after him and make records. There seemed to be so much confusion, no calm, and I didn't feel "at peace" at all.

I got to reminiscing about our time at St. Mark's and one thing I remember that I rather wish I could find again is this: Sunday evenings when we had big crowds and lots of singing and laughing at offering time. Then you would stand up and say, "There has been much tumult. No one is at peace within himself, so let us just be quiet for a moment." Then the fluttering of church bulletins, the movement, the very air seemed to be quiet and I would look up to the skylight and see the coming and going of the revolving cross light and everything seemed to be peaceful and quiet. Somehow I even felt soft and mellow inside and didn't try to think up what I could do to amuse myself. Well, that feeling is entirely obliterated by Dr. Edwards, people leave that church as they came in—hurried and not relaxed, not happy or content. At least, that is one person's opinion.[46]

Bill knew he was on a treadmill—five shows a week, every week of the month, every month of the year. By June 1939, he had completed his 420th show and was approaching his 500th broadcast as the year 1940 approached. Broadcasting was relentless. The fun and excitement of flying down to New York for the week, living in a hotel, and flying back to Boston for the weekend had long ago worn off. His radio ratings were high, he was making excellent money, and his reputation was soaring, but he was overworked and stale, having to repeat stories he had already broadcast because there was simply no time or opportunity to make new contacts, to interview new personalities.

Bill found that, try as he would, the pressure on him was almost unbearable. In one of his best broadcasts, he gave his listeners a piece of advice he had received one night when he was exhausted:

REST WHERE YOU ARE.

Not long ago at the end of a trying day I was visiting some friends. We were sitting before a wood fire and I was stretched out in a big arm chair completely relaxed with an end-of-the-day exhaustion.

The wife of my friend said to me: "You seem to be tired out." I replied: "I never felt so weary and done in."

She immediately left the room. I had an uncanny feeling that she was off to get me some medicine to relieve my weariness and I was always suspicious of such females; the type who are always wanting you to take some pet remedy to cure your ails. I have suffered much from such and I just didn't feel I had the male manhood that evening to resist such feminine advances. I probably would succumb without argument. And my suspicions proved to be correct for pretty soon she appeared with her remedy. Only much to my surprise and delight it was not a pill, not an effervescent drink to alkalize my body, not a stimulant, not a sedative—not even a Yeast Cake. It was a poem.

REST WHERE YOU ARE

[poet not known]

When spurred by tasks unceasing or undone
You would seek rest afar and cannot,
Though repose be rightly won—
Rest where you are!
Neglect the needless; sanctify the best;
Move without stress or jar;
With quiet of spirit, self-possessed;
Rest where you are!
Not in event, restriction or release;
Not in scenes near or far,
But in ourselves are restlessness or peace;
Rest where you are!
Where lives the soul, lives God;
His day, His world
No phantom mists need mar.
His starry nights are great tents of Peace unfurled;
Rest where you are!

As I read that simple poem with its practical suggestions, I felt a great sense of relaxation and peace come to me; and I actually felt rested.

I liked particularly several of its suggestions, one of which was that single phrase, "Neglect the needless." How we need to learn that lesson in life. I remember once that Peter Clark MacFarlane, a novelist of ten years ago, said to me in my early ministry: "Bill, you must quit gathering Goat Feathers." I smiled, but did not know what he meant. He smiled back and said: "Don't you know what a Goat Feather is?" I admitted that I did not. Then he presented me with a little booklet entitled "Goat Feathers." It was written by Ellis Parker Butler, he of the "Pigs Is Pigs" fame. It told the universal story of a certain type of man who is continually neglecting his main business of life by serving on Street Paving Committees, running errands for the whole town; acting as chairman of this and that; collecting dues for lodges; acting as agent for every conceivable sort of a movement; being secretary to every type of a meeting. That man finally awoke to the fact that he was being imposed on and wearing himself out doing everything but his own work; and, as a result, his own business was going back.

In other words, he was gathering "Goat Feathers." So he decided that he would begin a disciplined regime of neglect of the needless. If most of us started a regime of neglecting the needless things we do in a day we would save ourselves much wear and tear. I have tried it. I tried reading only one newspaper for a week instead of three and four and found that at the end of the week I was just as wise as if I had read four papers. I found that I was doing fifty definite things in a day that were utterly needless so I decided to take away that much wear and tear on my time and energies.

"Neglect the needless, sanctify the best"—give yourself more completely to the things worth doing. That is one of the fine arts of resting where you are; in the very midst of your work. Give the best you have to the things you ought to be doing. It is not in release from responsibilities that true rest comes but in learning to select our tasks and do them well. It is not in "scenes near or far"; not in climbing the fence into other pastures but in learning to rest in the midst of work.[47]

The closing piece of music for this broadcast was "Peace, Perfect Peace," which Bill had heard in New York City on the Sunday before he left for the front lines in France.

Two events now occurred in Bill's life—some months apart—that affected him vitally. Earl Marlatt, in his second year as tenure as dean of the School of Theology, decided to have young Ensley take over officially from Bill as head of the Homiletics Department, beginning with the school year starting in September 1939. Though he had no time to spare for teaching, Bill had been the department head for eleven years, and it was a credential of some importance to him.

The second event was catastrophic. Bill was informed that Fleischmann's Yeast had decided to pare its 1940 advertising budget significantly. The consequence for Bill was that

Getting the Most Out of Life was canceled. The remainder of his thirteen-week contract was to be honored, but after that there would be no more broadcasts. The economy still languished; it was unlikely that another sponsor could be found.

Throughout his life Bill had been running hard, achieving whatever goal he set out after, beating his competition in the number of members in his congregation, the number of books published, the number of articles placed in leading magazines, the number of listeners to his radio programs. He had existed on a superabundance of energy drawn from some mysterious source within, a force that was driving him forward on the upward arc of his life.

Slowly it dawned on him that now he had nowhere to go. There were no more hills to climb. The baton had been passed to younger men, like Ensley, whose turn it now was to race to the top. Edwin Markham, thirty years his senior, had preceded Bill to the peak; now Markham, an old man, was caught in the inescapable gravity of the downward arc of life. Was Bill in Markham's track? To have his radio program taken away was a devastating blow, since he had poured most of his energy into radio for nearly a decade. True, he had a teaching job to return to, but now he had no church or faculty chairmanship to fall back upon.

Dimly, Bill sensed also that if a second major war occurred—as seemed increasingly likely, with Hitler at the head of a militant Germany—it would not be for him. He was now too old to be allowed "at the center of immensities."

The mysterious source inside him that had supplied his seemingly endless energy was now dry, exhausted by a lifetime of use and at least a decade of overuse. Darkness closed in around him; insecurity and indecision became his reigning moods.

In March 1940, Bill returned to Boston confused and, for the first time in his life, directionless. His sense of humor had vanished; his intense curiosity about people around him was gone; and the lively man known to so many as Bill Stidger was lifeless and sadly inert.[48]

Notes

1. *Church of All Nations Bulletin,* November 4, 1934, 3.

2. "A Morning Antidote," *Times–Minute Man,* Editorial, reprinted in Morgan Memorial Goodwill Services promotional brochure, undated.

3. Letter dated October 23, 1934, from Jack Hyland to William L. Stidger, author's collection.

4. Betty Stidger diary, author's collection.

5. Telegram dated December 8, 1934, from Mr. and Mrs. William L. Stidger to Mr. and Mrs. Jack Hyland, author's collection.

6. Letter dated December 17, 1934, from Iva B. Stidger to her family, author's collection.

7. William L. Stidger, "Hitler Planning to Be Kind to the Jews?" *Liberty,* May 30, 1936, 16–17.

8. William L. Stidger, "Row on Hitler Planning to Be Kind to Jews," *Liberty* (date not known).

9. "Great Personalities Broadcast," Morgan Memorial promotional brochure, January, 1937,

10. Joseph Alsop and Robert Kintner, *Men around the President* (New York: Doubleday, Doran, 1939), 102–103, 108–109.

11. "Vandenberg Twits 'Good Neighbors,'" *New York Times,* June 20, 1936, 2.

12. Stanley High, *Roosevelt—and Then?* (New York: Harper and Brothers, 1937), 256.

13. High, *Roosevelt—and Then?* 255.

14. William L. Stidger, *These Amazing Roosevelts* (New York: Macfadden, 1938), 5–6.

15. Stidger, *These Amazing Roosevelts,* 3.

16. Stidger, *These Amazing Roosevelts,* 27–28.

17. Stidger, *These Amazing Roosevelts,* 32–33.

18. Stidger, *These Amazing Roosevelts,* 33–35.

19. Stidger, *These Amazing Roosevelts,* 28–31.

20. Stidger, *These Amazing Roosevelts,* 57–58.

21. Stidger, *These Amazing Roosevelts,* 55–56.

22. Stidger, *These Amazing Roosevelts,* 4.

23. Stidger, *These Amazing Roosevelts,* 80.

24. Stidger, *These Amazing Roosevelts,* 80–81.

25. Franklin D. Roosevelt, second inaugural address, January 20, 1937, in James MacGregor Burns, *Roosevelt 1882–1940: The Lion and the Fox* (New York: Harcourt Brace, 1956), 291–293.

26. Stidger, *These Amazing Roosevelts,* 13–14.

27. Stanley High, "Whose Party Is It?" *Saturday Evening Post,* February 6, 1937.

28. Alsop and Kintner, *Men around the President,* 111.

29. "Talk of the Town—Stidger," *The New Yorker,* March 2, 1940.

30. William L. Stidger, *How to Get the Most Out of Life* (Chicago: Rodeheaver, Hall-Mack, 1939), 5.

31. Stidger, *How to Get the Most Out of Life,* 1.

32. "Neglect the Needless," *Time,* December 6, 1937, 56.

33. Paul K. Conkin, *The New Deal* (Wheeling, W.Va.: Harlan Davidson, 1967), 96–97.

34. William L. Stidger, "Getting the Most Out of Life," first radio broadcast, *Fleischmann's Yeast Program,* Yankee Network, September 27, 1937.

35. Letter from radio listener to William L. Stidger, undated, author's collection.

36. Letter dated January 11, 1939, from "Jimmy" Darou, Cheerio Service Station, to William L. Stidger, author's collection.

37. Stidger, *How to Get the Most Out of Life,* 47.

38. Telegram from William L. Stidger to Betty Stidger Hyland, undated, early February 1938, author's collection.

39. Announcement, undated, early February, 1938, from William L. Stidger, author's collection.

40. Telegram from William L. Stidger to Betty Stidger Hyland, undated, early February, 1938, author's collection.

41. Letter dated March 4, 1938, from William L. Stidger to Dr. E. J. Helms; *Church of All Nations Bulletin,* March 20, 1938, 3.

42. William L. Stidger, "The Heart, Too, Must be Fed," "Getting the Most Out of Life," radio broadcast, *Fleischmann's Yeast Program,* Yankee Network, January 10, 1939.

43. William L. Stidger, "A Boy Whistled," in *There Are Sermons in Stories* (New York: Abingdon-Cokesbury, 1942), 215–16.

44. William L. Stidger, "The Wind of the Next World," "Getting the Most Out of Life," radio broadcast, *Fleischmann's Yeast Program,* Yankee Network, January 28, 1938.

45. Letter dated April 22, 1938, from Edwin Markham to William L. Stidger, author's collection.

46. Letter from Betty Stidger Hyland to William L. Stidger, author's collection.

47. William L. Stidger, "Rest Where You Are," "Getting the Most Out of Life," radio broadcast, *Fleischmann's Yeast Program,* Yankee Network, October 25, 1938.

48. With some irony, *The New Yorker* published an article on Bill in its issue of March 2, 1940, as "Getting the Most Out of Life" was ending. The text of the article follows:

The highest-paid minister in the world—if we are not being too disgustingly mundane—is probably the Reverend Dr. William L. Stidger of Boston, who conducts a fifteen-minute radio program between 11:45 and 12 noon every day except Saturday and Sunday, over WJZ and fifty-five affiliated stations in the United States and Canada. He is sponsored by Fleischmann's Yeast and gets a thousand dollars a week, more or less. His program, which is appropriately called *Getting the Most Out of Life*, features every week an original hymn, words by Dr. Stidger and music by Frank White, his organist. Copies of the hymns are mailed free to any listeners who request them, and one of Dr. Stidger's numbers, "Judean Hills Are Holy," drew thirty-eight thousand such requests. His sponsors have figured, from the Stidger mailing list, that the Bible Belt is moving up into Canada, and they have accordingly bought time on twenty-nine stations in the dominion. Trends, trends!

Dr. Stidger is the inventor of a revolving, illuminated cross for church steeples. There are now three hundred and eighty of these in use in the United States; the patent royalties bring Dr. Stidger something between four and five hundred dollars a year, which he devotes to foreign missions. He invented this cross back in 1913, when he was given his first church, which stood on a sand dune outside of San Francisco and had a congregation of three people. It packed 'em in. Dr. Stidger drove a YMCA truck during the last war, and afterward settled down in Detroit, where he got to know Henry Ford. For many years he had a monopoly on interviewing Ford for International News Service. He delivered the first political speech for Frank Murphy, when Murphy was running for judge of the Recorder's Court in Detroit. When the Knights of Columbus gave Murphy a dinner in Boston last year, Murphy insisted that Stidger be invited. It was probably the first time a Protestant minister had ever attended a K. of C. banquet in Boston. Another exploit of Dr. Stidger was a half-page advertisement in the Detroit *Times*, an appeal for money headed "I'm Whistlin' in the Dark." It brought him a $ 25,000 contribution for an organ.

Dr. Stidger next spent three years, from 1925 to 1928, in Kansas City. This period was brightened by Sinclair Lewis, who came there to consult Dr. Stidger on the technical details of a novel about ministers. He was the Stidgers' house guest for several weeks, a period during which—à la "The Man Who Came to Dinner"—Lewis was visited by Ethel Barrymore, Edwin Markham, William White, Gilbert Frankau, and Harpo Marx, in a body. They all decided to be witnesses at the wedding of the Stidgers' colored maid and gardener—a ceremony which Dr. Stidger had planned to conduct quietly, in his house, since white ministers in K.C. were not supposed to marry Negroes. Lewis slipped out and telephoned the newspapers, however, and the wedding made the front pages. Lewis then retired to an apartment in Kansas City, and in two months wrote "Elmer Gantry," which of course was not what Dr. Stidger had had in mind for him at all.

For the past eleven years, Dr. Stidger has been chairman of the Department of Homiletics at the Boston University School of Theology. During the past year and a half, since his broadcasts have been emanating from New York, he has been on a leave of absence. He was "discovered" by a Mr. Murray [Morris (sic)], an agency man, who was looking for a radio voice with the same "tired" quality (we use Mr. Murray's expression) as W. J. Cameron's. Mr. Murray happened to tune in on a non-commercial Stidger broadcast while driving in New England and signed him up right away. Dr. Stidger now has a long-term contract with the yeast people, with the usual thirteen-week option clause. His Crosley rating is 1.61. *Variety* knows of no other preacher under a commercial radio contract except Jacob Tarshish, a rabbi, who broadcasts as "The Lamplighter."

Twelve

Rest Where You Are

With Bill out of action, Iva had no recourse but to take charge. He lacked the self-confidence even to attend the funeral service of Edwin Markham—his friend of twenty-five years—or to preside at the marriage of Fred Stone's daughter, which the well-known comedian had gone out of his way to ask Bill to do. Of his condition Bill later wrote, "Two years ago, after ten years of ceaseless work in public speaking, teaching, writing and radio, I was shot to pieces and had to take a year off for a complete rest. It [a nervous breakdown] expresses itself in restlessness, irritability, lack of poise, anger, jealousy and suspicion. In some cases it gets so bad that a strong man is afraid to cross a city street."[1]

Iva reached out to Mark Hopkins, a doctor in San Jose and friend of many years. Mark, whom Bill had praised as a symbol "of all doctors who have the spirit of Christian service in their hearts," invited them to come to California. Therefore, in early March 1940, Iva drove Bill to San Jose, stopping en route in Ligonier. Her niece, Jane McIntyre, later recalled that she was shocked to see her "Uncle Bill" sitting glumly on the sofa, quiet and unable to participate in the conversation. It was as if the light that had burned so brightly in him had gone out.

Mark gave Bill and Iva "a restful cottage by the sea, administered costly injections of hormones and vitamins several times a week," and, as Bill wrote, "cared for me like a father and then laughed when I suggested payment for professional services."[2]

Weekly, Iva would drive Bill from their cottage in Rio Del Cruz to Mark's office in San Jose. A new road was being built in the narrow mountain pass between the two towns, and the existing road had been torn up. To Bill, the first trip seemed to be fifty miles, although he knew it was only a mile or so. "Bump, bump, bump, up and down the ruts, cross and criss-cross holes. To one in my nervous condition it was about as trying as anything could possibly be. I fumed, fretted and complained—and all but cursed the State of California, Santa Cruz County, the climate, the Highway Commission—everybody but Iva—and I had a sneaking feeling that she was partly to blame for that road, although I never told her so to her face. That first day, I was just about at the end of my patience, when through the almost blinding dust I saw a sign, which some imaginative contractor had put on the side of the road where the ruts were deepest, and it read: BE PATIENT WHILE WE BUILD YOU A BETTER ROAD, FRIEND! In spite of myself I had to chuckle over that sign, for it had a symbolical meaning for my own recovery."[3]

Despite the rest, medicine, and California sunshine, Bill made scant progress in his recovery. One evening, however, he was invited to go up to the top of Mount Hamilton to visit Lick Observatory. He was frightened just getting there: the long, winding mountain road had, he recounted, 365 corkscrew turns, one for each day in the year. Scared or not, he made it. Then, through the telescope, for the first time in his life, he saw the stars, in planes behind planes. As he said, "I saw front yards full of stars, backyards, meadows and fields of stars, rivers of stars, forests of stars, long mountain ranges of stars—stars behind stars. The friend who took me up there told the astronomer about my illness, and I saw that scientist's eyes sparkle as he said, 'This is the best cure for nerves I know.' That young astronomer swung his telescope around to a pinpoint in the universe and said: 'Look at that, doctor. Look at that!' I looked. Then he said: 'That is Alpha Centauri, a star which is practically sitting on our back doorstep. It is only four light years away. That means that its light, which travels 186,000 miles a second, takes four years to reach us.' When I came down from Mount Hamilton that evening I had several things to do that had before seemed important. But now they all seemed picayune and trivial. I was astonished that I had ever considered some of them important at all. For the moment I forgot my nerves and myself, lost in silent wonder and amazement at that universe I had seen from Lick Observatory."[4]

Under Mark Hopkins's orders, Bill was not permitted any telephone calls, and he had not felt capable of writing letters, even to Betty. She wrote herself, however, sending him this letter on his fifty-fifth birthday:

Dearest Dad,

Last week I was in downtown Cleveland and I thought how wonderful it would be if I could give you a nice leather bound volume of poetry. I looked at them and priced them and decided on three little volumes of Emily Dickinson. Then I walked away, knowing that you would fully understand what I wanted to do but couldn't afford.

So the next best thing was to write a poem to you myself. I have had all the most worthy intentions these last two weeks, but here it is—the deadline—and the poem is still in my heart or head. It is way back there somewhere, buried underneath wallpaper, paint color for the woodwork, the number of closet shelves, curtains, screens and in fact all the decisions needed for my new house, not to mention being buried beneath my concern for my "three" fine boys.

So the poem will have to wait. But the thoughts don't. They can tumble out forever and eternally. What is all this preamble? Do you remember? Fifty-five years ago a redhead was born and that redhead-smashed-nose fellow turned out to be a real great guy. I'm afraid that you didn't do so well on "production," but the quality of the single product that you can claim is great and really proud of what she belongs to.

Gifts are funny things, aren't they? You've always been so very generous with what you have had—a sort of outward and visible sign of an inward and spiritual grace. And Dad don't ever get the impression that I—we—don't appreciate those signs of your love.

But do you know, today, driving home, I tried to analyze the best gifts that I have ever received— the ones that make me love you and make me glad there are always more birthdays to come. First, there are very few girls who know that if there is trouble that they can call on their family and that family will be willing and interested in helping. Isn't this more important than a blue bike?

Secondly, isn't it more important than a trip to Europe to have memories of long walks on winter nights, of touching hands around the trunk of a giant tree to measure it—to look up at the stars or go to a show together?

Thirdly, wouldn't you rather know that no matter what you've done you can always tell the truth about it and get good advice more often than tirades?

Fourthly, to have some man as your Father who understands how you feel about children, who accepts them as his own, isn't that more glorious than a weekend in New York to see shows?

Dad—to me these things are why I'm glad you were born. Now don't let me build you up too much, you have your peculiar traits, everyone does. But you have given me so many wonderful things, the inward and spiritual things, I mean. I hope that my boys will have the same perfect freedom as I have had. It isn't anything I can ever cultivate or learn—but however much of the understanding heart that I have comes from you and no one else but you. Mother has given me things to grow on too, but the gifts that I have been talking about are your personal ones to me and, Dad—they will never be taken away from me—they grow bigger and will continue to grow bigger as I try to pass them on to my boys.

I'll never forget "Abide With Me" sung by you to me in the back bedroom on East Jefferson Avenue; your giving me the elephant's tooth to play with in your office, after you comforted me when I felt alone while Mother went shopping; the poetry contest in the car as we were driving to Colorado Springs; the walk to the mill in that funny little town in Scotland or England—I can't remember which, but I can remember the long twilight and the beautiful flower beds; and the dedication of your book of verse to me when I graduated from Smith. Finally, I'll not forget how you never asked Jack about money but only insisted that he love me and make me happy. You're a great guy Dad—up or down—I'm glad I'm part of you,

> *Happy, happy birthday,*
> *Love,*
> *Your daughter Betty* [5]
> *March 12, 1940*

This letter helped shake Bill out of his torpor, for it made him aware of all that he was missing. Jack and Betty were in the midst of building a new house in Chagrin Falls, a suburb of Cleveland. Life was moving on, and he was not a part of it.

Compulsively, he began grabbing every church bulletin or magazine he could get his hands on, combing through them to find pictures and poems to make a scrapbook for Betty. When he completed it, on March 29, 1940, this collection contained over eighty poems, most of them with photographs, but all were centered on the topics of family, home, sunsets and sunrises, streams and rivers. They conveyed the sense of beauty and peace that a happy family with its own roof over its head can have. With each poem or photograph, Bill scrawled an additional message that linked it directly to the Hylands, or to Betty, or to "Treetops," her new house. The inscription that he pasted into the book was:

Dear Betty and Jack: Here is a Scrapbook for the Hyland Home and with it come my poems and my love—Dad[6]

It took another five or six weeks, however, for Bill to feel strong enough to engage in a one-on-one dialogue with Betty, even though it was only by letter, dated May 4, 1940:

Dearest Betty and family:

Well here's my first letter and am I excited? I am! I have felt terrible not to be writing to you—I, who, all these years, have written you so regularly. However, I know you have understood, kid.

Mother and I have been to two or three picture shows recently and that was also an achievement for me. All of which means that I am feeling better, praise be! I have read your letters with great eagerness and the news of Billy [Betty and Jack had adopted a child and had given him the name William Stidger Hyland] thrilled me deeply. I have also been anxious about his collic and exhaust and what have you, but to be truthful the thing that has worried me most is the fact that it has brought additional burdens to you. However, you are young and strong and have had a maternal urge strong enough to plunge you into taking on this new responsibility and that will carry you through with good old Jack's backing. I love that "How are my boys?" Hurrah for Jack and you too!

I have Jacky's new picture on my dresser, and the first thing I see each morning is his smile and it cheers my heart as much as the California sunshine.

Mother is a wonderful person. I have always known that but these weeks have given me an insight into her courage and good spirits and character I never saw before. She is like a great rock in a weary land to me. I love her so and you and Jack and "our boys." Am crazy to see red-headed Billy and the time can't come too soon to suit me.

I am sleeping now [i.e., am able to sleep] and have been without sedatives for three weeks and there are other signs of improvement, so I am heartened. The one thing that is hardest to bear for me is to feel so far away from you and to be out of telephone touch. But it must be seen through. I wish I had words to tell you how we love you and miss you, old darling.

Love,
Dad[7]

Less than a week later, on May 9, 1940, Bill wrote a second letter:

Dearest Betty and Jack:

I want this to get to you for Mother's Day for if ever you deserved recognition on that anniversary it is this year and your Dad gives it to you. You are now a mother by the normal procedure and mother through going out of your way by adopting and that makes it complete. It might even be a good procedure for all mothers to go through that experience of home-making.

    In any case, you have [adopted a baby], sincerely, maternally and with love in your heart. That can't go wrong and your mother and I are happy about the whole thing the more we think about it, darling!

    We get very lonely to see you, but we rejoice in your lively, newsy letters and eagerly grab them when they arrive. It seems to us that, with all your problems in getting Billy started and the care of Jacky, you are coming along well, you old dear. Hurrah for you!

    It was funny, wasn't it, that when your last letter crossed with mine and yours had in it a declaration that I must write you, that the very next Monday you got a scribbled letter from me? It must have been telepathy. I had a sudden impulse that Monday to write to you just as I have today. I'll try and do better now.

    I am endorsing a small royalty check I just received from Harpers. It is for you—a combination Mother's Day and birthday gift. Get something for your birthday or do what you want with it. I wish it were ten times as much, as it has been in the past and will be again some day. But for the moment it carries all my love and then some—a love so deep-rooted that it goes down into my very life. I think you understand. Mother and I are getting along well keeping house, loving each other, building memories and getting well, at least, I am. Mother doesn't need to get well—she's there and has arrived at her distinction—like a circus with banners.

    I hope this air mail special reaches you by Sunday so you'll know that we have been thinking about you dear.

All my love,
Dad[8]

Iva also wrote a letter to Betty on the same day as Bill wrote his:

My dear, dear Betty,

When you arrived at our house last year, I thought all honor was due me on Mother's Day, but you have sneaked up on me and stolen most of my honor. You are the real little mother. I am so proud of you, for you have really chosen your task. It's such a big one, and such a worthwhile one. There is so much of it hard and drab—and it can't be laid aside once it's started. I know you'll be all the word implies—a mother.

    How I would love to see you all, be with you on Sunday and play my role—grandmother, also mother to Betty and Jack. For although you are stealing my honors, I am still mother to you two. And I burst with pride in that. It sort of sounds as though I'm slopping over, but I feel sloppy anyway.

    Dad is sitting opposite me scratching away. He hasn't had a good morning since last Saturday when he wrote you. He gets pathetically lonely and homesick for you. Maybe writing you will help. It makes him happier for the time anyhow.

    My deepest love and affection to my two children and my two grandchildren.

Mother[9]

Bill's recovery seesawed back and forth between forward movement and retreat. There were times when he fell backward into fear, insecurity, and withdrawal. He depended on Iva primarily, but also on Mark, whose strength and constancy gave him courage and the will to fight his way back up from the depths. Bill later wrote:

> The one universal law I have discovered about human beings is that they have an infinite capacity to come back from depression, despair, defeat and tragedy. All that the average human being needs to make a comeback that will astonish the world is for somebody to have faith in him. Faith is the victory that overcomes all obstacles. I have seen men who were down and out, seemingly beyond redemption of any sort, brought back to self-respect and achievement because a woman, a friend, a child—even a dog—had faith in them. I have seen human beings shot to pieces with disease, seemingly beyond hope, make a quick comeback to usefulness because some human being had faith in them, or because they themselves had an awakening in their own souls of faith in themselves.[10]

A change he discovered in himself was that his once-driving interests in writing, speaking, and broadcasting had faded in their priority to him. What replaced them was his knowledge that certain people now stood at the center of his world; he realized how essential Iva, Betty, and her family were to him. An adjustment as large as this occurred only gradually, but when it was accomplished Bill found an internal peace which he had not had before. Gradually, too, his faith in himself was restored. So indebted was Bill to his friend and doctor that he dedicated the first book he published after his recovery to "Hazel and Mark Hopkins, who in 'the winter of my discontent' made me see that 'if winter comes, can spring be far behind?'"

Bill and Iva remained in their cottage in Santa Cruz throughout the summer. Eventually though, it was time for Bill to return to Boston if he was going to teach in the school year starting on September 19, 1940. They drove back home and Bill—with some hesitation—took up his teaching. To say that he was healed would have been premature; he remembered "my shyness in going to visit good friends on Labor Day," contrasting it with his condition a few years later of "egotistical, full of energy, complacent self-sufficiency."

As Bill eased back into his life in Boston, he had occasion to read William Allen White's biography, which revealed that White had had a nervous breakdown that lasted the better part of a year and that he too had spent time in recovery in California. Bill found that it was comforting to be in such good company. Still "feeling a bit cautious and fearful about my activities," he received a letter from an old friend, Bishop George A. Miller:

Now that you are back in the harness, all of your friends will be telling you to be cautious and not to do it again. I'm telling you nothing of the sort. Go to it! We all have to enter the doors that open before us, and Owen Meredith in Lucile *says something about the fellow who knocked at all the doors of life cautiously and entered none. Finally, life became to him a noisy affair of the banging and the closing of doors all around the circle of life. He knocked at all the doors of life and entered none.*[11]

To Bill, Miller's message came "just when I needed it most." Furthermore, the aspect of White's biography that impressed him most was "the fact that the great events of his [White's] life—the glory and the honor, the power and the influence which he has enjoyed, two of his great novels, his national and international reputation—all came after he had that year of illness and was laid aside and expected never to do anything again. . . . He started right in knocking at all the doors of the White House as confidently as he walked into the door of his Emporia home. He walked into the life of Woodrow Wilson and wrote a great work about him. He walked into the tightly shut door of Calvin Coolidge's life and wrote not one, but two, books about him. Never could it be said of that smiling, happy, busy man that 'he knocked at all the doors of life and entered none.'"[12]

Bill wrote to Betty, telling her of his new order of priorities in life:

Well, seriously, on this Thanksgiving morning, I find that, down deep in my heart, I am most thankful of all the things that life has brought me, for Mother and you and Jack and the boys. Around you kids my life centers. Your happiness is MY happiness; your sorrows are MY sorrows; your anxieties and problems are MINE. If you remain happy, I remain happy. The older I get the clearer the focus of the important things comes out in clean cut lines and in burning white; and the focus in this case is on you and your gang. Morning, noon and night I think of you; wish for your happiness; center my thoughts and prayers and wishes on your little group and on Treetops.[13]

At the end of January 1941 Bill wrote: "Yesterday we started school again and I have large and enthusiastic classes and am looking forward to this semester. Time flies so fast that it seems that we barely get started in one semester than we have finished it and have plunged into the second. I suppose that, with me, this is more apparent because I have so many speaking engagements and so much writing in between classes." Zest and joy had indeed reentered Bill's life.

Once England and France declared war on Germany on September 3, 1939, neutrality, as declared by Congress two days later, seemed hollow and tenuous to many people in the United States. Moreover, in the Far East, aggressive moves being made by the Japanese (the early evidence of which Bill had witnessed in China and Korea in 1920) picked up in intensity, in lockstep with the actions Germany was taking in Europe. On September 27, 1940, just as Bill resumed his teaching duties, Germany, Italy, and Japan entered into a ten-year military and economic alliance, thus forming the Axis. For sophisticated observers, it was now only a matter of time before the United States would be drawn into war. Yet, despite all this forewarning, the lightning strike by the Japanese on Pearl Harbor, on December 7, 1941—virtually destroying the American naval force in the Pacific and killing over two thousand men—rocked the United States to its core. On that day, the Japanese bombed not only Pearl Harbor but the Philippines, the international settlement in Shanghai, Thailand, and Hong Kong.

Roosevelt's speech to Congress the next day informed the lawmakers that as commander in chief, he had directed all measures be taken for the country's defense, and that as president, he was formally asking that war be declared. His opening words became almost as famous as the attack itself: "Yesterday, December 7, 1941—a date which will live in infamy—the United States of America was suddenly and deliberately attacked by naval and air forces of the Empire of Japan." Congress immediately declared war on Japan, even as Japanese troops were occupying the province of Luzon in the Philippines as well as Guam. Two days later Congress also declared war on Germany and Italy. Life, overnight, was changed for all Americans. As one of Bill's students wrote,

When the attack on Pearl Harbor occurred, Dean Marlatt called the students together and said, "Men, we are at war. Our soldiers are dying. You will find your assignments doubled and our grading twice as hard. Now go, get busy and remember why you are here." We thought this was "Deanly overstatement," but at the next class we were confronted with a tough pop quiz. The professor assigned us not 40 pages of reading, but 85 pages. Times became tough in many ways. Rationing was very strict and limiting. With my job we had $7 a week to live on. I still have our ledger book with all expenses detailed down to a 3 cent stamp. Blackouts and oil shortages along with tanker sinkings [in the months after Pearl Harbor German U-boats operated extensively near the U.S. east and Gulf coasts, frequently torpedoing vessels in sight of land] were haunting aspects of this period.

Heat in our apartment came on at eight in the morning and went off at four-thirty every afternoon. Fortunately, my wife's romantic nature had led her to choose a small apartment with a working fireplace, which saved us. I bought broken furniture from Goodwill Industries for firewood. With a fire for warmth, several other couples came over to our quarters to study. Our wives kept warm in our old bed while we studied. Our last year at the school, we had no potatoes. Our meat was horsemeat. On Saturday nights after thirteen hours of work, I would walk to Haymarket Square when the merchants were closing up shop on their horse-drawn carts. There I could buy a week's supply of fruits and vegetables at good prices.

Our stove was 1885 vintage, with no oven thermostat. Our refrigeration was an insulated orange crate nailed to the outside of our window sill. Despite these "amenities," my wife still had the nerve to entertain faculty members and their wives in our tiny quarters. She worked for Morgan Memorial in their nursery and managed the Park Square Antiques store. I taught at the Church of All Nations, organized a cub scout troop, did leather and wood craft work with kids of school age. These were special years.[14]

At fifty-six Bill was too old to be on the front lines or even in the war at all. His son-in-law, Jack, at thirty-six, was also too old to serve and was assigned the job of air raid warden for Chagrin Falls, Ohio. Every citizen, however, whether in the active forces or not, felt the effects of the war, ranging from rationing to sharing with friends the loss of sons killed in action. Bill wrote Betty: "War psychology accounts, in part, for the seemingly swift passage of time. We are watching that huge spectacle, as well as attending to our daily chores so that the hours are full and fly by swiftly. Life becomes more exciting in wartime. You must find it so."[15]

Bill sent his extra rations of cigarettes by mail to Betty as well as candy and various toys to his grandsons, then he would chide her for not telling him how each gift was received. He also sent money, as well as this advice:

You told us that Jack had gotten a bonus of $500 and that was gloriously good news to us. Of course it went, as Pat McConnell says, "like spit on a red-hot stove." But that was what it was for. After all, money is to get debts paid and there's nothing to worry about over the fact that the bonus is now "gone with the wind." Don't spend any of your energy worrying about that doctor's bill for that too will get paid. We'll help you as much as we can. In any case you KNOW that you have us back of you all the time, so why worry? We'll never let you get into a hole from which you cannot ultimately extricate yourselves—you know that. And what's more, it's a joy and delight to us to do it and neither of us ever has a single feeling of complaint over helping you two. We love to do it.

Mother and I were talking at breakfast this morning and she was bemoaning the fact that we are not buying more War Bonds. Then she happened to think that I send my sister May $25 a month and if we didn't do that we could buy at least a bond a month. But that is a moral and family obligation that is mine to meet and I shall meet it as long as May needs me. That is my conception of family responsibility and of Christian and moral integrity. I'm not a very Fundamentalist sort of a Christian, and I do unorthodox things. A lot of people do not look upon me as a Christian of any great perfection from their standards of what being a Christian is: BUT I meet my moral, family and ethical responsibilities, and I do it with good . will. My guess is that this is about as definite and as final an expression of real Christianity as we can attain in this life. So I don't worry, and I have no regrets at sending that money to May. Much less do I have any regrets or qualms about the little that goes to you. I wish it were twice as much.

Bill also related some of the new war's sad moments: "What a day we had yesterday— I received a phone call from Ted Booth [Dr. Edwin P. Booth, professor at the School of Theology] that his son Bray is missing-in-action; I went out there immediately to comfort them and spent two hours. I realized then that my problems—or your problems— all seem trivial when compared with a son 'missing-in-action.'"

Bill's writing resumed, and he published a book of poetry in 1941 (*Rainbow-Born Is Beauty*); in 1942, he published a collection of stories from his radio program (*There Are Sermons in Stories*); and in 1943, among others, the following story appeared on Sanders Wilkins, the longtime janitor at the School of Theology, who retired that year:

WHEN THE HIGH HEART WE MAGNIFY

For many years I have been specializing in interviewing famous men and women. It has been a thrilling experience. I have put the material into a national broadcast under the title "Great American Personalities."

While carrying out these journalistic chores, I have been guided by a little quatrain from John Drinkwater, who said in his drama, "Abraham Lincoln":

> When the high heart we magnify,
> And the sure vision celebrate,
> And worship greatness passing by,
> Ourselves are great.

Side by side with that English poet's observation, I have always placed an immortal Tennysonian definition of true greatness, which runs:

> In me there dwells
> No greatness, save it be some far-off touch
> Of greatness to know well I am not great!

Therefore, it is of another group that I wish to write now—the near-great, the humble great, the great who do not know that they are great, the heroic, humble people who have lived like Christ and whose names have never got into any Who's Who.

One of those great souls happens to be a Negro whom I have known for thirty years. He is a janitor by occupation. His name is Sanders Wilkins. He was the janitor in the Boston University School of Theology for more than thirty years. I knew him first when I was a student in that school back in 1909 and 1910. Now that I have been a teacher in that same school for fifteen years, I feel that I am able to judge this man fairly.

First of all, Sanders Wilkins never had any education himself, and he has always worked with his hands and muscles, although he is intuitively and mentally a smart man. His usual hours, both in winter and summer, were from four o'clock in the morning to ten o'clock at night; and he is still, in spite of retirement, on that same schedule, because he wants to be.

Second, Wilkins has raised a family, and one of his sons, a college graduate, has attained a high place in the ranks of science, and in the service of his nation he wore the insignia of a captain. Another of his sons graduated from college, came to the same school where his father was janitor, and was graduated with honors. He is now the pastor of an important church in Nashville and is honored and respected. And my guess is that this father has never in all his laboring life had a wage that was more than one hundred twenty-five dollars a month. Yet he has managed to do all of this and see two sons through college and into positions of trust and service in the life of the Church and the nation. And I call that true greatness in the best sense of that word.

Third, this humble man is one of the finest Christian gentlemen I have ever known—bar none. And though there are twenty professors in this school of theology—most of whom are or have been preachers and are expected both to teach and to live the highest type of a Christian life—I do not believe that there is one of us who would not be fair enough to say of this janitor, in the immortal words of Kipling, "You're a better man than I am, Gunga Din!"

And if by chance there might be a single professor among all of those ministers who would hesitate to give a high place among the saints to this janitor, of one thing I am certain—there are no students who would deny him the honor. What I am trying to say is that a Negro janitor in a Methodist theological school outranks us all as a Christian. Sickness, suffering, defeat, financial struggle, disaster, disappointment and unkind and unjust treatment have been his lot through a long life of friendliness and good will. And yet I have never known him to speak unkindly of a student or of any person who did him ill. He has been the perfect example of a man who knew how to forgive, and did forgive, those who treated him unkindly, and he has heaped more coals of fire on more bald and haughty heads than any single person I have known in my lifetime. I have yet to see my friend in a vindictive spirit or seeking revenge for any evil that has been done him. He is always smiling, always friendly, and always has a sense of humor.

During these thirty years Sanders, our friend and janitor, has worn the cast-off clothing of professors, preachers and bishops; but he makes no apology for that, because he has done it through sheer necessity—the necessity of getting his children enough to eat, providing them their early education and, finally, putting them through college and into positions of responsibility. In fact, he wears those cast-off clothes with rare dignity and good humor. He honors the clothes he wears, and he is grateful for them.

Also, during these thirty years, Sanders has seen literally thousands of students graduate from the halls of Boston University School of Theology, many of them to become college presidents, bishops and pastors. The friendship he won while they were students because he was always the Christian gentleman he has maintained ever since.

These leaders honor him today. And when I go out to speak in their churches, the first man they ask about is not the dean of the school, the president of the university, or any of the professors. Instead, they first say, "How is good old Sanders?" When they come back to the old halls for a visit, the first person they want to see is the janitor, and they make their way down four flights of stairs into the dark recesses of the boiler room for a friendly reunion.

Sanders Wilkins has won an immortal place in the hearts of the graduates of Boston University School of Theology because he has literally lived all these thirty years by the spirit of the text, "The Son of man came not to be ministered unto, but to minister, and to give his life a ransom for many." Sanders has certainly lived heroically for Christ.[16]

During the summer of 1944, the mood in the United States about the war became increasingly upbeat. On Tuesday morning, June 6, 1944, Betty wrote in her diary, "We awakened and turned the radio on—the Allied invasion of Europe had started at 3:42 A.M. this morning. We began calling our neighbors at 6 A.M. Jack went outside to ring the bell." In July, there was an unsuccessful attempt to assassinate Hitler; on August 25, Paris was liberated by the Allies; and on October 20, Gen. Douglas MacArthur began the invasion of the Philippines. The Allies were making headway in both Europe and the Far East. The year 1944 was also an election year. Bill wrote Betty that he would support Roosevelt, who was running for an unprecedented fourth term:

[Gov. Thomas E.] Dewey [of New York, the Republican presidential nominee] was here this week and your excited Mother went downtown and stood on the curbstone for hours to see him. That to me is the low in imbecility. The president is to be here this evening at Fenway Park, and there is the usual "Roosevelt Weather," sunny, crisp and favorable. We shall see what we shall see in a few days. In either case this nation will go on as usual and we shall be safe and sound. I think that the president will be re-elected by a huge majority but I shall not feel smitten with a club if Dewey is elected. Both have their good points, and in either case I shall be satisfied.

On November 7, 1944, Betty wrote: "Election Day is here and gone! Roosevelt won. Dewey conceded at 3:15 A.M. in the morning. We heard it!" By the turn of the year, there was a presumption by the Allies that victory in Europe was only a matter of months away. Roosevelt was inaugurated on January 20, 1945, and two weeks later the tired and increasingly frail president departed for the Crimea for talks in Yalta with Joseph Stalin and Winston Churchill over the postvictory plans for the occupation of Germany. At this conference the Soviet Union agreed to enter the war with Japan once victory was won in Europe, which would help to assure a quicker victory over Japan. Bill wrote Betty a letter reacting to news about Roosevelt's trip:

Last night I started from the Seminary at five in the afternoon and didn't get home until nearly seven, a trip I ordinarily make in half an hour or less, due to a terrific blizzard that blew up with heavy wind and two inches of snow which fell in that same period. The streets were clogged, people couldn't see; their cars skidded all across the streets, several died (six, the papers say). Drivers would get stuck on the slight hills between here and Boston; and for miles cars were in a jam. And all the while that blizzard was blowing and snow simply sweeping down, there was the most beautiful crimson, golden sunset in the west. Then it turned bitterly cold and last night the temperature was ten degrees below zero. As I write this letter it is still zero but a bright warm sun is pouring in my study window so it will surely warm up before the day is through. Our house is warm and cozy and Mother is in the cellar washing clothes (of all things).

Life is like that: cold, wind, blizzard, sunsets, sunshine, washing clothes, writing, teaching; and, in between times, raising boys, having problems that baffle us; getting along with husbands and wives; making ends meet (maybe?); going to war; getting wounded; being away from people you love; lonely; in danger; losing legs and arms; and climbing into a plane when you are suffering with polio and can't use your legs, and you are old and tired, and harassed, yet flying to Russia or some far away spot to try to help settle the destiny of the earth; confusion, bitterness, hate, death and wounds for millions of boys; and yet out of it all something will emerge which will make a better world.

That is the way life moves along internationally, nationally and in families: full of problems, full of laughter and delight, full of satisfaction, full of evolution. So we take it as it comes, do the best we can, face up to it: our ultimate goal, the happiness and raising of our children and playing the game out to the end, enjoying whatever we may along the way. But to my way of thinking, OUR lot has been mostly cast in pleasant places compared with most human beings on this earth and why should we complain?

Thus endeth the Scripture Lesson and the Sermon for this morning.

The war, the weight of his responsibilities, and his frail health finally took their inevitable toll. On April 12, 1945, Roosevelt died in Warm Springs, Georgia, and the nation—which had lost the man who had led it for twelve years, guided it through the Depression and a world war—went into a state of shock. Bill admitted that he was depressed: "Every time I sat down at the radio listening to the proceedings of the president's funeral, I found myself weeping. Pat McConnell feels the same way. He is really down. I never saw him weep before in all my life—but the other night when we were listening to the radio I saw two tears run down old Pat's cheeks—and looked the other way so as not to embarrass him." Bill continued in his letter to Betty:

Yesterday, fortunately for me, I was free and we sat at the radio, listening and reading the news-papers all day. I doubt if there will ever be a radio day like it. The radio certainly did sense the people's feelings, and they certainly DID rise to the occasion in great style: no commercials, no comedy, no frivo-lity; all music, drama, serious programs, great hymns, prayers, religious talk; it was splendid. Last night we just happened to tune in the Jack Benny Hour, and that was the beginning of the greatest two hours I have ever heard on radio. It ran until nine o'clock: Bing Crosby; Jack Benny; Charles Laughton—reading Walt Whitman's "When Lilacs Last in the Dooryard Bloomed"; Ingrid Bergman reciting the prayer the president used in his Pre-Election Speech; Bette Davis in a marvelous talk to a son who had just turned twenty-one and was off to the war. It was the most powerful and appealing two hours, and I was hoping that you and Jack had tuned in as we had. It was not announced in advance so you had to get it by chance. I just sat and wept all through the two hours because it was so high and fine and understanding.

I never was so proud that I had been a Roosevelt supporter from his First Inaugural; and that I had not wavered during all that time; although Dan Marsh and more than two-thirds of our trustees were bitterly opposed to him. But that is all past now. Even those who opposed him are beginning to see that he was a great man and a great president, perhaps will turn out to be—when history records his final place—the greatest we have ever had; for, in a sense, he was a world figure and leader as none of our former presidents has been. They made a survey of his statesmanship last night on one show and it was overwhelming how he has led us, carefully, surely, through these years—always a year ahead of the people and yet tactfully leading us in getting ready for the war and leading us through it; always with ultimate world peace in his mind, his plans and his goals.

Now all the boys who referred to him as "That Man in Washington" will be relieved—some of them happy—and that is all right for that is the way of a democracy. I think that [Harry] Truman [who as vice president had succeeded to the presidency] will do well for he is honest, he is an interna-tionalist, he is conciliatory—and he is fearless. He never went to either high school or college—but at that he has had more education in schools than Lincoln, and Lincoln didn't do so badly in his day. I trust Truman.

I am to speak on the president at Copley Methodist Church Sunday night in a memorial service, and I spoke at Chapel in a like service Friday noon. Last night we tuned in accidentally just in time to hear the funeral train pulling into and out of Charlotte, North Carolina—children singing "Onward Christian Soldiers," people weeping, taps playing, and an announcer describing the whole train with its two engines and its darkened last car in which the president's body lay quietly. It reminded me of the

Lincoln Funeral Train which was going to Springfield from Washington and the crowds along the way, only this time we have radio to make it more universally impressive and dramatic and vivid. It is really a great historic event we are passing through.

But, enough of that. Now to more personal things: we loved your letter telling about Glen's taking you all for an airplane ride; about Billy's wanting to go up again—and what an experience for the kids. I told Pat about it, and we both remembered that neither of us had even been in an automobile until we were college students. The world does move along and Jacky and Billy will be as familiar with planes as we were with autos.

Within the space of four days, only two weeks after Roosevelt's death, the war in Europe ended: Mussolini was captured and executed on April 28, 1945; the next day, the German armies in Italy surrendered unconditionally to the Allies; and, on the third day, Hitler and his mistress Eva Braun committed suicide in a bunker in which he had been sequestered since January 16, under the Reich chancellery in Berlin. On the fourth day, May 1, the new German commander in chief, Grand Admiral Karl Doenitz, futilely trying to hide Hitler's suicide and keep German morale up, somberly announced over the radio that Hitler had "fallen this afternoon fighting at the head of his troops." With their leader gone, however, there was no will to continue fighting a hopeless battle, and Germany capitulated one week later, on May 7. Victory in Europe, signaling the end of the war, was formally achieved on May 8, 1945.

As the summer of 1945 progressed, so did the prospect of a victory by the Allies against Japan. In July, battle for control of the Philippines was written about in the newspapers and talked about on the radio. Bill followed the events closely and wrote Betty:

With the good news of the fall of Manila, I went up to the attic and dug out some of my articles which I wrote for The Dearborn Independent, *and I found two copies of my article on the dog market at Baguio in which—even that far back—you were one of the heroines when you were seven years old, which is just Jacky's age. The boys might enjoy hearing this story of a dog market and your defense of the dogs so I am enclosing it in this letter.*

It was very interesting to go over these articles and some old maps of Luzon which I had marked showing every town and section of Luzon that I had visited, and that included the exact line of march that MacArthur's troops took on their way to Manila. I spent a night in the town where the commandos released those prisoners (Tarlac). It's fascinating to watch troop movements when you have been over every foot of the terrain they have taken. I remember vividly one beautiful evening sitting on the bamboo upper porch of a missionary's home looking down over the expanse of white sand of Lingayen Beach and Gulf. It ran for miles, pure white sand, a beautiful crescent beach, fringed with millions of palm trees. It was on this beach that our troops landed and started their march on Manila. You will probably remember the Lunette and the band concerts in Manila, or the streetcar accident in which a car ran into one of those funny little horse-drawn carts.

August 6, 1945, turned out to mean much more to the Stidgers than Iva's birthday: it was the day when the U.S. Army Air Forces dropped the first atomic bomb. It destroyed virtually all of the houses and other buildings in Hiroshima and set in train a swift succession of events—the declaration of war on Japan by the Soviet Union two days later, on Wednesday, August 8; the dropping of a second atomic bomb, this time on Nagasaki, on Thursday, August 9; and the unconditional surrender by Japan five days later, on August 14, 1945, thus ending the Second World War.

The formal ceremony, V-J Day, took place on September 2, 1945, when Japan signed the surrender papers aboard the U.S. battleship *Missouri* in Tokyo Bay. Bill's hymn "Rise Up O World" was distributed to all Protestant churches, this time for the V-J Day celebrations, as it had been for the V-E Day celebrations. He said, "Millions of copies have been sent out; it has been sung all over the nation; and played on the radio several times, but, with all of this singing, I have not yet heard it."

Betty and Jack moved to Cincinnati in 1945 and to Philadelphia three years later as Jack was successively offered higher positions in leading commercial banks. Selling their house in Cleveland could have caused Bill some anxiety, because he had been so focused on the building of Treetops while he was recovering from his nervous breakdown in 1940. Instead, Bill wrote Betty the following:

It was fine to have that good talk with you on the phone this morning and to hear that the "die is cast"; the Rubicon is crossed; and we are on our glorious way to a new chapter in the living book of the Hyland clan. I LOVE Treetops as much as you do, and I thought, when you first talked of moving, that I would dread your going; but I find that I do not; that, on the contrary, I am excited over the new opportunities, the new adventure; just as if I were moving and changing myself. I am completely satisfied that Jack is doing the right thing and that you will soon have just as nice or even nicer home than you have had, and that the next chapter will be the best chapter of all.

Whatever you do, you know that we are back of you—and interested—and willing to help in this new adventure or in any other one for we love you and what is ours is yours, anytime you need it and want it. As long as we live that will be true as it always has been; and, when we go, there will be money for you if you need it and whether you need it or not. That is one of the objects of my life: to leave you something for the boys and yourself. I am not planning to go soon (I hope, I hope, I hope) for I am having such a darned good time—but when a GUY gets to sixty he naturally thinks of such matters (not a lot, but some). I have never had so long a fulcrum to lift the loads of life—never was happier; never had more assurance; never enjoyed the general adventure of life more.

On his return from a speaking engagement in New York, Bill wrote Betty:

Had a cool, nice day at Marble Collegiate Church with huge crowds morning and evening; and who should show up but Bishop and Mrs. Welch who sat in the front row and took me to lunch after the morning sermon, and we had a wonderful visit. He is 87 and still running our Methodist Foreign Relief and she is 85 (blind almost), but young and sprightly in spirit. Just before we climbed onto a Fifth Avenue bus, since I was to get off at 28th Street and they were to go on, Mrs. Welch said: "Now kiss me goodbye, Bill, for you won't get a chance on the bus."

Bishop Welch said: "You silly sentimental old woman. You still think Bill is young and handsome like you remember him in Korea; but if you weren't blind you'd see that he is just an old man like I am." Mrs. Welch replied: "He may look old but he doesn't act like an old man like YOU do."

I signed my contract for the Fleming H. Revell book which we are to call Human Adventures in Happy Living. *I am very pleased to do this book, and it will be my fifty-second. Not bad, eh? I also just wrote your elder son a letter, as I do every other day for he seems anxious to get them, even though I have received NONE in return, hearing about his activities only from the letters you have sent on to me. But I know how it is in camp when mail time comes, and if a Guy doesn't get a letter he feels left out and disappointed.*

I am enclosing some pictures of me that I received from Nona [Bill's sister]. When I showed them to Mother I said: "Can you imagine that you EVER had a slender, romantic, handsome, young boyfriend like that one with red hair and a concave tummy?" She just grunted in a disgusted fashion and passed the question up without comment.

On September 13, 1948, Bill wrote Betty that classes were to begin that Wednesday and that: "I go back to schoolwork feeling fifty percent better than I have in years, with NO anxiety, no regrets, rested and eager for the adventure of a new school year." And he concluded with:

Yesterday I received a request from George Carl, who has a wealthy member of his congregation in Chicago who is presenting his church with a stone baptismal font, to carve on that font my little verse of four lines:

> *In the breast of a bulb is the promise of spring;*
> *In a little blue egg there's a bird that will sing;*
> *In the soul of a seed is the hope of the sod;*
> *In the heart of a child is the Kingdom of God.*

That's the first time I ever had anything carved in stone with the consciousness that it will live far beyond me, or you, or even Heather [Betty and Jack Hyland had adopted their third child], and it's a new experience. I do believe, however, that I have written some things which are carved in the hearts of humanity and that they will also live far beyond me and my day, and you and yours. So that's that!

The end of the year was soon in sight, and Bill reported to Betty, on November 14, 1948:

This morning I went to Fitchburg [Massachusetts] at the invitation of Station WEIM, a local station and an affiliate of the Yankee Network, to make two or three records for them for which they paid me $25. They were so thrilled by the records I made (five minute segments) that they had the whole staff come in to hear them. The president said: "If you'll do it, we would like to send a recording instrument to your home every Monday morning and have you make five five-minute records for us to use each day of the week. We'll pay you eighty dollars a month and run the segments as a Sustaining Program. Then, when we get a sponsor for the program, we'll increase your pay and we'll make a real effort to syndicate the show."

I agreed to the arrangement, and we start next Wednesday. Eighty dollars a month for about two hours' work in one day here in my home isn't bad, Mother and I both think. The president of the

I will meet Thy tryst at twilight
When the silent shadows sleep
And all birds and beasts and children
Into dreamland softly creep.

I think that this is real poetry, and the music fits it perfectly. It is thrilling to hear a large audience sing it, especially that last verse softly. There is always a hush that comes over people when it is sung.

This morning our School started again, but it only runs one week and then we are into first Semester Examinations. I had my first class and LOVED IT. In fact the longer I keep at this job of teaching, the more I love it. Those young fellows are so appreciative, so enthusiastic, so friendly that they warm my heart, and I can hardly wait until it is time to start in again. They also seem to share that feeling, and that makes for joy in my job. Five different boys came to my room with bundles of my books; four titles for me to autograph. They get them through the GI Bill of Rights [education benefits for veterans], which pays for them, so I am the benefactor. But it gives me great pleasure to put personal messages in the flyleaves for these aspiring young ministers.

Last night I got to rummaging around in the attic and unearthed a pennant which was stuck full of medals that I had won in college for the 100 yard dash, the 220, the quarter mile; one medal for winning an Oratorical Contest (gold, and still untarnished—an elaborate affair); and one for debate. I took all this down to show Mother and dangling it under her haughty nose said: "My legs may be bad now, temporarily, but they used to be good enough to win medals, kid." She just sniffed and replied: "I'm not interested in history; it's NOW that counts!" Tell Jack that this is what he has to look forward to with a woman who has as much of Mrs. Iva Berkey Stidger in her as YOU do. Of course, there is always the saving grace and ameliorating circumstance that you also have some of me in you, and that will save him many a bump in his declining years. Now I'm on the prowl for a group of about ten letters Mother wrote me in our first days of courtship when she addressed me as "My Dear Mr. Stidger." They were fairly imperious letters, and I intend to find them and dangle them in her face to see what happens.

In his next letter, Bill told Betty that he had been going through his files, "taking the first research step in getting material ready for an autobiographical book. I have the material filed by cities: San Francisco, San Jose, Detroit, Kansas City and Boston. That will do for the present status of the book." He added that he had been hounding Iva to make a date with her doctor for her physical examination, "and I might suggest MENTAL EXAMINATION, for that is what she needs more than a physical. And, talking about examinations, I go to the Mayo Clinic this afternoon for what I hope will be a final check by Dr. Norcross. I have been going now for a year and a half and they certainly have done a thorough job on me. My legs are much improved and I feel better in every way. I'll tell you more in my Wednesday letter."

By Wednesday, January 12, 1949, Bill could report to Betty, "I have at long last bulldozed Mother until she actually has an appointment to have her doctor give her the once over, check her urine (if you'll pardon the word?) so that we can find out what ails her. Then we can be satisfied that she is not falling into a diabetic, cancer, fallen arches, falling hair, change of life and mind. This morning she came into my office in her corset (and nothing else) to show me that the corset she had bought from Stern's a year ago—and was tight for her then—now fits her like the new paper on our walls, even like the paint on some of our walls. In fact she looks like she used to look at Allegheny College when I first fell in love with her. We'll find out after she has had her physical examination what this weight loss thing is all about. As for me, I had a most satisfactory checkup with my doctor and came home elated, took a longer than usual walk and my legs didn't bother me a bit; am I happy? The answer is that I am, and how!"

Iva proceeded with her physical examination on Saturday, January 15, 1949, and was asked to go to the Newtonville Hospital for an additional test on Monday morning. On Wednesday, January 19, 1949, Bill wrote Betty:

Your lovely, newsy letter came just after the doctor left. He gave your Mother her first shot of insulin. It all went easily, and she didn't mind it a bit, saying it didn't hurt. Then we had breakfast. She is to take her insulin and then eat within fifteen minutes. I have to boil her a half-cup of oatmeal which she eats with cream; she has to have a boiled egg, a slice of toast, half a glass of orange juice and all the tea she can swill down.

I purchased a "Manual on Diabetes" written by Dr. Joslin yesterday and both of us are reading it. The book is fascinating and proves that diabetics can live normal lives and may even live longer than the rest of us because they have more scientific and regulated diets. Sunday at three she goes into The Deaconess Hospital to stay a week for an educational course on diet and on administering the insulin to herself. She will have to put the needle into the muscle of her ample thigh (and there is plenty of room). She has to have a shot only once a day, in the morning, fifteen minutes before breakfast. Following our first experience when the doctor administered the shot, she washed the dishes, did the beds and other minor chores, telephoned a lot, and is now off to a luncheon—so it doesn't seem to have changed any of her schedule or spirit.

There is absolutely NOTHING for you to worry about, for WE are not worrying. We shall call you about nine on Sunday morning and report what the three or four days of our own administering of the insulin has done; and have a talk. In the meantime, don't be calling her in an excited fashion, for that would upset Mother. If YOU will just take it calmly, as a matter of course, as we are taking it, everything will go smoothly. She was a bit upset when she first discovered that the tests were positive, but now she is all over that. The doctor wants her to live a normal life, and get all the exercise and activity she can, for exercise helps to eat up the sugar in the body. We now walk two times a day.

To tell you the real down right truth, the hardest thing for her to face is the necessity of eating a dish of oatmeal, a boiled egg and a slice of toast at breakfast when, for years, she has been eating only one slice of toast, a glass of orange juice and a gallon or so of tea. This morning she said she felt like a stuffed pig after breakfast, but this will soon level out, for her other two meals will be smaller than she usually eats. Well, that is as complete a story as I can tell you but we'll have a phone talk Sunday morning. We love every derned one of you, from the BIG BOY (Guide and Mentor and Banker) down to that bright-eyed Heather Hyland.

Your affable and affectionate,
Father

Bill's letter to Betty of Monday, January 24, 1949, thanked her for a letter she had sent that had meant much to Iva:

Dearest Betty:

Your beautiful, comforting, Special Delivery Letter came to Mother yesterday and gave her a lot of joy. It WAS a lovely letter, such as only you could write, and it sent her to the hospital with little songs singing in her heart. In fact she took it with her, as she said: "So that I can read it over and over again." She calls it her Tower of Pisa Letter because you said in it that she had always been a "Tower of Strength" to YOU (as indeed she has always has been to ME). Then she said to me: "I may be a Tower to Betty but just now I feel like the Leaning Tower of Pisa." To which I add this beautiful "Thought for the Day" which no man ought to hand on to even his gentle, cultured, delicately-minded daughter (but I can't resist it, it's so good): "Yes, you are a Leaning Tower because of Sugar in your Pisa." Isn't it awful? But true.

That's Mother. She won't break; but she may lean or bend a bit in the storm.

Later I returned home and got my supper, listened to my usual Sunday evening broadcasts which were all punk (as usual), maybe more so last evening because she wasn't here to share them; and the house was, as I told her, "as empty as a shell with the NUT gone." Then at nine I called her, had a good talk, found her cheerful and contented, so I went to bed and slept like a top. Up this morning to breakfast, did my leg exercises, read the newspapers, phoned Mother finding her once again cheerful. Today she is busy with lectures and tests, and I guess she will be taken care of all right.

Now who could make a more complete report than this has been, kid? AND don't give me any of that BUNK about my having SHOCKED you in writing about Mother's sugar content. I gave you the facts. What did you want me to do: feed them to you with a spoon, a little in each letter until, at last, I had informed you that she has diabetes? That's all for this morning "Child of my heart." Your lovely Mother is all right and my guess is that eventually she won't even have to take insulin, for she is responding to treatment so well. And, hereafter, I'M THE TOWER OF STRENGTH in this family; and, if you don't believe me, ask HER.

Your light-hearted and loving,
Dad

On Saturday, January 29, 1949, Bill wrote Betty to tell her of Iva's status and to admit how dependent on her he really was:

At this very minute, this letter was interrupted by the phone and it was Mother calling from the hospital to say that she will be released at 12:30 P.M. and that I am to come for her; that she is entirely free of sugar; that she only has to take insulin once a day (it had looked for awhile as if she would have to take two shots, and she was anxious about that). Later she may not have to take any. She is happy, and I am happy. The world is beautiful again, and in my own quiet way I am hilarious over having Mother home again for, gosh, this old house has been a lonely place this week.

I have developed my own system of washing dishes in her absence: I wash each dish as I use it. For illustration, when I have finished my egg plate I get up, run hot water over it, give it a swipe and lay it down. No wiping, no putting it away in the closet. I leave 'em out where they are handy to get at. I do it with a minimum of effort; on an efficiency basis. However, I did notice one thing: that the bottoms of my dishes stick to the top of the sink, and I have to pry them loose when I want to use them at the next meal. I have slept in the same sheets all week, and I noticed last night that one of them was tangled around my torso more than it is when Mother makes the bed. In any case I'll be glad to have her home again. "You never miss the water until the well runs dry" is what I have to say on this subject.

A month later, Bill wrote:

From now on until Easter, I have a heavy schedule, but I feel fine and am able to do it and am look-ing forward with great joy to doing it; all of which ends up with my preaching to more than three thou-sand people in Atlantic City on the Steel Pier on Easter morning, for $100 and expenses. Bromley Oxnam did it last year, and it is considered a great honor in the church world, and I am pleased to be invited. I shall see you at that time, and it just may be that you can all drive over and we'll have dinner together in Atlantic City at some hotel. Then I'll drive back with you and stay the day and possibly the next day. If, though, it is too much of a drive, don't consider it. I don't yet know what time the service is, but I'll know in plenty of time to tell you.

As the speaking engagement on the Steel Pier in Atlantic City drew nearer, Bill was surprised by the extent of the national publicity surrounding the event. He told Betty about it in a letter dated Sunday, April 9, 1949:

On Thursday, my Radio Class had a surprise for me. When I went into the Seminar Room, there was a cake with "Thirty-eight" candles (a la Jack Benny); a quart of ice cream; a poem they wrote to me; and a hilarious crowd singing "Happy Birthday to You."

Overall, I received at least fifty cards and letters from all over creation and a box of cookies from one of my favorite student wives. A week from this morning, "God willing and it doesn't rain" as the Ligonier saying goes, we shall be with you. I have added a speaking engagement at Margate, a suburb of Atlantic City. You will be interested that I have been getting United News and Associated Press Service clippings from all over the nation: California, Niagara Falls, Georgia, Texas, Virginia, announcing my speaking at the Steel Pier and referring to me as "Dean of Boston University School of Theology" and just this week referring to me as "President of Boston University," all of which goes to show how the promotions are flying at me thick and fast this spring.

Easter Sunday, April 17, 1949, and the visit to the Hylands came and went swiftly. Bill wrote Betty on the next Wednesday, April 20, 1949:

Well, here I am, on my old schedule of writing to you, right on the nose with my usual efficiency. We had a wonderful visit with you; so much fun, so many times when we had good laughter together. Because we talked about you and your family all the way home, the trip seemed very short, and in fact it was fast driving, for we ran along at an average of 60 miles an hour on easy, smooth roads in perfect weather. My trip to Atlantic City was an unusual adventure, if for no other reason than getting up at four in the morning and preaching in a temperature of 35 degrees at five thirty A.M. to a crowd of

3,500 people who were already frozen numb. That put a greater test on my ability to capture an audience than any test I have ever submitted to, and what's more: I DID it! I shall finish your book this week and get it off to a publisher. I didn't want to do a careless hurried job on it and, because of that, left it until after the Easter speaking rush was over so that I could do it carefully.

Bill's letters, as the following one, written to Betty on Sunday, April 24, 1949, shows, usually began in a chatty manner but inevitably concluded with an important emotion or thought that was on his mind:

On Friday night we went to our Allegheny College banquet and had a glorious time: fifty-five were present (our largest group) and the new president spoke. We met a lot of old friends and came home refreshed and exhilarated. Your Mother was the best dressed, best looking and "oldest living alumna who could still walk unassisted," which was MY designation of her when I spoke.

My lilies-of-the-valley are up in the backyard, about three inches tall and beginning to show clusters of buds nestled down between the green, slender leaves. I watch them come out each year with such a joy as I cannot easily put down on paper because at Allegheny we had a cluster of them in front of our fraternity house, and I loved to pick them and carry them to that slender, attractive, fascinating person known as Iva Berkey. Since those days lilies-of-the-valley have always been associated with Mother and our romance. And I love them still. This little cluster in our backyard, which I myself planted and have tended through several years, means a lot to me (and to her also, although she will not admit it).

Yesterday afternoon (Saturday) we lay on our bed and listened to the Red Sox lick the Yanks in a tight game and enjoyed it. I went down [to Fenway Park] for the opening game on Thursday, and it was so crowded that I couldn't even get into the park: 34,000 people, the largest attendance at an opening game, ever. I have passes to both the [Boston] Braves and the Red Sox, so I am all set for the summer.

We are still talking about and reveling in the delights of our visit with you. Mother is much better, alert and feeling her old self, and I am sure that our visit and her discovering that she could take care of her self away from home account for her change in feeling.

Well, Child of my Heart, all I can hope for you and Jack is that you two grow into as beautiful and as enduring a life-long friendship, mutual respect and affection as Mother and I have. And YOU WILL—for you have something that even we did not have: a family of three fascinatingly different in temperament children—a binding strength. All we had was YOU; not bad, but three children are better any time.

Love and a large load of it,
Dad

The end of the 1949 academic year was a particularly emotional one for the faculty of the School of Theology, because it was the end of an era. Over the summer, the school was scheduled to move from its old quarters to a new campus along the Charles River adjoining the rest of the university. Iva was asked to preside at the school's "final tea," as Bill wrote Betty, on Wednesday, April 27, 1949:

This is a busy day: Mother has the final "tea" at the Theology School and what a tea it is to be; a bang-up cookie, sandwiches and what-have-you tea; and she has been working on it for days, hammer and tongs. In addition to that she has been cleaning every keyhole, corner shelf and drawer in this house in anticipation of the 24 hour visit of Mary [Iva's sister] and Turney McIntyre as well as Jane [Bill's niece] and her husband. You would think the duke and duchess of Windsor were paying us a visit. As for my own chores today, I had one of my students on the radio this morning, two classes this afternoon, and then I go to Beverly [Massachusetts] for a Chamber of Commerce banquet (Ladies' Night) where I address them in my own inimitable fashion and collect $60 so that Mother can pay Lucy for helping her clean this house to within an inch of its life to impress her family. Ah well.

Bill could not refrain from telling Betty—with sadness—that Robinson Chapel, the most beloved building of the old campus, would soon be history:

This morning I am to make my last talk in the old Chapel, and I am telling the story of your marriage there with that wonderful phrase: "Daddy, this is the most beautiful spot in all the world," as my closing words, because that Chapel has been and is the most beautiful spot in all the world to a lot of people. It is really a strange, lonely feeling that we all have. Your beloved Chapel, where you and Jack shook hands, will be owned by The New England School of Pharmacy next year, and we shall be in the new building on the Charles River. Life moves along with a rapid stride. . . .

Everybody feels a sense of loneliness for most of us have been connected with Beacon Hill and these buildings for twenty to thirty years and one doesn't build up a background of memories, connected with the location and building, and lightly leave them all behind. However, the new theological building and chapel on the Charles River are beautiful, white stone Gothic structures, equipped with every modern convenience and new, attractive furniture. I was in the building yesterday and the two lower floors are already plastered and ready for the final touches while work is still being done on the three top floors. It's a thrilling adventure to see those two grand buildings arise on that river.

The manuscript of a book by Betty, *Those Heavenly Years,* had been in Bill's hands to critique since before Easter. He had found one excuse after another not to delve into it in deep detail, which kept Betty on edge, worrying that he either did not like it or—even worse— did not like her writing. Finally, on Tuesday, May 31, 1949, he sent her the following:

I got so wrapped up in your book manuscript yesterday that I forgot to write my usual Monday morning letter to you—but that's a good sign, I'd say. The book IS interesting. In fact, it is well-written; your character delineation is clear-cut and full of meaning; your ability to reproduce certain atmospheres is excellent, such as your entrance into Smith College, that fear of having a baby episode, the cigarette coat- burning story, and a dozen others. You have a real style; the short, short sentence, and I like it.

Your book demonstrates that you have talent and ability to write, much more than I have EVER had. I am pleased and proud of you. As to whether it will be accepted by a publisher, neither I nor anyone else can know. That is always and largely a pure gamble. After reading I Wanted to Write, however, as well as a dozen books of that type, I have discovered that very few writers have their first book accepted (your own poor father didn't even get his novel Mother Man past those toughest of all censors, his family—thank God for that!)

The business of writing is a long, hard struggle, and only those succeed who keep themselves in the race, have stamina and a driving desire to write. All I can really say at this stage of your book is that YOU REALLY CAN WRITE. Whether you go on with it or not will be entirely decided by whether you WANT to write badly enough. Or, in other words, whether or not you can KEEP yourself from writing. It is a long, hard—but intensely satisfying—apprenticeship.

I have never been a great writer in any sense, and, what's more, I KNOW IT. I have written a few poems which will undoubtedly live far beyond MY day and long after any of my confreres or contemporaries have been forgotten. Edgar Brightman, the highest-paid professor on our staff, has written books on philosophy; Harold deWolfe has written in the field of theology; Paul Johnson in the field of psychology; but, as Ted Booth said in speaking of me at the senior banquet, "Likely Bill's poems will be living when the rest of us are in our graves and all that we have done has turned to dust." I was pleased that he said that, and I verily believe that it is true. "I Saw God Wash the World" is one of those imperishable things which came like a flash of inspiration to me and expressed an universal feeling and emotion; and, as a result, it will likely live far beyond my day. A man (or woman) has only to write one such thing to achieve a certain immortality.

And yet doing that simple poem which came to me in a moment of inspiration did not need one thousandth as much work and sweat and toil as you have put into your book. That moment occurred one sunny morning; in fact, it was such a morning as this May morning happens to be—clear and sunny after a rain-washed night.

Now I must hop, for we have our final faculty meeting in the old building this morning at 10:30 A.M., and I want to be there.

All my love,
Dad

With her permission, he submitted Betty's book to Houghton Mifflin. For a number of weeks, he heard nothing. In early June 1949, Betty attended her fifteenth reunion at Smith College, while Iva went to Philadelphia to take care of Betty's children. Bill wrote Betty:

My guess is that you will never be the same again after seeing how those gals have aged over the past fifteen years, grown fat and bulky, baggy-eyed and decrepit. From now on, you'll probably be more grateful for your Dad and Mother, your fine husband and your three wildcats, for my guess is that YOU looked the youngest and freshest, the least-aged and are perhaps the happiest of them all.

I am having one of my great days—I wrote a poem for the laying of the cornerstone of the new Theological School, and I am to read it this afternoon. Not only that, but with great ceremony yesterday, when I went to Dan Marsh's office at his phoned request to talk it over, he put the original copy of my poem in a sealed envelope (pigskin as if that mattered?) after asking me to sign it and then placed it in the copper box which will be "hermetically sealed" (his own impressive words) and "will not be opened for two thousand years." Now, ain't that something? What the hell do I care when it's opened? Even you with all of your youth ahead of you—and the children's also—will by that time be "hermetically sealed" yourselves.

Lots of love,
Dad

When Betty returned from her reunion, she tried to have Iva stay a few extra days, a request to which Bill shot the following reply:

Well, I think that I have done pretty well by you this weekend, and still you tried to talk me into letting Mother stay longer. I have had a very satisfied, happy feeling over her being there with the children while you attended your fifteenth. But it is over, and you are back, and it's time to send Mother back to me. I have had an exciting time during Mother's absence reading my poem at the laying of the cornerstone of our new Chapel. I was generously acclaimed for the poem itself and the way I read it. Pat said after the ceremony was completed: "I hate to admit it, Bill, but that was tops. Both the poem itself and the way you read it." The general reaction was similar to Pat's and so many people requested copies of the poem that Dan Marsh asked the editor of Bostonia *to publish it in his next issue.*

Bill's letter to Betty of Wednesday, June 22, 1949, apologized for a gap in his letter writing caused by his being away for more than a week:

Well, it's about time, and the first thing I'm going to do now that I am "at long last" back in my office is to write to my sweetheart. Not that you deserve it for, after reading that thank you letter you wrote to Mother and the low place you give me in that episode, I really ought to cut you off my mailing list. So it's your Mother and not your Father to whom you want to turn in time of trouble, is it? And not me? Well, I'll have to say to you: "Who in hell IS it who furnishes the money—and incidentally the IDEA in the case of Mother's journey to Wynnewood—for these expeditions of service and love?" I ask you, WHO IS IT?

Now, having settled that important domestic matter to MY entire satisfaction, I must tell you about your honorable Pop's doings the last ten days: First, I took the trip down through your town to Washington on my way to Bristol, Virginia. I spoke at a beautiful girls' college, Sullins; slept under blankets every night; the roses were in full bloom, and the mockingbirds and thrushes sang every morning and evening. I was the main speaker every night to packed audiences (600) and lectured three times each day to about 100 preachers. 450 copies of my books were sold, every one of which I autographed. It was the most successful and most satisfying week I ever spent for I was the "Big Boy" of the conference.

I returned on Saturday passing through Pawling, New York, where I was entertained in Lowell Thomas's home, along with General Lucius Clay; the new U.S. High Commissioner for Germany, Mr. John J. McCloy (his picture was on the front cover of last week's Time *magazine); Finn Ronne [Captain, U.S. Navy], Chief of Staff of Richard Byrd's Antarctic Expedition; Dr. Fleming, the new president of Ohio Wesleyan; and the president of NBC. They, along with Governor Thomas Dewey and his wife, were all at church on Sunday morning when I preached. It was the most distinguished crowd I ever spoke before, and my sermon went over with a bang. Every man in that gang said something fine and appreciative to me about it. On the prior evening, Finn Ronne lectured and showed wonderful pictures of his expedition to the Antarctic, after which Lowell gave a speech which he ended by saying: "And, anybody who is strong enough to enjoy our Barn Dance tonight is strong enough to make it to church tomorrow morning." And they WERE THERE, so many of them that the church was packed.*

I forgot my bag and this morning I got a wire from Lowell: "No trouble at all. We discovered your zipperless zipper bag last night and put it in a box and it is now on its way. Everybody is talking about your magnificent sermon. Best wishes and many thanks from all of us on Quaker Hill. Lowell Thomas."

I've missed writing to you at my regular times and shall keep to the schedule the rest of the summer. You are a dear girl and my favorite female of them all.

Love and HOW,
Dad

Bill finally received a letter regarding Betty's book from his publisher and sent both the letter and this advice to Betty:

"At long last" I have a report on your manuscript from Houghton Mifflin, one of the top publishers of this nation. I am enclosing Diggory Venn's letter and to my way of thinking it is a wonderful letter to get from a big publisher on a first book. Many writers have rewritten a book twenty times before it landed; and the difference between a real writer and a mediocre one is just that tenacity in writing and re-writing and sticking to it until it DOES come through. That is what we all have to learn to do. Personally, I think that you have a right to feel greatly encouraged over this editorial reaction from them for they are the keenest and most exacting editorial staff in America.

The publisher had said, in part:

I sent your daughter's manuscript down to our editorial department with pleas for extra careful consideration. It was a pleasure to do this because you have been such a good friend to Houghton Mifflin Company, and done more than your fair share of helping bring the attention of the public to our books. As a result the manuscript was gone over by our managing editor after a preliminary reading. The verdict is that your daughter comes through to the reader as a lovable, warm and vital person, but that she needs a good deal of practise before achieving a professional sense of incident. She needs to see how each chapter of the book can be a polished little drama in itself.[17]

Following receipt of Bill's letter, Betty wrote Bill, and he replied to her in turn:

Talking about books, I am pleased that you take the news of the Houghton Mifflin rejection of your book like an "old timer." Your attitude toward that rejection is exactly what I wanted to see; is exactly the way I would have taken it; and that means that you are really a "Trouper" and that you will ultimately do something in that line worthwhile. I shall send it. . . .

On the last Sunday of July, Bill summarized for Betty what he had been doing. The Hylands were on vacation in Harvey Cedars on the New Jersey shore and would return in a week:

My Dear Betty:

We have just been sitting on the back porch where it is coolest—86 degrees at eight o'clock in the morning—and thinking about you this Saturday morning taking one last plunge into the surf, hurrying around getting the cottage ready, packing up kit and caboodle and starting off for home. By the time you receive this letter, all of that packing up is over and you are settled down in your own home again. There will be advantages to it for I am sure there won't be sand all over everything; you will have your dishwasher, your clothes washer and be comfortable in your own familiar surroundings.

    I preach at Quincy [Massachusetts] Sunday morning, and it is broadcast over the radio, then I am free for the day and it is a good feeling for I have been traveling the last four Sundays and that is not pleasant in hot weather. This week I have done a lot of writing: getting caught up on my newspaper syndicate (22 pieces); three for The War Cry; *a Christmas sermon for* The Christian Herald *which has already been accepted and for which I am to be paid $50; a sermon for* The Upper Room Pulpit *which has been accepted and for which I am to be paid $25; so it has been a profitable week above the hot weather and preaching. I also got a check for $40 from Cook Publishing Company for the first month of a new column I am to write for one of their weekly magazines. That is an assignment I love and will bring me $40 a month over everything else. Now I have the monthly Stidger Storiette for* The Christian Herald, *my weekly story and my daily newspaper syndicate.*

On Saturday, August 6, 1949, Bill wrote the following letter to Betty:

Dearest Betty:

This is an eventful morning: the Atomic Bomb Day and your lovely Mother's birthday: an event in history and time. I said to her this morning at breakfast: "Well it looks as if your daughter has forgotten that it is your birthday."

    She said: "Well of all persons to forget, she is the last one who ought to, for she is so insistent upon us remembering HER birthday." That's all that was said but it is significant. As for me, your Pop, he doesn't give a hoot whether anybody remembers his birthday or not.

    My present to Mother is (and I thought it up myself) that I start today, lay aside six cigarettes, smoke two of them after breakfast; two of them after lunch and two in the evening; thus cutting down on my smoking. That seems to be the one thing that she wants more than anything else, so I'm presenting that to her as her 65th birthday present. Some gift, don't you think? So far—it's ten minutes after breakfast—I'm getting along fine.

    Tomorrow I preach at Wesley Methodist Church in Worcester [Massachusetts] so it is not such a chore as my trips farther away from home. I am preaching on "I Will Pray" which is based on my hymn of that title which I enclose in case you have forgotten it:

    I will pray, dear God, when darkness
    Throws its vesper shadows 'round,
    In the shadows I will listen,
    Kneeling on Thy Holy ground.
    I will meet Thy tryst at twilight,
    When the silent shadows sleep
    And all birds and beasts and children
    Into dreamland softly creep.

Those last four lines are my favorites of all the lines I have ever written. Somehow they give me a deeper satisfaction than even "I Saw God Wash the World." I even like "I Saw God Make a Morning" better than my famous poem. Lest you may have forgotten that one I enclose a copy of it also. Why not read it to the children and give them a conception of God in Nature and dawn? That's the way to build a spiritual, unconscious reverence in their souls.

Last night we listened to the Red Sox beat the Detroit Tigers 9 to 0. It was a magnificent game and a shut-out for [Jack] Kramer. We are HOT just now and have won our last seven games in a row and Dom [Joe] DiMaggio has hit safely in thirty-three straight games. The whole of New England is excited about this, and none more than your Mother. That woman knows every player—his record, his batting possibilities when he comes up; yells at him—while lying on the bed, listening to the game—to "make a hit!" This has all developed this summer, and I am glad of it. Remember my story in The Ladies' Home Journal, *"What I Saw in My Wife to Marry Her" for which I won a prize of $200 ? (I bought her engagement ring with that money.) Well, the thing that I saw in my fictional gal friend (and it was purely fictitious in Mother's case) was the fact that she KNEW baseball. Now, "at long last," she DOES know baseball, but it has taken me forty-five years to teach it to her, and that's a long, long time to vindicate myself as to "What I Saw in My Wife to Marry Her."*

Well, old kid, this must be all for this broadcast. Listen in again, on this same station, at this same time, come next Monday.

> *Your ever faithful and fulsome,*
> *Father*

 But there was no "listening in again, on this same station, at this same time," for these were the last words that William (Bill) Leroy Stidger ever wrote. On the next morning, after breakfast, as he was preparing to leave for Worcester to deliver his sermon, "I Will Pray," he complained of chest pains and said that he wasn't feeling well. He lay down on the sofa in the living room while Iva went to the kitchen to call the doctor. When she returned, he was lifeless and still. The Bill whom Iva loved and with whom she had shared forty-three years was gone; perhaps he had already moved gloriously on to try and catch up with the heroes and giants whom he had met in his life and in his reading—but he was gone from her, nonetheless. The doctor pronounced Bill dead of a massive coronary. It was August 7, 1949, his sixty-fourth year.

Iva predictably pulled herself together, as Bill would undoubtedly have wryly pointed out in his next letter to Betty—if there had been one—drawing on her inexhaustible reservoir of strength and courage. She called Pat McConnell and Walter Muelder, dean of the School of Theology. Muelder telephoned the church in Worcester, and then he and his wife drove to the Stidgers' house, where they spent the rest of the day helping Iva with the details that accompany a death, as well as keeping her company. Pat spelled the Muelders and stayed late into the night. Betty caught the first train to Boston; she stayed with Iva for a month.

The ritual events of the funeral service and the attention that friends paid to her preoccupied Iva, staving off the rawness and pain of her loss until much later, when she was alone. Bill's death was widely noted in newspapers around the country; telephone calls, letters, and visits paid filled her days in the immediate aftermath of the event. Betty, being there continuously, was of immense consolation.

The funeral service was held two days after Bill's death, on Tuesday, August 9, 1949, at his old Copley Methodist Church. Dan Marsh, president of Boston University, presided; the opening prayer and Lord's Prayer were read by Bishop John Wesley Lord, the Methodist bishop in Boston; Walter Muelder read the Twenty-third Psalm; Bishop Lewis O. Hartman, former bishop for Boston, read "And I John saw" (Rev. 21:2–4); and the benediction was given by Professor Edwin P. Booth. The music was planned and led by Professor Jim Houghton. The address, made to the packed church, was given by Pat McConnell:

TRAVELING HUMAN

Thirty-five years ago there appeared in the *Epworth Herald* a series of articles entitled "Traveling Human." They were stories of people picked up by a traveler who was alive to what was going on around him. A crying baby was the center of one interested and annoyed group. An old couple going back to visit the hometown of their birth had a story to tell. A drinking roisterer was the maker of a disturbance. They had no plot and pointed no moral. They were flashlights turned on human faces with care, joy, annoyance, written for anyone who knew the language of life to read.

Early in the past year a book appeared bearing the title "Adventures in Understanding" which closed a lifelong series about people of worldwide fame and obscure watchers of sky and field. They were set down by one who traveled human. Sometimes it was in poetry, sometimes in prose but always in winged words.

There are people who bend their energies toward a set goal: it may be a million dollars and they become the richest men in the cemetery. It may be some high goal of scholarship and they end up in the insane asylum as the most learned inmate. Life is to them a destination and they travel in a compartment with shades drawn to shut out the beautiful but distracting scenery. The man who traveled human never missed a sunset, a tree, a flashlight on the seven seas or a sermon in a stone. His ears were tuned to the chirp of the cricket or the thunder's roar. He could see the far horizon as clearly as the tired look in the travel-worn mother's eyes who had walked four days and nights with two small children to meet her soldier husband. The man who traveled human saw life as a journey and not as a destination.

Anyone who sees life through human eyes can not long be content as a reporter or as a journeyman storyteller. He has to lay down his pen and render first aid to some other traveler who has been overtaken by a fault. Once it was a man about whom his enemies chose to believe the worst and swarmed over him for the kill. The man who traveled human roamed far and wide in his friend's defense.

It was a long, long journey that the man who traveled human took. It carried him into the far corners of the earth in peace and war. Up and down the world he went poking his flashlight into the nooks and crannies of continents and back roads. But he was not only interested in geography but in folks. Always it was a man, woman, or child in the picture. Once it was a silhouette of a soldier against a flaming battle front. Over fifty books were filled with stories. The little people were never nudged out by the big folk. Multimillionaires shared his pages with Miss Mary of Moundsville.

He saw God wash the world and hang it up to dry. And that was not all he saw in God's great world of birds and trees and sky. As human traveler he had some of the reverence for life that Albert Schweitzer has. The flash of a scarlet tanager held as much interest for this man who traveled human as the southern cross.

While life is not a destination but a journey, there comes a time when it changes form, and as we know it there comes an end in the journey. That is what the skeptic thinks, but never does it enter a Christian's mind that "life is a meaningless journey between two unknown continents—birth and death," as an atheist once said in his despair. There are those who would say that our fellow traveler passed on last Sunday morning as he was about to leave his home to preach a sermon on prayer. We believe that somewhere in God's kingdom he is engaged in the activities and is having the experiences which belong to that unseen realm. "For death," once said Borden P. Bowne, "is only an incident in the existence of an immortal spirit. . . . It is a passage from a lower to a higher phase of our continuous life. . . . And if at the end of it all, we emerge from life's work discipline crowned souls, at home anywhere in God's universe, life will be a success."

These words of wisdom are but an echo of far greater and more comforting ones spoken to the troubled heart by a man who traveled human on the roads of Galilee: "Let not your heart be troubled: ye believe in God, believe also in me. In my Father's house are many mansions. If it were not so I would have told you. I go to prepare a place for you, I will come again and receive you unto myself; that where I am there ye may be also. And whither I go ye know, and the way ye know. Thomas said unto him, Lord, we know not whither thou goest; and how can we know the way? Jesus saith unto him, I am the way, the truth and the life: no man cometh unto the Father but by me."

It turns out that the one who travels human has a fellow traveler who knows the way to the Father's house, which we deeply believe can be reached at his journey's end, or beginning, as you would have it.[18]

Bill seemed incapable of death, at least in the minds of some people. On August 17, 1949, *Zion's Herald* printed a letter he had written to Emory Stevens Bucke, the editor, which made it seem like he was still in his study, spewing forth letters in all directions:

DR. STIDGER'S LAST NOTE

During vacation months I have time to be a Christian; and this morning, I want to be a Christian enough to say to you that your editorial "With Reverence For Life" is a knockout; tender, factual, full of strong characterization of a man, and with youthful enthusiasm enough to make it contagious. You are learning not only to edit but to write and that is important.

William L. Stidger
Newton Center, Mass.[19]

In the same issue, *Zion's Herald* stated that it was carrying "the sad news of the passing of William L. Stidger. The modern generation of Protestants has been inspired by the ministry of this man, and his death leaves us lonely indeed. Poet Stidger was a great writer because he involved himself in everything he wrote. There are few preachers in Methodism who have not used one or more of Bill Stidger's stories or poems, and there are few laymen who have not read repeatedly his greatest poem, 'I Saw God Wash the World.' This editor counts it one of his highest opportunities to have known Dr. Stidger intimately. Hardly a week passed without a visit or a note which enthusiastically approved—or disapproved—of an editorial or an article that appeared in *Zion's Herald*.

"His friendships were legion and in every conversation he would pull stories from these friends. He loved children and delighted in finding out what kind of things they did and what they talked about. When issues were being discussed, Bill would frustrate the most ardent crusader by asking some apparently irrelevant question and then bring the humanity of the matter to the fore: he wasn't interested in issues, he was interested in people."[20]

Letters from readers streamed into *Zion's Herald*, where Bill's weekly column "Getting a Kick Out of Life" had been the most popular feature and had been running for over five years:

BILL IN PARADISE

In the passing of "Bill" Stidger we have lost a gay heart and a grand spirit. His homiletic daring, and his vivid imagination stirred me beginning with the first day I set foot in Boston University School of Theology in '29, the year he began there, and his writings have helped to keep me alert across the years. A daring preacher, he was always subject to sharp criticism by those who aspired to preach, yet even those who scorned his methods held secret admiration for his preaching skill. As much as he loved to write and to preach, he loved people more, and it was through his human touch and his heart of overflowing kindness that made him such a winsome interpreter of things divine.

What a time Bill will have on Paradise Boulevard in the Celestial City. He will get a kick out of his old friends, and how thrilling it would be to have his report on how things have been with [Bishop] William A. Quayle, the "Skylark of Methodism," Fred Winslow Adams and Henry Ford.

(Rev.) W. Ralph Ward, Jr.
Pittsburgh, Pa.[21]

OPEN LETTER TO BILL STIDGER

Dear Bill:

You were always a great one for letters. I'll miss not getting any more of them. But, I've got several, signed with that scrawling "Bill," carefully tucked away to look at on gloomy days.

Mostly, however, I'll miss your hearty greetings which always swept the clouds right out of the sky. Also, I'll miss your honest interest which you always took in any little thing which I happened to be doing. You could make that little thing the most important and worthwhile in the whole world. Yours never was the criticism which spreads despair. Yours was the optimistic encouragement which fills the horizon with glowing mountain peaks and inspires the most downcast to start for the top. When you looked at those peaks I knew that I, even I, could get going. You made my reach fit the steps.

You were a friend to so many that I could never be jealous of your friendship. I sometimes called this your one fault. (You must have had others, but they were dimmed by the bright light of your better self.) I like to be greedy and exclusive about affections. You could never allow that. There was so much room in your heart.

There are a lot of people these days talking about your sudden death or how you passed away so unexpectedly as you were preparing to leave to preach that Sunday morning. (Your subject, I believe, was "I Will Pray.") Somehow, though, I can not associate "dying" or "passing away" with you. No, I'll tell you what I believe. I believe that you poked around so much in this life and you found a multitude of fascinating, good and wonderful things in it—lived it so fully—that you had to have more space. You had to go somewhere bigger. . . .

As the days pass I like to indulge in a fantasy about you. I like to see you vigorously busy in your new world. There is so much of the good, the fine, and the noble there for you. What a place for stories and poems worthy of your telling! What a delightful time you are having! I know now, Bill, when I join you everything will be beautiful and good—even touched with a tinge of wholesome humor now and then—because you will be there to make it so.

*(Rev.) John D. Erb,
Worcester, Mass.* [22]

A STUDENT'S TRIBUTE TO "BILL STIDGER"

To a young minister there is often a man outside of his father who is a special advisor, confidant and friend. Bill Stidger was such a man to me and to many other young ministers. He will certainly be remembered for his great contribution to homiletics, magazine writing and poetry, but I shall always remember Bill for his unselfish friendship and brotherly love. As one of his students, who has been accused of "majoring in Stidger," I bear testimony to the worth of a man who never seemed any older than his students.

I heard the news of his passing with a great numbness, but upon reflection I know that Bill Stidger can never die. He was so full of life, energy and spiritual effervescence that he infected all who were associated with him. I loved Bill Stidger for the studies which he taught, but also for his ability to make me see a new facet of the pastoral ministry. He has given me a fierce pride in being a Methodist minister. He taught me that the ministry can be the greatest and most compelling calling to which one should always testify, and that this calling should be presented in the most modern and successful media of communication and advertising. . . .

I shall miss his advice and his wonderful letters which were full of friendship and nonsense, but his familiar figure, with his hands stuck in both back pockets, will never leave the minds of us who knew him. As one of "Bill's Boys," I can remember several lines of the Lincoln poem by Edwin Markham which apply to Bill Stidger:

And when he fell in whirlwind, he went down
As when a lordly cedar, green with boughs,
Goes down with a great shout upon the hills,
And leaves a lonesome place against the sky.

Bill Stidger has left "a lonesome place against the sky," but his spirit among us will fill that gap for many years to come.

(Rev.) Ronald A. Mosley,
East Natick, Mass.[23]

Of all the tributes, however, the one that Bill would certainly have enjoyed the most and would have been the most surprised about appeared in the *Boston Herald*, written by its prominent sportswriter, Bill Cunningham:

It seems strange to be referring to the friendly man who always signed his wonderful letters "Bill" as the Rev. Dr. William L. Stidger. It's stranger still to try to realize that his friendship, his inspiration, his keen interest in people and things, patterns and pictures that included all living, even the sports kind of living, are ended.

Dr. Stidger was truly a distinguished clergyman. A Methodist, nationally known through his coast-to-coast broadcasts, his books, his lectures, his extensive travels, his basic affiliation was with the faculty of the Boston University School of Theology. That's what the formal obituaries say, and they go on to list his honors, his degrees, his accomplishments and emoluments.

What they can't list, however, is the lift he gave all who knew him, the stronger belief in some finer way, the breadth of vision, the respect for decent things, belief in God and all that a clergyman should represent and be, but, above all, perhaps, on the layman's level, the living example that a man can be a Christian, not only a clergyman, but a teacher of clergymen, without sacrificing contacts, interest, humor nor happiness in the workaday world as the rest know it. Proof of that is the name by which most of us knew him, Bill Stidger. I never knew a name that fit a man so exactly.

Dr. Stidger was interested in a great many things. He would have made a great reporter. In fact he was a great reporter. That is proved by his writings, and likewise by his sermons and lectures. But all his reporting wasn't confined to the formal products. Some of it was in letters that came to this office. Keenly interested in people, all kinds of people, he sometimes encountered athletes of major or minor import in his travels.

Interested in how they lived, what they thought, why they did it, he generally managed to draw them out. His interest was so sincere, his approach so sympathetic, albeit, so masculine, that they generally confided far more to him than they ever would to a sports writer. So far as I know, he never violated real confidences, but he occasionally did pass on some of his observations and conclusions in letters to this office.

These weren't always in the interest of just helping out a friend, either. Sometimes they amounted to correction, a taking of the other fellow's side. I remember the case of a prize fighter who seemed to have fouled the general code. He was a pretty prominent character, and controversy developed. I was lambasting him with all I could throw. Suddenly, in the mail, came a letter from Bill Stidger. It was one of these now-you-looka-here letters. I wasn't being entirely fair, the noted clergyman advised.

He'd met this young fellow not too long ago, he said, and they'd had quite a talk, and while he may have done wrong in this particular instance, he was definitely not all these things I was saying. He was a young man with a lot of problems, and what he needed was help and encouragement, not banging around. Bill Stidger was a husky man. He could be husky in letters. He didn't hesitate to punch, especially when he thought some underdog could use a spot of help.

Those who read this column, however, will probably remember best, of the references made to him here through the years, the summation of a radio talk he once made. It was entitled "Rest Where You Are." That was likewise his philosophy and practical prescription.

There was nothing religious in this particular message. Spirituality wasn't even involved. It was nothing but a small dose of common sense—a practical suggestion in the business of living.

The gist of it was that we could all save energy in this hard-driving world if we'd only learn completely to relax in the many opportunities all of us have in even the busiest routines. Instead of staying tense all the day, and all the way, the saving trick is to relax every muscle, and every nerve, completely as the opportunity offers.

And where and what are the opportunities?, he asked.

There are many. Some are brief, but they're enough. If you're sitting in your car waiting for a traffic light to change, for example, there are a few seconds. That's an opportunity. Simply relax. Let everything go. If you're waiting in an office for an appointment, there's an opportunity. Instead of sitting tensely, relax every muscle, and the mind with it, if you can. And so on through all the day's activities. Simply "rest where you are," and you'll find yourself better, less worn, more alert at the end of the day.

It would be hard to tell how many millions have benefited, and are still benefiting, from that simple suggestion. During the grinding years of the war, without even asking his permission, I revived "Rest Where You Are" here, giving him full credit, of course. From here, it literally went 'round the world. Other papers and publications reprinted it. The Armed Forces immediately appropriated it. Soldiers and sailors mailed it back from where their theater, post or unit publications had featured it in all parts of the globe. They even had a name for it—"Stidgerizing."

Bill Stidger was interested in photography. He was interested in sports. He knew his baseball, and he knew it from away back. Not too long ago I got myself into a controversy of sorts with the veteran Ty Cobb. The now apparently mellowing old Georgia Peach, a terror on the base paths in his time, was insisting belligerently that he'd never played rough, that he'd never deliberately charged an opponent, nor come in with high spikes.

"Don't back down on him," wrote Bill, "why, I remember one time, when with my own eyes, I saw. . . ."

There's not much you can say when the Lord calls His own, but here's one case, certainly, where death is not the end of the living. Today they will bury the mortal remains of the fine friend, the great preacher and the teacher we knew. But as long as those who were privileged to share his friendship themselves continue to live, all that was warm and human and inspirational and Christian in Bill Stidger will live. Men such as that don't die; they merely pass on.

Rest, sweet rest, where you are.[24]

As if to fulfill the wishes of so many of his friends that he not die, Bill remained alive in the pages of *Zion's Herald* for almost an additional five months. He had written Betty, just before he died, that he had completed twenty-two stories for his column "Getting the Most Out of Life," and with Iva's permission *Zion's Herald* ran these stories until the supply was exhausted at the end of December 1949.

For Iva, however, Bill was most sadly and horribly gone. At the end of her first week of being alone, after Betty had returned to her family in Philadelphia, Iva wrote:

Dear Betty and Jack—

It's ten o'clock Friday night. I have found every excuse to keep me out of this sunroom and away from the letters, but I finally thought, "Why, I want to write Betty and Jack," so here I am. It's raining pitchforks. Lucy [Iva's cleaning lady] is over at Waltham visiting some friends, and her sisters will bring her home. I really like having her here. She is so nice to me; looks out for everything—so she has helped me through this first alone week, as have so many people. Indeed, I have not gotten anything done—just little tries at this and that, but I'm sure the day will come when I can get at it, and then I'll move mountains.

To have you four weeks with me and then all gone and a house so still and quiet was very, very hard for me. I knew that I had to face it, so when you drove off, I had myself my first real cry. Then I tore into washing dishes and straightening the house—and finally the day got over.

I do wish I could tell you both what you meant to me. In spite of each minute seeming long and terrible you did get here so quickly when I needed you so badly. You were both so kindly, so thoughtful and so comforting, I kept saying little grateful prayers that I had you to lean on.

Dad's going was so startling and so sudden and so final. I still wonder if I'm not just in a bad dream, but then the awful truth overwhelms me. We have to go on, and every day we'll be given courage and strength to do it. His goodness seems to grow every time I think of him. Life with him looks very beautiful from this angle. He was a kindly father, an indulging, unselfish and loving husband, a great man. Oh, how I loved him and how I revere this memory of him.

Betty dear, yours is a rich heritage and "you are worthy of your lineage." I can scarcely keep from calling you, but I must control myself. However, I'm going to call some night this week, I'm sure. Life wouldn't be worth living without you all. I love you so very much. You were all that a daughter and a son could ever be to a mother in deep need. I am so grateful for the weeks you spent with me. It helped more than anything ever could have.

Always, I love you all,
Mother
Friday last week; and
Wednesday this week [25]

Shortly after her letter, Iva realized that Betty felt Bill's death as poignantly as she did herself. Her second letter embraced this sadness:

Dear, dear Betts—

I must tell you right off that I have been miserable every minute since I talked with you for I know how restless and unhappy I am and how restless and unhappy you are about old Dad's leaving us. You have been so thoughtful of me and every letter from you I am so grateful for, that for me to not do my part to help you is so unkind. And, of course, I should have written very often for you miss Dad's letters and his regular writing. Darling, I'll be more careful.

Physically I think I'm well—people tell me I look better, then the next time I see them they say "You look better" again. I know I don't look well, but I feel all fine. When I can face the world mentally I'll be fine.

Although this place on Lake Winnipesaukee is very peaceful I am anxious to get back home. I felt when I left that morning that I was turning my back on my home and on Dad. It was terrifying for awhile. As I said, I am so anxious to get back home—and then on to you. I had a letter from David Cook Company asking me if they could use some of Dad's stories. I said yes. The money would be very acceptable. I am still getting 4 or 5 letters a day from his and my friends, and from people I don't even know.

I must close. I do love you all so much. I wouldn't dare try to write you about how I really feel. I suppose it's best that I feel I never can just give way to my feelings, but I am so lonely and so lost. Sometimes I think I miss Dad more every day. Wasn't he a wonderful old dear? If he could have only stayed with us longer.

Lovingly,
Mother [26]

But life does go on. Wounds as deep as those inflicted on Iva by Bill's death never heal, but the pain they cause gradually loses its sharpness and becomes only a dull ache. It was the same for Betty. They agreed to bury Bill's cremated remains beneath a simple flat marker in a peaceful plot under a white birch tree, so Bill would be shaded by its leaves, in the Sleepy Hollow Cemetery in Concord. It was Bill's favorite cemetery, and he had visited it many times in the past; he had even written about some of the famous—and not so famous—people buried there.

Almost exactly one year later, Jack Hyland died, just as suddenly and abruptly as Bill had, although Jack was only forty-three. This time, it was Iva's turn to go to Betty's side and give her the support she needed. Later, when Betty had dealt with her loss as best she could, she and Iva decided that Iva should move to Philadelphia to help Betty bring up her three young children.

Therefore, on Sunday, October 1, 1950, just a little more than one year after Bill died, Iva visited Sleepy Hollow with Pat and Lucille LeSourd (Dr. Howard M. LeSourd, dean of the graduate school affiliated with the School of Theology, and his wife, Lucille, were close friends of the Stidgers) to pay their respects to Bill's memory and for Iva to say good-bye before leaving Boston to live with Betty. Lucille wrote the following letter to Iva after their day spent together:

My dear—

At the end of this perfect day I must share some of my thoughts with you. I was too full of tears to say all that was in my heart. Somehow the day was a tribute to Bill—a trip to his favorite haunts. His presence hung over us like a sacred benediction. I felt the windows of Heaven wide open, as we stood on the hallowed ground at Sleepy Hollow and Bill smiling down upon us.

I was so moved by the stillness—the peace, the feeling of security leaving him under the old, white birch tree but oh-oh-the heartache!

I thought as I sat in church—what a heritage Bill has left, wealth untold in the inspiration of his poetry and books and all the lovable, livable tributes he paid each one of us in word and deed.

Our lives have been so enriched by both of you—the enrichment hurts so very much these days and yet there must be no sadness of farewell—just a wave of the hand from a heavy heart and so much longing that it will be only a temporary separation.

I can only thank you from the depths of a grateful heart for friendship that "passeth all understanding." You have given us of yourself and your example of triumphant living will be cherished always.[27]

Iva joined Bill in 1961, twelve years after his death in 1949. She rests quietly—and I know happily—beside her husband, the true love of her life. Betty lies beside her Jack; she died in 1969, while reading from her book *Those Heavenly Years* to a women's club. Bill would have been stirred by the tribute that Betty paid him—her "father and pal." It was this tribute that she was in the midst of reading to her audience in Philadelphia when her final heart attack overcame her. She peacefully placed her head on the table and quietly and serenely joined Iva and Bill, Jack, and her young son—my older brother—forever. This is what Betty had read to the women's club:

THE MOST UNFORGETTABLE PERSON I EVER KNEW

He is fat and bald—has been ever since I became aware of him. His eyes are sailor blue and twinkle with joy or flash with indignation.

He is the most impractical man I ever saw. Why once, when he was younger, and very very poor, his wife sent him to the store with their last five dollars to buy some food for them and their baby daughter. He came home, hours later, with no food at all but jubilantly carrying a set of bronze dinner chimes.

He is also absent-minded. Once his daughter called him at home on the phone and said "Dad, I have a flat tire, and I didn't bring any money. What shall I do?"

"Stay right there and I'll come and get you." He hung up the phone, rushed right out, borrowed a friend's car and spent an hour driving around hunting his daughter until suddenly he realized he couldn't find her because he didn't know where she was.

Another time, he took some friends to the Boston Pops [orchestra]. At the close of the program they saw that it had started to rain, so my friend insisted that the others stay by the marquee while he went for the car. An hour passed. Everyone had left the hall. The marquee lights went out and still the little group waited. They were just trying to decide whether to call a cab or a policeman when my friend showed up. He had completely forgotten that he had a new car and he spent the hour hunting his old one. He had passed his new Nash many times and finally when all the other cars had been claimed and the Nash was the only one left he realized that this was his.

This friend of mine is a preacher, and a very good one too. He never tries to push the idea of God onto anyone. But he has brought hope and comfort to more people than tongue can tell. He believes in living his religion. He trusts everyone and he has seldom been hooked.

He and I were very good friends when I was young. We did many things together. One thing has always stayed in my heart. One November night we took a walk. A new moon was cutting its way across a starless sky. I complained that there were no stars and suddenly my friend clutched my arm.

"Betty, look, cradled in the heart of that moon is a bright new star. The crescent moon is guarding it, and that is what I always want to do for you. As that moon cradles that star so my love will always hover about you. Let it be then, whenever we are apart, that if you will look at the moon and the stars, you will remember me and will know that somewhere I, too, am watching those same stars and I am thinking of you."

Of course I grew up and married and moved away from my friend. I saw him often enough but I was so wrapped up in my own new existence that his words seemed old and shopworn.

The second spring of my marriage, I became an expectant mother and I told my friend, and he was jubilant. My friend started sending me letters. One almost every day. Letters filled with pictures of mothers and babies, miniature oils of madonnas, cartoons from papers and magazines. Literally hundreds of warm happy letters to let me know the joy that my baby would mean to him.

My little son arrived one August night in the midst of a terrific thunderstorm. It took him a long time to come and the journey must have tired him for he soon went back into the nowhere.

My friend came to me then and said "Betty, do you remember the stars? Your Mother and Dad have always tried to shelter you from the hard things of life, and now comes the hardest and they cannot shelter you. But when you are bitter and blue try to remember the stars and then you will remember that your Father loves you and is as loyal as those stars."

Yes, my friend is my Father, loving, absentminded, crazy, angry and happy. Ask many a nobody, ask his millions of parishioners, ask the famous people he knows, ask me, his daughter, for Dr. William L Stidger is the most unforgettable person I ever knew.[28]

Here is the poem that Bill and Betty created and the story that Bill wrote about their experience:

A CRESCENT MOON AND A CRADLED STAR

William L. Stidger

I pointed out that beautiful sight to Betty and said: "See that, Betty: a crescent moon and a cradled star. That ought to be put into a poem."

Betty replied: "Why not? Let's do it." And we did. On the spot the two of us got the first two lines, and to save my life I can't remember who got those two lines, for Betty is also somewhat of a verse writer. Then we went home and she insisted that I seclude myself in my study until that poem came and I did and it did—and here it is:

There's a crescent moon and a cradled star
And a sense of the beautiful things that are
Where the golden crest of a cloud swings high
In the lonely west of an amber sky.
There is fatherhood and the flowing stream
Of a mother's urge and a mother's dream.
There's a love for home and the kindly ways

Of a hearth that burns with a cheerful blaze.
There is truth that tramps with a mighty tread
Where the martyrs lie with the living dead;
There's a dream of dawn that will lift its soul
To the lofty trail where the planets roll.
There's a Christ who lived and died that we
Might dare all death and tragedy,
And a Christ who rose that the world might know
That the tides of time have ebb and flow.
That the tides of time and the streams of truth
Are the tides of dawn and the dreams of youth;
That the winter goes and the spring draws near
In the flow and the flood of the tidal year.
There is Jesus Christ and a rough-hewn cross
And a glimpse of the poor world's greatest loss,
There's a crescent moon and a cradled star
And a sense of the beautiful things that are![29]

I have always believed that somewhere, out there in the evening sky, there is a crescent moon and a cradled star, "and a sense of the beautiful things that are." There is a whisper that can be heard in the shadows of that beautiful summer night, although it may be no more than a warm breeze stirring as the light fades from the sky, and I like to think that the whisper is the sound of a younger Bill saying to his much younger daughter, as he points upward, "Betty, hereafter, no matter where you are or how old you are, whenever you see that moon and star, you must think of this night and remember that your Dad loves you—and always will." And I believe that if it is Bill who is speaking to Betty, then Iva stands beside him, smiling.

Notes

1. William L. Stidger, "A Look at the Stars," *More Sermons in Stories* (New York: Abingdon-Cokesbury, 1944), 62–63.

2. William L. Stidger, "A Tender Case That Nothing Be Lost," *Human Adventures in Happy Living* (New York: Fleming H. Revell, 1948), 35.

3. William L. Stidger, "A Better Road," *Human Interest Stories in Christian Stewardship* (Chicago: Methodist Church, General Board of Lay Activities, 1947), 59–60.

4. Stidger, "A Look at the Stars," 63–64.

5. Letter dated March 12, 1940, from Betty Stidger Hyland to William L. Stidger, author's collection.

6. Scrapbook dated March 29, 1940, prepared by William L. Stidger, presented to Betty and Jack Hyland, author's collection.

7. Letter dated May 4, 1940, from William L. Stidger to Betty Stidger Hyland and her family, author's collection.

8. Letter dated May 11, 1940, from William L. Stidger to Betty Stidger Hyland, author's collection.

9. Letter dated May 11, 1940, from Iva Berkey Stidger to Betty Stidger Hyland, author's collection.

10. William L. Stidger, *How to Get the Most Out of Life* (Chicago: Rodeheaver, Hall-Mack, 1939), 7.

11. William L. Stidger, "At All the Doors," *More Sermons in Stories,* 136–37.

12. Stidger, "At All the Doors," 136–37.

13. Thanksgiving letter, undated, from William L. Stidger to Betty Stidger Hyland, author's collection.

14. Letter from former student of William L. Stidger to author.

15. This passage, and those below not otherwise cited, are from various letters from William L. Stidger to Betty Stidger Hyland, author's collection.

16. William L. Stidger, *Human Adventures in Happy Living* (New York: Fleming H. Revell, 1948), 124–127.

17. Letter dated June 23, 1949, from Diggory Venn, Houghton Mifflin Company, to William L. Stidger, author's collection.

18. Charles M. McConnell, "Traveling Human," *Zion's Herald,* August 17, 1949, 13.

19. William L. Stidger, "Dr. Stidger's Last Note," *Zion's Herald,* August 17, 1949, 2.

20. Emory Stevens Bucke, "The Poet and the Prophet," *Zion's Herald,* August 17, 1949, 6.

21. W. Ralph Ward Jr., "Bill in Paradise," *Zion's Herald,* August 17, 1949, 2.

22. John D. Erb, "Open Letter to Bill Stidger," *Zion's Herald,* August 31, 1949, 2.

23. Ronald A. Mosley, "A Student's Tribute to 'Bill Stidger,'" *Zion's Herald,* August 31, 1949, 2.

24. Bill Cunningham, "Rev. Stidger Gave All Lift," *Boston Herald,* August 9, 1949, 8.

25. Letter, undated, from Iva Berkey Stidger to Betty Stidger Hyland, author's collection.

26. Letter, undated, from Iva Berkey Stidger to Betty Stidger Hyland, author's collection.

27. Letter dated October 1, 1950, from Lucille LeSourd to Iva Berkey Stidger, author's collection.

28. Betty Stidger Hyland, "The Most Unforgettable Person I Ever Knew," undated, author's collection.

29. William L. Stidger, "A Crescent Moon and a Cradled Star," *How to Get the Most Out of Life,* 17–19.

The Relevance of Reverend Bill Stidger

Walter G. Muelder

B ill Stidger was a fearless and creative preacher who adapted his preaching to his own talents and to the age in which he preached. He was essentially a preaching minister, coming from an era when to be a minister, a clergyman, meant to be a pulpiteer, one who had mastered the preacher's art. He could do much more than preach, for he was a writer, a journalist, and a poet; fundamentally, however, Bill Stidger showed his students the relevance of culture to the proclamation of the Word and the relevance of the Word to the many modes of communication, persuasion, and action.

I have argued that every well-trained minister should be able to do five essential tasks: conduct worship and preach, administer religious education, counsel people in the crises of life, manage a church organization, and relate the gospel effectively in community service and for social change. The talents and gifts of each clergyperson lead each to approach those ministries differently. Bill was especially creative in worship and preaching. It is still an essential skill, especially in a church with only one pastor, which is the most common type. Stidger was creative in all the arts of ministry.

In pursuing his craft, Bill was open to the full range of cultures and incorporated their leading edges in his style of promoting the gospel. Many ministers are confined to those aspects of contemporary culture in which they feel most comfortable. Bill was not afraid of the changing styles of life and expression in the visible arts—in music, theater, literature, dance, and unconventional modes of communication. All culture invited him to make it serve the purposes of the gospel. He was not afraid of the culture in which he lived. He was at home in the secular world.

One of his responses to the challenge to find new styles of preaching was his famous "symphonic sermon" device. There were many great preachers in his generation, and each tended to develop a characteristic shape or method of sermonizing. Bill was adaptive, but one of his successful forms was symphonic. Essentially this meant that the various parts of the sermon climaxed symphonically in a repeated couplet or quatrain that would sing itself in the listener's mind throughout the week after the service. Such, for example, is "The soul can split the sky in two and let the face of God shine through."

In other words, Bill Stidger was inventive. He was not an imitator of classical styles of sermons. He also wrote verse, poems, hymns, and stories, trusting in his own genius and gifts.

That he drew inventively from the modern poets illustrates that Bill acquainted himself with the literature of the day and with those who produced it. Many members of the clergy have narrow circles of professional contacts. Many have forgotten the art of relating the gospel to the spiritual values of world literature. Bill Stidger was unconventional in that he made the personal acquaintance of actors and performers, even used them in the life and programs of the church. He became a living bridge between reporters, actors, players, and their modes of communication in their venues, and the chancel or platform in which he was so creatively at home.

Often the church is a half-generation or a full generation behind the leading edge of technology and the media. Bill fearlessly used the latest in journalism, advertising, showmanship, and the radio, adapting his messages to what was most effective. Yet he quite consistently retained the integrity of his message. He did not, like some, sell out the gospel to the popular clichés of the day. He never forgot that he was a Christian preacher. He was deeply wounded when his sometimes exaggerated style was misinterpreted. In his excursions into flamboyance, Bill never knowingly drifted far from his spiritual center of gravity.

Bill's relevance as a pastor included his great capacity for friendship and his personal caring. When theological students were dismayed by their limitations in grasping the subtler dimensions of the theoretical theology, of Christian doctrine, Stidger had a way of building up their self-confidence. On the other hand, he could prick the bubble of arrogance in a budding preacher who had developed a false sense of self-importance. His loyalty to friends and colleagues was widely known. His words of encouragement were common and timely. He expected excellence in others and did not hesitate to praise it in them.

Wherever he had a pulpit or became the pastor of a church, he fearlessly faced the social issues and crises of the day. Whether it was ministering to soldiers at the front in

World War I, opposing corruption and decay in morals in an urban setting, or support-ing labor's struggle for economic justice in industry, Bill took the social teachings of the prophets and of Jesus with great seriousness. In the inner city, he found a ministry to the theater district, to the multiethnic, recent immigrant sections, to the power structures, and to the neglected. He knew how to dramatize the plight of the deposed in the Great Depression and the callousness of ordinary citizens toward the inhabitants of flop-houses, how to combine empathy and confrontation in his inclusiveness.

Stidger recognized that most of the work of the church is outside the four walls of its sanctuaries. Obviously, he was a master pulpiteer, with unique techniques for draw-ing audiences, but his total ministry made the example of the Good Samaritan a daily assignment.

Bill thus made the whole of society and its culture his parish, but he never forgot the spiritual core of his discipleship. There is no bifurcation between the personal and the social gospel. At all times he was an apostle of Jesus Christ. Any substitution of a good social cause for the "spiritual" disciplines of devotion was contrary to his com-mitment. The gospel was for him a seamless whole.

To accomplish his goals as a preacher and pastor, he was willing to risk innovation; he approved of attention-getting devices. He exploited so-called secular media. He wrote voluminously. He sacrificed scholarship for journalistic effectiveness. He made relevance the benchmark of his preaching and teaching.

Walter G. Muelder
Jamaica Plain, Massachusetts
September 2000

WALTER GEORGE MUELDER (1907–), Dean Emeritus of Boston University School of Theology, is an educator, personalist, ecumenist, and ethicist. He attended Knox College (B.S. 1927) and Boston University (S.T.B. 1930, Ph.D. 1933), with studies in Frankfurt, Germany, in 1931. He taught at Berea College (1934–1940) and the University of Southern California (1940–1945) before going to Boston University to serve as Dean of the School of Theology and Professor of Christian Theology and Christian Ethics (1945–1972). He served the World Council of Churches for many years and served in various capacities with Faith and Order, including Chair of the Commission on Institutionalism (1955–1963), and Chair of the Board of the Ecumenical Institute (1961–1968). He began teaching and writing in general philosophy, editing *The Development of American Philosophy: A Book of Readings* (1940, rev. 1960), but is best known for his later works in ethics: *Religion and Economic Responsibility* (1953), *The Idea of the Responsible Society* (1955), *The Foundations of the Responsible Society* (1959), *Methodist Social Thought and Action* (1961), *Methodism and Society in the Twentieth Century* (1961), and *Moral Laws and Chrisitan Society Ethics* (1966).

Appendix

Published Books by William L. Stidger

1911   *The Lincoln Book of Poems* (Gorham Press)
        The Old Wolf Spring (Schoolcraft Press)

1918   *Giant Hours with Poet Preachers* (Abingdon Press)
        Soldier Silhouettes on Our Front (Charles Scribner's Sons)

1919   *Star Dust from the Dugouts: A Reconstruction Book* (Abingdon Press)

1920   *Outdoor Men and Minds* (Abingdon Press)

1921   *Standing Room Only* (George H. Doran)
        Flashlights from the Seven Seas (George H. Doran)

1922   *Flames of Faith* (poems) (Abingdon Press)
        There Are Sermons in Books (George H. Doran)
        The Place of Books in the Life We Live (George H. Doran)

1923   *Henry Ford: The Man and His Motives* (George H. Doran)
        Adventures in Humanity (George H. Doran)

1924	*That God's House May Be Filled* (George H. Doran) *The Epic of Earth* (Abingdon Press) *Symphonic Sermons* (George H. Doran) *A Book of Sunsets* (poems) (Abingdon Press)
1925	*Finding God in Books* (George H. Doran) Contribution to *Best Sermons of 1925*
1926	*Pulpit Prayers and Paragraphs* (George H. Doran) *Building Up the Mid-Week Service* (George H. Doran) *Building Sermons with Symphonic Themes* (George H. Doran)
1927	*God Is at the Organ* (Abingdon Press)
1928	*The High Faith of Fiction and Drama* (Doubleday, Doran)
1929	*Preaching Out of the Overflow* (Cokesbury Press) *Personal Power* (Doubleday, Doran) *If I Had Only One Sermon to Preach on Immortality* (editor) (Harper & Brothers)
1930	*The Pew Preaches* (editor) (Cokesbury Press)
1931	*Men of the Great Redemption* (Cokesbury Press)
1932	*Planning Your Preaching* (Harper and Brothers)
1933	*Edwin Markham: A Biography* (Abingdon Press)
1934	*I Saw God Wash the World* (poems) (Rodeheaver Hall-Mack)
1938	*These Amazing Roosevelts* (Macfadden)
1939	*How to Get the Most Out of Life* (Rodeheaver Hall-Mack)
1940	*The Human Side of Greatness* (Harper and Brothers)
1941	*Rainbow-Born Is Beauty* (poems) (Cornell College Chapbooks)
1942	*There Are Sermons in Stories* (Abingdon-Cokesbury Press)
1944	*More Sermons in Stories* (Abingdon-Cokesbury Press)
1946	*Sermon Nuggets in Stories* (Abingdon-Cokesbury Press)
1947	*Immortals of the Christian Ministry* (publisher unknown)
1948	*Human Interest Stories in Christian Stewardship* (General Board of Lay Activities, Methodist Church) *Human Adventures in Happy Living* (Fleming H. Revell) *Sermon Stories of Faith and Hope* (Abingdon-Cokesbury Press)
Unknown	*Keeping the Soul of the World Alive* (publisher unknown) *Greatness Passing By* (publisher unknown)

Index